A
New Essay
concerning the
Origin of Ideas

ANTONIO ROSMINI

A
NEW ESSAY
CONCERNING THE
ORIGIN OF IDEAS

Volume 1

Translated by
ROBERT A. MURPHY

ROSMINI HOUSE
DURHAM

Translated from
Nuovo Saggio sull'Origine delle Idee
Vol. 1, Intra, 1875

Typeset by Rosmini House, Durham
Printed by Bell & Bain Limited, Glasgow

ISBN 1 899093 55 9

Note

Square brackets [ ] indicate notes or additions by the editors.

References to this and other works of Rosmini are given by paragraph number unless otherwise stated.

Foreword

A New Essay concerning the Origin of Ideas is the first complete English translation of Rosmini's[1] *Nuovo saggio sull'origine delle idee* since the publication in 1884 of a similar three volume work by William Lockhart.[2] The aim of the present edition is to offer English-speaking readers an opportunity to share in the renewed interest in Rosmini currently underway in Italy especially, but also in North and South America. This aim is, of course, dependent upon a belief that Rosmini has something to offer today. The work is not intended solely as a contribution to the history of philosophy.

A New Essay, despite almost total neglect in English-speaking philosophical circles, marks a watershed in philosophical development.

---

[1] Antonio Rosmini-Serbati, born at Rovereto (Italy) 1797, died at Stresa (Italy) 1855. A saintly priest, polymath, philosopher and theologian, he was the founder of a religious congregation, the Institute of Charity. Revered by many in the Church, and reviled by many more, he was the subject of philosophical and theological controversy from 1841 until his death. Two of his works, *The Five Wounds of Holy Church* and *A Constitution according to Social Justice*, were placed on the Index of Prohibited Books in 1848. In 1889, forty propositions, taken in part from posthumous works, were condemned by Pope Leo XIII. An active process of rehabilitation within the Church is underway, and has clearly been reaffirmed by Pope John Paul II in his encyclical, *Fides et Ratio*: 'The fruitfulness of this relationship is confirmed by the experience of great Christian theologians who also distinguished themselves as great philosophers, bequeathing to us writings of such high speculative value as to warrant comparison with the masters of ancient philosophy. ...We see the same fruitful relationship between philosophy and the word of God in the courageous research pursued by more recent thinkers, among whom I gladly mention... John Henry Newman, Antonio Rosmini, Jacques Maritain, Étienne Gilson and Edith Stein... Obviously other names could be cited; and in referring to these I intend not to endorse every aspect of their thought, but simply to offer significant examples of a process of philosophical enquiry which was enriched by engaging the data of faith' (no. 74).

For Rosmini's life, *vide* Claude Leetham, *Rosmini, Priest and Philosopher*, New York, 1982, and Denis Cleary, *Antonio Rosmini: Introduction to his Life and Teaching*, Durham, 1992.

[2] *The Origin of Ideas*, 3 vols., London, 1884.

In the work, the whole of Western thought on epistemological problems is evaluated (volume 1), a coherent theory about the origin of ideas is set forward (volume 2) and the nature of certainty is examined (volume 3).

The evaluation of philosophical theory about the origin and nature of ideas takes into account two classes of thinkers: those whose work errs by defect, and those who err by positing more than is necessary for the solution of the problem. Locke, Condillac, Thomas Reid and Dugald Stewart stand on the deficit side of the divide; Plato, Leibniz and Kant on the other. Rosmini then bridges the gap between the two by positing a single, innate idea — the idea of being — as the necessary foundation of all thought. As an innatist, therefore, he stands with Plato. At the same time, he accepts, with Locke and Kant, the need for sense experience to determine and concretise this idea through the judgments we make about the existence of things. Finally, on the basis of the naturally intuited idea of being, which as the light of reason forms the capacity possessed by the human mind for looking out on all being, Rosmini writes at length about certainty, the only final resting place for human thought.

It is clear that the idea of being is for Rosmini 'the final reason for every concept...' It contains everything embryonically ('virtually', as he would say) and as such is the 'mother-idea'.

The motive prompting Rosmini's work was complex. Since his youth, he had been enamoured of truth which, according to him, would be expressed in systematic knowledge by establishing 'uni-totality' (one self-evident principle as the basis of all on-going knowledge) as the aim of the 'system of truth'. In other words, all development of knowledge must depend upon a single, self-evident principle as its basis. For him, the only worthwhile exercise in epistemology lies in seeking the mediate principles arising from truth, and developing the relationship between these principles and their conclusions in an orderly fashion. A non-philosophical example would be the principle of the wheel, which contains within itself the seed of all applications of the wheel. Similarly, the intuited idea of being, the sole foundation of truth, is that from which all determined knowledge, direct and reflective, has to be drawn.

As Rosmini completed *A New Essay*, he was confident that he had laid the groundwork for everything that could validly be encompassed within the ambit of knowledge, although he had no illusions about the actual paucity of human knowledge compared with what always remains to be made known through advances in every branch of science. He insisted, however, that everything contrary to the idea of being — anything which *is not*, anything which is opposed to being — is an impediment to knowledge. Error, the antithesis of knowledge, 'consists in a thought, and hence in a word, about things which are not, that is, which do not have being.' Descartes with his doubt, Locke with his philosophical sensism, and Kant with his categories, destroy the unity of being and fragment the totality sought by the human mind.

It is clear that such an epistemology would not be complete without a metaphysics of being. This conviction, deeply embedded in Rosmini's considerations, would lead him to further work intimately connected with ontology, and still incomplete at his death. This need not concern us here. What does concern us, however, is Rosmini's maturing approach to the work we are reviewing. Although he was subject to Lockian influences in his first philosophical formation, and had been engaged in ontological speculation since at least the age of sixteen, his first major attempts at formulating a Christian Encyclopaedia in active opposition to the French Encyclopaedia show active and reasoned distaste for Locke and sensist philosophy. In particular, he saw sensism as destructive of society, a matter of particular concern to him as he surveyed the rejection of moral values and responsibility following upon the Enlightenment, and actively developed during the French Revolution and its aftermath. As he came to grips with the philosophical problems inherent in a world where society was, as he saw it, on the brink of collapse, he realised that little or nothing could be achieved for society's renewal without first providing a reasoned and explicit answer to the epistemological problems underlying the symptoms of uncertainty threatening the social fabric. Consequently, he set aside work previously undertaken on the nature of civil society to devote himself to the production of *A New Essay concerning the Origin of Ideas*, where the reference to Locke's *An Essay concerning Human Understanding* could scarcely be missed. When he had published the work in 1830, he was able to return to his former studies, consolidate his ideas on the human person, and move forward on a broad philosophical front embracing ethics and conscience,[1]

---

[1] *Principles of Ethics*, Leominster, 1988; *Conscience*, Durham, 1989 (these texts, together with other English translations of Rosmini's works, may be viewed at: 'www.rosmini-in-english.org').

philosophical anthropology and psychology,[1] the whole field of human rights[2] and the philosophy of society[3] and metaphysics.[4] Towards the end of his life, he made use of all this work, but especially of his metaphysical speculation, in revising important aspects of *A New Essay*.

The remote preparation for such an undertaking was completed during Rosmini's youth. By the age of twenty, he was thoroughly conversant with classical literature, at home with Greek philosophy, Socratic and pre-Socratic, and very familiar with the Fathers of the Church, especially St. Augustine. In addition, his knowledge of the Scholastics, and of Aquinas in particular, was profound. His early attitude to Plato and Aristotle, whom he views together as the key to Western philosophy, is seen in his conciliatory attempt, in *A New Essay*, to examine Aristotle by comparing him with Plato, rather than by viewing Aristotle in himself. Later, he would undertake a more intense study of Aristotle which reached its culmination in two works[5] which favoured Plato to the detriment of Aristotle.

This very brief outline of Rosmini's preparation and motive for writing *A New Essay* is a simple, schematic introduction to the work. But we may still ask ourselves why Rosmini is being resurrected in English today. The answer is found in the destructive individualism proper to our post-modern world and the need for an antidote to the intellectual debility and chronic uncertainty characteristic of post-modernism.

We live in an age of uncertainty. Even the great strides towards domination over nature taken during the past two centuries have contributed in bringing Western civilisation to a paradoxical condition in which intolerable mental confusion is often combined with considerable intellectual arrogance. Inevitably we look for salvation, and find it at best in strong, decent guidance, at worst in any

---

[1] *Anthropology as an Aid to Moral Science*, Durham, 1991; *Psychology*, 4 vols., Durham, 1999.

[2] *The Philosophy of Right*, 6 vols., Durham, 1995.

[3] *The Philosophy of Politics*, 2 vols., Durham, 1994.

[4] Cf. in particular Rosmini's incomplete philosophical meditation on being, published posthumously in *Teosofia*, Turin, 1859. An English translation of this work is in preparation. All six volumes of the study are currently being republished in Italian as part of the critical edition of Rosmini's edited and unedited works (*Opera edite e inedite di Antonio Rosmini*, Rome/Stresa, 1979–).

[5] *Logica*, Turin, 1853, and *Aristotele esposto e esaminato*, Turin, 1857.

distraction promising relief from the need to accept our individual responsibilities.

The chief factor leading to this disorientated living is widespread scepticism about the value of human reasoning. Not long ago, such an attitude would have been found only in philosophical circles, but greater instruction, better communications and the loss of our ability to concentrate on sustained argument have enabled it to spread throughout society at great cost to objectivity. Subjectivity, however, affords no solid basis on which to found a consistent way of life and fulfil human longing for freedom and dignity.

Rosmini's work on the problem of knowledge places 'the objective *light* of reason', not reasoning itself, at the centre of thought. This necessarily objective light, revealing itself to human beings as the objective source of all knowledge, is the sure element upon which all reasoning depends. Without this illumination, even scepticism would be at a loss to express the contradiction inherent in its affirmation of universal doubt.

Moreover, the light of reason is not a transient feature in human life. It shines before individuals unchangeably, whatever use they make of it, and even when they endeavour to turn away from it. As a stable feature it allows human beings to share unceasingly in its eminent characteristics. Without entering their existence as part of their subjective being, it is the fount of their dignity, their duties and their rights. As something seen by all who share human nature, it is the source of our essential unity and brotherhood. And it draws all human beings to rise above themselves, inviting them to search for that of which human nature is an image.

In addition, Rosmini's investigation into the source of human knowledge provides, amongst other things, an examination of the relationship in the human person between the light of reason and feeling or sensation, and shows how these elements contribute the characteristics of objectivity and subjectivity to human existence.

Finally, Rosmini's theory offers not only a basis for certainty, but a criterion by which we may judge whether we do in fact possess certainty, defined by him as 'a firm and reasonable persuasion which conforms to the truth'. In the third volume of *A New Essay*, he deals at length with the question of certainty and its definition, and draws a number of corollaries about outstanding features of human understanding and will.

Because persuasion in Rosmini's sense depends upon the will, it is immediately clear that his definition places certainty where it really belongs, that is, amongst human acts. It is a human quality, not an attribute of truth. But it is connected with truth in such a way that it cannot be unrelated to it. Persuasion as the foundation of certainty must conform to truth; it cannot, according to Rosmini, be accorded to formal error and retain its capacity to serve as a basis for certainty.

A second corollary concludes that *formal* error, as a human, reasoning act, has its essential roots in the human spirit, where it springs first from an act of will, not of intellect. It is therefore avoidable, at least through willed suspension of judgment. In the last analysis, formal error is that act by which we refuse to acknowledge what we know for what we know it to be. As such, it takes on the quality of immorality.

A third corollary shows that logical principles are not the outcome of empirical understanding, but the most general application of the light of being, truth itself, to the things we know. Consequently, although they enable us to judge the validity of thought in so far as it expresses what is possible and what is impossible, they tell us nothing about the existence of finite things. They can, however, draw our attention to the necessity of an infinite existence, the supreme Being, as the only final explanation of the existence of the logical principles themselves.

Each of these great corollaries is challenging in its beauty and audacity, and each of them drives the reader back to the principle of unity on which the whole of Rosmini's theory of knowledge rests. The great call of his treatise on certainty, as a whole and in its parts, is to provoke final surrender to, or rejection of, the 'light of being'.

THE TRANSLATION

Beside the general description of the work attempted here, it is necessary to add some notes about the translation, which has been made from the 5th Italian edition of the *Nuovo Saggio*.

This Italian edition, reviewed in its entirety towards the end of Rosmini's life, contains a number of important changes from the first edition.[1] In particular, Rosmini's metaphysical studies had brought him to a better understanding of the importance of the distinction in Italian between *essere* and *ente*, pl. *enti*. *Essere*, used as

[1] Rome, 1830.

a nominal infinitive, stands for the Greek ἐιναι (German *das Sein*); *ente*, the supposed present participle of *essere*, was introduced — as in the Latin *ens*, pl. *entia* — to represent the corresponding τὸ ὄν of the Greek philosophers (German *das Seiende*). In English, both *essere* and *ente* would normally be translated as 'being' with consequent misrepresentation, in our case, of the sense of the author, especially in those places where Rosmini, in his final revision of *A New Essay*, has considerably refined his use of these words. The translators have decided, therefore, to use 'being' for *essere*, and 'ens', (*pl.* 'entia'), for *ente* (*enti*).[1] Some foundation for this will be found in the *Oxford English Dictionary* where 'ens' is listed, but without the precise philosophical meaning given to *ente*, a meaning which can be evaluated only within the ambit of Rosmini's epistemology and metaphysics.[2]

Another important feature of the translation is the transference of many of Rosmini's immensely long footnotes to an appendix within each volume. This has been done, in the first place, to avoid the need of inordinately long footnotes which sometimes run to three or four pages. But there is another, more important result which we hope will be of benefit to readers. These lengthy, transferred footnotes are not indications of sources, or passing references to other works, or snippets of information about the matter in hand, or an unworthy show of erudition. They are essays in themselves, and often throw great light on passages of other authors, especially of Aristotle and St. Thomas Aquinas. Read at a distance, as it were, from the text, their clarity takes on a value of its own without losing its appropriateness for the text to which it is being referred.

Special mention is needed, however, of no. 35 in the Appendix. This is not a displaced footnote, but originally appeared as a preamble to Rosmini's collected epistemological works, and was intended as a reply to G. M. Bertini's criticism of Rosmini's theories.

[1] The translators cannot agree with Lockhart, *op. cit*, Preface, p. xxviii, that 'the context [in *A New Essay*] will always tell which meaning to attach to our single [English] term, *being*.' For a more extensive discussion of the difficulties entailed in translating *essere*, *ente* and other words in Rosmini's philosophical vocabulary, see pp. x–xi, of the translators' Foreword to *Psychology*, vol. 1, *Essence of the Human Soul*, Durham, 1999.

[2] The following example may help to indicate the difficulty, and in part illustrate Rosmini's use of *essere* and *ente*. *L'essere è l'atto d'ogni ente e d'ogni entità* (being is the act of every ens and of every entity) (*Teosofia*, vol. 1, p. 215, Stresa, 1998). Translated as: 'Being is the act of every being and of every entity', the sentence would appear only as a regrettable pleonasm.

Although it contains a number of valuable insights into Rosmini's mind, it would be wholly inappropriate at the beginning of a modern English translation. We have, therefore, retained it, but in a position where it will not take first place in Rosmini's text.

Finally, some general consideration must be given to Rosmini's Italian. It has a number of precious qualifications, amongst which however brevity and conciseness do not take first place. There has been no attempt to reproduce in English Rosmini's often long, and sometimes tortuous journey through lengthy concatenations of phrases, although every effort has been made to retain all elements of meaning in the briefer sentences we have normally adopted. On the other hand, the gain in clarity from Rosmini's constant habit of summing up before taking a new step forward is a feature of his method which we have tried faithfully to preserve. All in all, we suspect that the modern English will be clearer today, even for English-speaking Italians, than the original Italian. We sincerely hope that this is the case 'although it is a risky business, stating what one has tried to do or, worse, the principles one has used'.[1]

DENIS CLEARY
TERENCE WATSON

Durham,
July, 2001

---

[1] Robert Fagles, Translator's Postscript to Homer, *The Odyssey*, p. 490, New York, 1997.

Contents

SECTION FOUR

False Theories Assigning a Superfluous Cause of Ideas

CHAPTER 3. Kant

THIS ESSAY
ON THE PRINCIPLE OF
HUMAN KNOWLEDGE
I DEDICATE IN GRATITUDE TO YOU
MY REVERED TEACHER
PIETRO ORSI
PRIEST
IN PERPETUAL MEMORY OF THE YEARS
1815 AND 1816
WHEN
BY TEACHING ME PHILOSOPHY
YOU BROUGHT ME TO LOVE OF VIRTUE
WITH THE POWER OF TRUTH
AND THE SWEETNESS OF FRIENDSHIP
AND SURROUNDED ME
WITH IMMORTAL BENEFITS
ON A PAR WITH THE RATIONAL SOUL

———————

ANTONIO ROSMINI-SERBATI
Rome 3rd May 1829

Preface

Principium, qui et loquor vobis
[The beginning, who also speak unto you.]
Jn 8: 25.

1. The present work is not about philosophy in its *search* for new truths but about its attempts to clarify and develop truths known to all. In writing this essay, my sole intention has been to invite people to observe their inner thoughts and feelings, the things they already know naturally, even though habitually they do not reflect on them. In other words, I want to write a commentary upon a *common-sense opinion* and offer a reply to the simple question: 'What is the light of reason?' — that 'light' whose presence is fully authenticated in mankind because it is found in all languages and ages, and used by all schools of thought and by ordinary people everywhere. It is the most obvious fact, the pre-eminent fact, from which every other kind of evidence is derived.

2. I was led to undertake this task when asked to clarify statements I had made in other writings about the origins of human knowledge. I said:

> In my opinion, pure human understanding is neither restricted nor limited. According to me, human beings possess only one form of understanding, the form of TRUTH. This form places no restrictions on the understanding because it is not particular, but universal (and indeed the most universal of all). It includes all possible forms and is the measure of everything limited. By reference to this single form and single type of assessment, I explain everything in the activity of the human spirit which transcends sense and experience.[1]

But without undertaking a long, thorough investigation into

[1] Cf. vol. 1 of *Opuscoli Filosofici*, p. 98.

the nature of human understanding, the object of the present work, I was unable to offer a full, convincing explanation of my assertion or describe the nature of this idea or primary form — what Dante calls 'The light connecting truth and intellect'.[2]

3. This *mediating* light, as Dante calls it, between the spirit and things constitutes and creates the very nature of the intellect. Nowadays, this nature and that of the senses have been so completely identified that philosophy appears willy-nilly to have reverted [*App.*, no. 1] to its childhood days in the period prior to Aristotle and Plato.[3] In the long history of philosophy, from the remotest times to the present day, there has never been to my knowledge a baser, more demeaning misconception for human nature than the one advanced by sensists in the last century. By restricting the divine light of human understanding strictly to sensations, which man shares with the beasts, they extinguished that light. Even those who, like Locke and Condillac, claimed to discern an immortal soul in human beings were unaware of the distinction between *sense* and *intellect*, between *sensation* and *idea*. Recently I wrote some critical but true strictures on these two philosophers and was sharply taken to task by one of my shallow compatriots who have grown old in servitude to 18th century ideas and who never tire of trotting out their feeble, outdated views.

4. However, in Italy's defence, it is only fair that I mention how, during periods of philosophical subjection, it preserved its intellectual freedom better than others, or was certainly less tainted by the spinelessness that bows before the latest philosophical mountebank to appeal to the masses. Condillac's thought was in fact candidly assessed by the soundest Italian critics at an early stage as we can see in *Memorie dell'Istituto nazionale italiano* where our young people were advised against deception by the unusually forthright, presumptuous

[2] *Purgatorio* 6: 45.

[3] These two philosophers pointed out and refuted the fundamental error of their predecessors, who were unable to distinguish feeling from thought, and made a single faculty from these two intrinsically distinct faculties. They ascribed this to lack of sophisticated observation on the part of the earlier philosophers whose observation of human nature they considered primitive and coarse.

style of Condillac who had held such absolute, tyrannical sway
for so long in France. Michele Araldi warned young Italians not
to yield readily or let themselves be swayed by arrogant, over-
weening, contemporary writers who proclaimed their superiority and their right to teach the whole of mankind. He spoke out
boldly at that time:

> The likelihood of attacks from many sides will not deter me
> from naming a respected thinker of recent times: I refer to
> Condillac. It seems that his appearance on the scientific
> scene was our good fortune. He had come, after all, to clar-
> ify matters. We believed him, and took everything he said as
> gospel. But it could well be that he became famous as a re-
> sult of his dogmatic outspokenness which made him con-
> tent with categorical assertions usually devoid of proofs.
> Perhaps his somewhat casual, rude attitude towards the
> philosophers whom he arraigned before his tribunal was
> intended to increase his popular appeal. In his *Logic* and
> *Grammar*, he scathingly takes them to task and, among the
> other accusations and faults he levels against them, re-
> proaches them again and again for leading ordinary people
> astray by their quibbling. He claims they have contributed
> to the dire situation whereby languages, as currently spo-
> ken, lack the analytical character he thought they should
> have. The only observation I shall make regarding
> Condillac's conceit is that in his posthumous *Works*, spe-
> ciously entitled *Language of Calculus*, he parades the same
> ideas, which he develops and comments on fulsomely, or at
> least at great length. His last work exhibits the same man-
> nered style; he laboriously goes over identical ground and
> comments on his own work. I could also add that his teach-
> ing — even disregarding its doubtful or erroneous proposi-
> tions — owes its appeal also to the metaphysical apparatus
> with which he adorns or suggests it. Once this is removed,
> we see his doctrine as it really is: repetitious and common-
> place. I hope these few examples are sufficient to offer the
> young people to whom they are addressed the means to cut
> the giant down to size and make a more realistic assessment
> of his worth.[4]

Thus Araldi, twenty years ago. What he said should count in

---

[4] *Saggio di un' errata di cui sembrano bisognosi alcuni libri elementari delle naturali scienze etc.*, Milan, at the Royal Printing Works, 1812, vol. I, p. 311 ss.

his favour with those who know how Condillac was revered and what scorn was poured on anyone who dared to doubt the great master or even mention any author prior to him.[5] Even now there are still survivors among us who confine all human wisdom to the superficiality of Condillac's system because that happens to be the only philosophical system they have to offer.

5. This present work is a continuation of other short works published earlier. It is simply a further step towards the sole aim of all my efforts: to contribute, to the best of my ability, to the restoration of true philosophy, which has suffered so much humiliation and neglect in our times at the hands of the very thinkers who claimed to be its most dedicated devotees. Mankind must recognise the abasement of philosophy as a cause of the serious ills which sorely afflict it and of the dire sufferings characteristic of our present age. In my view, mankind can neither recover from its sickness nor find a respite from its endless anxieties without true philosophy as an effective cure, or at least relief, from its unending sufferings.

6. It is true that the argument proper to this book is very abstract and apparently remote from mankind's immediate,

[5] Nowadays, even the French admit with disdain the presumptuous tone of Condillac and his school, which so scornfully lorded it over other philosophers. It is a pleasure to see in the following lines of Jouffroy how, after the disappearance of fanaticism, people clearly recognised, even in France, the truth which Araldi and other Italians had seen so long before. 'At the time when M. Royer-Collard began his lectures (1811), Condillac's was the only philosophy in France. Whether this philosophy is good or bad is not a question I wish to debate. I merely state that it had then acquired the authority of a dogma. It was the subject of commentary and development, and of attempts to present it more accurately and clearly. No one, however, attempted to challenge its fundamental principles. Condillac, it seems, had so faithfully delineated the forms of the human mind that studying the original had become a waste of time. Recapitulation of his wonderful analysis was adequate for all intellectual requirements. Condillac had done nothing to safeguard his followers from such blindness. Not only had he refrained from giving such a warning, but the whole thrust of his claim was that his system on the human mind fully registered and explained all the phenomena the mind could possibly contain. It was impossible to be a half-hearted follower. Merely to question or seek to complete a single issue was tantamount to rejecting his philosophy. One had to walk with him or be considered his adversary' (*Oeuvres complètes de Th. Reid*, published by M. Th. Jouffroy, Introduction).

practical requirements. However, when ills are deep-rooted, causes have to be sought deep down. Perversion and dissoluteness are no longer due to regrettable weakness and frailty in the moral fibre of the human being; they have pervaded, so to speak, vast tracts of the human spirit, risen to the mind and been transformed into thought-out, icy malice. They have waged war on the truth and, after assailing consequential and front-line truths, have pressed their attacks ever deeper. Truths that could not be destroyed were ignored, denied and derided. This campaign of derision and denial of truths was sustained until the very last was overthrown: the essence of truth itself was denied and blasphemed. In scepticism, that is, in utter human imbecility, the evil spirit found a suitable place to lay the first stone of the edifice of human malice and corruption. The proper thing now is not to adopt a superficial approach nor to conceal from ourselves the extent of our wounds by adopting purely palliative remedies. Instead, all good persons with the necessary ability and knowledge must readily co-operate to contribute to the rebuilding of knowledge itself. After that, morality must be rebuilt and then, finally, our shattered and dislocated society. Moreover, in rebuilding the whole edifice of learning, people must begin from the most basic truths, upon which depend all other truths, together with the good generated by truth. They must force *sceptics* to admit their utter inability to ruin human understanding and extinguish its light, and convince the *indifferent* openly of lying to others and to themselves when they declare or persuade themselves of their unconcern for the indelible truth which is the very life of rational beings, and for the eternal good ordained by God and inevitably drawn by nature.

7. The aim of the present work is therefore to trace back as far as possible the source of truth within us where the springs of the river of life are to be found, and derive from this primary source all human knowledge and certainty. In the process, we discover a single seed from which grows true philosophy — the philosophy essential to mankind's needs. This philosophy exhibits the twin characteristics of UNITY and TOTALITY,[6] characteristics

---

[6] See what I wrote about the nature of the philosophy which I intend to follow, and about the two characteristics which mark it off, in the two prefaces to vols. 1 and 2 of the *Opuscoli Filosofici*.

which I have elsewhere detected in philosophy. UNITY endows our cognitions with consistency and harmony; TOTALITY provides the immense pasture for which the human spirit longs and without which it cannot function. Whenever humans are deprived of some good essential to their mind, they inevitably fall into a sort of intellectual frenzy. The first truth, the *form* of reason, is of itself unique and extremely simple and inevitably bestows the most perfect UNITY upon all knowledge derived from it. All knowledge is derived from this truth which inevitably embraces all that is; this truth is the source of immense fecundity, and the subject of philosophy characterised by TOTALITY.

8. It is necessary therefore to attain the *essence of truth* as it is known by us in this life. This is the aim of the present work. I begin by dealing with the most obvious things and describing the most easily conceived systems in explaining the origin of ideas. I go on to point out the difficulties these systems leave unsolved. After that I outline the fruitless attempts of a number of worthy thinkers to overcome the difficulties. Finally, I expound the true solution and attempt gradually to introduce the most relevant conclusions and reveal clearly the thought I have been dealing with. Once truth is known, its characteristic as *essential unity* of all things is also known, together with its status as sole principle from which derives the unique philosophy we are seeking. At the same time, we know how this unique philosophy essentially embraces all that is. Truth is simply *possible being*. Outside of truth, outside of possible being, there lies only nothingness.

9. In actual fact, human beings have to satisfy two essential needs in themselves: one depends on the immensity of the heart, the other on its depths.

Even if we were given the whole universe to enjoy, we would not be satisfied. There is another requirement, over and above the many contingent beings on offer. The vast number of objects captivate and seduce us, but simultaneously weary and oppress us. We cannot be sated by a profusion of ungraspable, unsatisfying objects. In the end, we will seek some order in that profusion. We will look for something necessary and unique in it; we will never be fully satisfied until we have reduced and subdued the huge diversity and universality of things to a single principle. There, in the immutability of this principle, we will discover peace and calm of mind, where nothing remains to be desired because nothing else exists. In it, we are sated yet unwearied; in it, nothing is lacking, not even the most absolute simplicity.

10. When we have attained this absolute knowledge and arrived at a truth in which all is simplified and resolved, and beyond which the disquiet dependent on the pursuit of knowledge disappears, we remain calm and satisfied. We can also view calmly the position we occupy in the whole scheme of things and how we have to behold this place of ours if we are to avoid disrupting an order we have been pursuing for so long. We submit to the principle which unifies all things in order to enter this great unity without disrupting it — the unity we have recognised as the final desire of our intelligent nature and the term of our deepest needs. This all-embracing unity then provides a solid foundation for moral science. As long as the different branches of knowledge are taught separately, they are like disjointed fragments of a great temple shaken or shattered by barbarian invasions. In these circumstances, human knowledge will never keep step with moral virtue. Nor will an increase in enlightenment make people any better. And if we do not improve, how can amoral society be reordered?

11. I also affirmed previously my belief that this is the theory underlying the Gospel, and therefore the philosophy of Christianity. It is no surprise that a divine philosophy intended for humans should have its roots in human nature and correspond to the fundamental laws of the nature through which it is mediated. Indeed, I truly would not know where to find any teaching other than Christianity that combines in itself the most perfect UNITY with the most complete TOTALITY. But Christianity is not merely a theory pointing the human mind to the way of truth, or to truth itself, as one person can speak to another. It is also an invisible power taking possession of the human mind, where it displays and radiates new light and reveals other aspects of itself previously hidden from human gaze and barred by the limitations of human nature. It acts powerfully in the heart which it transforms and converts from the pursuit of the outward appearance of perishable good to a longing and love for the supreme good which in truth itself is made more obvious

and more attractive for us. It acts powerfully in our life renewed in conformity with our renewed mind and heart. It acts powerfully in the universe itself which tempers its laws, or rather has its laws already tempered *ab eterno* in obedience and service to truth that extends and triumphs in human nature.

12. That is why holy Scripture calls Christians: 'Those who have known the truth,'[7] as though this were their proper name. However, this truth — the principle underpinning the whole of Christianity — of which Scripture speaks and by whose *word* we are brought forth,[8] as Scripture says, is not merely the natural light of the mind (initial truth), but truth in its absolute fullness: first, subsistent truth. Thus it is not a cold IDEA of ours but all-powerful strength, the very WORD of God.[9] Consequently, holy Scripture tells us that *the grace of God is in the truth*[10] and that, by virtue of grace, we *walk* in the clear light of *truth*[11] in so far as we share, in our earthly life, in divine truth (the foundation of Christianity), and experience its power to fortify our intellect and rule our spirit. Yet even this fullness of truth, which operates within us with the utmost efficacy and sheds its radiance in our minds, is not fully revealed to us in its very essence, which is the essence of God. Here below, we must *believe* in its power in so far as we cannot experience it. In this sense, faith is the primary virtue of Christianity. Faith, says Scripture, is open to truth, and anyone who refuses to believe truth itself is essentially subject to the damnation springing from a lie.[12] Note that the only reason given by Christ to explain why human beings do not recognise his voice is their love of lies and their prior rejection of truth.[13]

13. The single principle of Christianity is TRUTH: and TRUTH is

---

[7] *Qui cognoverunt veritatem* (2 Jn: 4).

[8] *Genuit nos verbo* (Jas 1: 18).

[9] *Ego sum... veritas* (Jn 14: 6).

[10] *Gratiam Dei in veritate* (Col 1: 6).

[11] *In veritate ambulare* (3 Jn 4).

[12] *... elegerit vos Deus... in fide veritatis* (2 Thess 2: 12 [13]) *... Ut judicentur omnes qui non crediderunt veritati* (*ibid.*, 11 [12]).

[13] *Quare loquelam meam non cognoscetis?... Quia non potestis audire sermonem meum. Vos ex patre diabolo estis... quia non est veritas in eo* (Jn 8: 43–44).

also the principle of philosophy. In philosophy, truth is found only as a rule of the mind; in Christianity, it comes to us complete and entire, and self-subsistent as a divine person. In part, this person is light within us, operating with the utmost efficacy in the very essence of our spirit; in part, this person is veiled and hidden, and as such forms the revered object of our faith and the infinite reason for all our hope. It follows that philosophy, to be authentic, must consider itself as nothing more than a propaedeutic to true religion. We will be more fully open to worship and faith the further we move away from error and the more we recognise and cherish even the 'preliminary outline' of natural Christianity (if I may use that term) which in us is natural truth and a veiled form of the divine Word, as I would be tempted to call it.[14]

14. This utterly simple principle, which gives such UNITY to Christian theory, is also the extremely fertile principle from which arises ALL the good bestowed by Christian theory. Even the different branches of science do not prosper steadily and harmoniously unless they are shoots of the seed and branches of the solid root of Christianity. This explains how Christianity brought civilisation — one of its natural by-products — to our world and made it as indestructible as itself. Christianity, working its way ever more deeply into society, planted in it a seed of unlimited perfectibility. But we, in our pride, are always heedless of the good things done by others, always ready to appropriate others' success. We attribute to ourselves the perfectibility which pre-Christian nations had not known. Christ alone, as Isaiah boldly said, 'destroyed the bridle of error that was in the jaws of the people'.[15] Human self-assurance, which can harm individuals. is now powerless to corrupt the whole of humanity. All the powers of hell in the last century have only served to offer further proof of human nothingness and of the omnipotence of our Redeemer, who has healed the nations.[16] For him, every obstacle is a necessary, premeditated expedient helping to accomplish the inescapable purposes of the Gospel. Despite momentary

[14] *Lux vera, quae illuminat omnem hominem venientem in hunc mundum* (Jn 1: 9).

[15] *Fraenum erroris quod erat in maxillis populorum* (Is 30: 23).

[16] Wis 1: 14.

appearances to the contrary, it can nevertheless be safely said that nothing halts or holds back the progress of Christianity. On the contrary, even today we can repeat St. Athanasius's words: 'Henceforth pagan wisdom makes no progress. Rather its former wisdom is gradually disappearing.'[17] The efficacy and reliability of the word of God were for the Fathers of the Church the proof and the seal, as it were, of its divine origin; God's word is sure to be implemented. Christ himself referred to this characteristic when he said: 'All who came before me are thieves and bandits, but the sheep did not listen to them — I am the good shepherd. I know my own and my own know me.'[18] And: 'I did not lose a single one that you gave me.'[19]

15. All the effects of Christianity (and when I say the effects of Christianity I mean all possible good for mankind) stem in profusion from the single root of subsistent truth. The nature of this sublime institution, therefore, is such that it only needs to tend its roots to produce its wonderful effects. This explains Christian *simplicity* which seems intent on a single transcendent purpose and yet leads unexpectedly to happiness in the present life. Moreover, societal perfection, brought about in a hidden fashion, appears of itself on earth. Hence, the Gospel says that Jesus Christ, although he taught neither crafts nor natural sciences, 'taught *all truth*'.[20] Because the Fathers of the Church possessed this radical power of Christianity in all its abundance, they exhorted their neighbour to renounce secular knowledge. The philosopher and martyr, Saint Justin, exhorted the Greeks to espouse Christian wisdom when he described its true nature:

> Our captain, the Word of God, who is in charge of us, does not require bodily dexterity or good looks or high-minded persons of rank. What he does require is purity of soul and holiness. Through the Word, such power pervades us all, constituting a perfect means for avoiding serious

[17] *Nullos item progressus habet Gentilium sapientia: sed potius quae antea erat sensim evanescit* (St. Athanasius, *De Incarnatione Verb. Dei*, no. 55).

[18] *Omnes quotquot venerunt fures sunt et latrones, et non audierunt eos oves ... Ego sum pastor bonus, et cognosco meas; et cognoscunt me meae* (Jn 10: 8 and 14).

[19] Jn 18: 8.

[20] Jn 16: 13.

consequences and extinguishing the inflamed, native ardour of the soul. This power does not make us excellent poets, philosophers or orators but through inner teaching renders mortals immortal and human beings Gods. Come then, Greeks, learn and become as I am, since I too was once like you until the invincible power of the teaching and efficacy of the Word took hold of me. Just as an expert charmer drives away a dangerous snake once he has lured it from its nest, so the Word drives out base feelings from the inner recesses of the heart, especially covetousness, which gives rise to bad feelings, antagonisms, quarrels, envy, rivalry, anger and similar powerful feelings. Once covetousness has been driven out, the soul attains peace and calm.[21]

Thus, as a result of our renewal, of our being joined to God once more, of our becoming immortal and god-like, Christianity has made us — as a kind of small favour added to a huge one — the successful founders of human arts and happy promoters of the sciences, capable of forming a free, peaceful, happy society here on earth, similar in certain respects to a heavenly society. In a word, we can form Christian society, which embraces the whole world and grows to perfection as the ages pass.

16. The Church Fathers, while showing this UNITY of Christianity to be in its principle uncreated truth, also defined it as the power of the Word coming into us, but not for the sake of making us poets, philosophers, outstanding orators. They felt the TOTALITY of its effects, in which were necessarily included all dependent truths, but they also realised that every truth fell within the ambit of Christians, who worship subsistent truth. No aspect of true wisdom was ruled out, although all the pagan arts and sciences were to perish naturally as branches of a rotten, transient shoot, that is, of the human mind abandoned to its own resources. The prophecy of Jesus Christ was to be fulfilled: 'Every plant that my heavenly Father has not planted will be uprooted.'[22] All plants were to be renewed as they grew out of a Christian root, and were themselves to become Christian. According to Saint Justin:

The reason for abandoning the heathen authors was not

[21] *Oratio ad Graecos*, no. 5.
[22] Mt 15: 13.

because Plato's basic teachings are hostile to Christianity but because, along with the teachings of Stoics, poets and historians, they are not identical with Christianity. For whenever as individuals these authors recognised some aspect of divine reason that was consistent with itself, they wrote in a most noble fashion. When however they fought over really serious issues, they showed openly that their knowledge was no more sublime than that of other thinkers and equally open to attack. Everything excellent written by others belongs therefore to us Christians. We worship and love, according to God, the Word born from the uncreated and ineffable God, who became man on our behalf so that, by sharing in our sufferings, he might heal them. Yes, all authors, in virtue of the seed of reason implanted in them, were able to see the truth, although somewhat darkly. The seed[23] of something and its imitation, bestowed according to various powers, is one thing; the same thing, communicated and imitated in accordance with divine grace, is another.[24]

It is the common view of the Fathers that Christians have quite a special ownership of, and right to, all truths and all sound teaching. This is due to their profession as Christians. The Fathers also defended this right, which they made a point of Christian honour to maintain. As St. Augustine says:

If those whom they call philosophers utter truths in keeping with our beliefs, we should take them from these unjust owners, and claim them for our own use.[25]

17. This explains Clement of Alexandria's affirmation. Conscious of the efficacy and fruitfulness of the Gospel and its world-wide penetration, he maintained that Greece and Athens were no longer destined to be the seat of wisdom. From then on, the whole world was Greece and Athens, and the great need was not to resort to the heathen schools, but to listen to the

---

[23] The *seed* mentioned by St. Justin corresponds to *initial* being, the term which I use for the light of reason.

[24] *Apologia secunda*, no. 13.

[25] *Qui philosophi vocantur, si qua forte vera et fidei nostra accommoda dixerunt, ab eis tanquam injustis possessoribus in usum nostrum vindicanda sunt* (*De Doctrina Christiana*, 2: 40).

Word himself who had come to live among us.[26] Pagan arts and sciences were sterile, but those producing shoots from the Word of God were themselves divinised and incorporated into the *knowledge of truth*.[27] Consequently, Christianity demands and exhibits not just UNITY — and in unity the TOTALITY of what is known — but ORDER and the rightful origin of cognitions without which totality cannot be perfect, nor knowledge lasting and efficacious among human beings. In fact, pagan civilisation, centred almost wholly upon Greece, was short-lived; the civilisation springing from Christianity quickly spread throughout the whole of Europe, although it would be inaccurate to call it European. Its enduring tendency to spread throughout the world is so obvious that it can only be called catholic, a sign characteristic of the religion which produced it.

18. This sublime religion, which abolished slavery and brought together the great company of free men that is the Catholic Church, accomplished its task without any violent effort simply by communicating to mankind the knowledge of divine truth in accordance with the prediction made by the Church's founder: 'You will know the truth and the truth will set you free.'[28] This is true freedom, the first fruit of virtue according to the teaching of her divine founder: 'Truly, I say to you, anyone who sins is a slave to sin.'[29] True servitude to God is

[26] *Quam ob rem, ut mihi videtur cum ipsum Verbum ad nos venit caelitus, non sunt nobis amplius frequentandae hominum scholae, nec Athenae, aut reliqua Graecia, aut etiam Ionia studiorum causa adeundae. Nam si hoc utamur magistro qui sanctis virtutibus, opificio, salute, beneficio, legislatione, vaticinio, doctrina complevit omnia; nulla est doctrina quam is non tradit, ipsique, hoc est Verbo, universus iam orbis terrarum Athenae atque Graecia factus est* [Therefore, since the Word himself has come down to us from above, it seems to me that we need go no longer to pagan schools or resort to Athens, or anywhere else in Greece or even Ionia in order to study. For if we follow this teacher who has filled all things with holy virtues, with his works, with salvation, beneficence, law-giving, prophecy and doctrine, we find there is no teaching which he has not given. For him, that is, for the Word, the whole world has become Athens and Greece.] (*Cohortatio ad Gentes*, 11).

[27] *Scientia veritatis:* this is the precise definition of Christianity in holy Scripture. Cf. St. Paul, 2 Tim 3: 7.

[28] *Et cognoscetis veritatem, et veritas liberabit vos* (Jn 8: 32).

[29] *Amen, amen dico vobis quia omnis qui facit peccatum, servus est peccati* (Jn 8: 34).

that alone which can free us from servitude to one another. Mankind's decree of emancipation is thus contemporaneous with and identical to the first of the Ten Commandments, which involves the worship of God, who set up worship of himself and promulgated freedom in these solemn words: *Dominum Deum tuum adorabis et ILLI SOLI servies* [You shall worship the Lord your God and HIM ONLY shall you serve].[30] Truth, then, is the principle of *justice* because we become holy in the truth.[31] The fruits of justice, in which the worship of God mainly consists, are freedom, peace and happiness for society. The Catholic Church, the society formed by truth, is therefore essentially free although the unjust world, which 'detains the truth of God in injustice',[32] is constantly endeavouring to bind it in chains. This essential freedom is the necessary effect of the principle of Christianity which is *truth*. And as the development of truth among human beings can no longer be halted or slowed by human efforts and the perversity of the devil, so the progress of freedom for the Catholic Church cannot fail to continue and become even clearer. Some unhappy souls, overcome by love of fragile, temporary power here below, think they can dominate the Church, which is subject only to God. But generous souls who fight God's battles to obtain freedom for the Church are blessed. Their names will always be honoured and remembered in the society of the just with everlasting, unfailing love.

19. Such are the effects of truth, the principle of religion in so far as it is complete, divine and naturally hidden from mankind but, by God's action, now a well-spring of grace and an object of faith. It is also the principle of philosophy in so far as it naturally radiates in our minds either as an initial idea or as a norm of judgments. Philosophy, therefore, cannot be confused with religion with which, however, it is remarkably consonant and for which it provides a very useful service.

This is the relationship between philosophy and Christianity set out in this book. In expounding it, I have tried to fulfil the duty incumbent on all authors to reveal candidly from the start

[30] Lk 4: 8.

[31] *Sanctificati in veritate* (Jn 17: 19, 17).

[32] *Qui veritatem Dei in iniustitia detinent* (Rom 1: 18).

their own personal stance and make themselves known clearly to their readers. I have always thought it shameful to hide behind anonymity in the manner of some good, but overtimid authors, or other treacherous, untrustworthy and dishonest writers whose concealment and dissimulation of their feelings can in some way be condoned. In my view, I owed it to Christian society, to which the majority of my readers belong, to point out how my philosophy is related to Christian philosophy. It is only fitting that Christians, when presented with a new work of philosophy, should immediately ask how it is related to the religion they profess, in which they place their greatest hopes and their fundamental good. They have a right to be given accurate information. However apathetic our age may be, and however much religious fervour has declined, it remains a fact that baptised people, taken as a whole, do attempt such a quest, at least implicitly in the depths of their hearts. The impression made on human nature by Christianity is so profound that people often do this involuntarily, without being aware of it. Consequently, I owed such a declaration to the great society of Christians and especially to my beloved Italy which besides giving me life and speech, devoutly preserves the faith of its true forefathers and takes its greatest pride in such fidelity. I owe it also to the Eternal City where I am now writing, the foundation stone of the edifice of the Church to which people of all nations converge. Here Christians mingle as citizens of a common motherland and, as believers from the four corners of the earth, meet and embrace at the feet of a common father in whose features they see the living image of Jesus Christ.

20. Having done my duty by indicating the spirit of the philosophy I profess and which I hold to be the only true philosophy beneficial to mankind, it is worthwhile pointing once more to what I see as major obstacles to its progress. I will do this briefly.

I have no intention of speaking about the continuous opposition on the part of the wicked to the progress of truth or about the continuous persecution to which the world subjects the Church. Obstacles of this nature are not subject to our will but controlled by divine Providence, which guides them with ineffable wisdom to achieve the greatest glory and the foreordained triumph of Christ. I intend to speak of the obstacles which we ourselves raise to the progress of the philosophy for which the world feels such a need and for which religion asks and urgently pleads today to safeguard people from books full of false, dangerous teaching often openly irreligious and impious.

These obstacles, often raised by good people who do not realise the harm they are doing, spring from unfamiliarity with the intimate nature of religion and philosophy and from complete ignorance of the condition and needs of modern society. Such people maintain that there is no need to debate difficult problems because the Gospel in its simplicity is perfectly adequate to human needs. I have already replied to this by reference to the teaching of the Fathers who knew the fullness of truth in the Gospel and also knew that after the Gospel, which contained all that was needed, pagan schools were useless.

But by this they meant that the Gospel contained teaching which essentially ennobled and elevated the moral and intellectual status of mankind. When ennobled by the Gospel and linked closely to God, Christians were, in a word, enabled to re-create on their own all the arts and sciences in a truer and more noble manner and to form society anew. Thus they no longer needed to go to the pagans and seek artificial, tainted wisdom full of dross and error. Progress in knowledge, rather than an obstacle to the Gospel, is its natural effect and fulfils the needs of all mankind. God himself assisted the development of doctrine by allowing unbelievers and heretics to contradict and attack the truth. In doing so, they forced good people to make it more widely known and uncover the depths of its riches. For the most part it is not we but our adversaries, more restless and shrewder than ourselves,[33] who bring to the fore the most arduous questions about human nature and God. In dealing with these pressing difficulties, we are obliged to acquire a huge treasure house of true and priceless teaching.

St. Hilary spoke against this type of obstacle in words which, although apposite for his own time, are even more appropriate today:

> It is wise to guard against philosophy rather than merely

[33] Lk 16: 8.

avoid works of human tradition[34] which have to be refuted. There is nothing that the wisdom of God cannot do; God can do everything in his wisdom. Moreover, because reason cannot be in opposition to his power and his power cannot be in opposition to reason, it is fitting that Christian preachers should refute the irreligious, imperfect teachings of the world with the knowledge of the wise, all-powerful God. As the blessed Apostle says: 'Our weapons are not those of the flesh; the power of God is able to destroy defences and contradict any opposing reasons and any pride that rebels against the knowledge of God.' God, therefore, did not leave faith shorn of arguments. For faith is indeed the principal element in salvation, but when bereft of teaching, cannot stand secure, although it has somewhere safe to flee when faced with danger. It will be like a camp for the wounded who have been put to flight; not like a camp for those who, compared with the wounded, still have undaunted and fearless courage.[35]

21. There is another category of good people who impede the progress of philosophy. Wearied by numerous, unsuccessful attempts and rendered uncertain about the outcome by the wide divergence of opinions, they abandon all philosophical study without realising that this weariness is caused by their own lack of individual drive. They then want to make a universal rule of the lethargy into which they have allowed themselves to drift. It is difficult for us to accept what happens to us as our own fault. We want to justify ourselves, and attribute our own shortcoming to a universal law of human nature and even of truth itself. Sometimes we impose this law on others by claiming that all have the same shortcomings as ourselves and are in the wrong if they are not like us.

But it is no wonder that our times should see the rise of weariness in philosophical argument when as early as the fourth century of the Church's history St. Gregory Nazianzen was writing:

[34] We see here that error also has its traditions, which the Fathers characterise by the name 'human', and justly so, because the human race, considered in itself, is so little capable of being the judge of truth!

[35] *De Trinitate*, bk. 12, no. 10: *Cavendum igitur adversus philosophiam est; et humanarum traditionum non tam evitanda sunt quam refutanda, etc.*

> Weary of our abundant problems, we have come to re-
> semble people with an aversion to food. Like people put
> off by one type of food, who then go on to refuse all food,
> we first become bored with one argument and then find
> all arguments distasteful.[36]

These people, therefore, unjustly inveigh against philosophy
and claim they can set aside what they call perplexing questions
which, according to them, are merely the cause of endless,
unedifying disputes. But people like this have little idea of
human nature and their own powers. They think they can draw
a line between one truth and another, and declare some truths
useful and others worthless. They do not realise that truth in all
its extension is an essential requirement of our nature which
longs more keenly for knowledge the more difficult, far off and
mysterious knowledge is. The powers of individuals are indeed
limited, but only in the sense that they are unable to deprive
mankind of the tiniest particle of truth. Mankind will never
accept the imposition of such an arbitrary, unjust limitation;
the pursuit of truth will always be on a par with the search for
light and air, and will be as accessible to mankind as God has
made it.

22. Weariness in pursuit of truth produces different effects in
different kinds of people, all of them detrimental to the development of sound philosophy.

In some, it leads to the rapid adoption of the first views they
hear. They forget that when eternal truths are applied to human
affairs, these applications, like human affairs themselves, are
capable of going awry; circumspection and conscientiousness
are required if we are to be convinced that such applications are
true and reliable. Minucius Felix made the same point:

> It is not difficult to show that in human affairs everything
> is doubtful, uncertain, unsure and probable rather than
> true. We cannot wonder, therefore, that some, overcome
> by the tedium involved in a thorough quest for truth,
> rashly fall in with any opinion rather than doggedly pur-
> sue the search.[37]

[36] *Oratio* 31.

[37] *Nullum negotium est patefacere, omnia in rebus humanis dubia, incerta,*
suspensa, magisque omnia verisimilia quam vera. Quo magis mirum est,

23. Others, endowed with greater intelligence and full of self-assurance, imagine they can put an end to all problems by devising their own simple, universal systems with an admixture of few concepts. But these are no better than the systems of their predecessors and cannot offer any better solution to the difficult problems posed by human nature. Such solutions arbitrarily rule out lengthy research and confine themselves to a narrow, extremely inadequate circle of cognitions assessed and determined in accordance with their own standards. Such thinkers are a considerable impediment to the advance of truth, especially if they present their errors in a magnificent, flowing style and flatter their readers by the ease, simplicity and magnificence of few, occasionally true, holy pronouncements. The disdain they heap on those who do not agree with them is another important impediment to truth. They are convinced that everything important for human nature is contained within the confines of their own declaration of doctrine, and their excessive zeal leads them to forecast the most dismal consequences for any views other than their own. Very often, they label heterodox or even atheistic all opinions differing even slightly from their own. Too many are led astray by the semblance of the good these people intend to attain, but from which they are debarred by their lack of prudence and their incapacity. Their errors are like rocks at sea, which should be carefully avoided. That is why I have chosen to describe them briefly. But because these people have good intentions, seeing themselves clearly in a mirror may be sufficient to alter their ways.

We should not believe, however, that this group, and others I have mentioned, have begun to exist only now. Is there anything new under the sun? Are there any flaws in human nature originating only today?

24. The fault I have described — and even the good fall prey to it out of weakness — is due entirely to arrogant confidence in our own powers, and to an exaggerated trust in our ability to rectify faults without difficulty. We think we can lead people along some great highway to achieve perfectly here below a goal which will be attained only after many centuries, or perhaps not

nonnullos taedio investigandae penitus veritatis cuilibet opinioni temere succumbere, quam in explorando pertinaci diligentia perseverare (In Octavio).

at all. We think that an idea which seems helpful in attaining such a perfect goal can occur to the mind only if it is already part of human nature and of the natural order of things. Those who view such an idea favourably immediately assume that it exists in human nature or in the order of things. Lured by the advantage it affords their thought, they firmly assert that it *is* a law of nature and already present in the natural order of things.

The theory which takes common agreement amongst the whole of mankind as the sole, ultimate criterion of certainty is one example of this. It arose from the thought that human beings would indeed find it useful to have a simple, universal criterion generating individual truths in a fine, expressive way without the difficulties inherent in the application of other criteria.[38] One thinker considered it would be useful to have a swift, simple criterion of truth, and concluded that universal agreement was this criterion. He did not inquire whether this was the case in actual practice. The appeal exerted by the usefulness of such a criterion was sufficient to proclaim its existence. What was the origin of Leibniz's confidence in the rules of logic, or Raymond Lull's or Giordano Bruno's trust in *arte magna*? Or the origin of the hope of rediscovering a universal oral or written language with which to carry every argument to its conclusion and true result? It was not a close examination of the nature of things — which would have shown these bold philosophers the length to which the Creator had gone to provide man with the tools required to solve the most intricate problems — but a vivid appreciation of the usefulness of such a universal sign. They reasoned that such a useful means must necessarily exist in the nature of things.

And what was the source of so many conflicting, strange theories put forward by publicists on the origin and nature of

---

[38] If you consult an authority to know the truth, and the authority is infallible, you are told the truth. A rational principle or criterion, however, does not furnish truth directly, but is merely the means of discovering or of inferring it by argument. Granted therefore an infallible authority, no other form of reasoning is needed to discover the truth. As a result, it was hoped that all philosophical systems might be eliminated and a great number of very difficult problems avoided by declaring mankind the infallible judge of all the questions on which we can attain certainty. But even after such a declaration, we remain exactly what we are, neither more nor less.

society? In most cases, these authors simply refrained from considering facts and satisfied themselves with conceiving whatever they considered most beneficial. They described the nature of society not as it was but as they determined it should be. The tragedian of Asti [Vittorio Alfieri] wrote with assurance and confidence that society should be organised so that we were no longer able to harm one another — thus arriving at the same concept as Kant, the sophist of Koenigsberg, with his 'jural status', because he thought it would be extremely useful. But he gave no consideration to investigating its possibility. It never occurred to him that human nature would reject the regulation, the wisest and most useful of all according to him, which his mind wished to impose upon it.

Finally, we cannot explain the arbitrary laws imposed by so many writers as the very laws of nature unless these authors considered them advantageous. This explains the many arbitrary decisions found not only in civil societies but even in the organisation of the fine arts. After all, even beauty itself, to be beautiful, has to bow down before the rules of art and see whether it conforms to them or not. All these errors, committed by learned people in pursuing the good not where it is to be found, but where they are persuaded it must be, depend upon two things. First, our authors have a high respect for the nature of things, rightly considering that nature has not been created haphazardly and stupidly, but according to wise law and sovereign goodness. But they have an even higher opinion of themselves. It never occurs to them that their law, which they consider so wise and outstanding, is not the law of nature. They are often led astray in this way. Sometimes — I should say always — nature's laws are wiser and better than those devised and desired by philosophers as laws of nature, although desire prompts them to declare their own better, and defend them doggedly. In fact, the infinite wisdom of nature far surpasses our limited wisdom. The law which we wish to impose upon nature as wisest and best is so often not merely foolish and wicked, but absurd! It is not sufficient to foster a principle of benevolence if this principle is unqualified by prudence and lies outside the direction of the type of wisdom acquired by humble observation of the nature of things.

In short, we have to become students of nature, examining

her laws without anticipating them or dictating them to her. We must not be dismayed if the laws observed in physical, intellectual and moral nature differ from those thought necessary by our vain prejudices. We have to remain faithful to a lively belief in a supreme wisdom which corrects and directs all. If we see no advantage in a law under examination, we must patiently continue our research. Pondering that law more deeply, we will either discover a wisdom which proves amazingly instructive or, if we still remain puzzled, enjoy even in the dark a greater light, which will gently overwhelm us. We will attain a philosophy which is not disdainful of humanity, nor proud and domineering, but in harmony with Christianity, since the author of nature is also the author of the Gospel.

25. However, in the present work I merely wish to offer the outlines of such a desirable philosophy. If this first, slight work is carefully based on nature's standards, if my intentions are honourable, if the spirit of philosophy which I put forward to civilised nations is in harmony with the spirit of their religion, let good people join me in my work by correcting my mistakes in a brotherly spirit and making up for my deficiencies.

A NEW ESSAY
concerning the
ORIGIN OF IDEAS

SECTION ONE
Principles Governing this Enquiry

CHAPTER 1
The two principles of philosophical method

26. The two basic principles by which I wish to be guided in my argument are:

First: 'In explaining facts connected with the human spirit, we must not make fewer assumptions than are required to explain them.'

The reason for this is obvious: unless we assume all that is needed, we can never say that we have succeeded in putting forward a sufficient cause, that is, a reason explaining the facts. For example, anyone who observes colour and sound, two facts associated with the human senses, and claims to explain both by referring to hearing alone or sight alone, does not explain fully the nature of these two facts because, in reducing both to sight, he will never be able to understand how the ear perceives sounds. If, on the other hand, he reduces both to hearing, he will never be able to explain colour-sensation satisfactorily.

27. Second: 'We must not make more assumptions than are needed to explain facts.'[39]

Any assumption over and above what is required for such an explanation is superfluous and completely gratuitous. But any statement made gratuitously can be refuted and denied gratuitously. For example, if we were to take two senses and use them purely to explain a single species of sensation, we would be mocked for attributing two causes to a single kind of fact. One of the causes will obviously be superfluous and introduced unthinkingly.

28. Thus, in considering the nature of the human spirit, we must acknowledge and admit 1. everything needed to explain all the characteristic facts provided by careful, complete observation; 2. nothing more must be admitted. In other words, we must acknowledge and admit the *minimum possible*. 'Of all complete explanations of facts connected with the human spirit, we should opt for that which is simplest and requires fewer assumptions than other explanations.'

[39] It is easy to see that these two principles, taken together, are simply the component parts of the principle of sufficient reason.

CHAPTER 2

Two philosophies, one popular and one scholarly, and their respective shortcomings

29. There are, therefore, two principles that establish accurate, true method in philosophical inquiries. Similarly, there can be only two types of defect in theories that have developed regarding the human spirit: some tend to offend against the first principle by not assuming enough to explain all the facts; others offend against the second principle by too easily admitting in the spirit things unnecessary to explain observed facts, and by fabricating hypotheses superfluous to requirements.

30. It is not easy to avoid these two dangers. Indeed, philosophy, when it evades both, may truly be considered near to perfection. Such completion cannot be attained 1. without full observation of facts; 2. until characteristic or specific facts have been accurately distinguished and isolated from others that exhibit only non-essential variants or barren repetition of identical facts; finally 3. until, on the one hand, the difficulties of explaining the facts have been discovered and weighed, and on the other, an assessment has been made of the force of the arguments assumed to explain the facts. If these two features are not accurately appraised and carefully weighed by the philosophical mind, the arguments put forward will either be invalid or contain unnoticed superfluities.

31. Although popular philosophy[40] commits errors springing

---

[40] I use the term *popular philosophy* for the imperfect form of philosophy still surviving among the mass of philosophers at a time when the world already possesses great and profound philosophical knowledge, such as that contained in so many books coming down to us from antiquity and subsequent centuries.

In the last century, an attempt was made to renounce the whole legacy bequeathed by our ancestors. Philosophy reverted to a state of infancy. This is what I would call 'popular philosophy', because people in general are accustomed to address questions in the form in which they first occur, despite changes in the state and nature of the questions when they become the object of more mature and profound philosophy. Descartes caused a scandal by choosing, single-handedly and with very little study of earlier philosophers,

from non-observance of one or all of these three points, such mistakes usually infringe the first of the two principles already indicated.

Popular philosophy is never based upon thoroughgoing observation; it is incapable of classifying the observed facts, that is, of distinguishing characteristic from uncharacteristic facts. It is quite satisfied to have gathered a large number of facts, without realising that the real value of observations depends not on the number of ordinary, similar facts but on the number of characteristic facts, that is, those marking out a species. Finally, popular philosophy does not penetrate the interior nature of the fact itself; it does not grasp where the difficulty of created being lies nor is it aware of how forceful its explanation has to be. Popular philosophy is imperfect and deficient in all these areas.

32. The defect proper to popular philosophy is easily perceived by anyone accustomed to reflect. We all have dealings of some kind with ordinary people and are able to observe in their way of thinking two apparently contradictory characteristics which, however, have the same cause: they lack the three conditions mentioned above as necessary for philosophical reflection.

On the one hand, ordinary people do not wonder at things which are intrinsically wonderful, because such things are familiar in daily life. Ask them the reason for these things, and ordinary people think they can give you an immediate, satisfactory response by pointing to what they think is natural and obvious. They will almost go so far as to smile at the naivety of your ignorance, or your apparent ignorance. That is why uneducated people ask themselves so few questions. They see only very few, extraordinary difficulties which they believe they can solve immediately by offering what they consider reasons, or are rather crude, incontrovertible assumptions.

to set up a philosophical structure despite that already constructed by previous centuries. His great intellect and the few ideas which he received from the Schoolmen — which he used profitably without acknowledgement, perhaps even without adverting to his debt — saved him from many errors. His work has its faults, but it is extraordinary, nevertheless, when considered as the work, I was about to say, of a single mind. Locke, much less gifted intellectually than Descartes, tried to exhibit the same outspoken approach, but is characteristic of the true age of popular, 'infant' philosophy to which I am referring.

[32]

On the other hand, you may succeed in raising doubts in their minds about their proposed solution and enable them to grasp the presence of some knotty problem. If so, their first reaction will be to take the exactly opposite viewpoint. Previously, they solved the problem without the slightest hitch; now, after having finally understood your objection, they will have great difficulty in seeing the reason capable of explaining the issue. Previously, they had no hesitation in accepting their own explanation; now, they find it practically impossible to accept any suitable explanation of the difficulty.

33. In other words, the error underlying theories which make use of inadequate, defective reflection to explain facts connected with the human spirit is in keeping with popular arguments. By contrast, the error of those who use more than is necessary to explain the same facts is typical of people who have already made some progress in philosophy. Using their philosophical insight, they have already seen some problems, but are as yet unable to explain them simply. This comes much later. First reasons, which are always conjectural, extremely complex and involved, are welcomed and accepted by the impatient human mind which on the one hand has nothing better to offer but on the other cannot endure a total lack of explanation.

34. Hence three philosophical periods, as it were. First, *popular* philosophy, which is undemanding in its approach. It either does not grasp problems at all or has only a vague grasp of them; consequently, it explains them by concocting crude, confused hypotheses. In the second period, philosophy has become *scholarly* and has by now fully grasped the difficulties inherent in its earlier hypotheses. As a result, it spurns ancient, popular theories. Ingenious, complex systems are created, which are usually as over-elaborate as the initial systems were inadequate. Philosophy is defective in each of these two periods. The first stage is inadequate because it is new to problems; the second because it is new to solving problems. As it gradually becomes more perfect, philosophy corrects these inadequacies by simplifying and completing its theories. It has then entered the third period, when it attains perfection.

CHAPTER 3

The shortcomings in Locke's philosophy

35. The radical shift in ideas brought about by Locke and his followers does not consist in any great renewal of philosophy, but in the successful rescue of philosophy from the closed precincts of the Schools and in its proclamation to ordinary people.

This I consider not so much the personal credit of Locke as a requirement of his whole age, for which alone it will always be remembered.

36. For myself, I can think of nothing more gratifying than being able to draw mankind to sublime teachings which elevate the mind and ennoble the heart.

On the other hand, I consider it depressing and most painful to see how the outstanding teachings that mankind cherishes most dearly are restricted to a tiny group of what could be called privileged persons who have made such teachings their own exclusive property. As a result of some unspecified right of conquest, all mankind, it would seem, is denied access to these teachings. There is something distasteful and irritating about this shady, academic branch of studies which seems to shun the light of day. It behaves rather like a sect, making use of language, or rather private jargon, to which ordinary people have no access. It behaves in an ambitious, odd manner which seems to conceal some secret, mysterious purpose. This self-absorbed philosophy is evasive, contemptuous of humanity, selfish and, it would seem, heaven-sent to the few whom the rest of mankind has to follow like sheep. The great body of humanity is thus deprived of any opinion on which its own nobility and happiness depend.

Such thoughts, which readily occur to an untainted spirit, make one extremely grateful to those who give their all to enable as many persons as possible to scale the summits of knowledge, to develop this knowledge, and to present it to the general public in the simplest and most obvious way. Even ordinary persons are thus able to enjoy these fascinating truths and reach a higher state previously attained by only a minority of the most clever, inquisitive and fortunate individuals. The greater part of humankind, like a stern, experienced judge, can then bring common sense to bear upon the interminable questions of scholars whom they summon back from the vain pursuit of fame to more worthwhile work and sounder views. I say 'vain' because such fame is achieved by hollow, momentary triumphs over opinion rather than any real contribution to the human spirit or to society.

37. However, despite being impelled by an irresistible power of good human nature to look kindly on such human views, we sense some inherent difficulty. Some nagging doubt restrains us perhaps from nursing exaggerated hopes. It is obvious that there are real problems in such an undertaking. The attempt to teach, in a short time, the majority of mankind to philosophise is surely absurd and an example of philosophical credulity.

I am referring, of course, to philosophising on the most difficult issues, about which few scholars have ever been able to agree and have frequently accused each other of not even understanding the point at issue. If the extension of elementary education — which is still not available to all children — has occasioned so much concern and given rise to so many problems, it is surely unreasonable to expect ordinary folk to understand philosophy properly even when it is expounded in language they can understand. I am not referring here to the odd views of those who would like philosophy to be judged by the populace (as though a case against the rulers of the literary world could be brought before the common people).[41] Such an

---

[41] It is repugnant, and a contradiction in terms, for uneducated people to judge their rulers, and common people their masters. It is obviously absurd to raise on high the lowest section of mankind; it means overturning order in everything. However, absurdities like this should not be confused with the approach of those who, as a general rule, feel obliged to invoke common sense as though it were a high judge. The whole thrust of this approach, when properly understood, is to check the foolhardiness and self-assurance of individuals and to enthrone society, mankind as a whole, so to speak. It does, however, leave the *order* in society and in mankind as the bond and form established by divine providence. But while I point out the difference between these two approaches and hold the former absurd and repugnant, I do not intend to attribute my interpretation of the latter to any particular writer. I am

attractive, rosy prospect for society, even if it is not a dream, is so far in the future and so vague that even the most discerning minds cannot envisage it in practice, although its possibility cannot be discarded without setting arbitrary limits to human perfectibility and divine Providence.

38. It was quite natural that anyone wishing to introduce philosophy in everyday language to the common people — who were not yet ready to receive it — would also have imparted to it an approach and a method of argument somewhat similar to that of his readers.

This is why Locke's philosophy 1. shows signs throughout of inadequate observation, especially of those facts which, to be grasped, require lively, constant self-reflection and, at times, a whole series of reflections on our reflection, for which the average person is completely unfitted; 2. shows little sign of discernment in establishing characteristic facts, that is, facts constituting a new species, and distinguishing them from similar facts which vary only accidentally (writers belonging to this school all suffer from the same fault: they are scrupulously accurate in gathering and amassing similar facts and multiplying examples but totally careless in indicating the different species into which the facts are grouped); 3. lastly, the members of this school hardly ever see the main issue of a problem. As a result, they readily exhibit contempt for the works of earlier philosophers and spurn the precious legacy of teachings transmitted to us down the ages. In speaking of the great philosophers who spent their energies on finding appropriate solutions to the most difficult problems, the members of this school dismiss them as dreamers. Because they do not understand the reason for their efforts, they do not see the need for the choices made by the ancients in responding to proposed questions. Theories are dismissed with a few seemly words, perhaps with a smile to indicate one's good fortune in being immune from the dreadful itch to philosophise!

The mistake made by this school, especially in its initial stage, depended far more on over-confidence in trying to explain facts of the spirit without adequate arguments than on the use of

referring purely to teaching. I am not pointing to the personal opinions of anyone.

[38]

unnecessary elements in explaining such facts. Soon, however, such writers, conscious of difficulties unnoticed by their early teachers, strove as hard as they could to resolve them, but without success.

39. This shortcoming in Locke's philosophy devalued it in the eyes of some of his great contemporaries.[42] Nevertheless, he won popular favour and gained the support of a party which even then was becoming powerful by passing itself of as the friend of the people. Locke's brief triumph was, in fact, almost universal. The conditions of the period in which he published his philosophical work were highly favourable. The philosophy of the Schools had been corrupted, one might say. Descartes, who had dealt it the final blow, offered in its place certain profound concepts which, however, were insufficient to produce the complete system required by society. Moreover, as people in general became more literate, and acquired greater weight in society, their opinion came to prevail in those areas involving not only their own interests, but philosophical judgment also.

40. A brief reference to the shortcoming I attribute to the school of Locke may be found in the problem I am about to discuss. In other words, to justify my attribution to human reason of a single form which I call the *form of truth*, I have to demonstrate that only with such a system can we avoid the twin reefs on which various modern theories have so far been wrecked. I must mention, first of all, the system proper to those who do not assume sufficient to explain the origin of thought; after that, the system of those who admit far more than is needed. Finally, I have to prove the theory of the SINGLE FORM OF REASON which steers an even course between these twin reefs and show that, of all the full explanations of the problem I am discussing, this is the simplest, that is, the one which assumes and presupposes less than the others.

[42] Leibniz considered Locke's philosophy a shabby system. However, while contradicting it, he realised that its popular character was advantageous and pointed this out in the preface to *New Essays concerning Human Understanding*: 'He (Locke) is more popular than me; occasionally I am obliged to be more esoteric and more abstract, which is no advantage to me, especially when writing in a living language.' Nevertheless, Leibniz did choose to write the *Essays* in French in order to make them popular. It proved too difficult, however, to make ordinary what is sublime.

However, since my purpose is not to offer a theory of all that can be observed in the human spirit but solely to explain the origin of ideas, I shall first need to explain as briefly and clearly as I can, the intimate nature of this fact, and enable my readers to understand the *status quaestionis* and the difficulty faced in solving it.

SECTION TWO
Difficulties in Explaining the Origin of Ideas

SINGLE CHAPTER
The difficulty outlined

41. The fact I propose to explain is the existence of ideas or of human cognitions.[43]

Human beings possess cognitions, think about various things, in short, have ideas. What these ideas are is not my present concern; I am quite happy to accept the everyday view shared by all. My question is: where do they come from, or why are they found in the human spirit? Anyone can ask himself this question but not everyone is equally capable of answering it. This is the well-known problem of the origin of ideas that has divided schools and philosophers down the ages.

42. To outline as briefly as possible where the difficulty lies, I argue as follows.

When we form a judgment, we already need universal notions in our mind.

For example, to say: 'This sheet of paper is white' or 'This man is wise,' we need to possess the prior universal idea of whiteness and of wisdom; otherwise we could not apply such predicates to one subject rather than another.

Demonstrating this by induction for all the different species of judgments would be a long task, yet it can be done accurately. As a result, we can demonstrate that a judgment is merely the

[43] Every idea imparts some knowledge, some cognition. It could be argued that pure ideas, which in themselves do not give information about real things, do not constitute any knowledge as such; something similar is found in Aristotle. Nevertheless, in the broad sense, 'knowledge' can be ascribed to all types of ideas. Moreover, ideas constitute the formal element of all types of knowledge, as we shall see.

operation whereby we unite a given predicate to a given subject. In doing so, we 1. distinguish between subject and predicate, viewing them as two mentally distinct things in such a way that we can concentrate exclusively on one and distinguish it from the other; 2. recognise that in nature these two entities are united, that is, we do not concentrate on each of the two terms separately but on their relationship of union in the subject.

This analysis of judgment enables us to see that in such an operation we first conceive a predicate as distinct from its subject. Without this we would be unable to make a judgment. Moreover, a predicate distinct from its subject always contains a universal notion since, until it is joined to a subject, it can be joined to a number of subjects, even to an infinite number of possible subjects. This is precisely what the word 'universal' means when applied to ideas.

However, if the human mind cannot carry out the operation called judgment without possession of some prior universal notion or idea, how does the human mind manage to form universal ideas?

43. It is easy to see that the human mind can form a universal idea in only one of the following two ways 1. by *abstraction* or 2. by *judgment*.

Abstraction enables us to derive a universal idea from a particular idea[44] on which our spirit carries out the following operations: 1. it breaks down the particular idea into its two elements, that is, a) what is common and b) what is proper; 2. it discards what is proper; 3. it focuses its attention exclusively on the *common aspects* which are, in fact, the universal ideas for which we are looking.

It should be noted that 1. these three operations of our spirit which we exercise on a particular idea are focused upon an idea

[44] Here I need to say a word about the expression 'particular idea'. An idea is particular only in so far as it is associated in my mind with a real individual. As soon as the idea is detached from the individual, it acquires or rather exhibits universality. When it is free, I can apply it at will to an infinite number of equal individuals. Accordingly, the only absolutely individual or particular element in the idea is the real individual with which it is associated. This is not part of the idea itself, but something foreign to the idea to which it is linked not by nature but by the action of the intelligent spirit. 'Pure idea', therefore, I take as 'universal idea'. All this will be fully clarified as the work progresses.

already existing in us, whatever its source; and 2. these operations are therefore aimed solely at observing the common feature on its own and in isolation, not to produce or generate it in our minds.

However, in order to observe what is common and universal in our particular ideas, we must assume that it is already present in them. Otherwise, we could neither observe it nor focus our attention upon it. And this common element is the pure idea.

Abstraction, therefore, is not adequate to explain how we form those ideas which are *per se* common and general, although certain philosophical schools maintain that it is. Abstraction merely enables us to *observe* such ideas where they already exist. It enables us to disentangle them, to distinguish them from every extraneous element, to bring them before our attention in perfect isolation.

44. It remains, therefore, that we form common or universal ideas by means of a *judgment* only.

But we have already seen that every judgment presupposes that we have within us some prior universal idea (cf. 42). A judgment is merely a mental operation which uses a universal idea, that is, applies it to a subject and, as it were, places the subject in a certain class of things which is determined by the universal idea. For example: when I judge that a person is good, I place him in the class of things formed by the universal idea of goodness. The same must be true of any other judgment.

Consequently, if we cannot begin to judge except by means of a universal idea, it is patently impossible to explain the *formation* of all universal ideas by means of *judgments*. We have to suppose that we are endowed with some pre-existing universal idea prior to all our judgments. With this idea, right from the start, we are able to make judgments and thus gradually form all the other universal ideas.

45. This is a brief outline of the difficulty faced by anyone who attempts to explain, uninfluenced by scholarly prejudice or common, arbitrary opinions, the origin of ideas. As we go forward, this difficulty will become increasingly obvious and seem too difficult to philosophers who consider they can deduce from the senses alone all the ideas which observation and consciousness tell us that we possess.

SECTION THREE
False Theories Assigning an Insufficient Cause of Ideas

46. The difficulty I have outlined has occurred in various forms to tax the minds of all the great philosophers, who have devised ingenious hypotheses to solve it. I shall begin, therefore, by examining the main systems to see whether any of them is satisfactory. The first system we encounter is Locke's.

CHAPTER 1
Locke

Article 1
Locke's System

47. It has to be admitted that Locke, although famous, was either less conscious of the difficulty I have mentioned than other thinkers or did not focus upon it. Nevertheless, we shall see that even he was to find it an obstacle to his progress.

Locke, unaware of any difficulty, directly derives all ideas from *sensation* and *reflection*, almost like spring water gushing from two great jets.

Article 2
In attempting to explain the idea of substance, Locke encounters the difficulty without recognising it

48. Having hit upon a system from the very start of his

argument,[45] Locke proceeds to apply it; he reviews the different species of ideas and goes on to show how they are all derived from sensation and reflection, and easily formed.

This is most commendable because application alone can confirm the system adopted and show it to be satisfactory, if it really is so; and if not, discover where the faults lie.

49. In fact, the nub of the difficulty came to light immediately. Among the various species of ideas that occurred to Locke was the idea of *substance*, and he vainly tried everything he knew to explain how it could be produced purely by sensation and reflection.

However, when he became aware of this obstacle, he refused to admit that the principle of his system was unsatisfactory and that his two sources of sensation and reflection could not produce all our ideas. Rather, he found another way to overcome the problem; he merely denied the existence of the idea of substance.

'I confess,' he says, 'that there is another idea[46] which would be of general use for mankind to have, as it is of general talk[47] as if they had it;[48] and that is the idea of substance; which we neither have nor can have by sensation or reflection.'

50. Locke's argument in dialogue form comes down to this:

Locke: Like everything else, the origin of ideas must be dealt with on the basis of facts.

---

[45] This is Locke's method: there are no grounds for thinking that he begins with facts and proceeds to establish principles. Indeed, he starts from assumed principles and derives from them the explanation of the facts. This method is followed more or less by all of Locke's school including Cabanis, Destutt-Tracy, Gioia, etc. Their merit, relative to philosophical method, consists however in constantly proclaiming that we should do the opposite, that is, start from facts and move step by step upwards to principles. Simply teaching what is correct deserves no small credit; on our part, we take whatever is good from any source and forget about the rest.

[46] An odd contradiction! An idea exists that does not exist!

[47] How can something that is not an idea be a subject of general talk? I see that some non-existent *thing* can be a subject of general talk, but not that some *non-thought thought* — something that is not even an idea — can be a subject of general talk. This is wholly unintelligible to me! It is a metaphysical mystery worthy of Locke.

[48] Again, people use an *idea*, which they introduce into all their conversations, but do this without having the idea! I leave the explanation to this class of philosophers, who pride themselves on their clarity and logical rigour.

Objector: I agree completely: but which facts form the starting point for explaining the origin of ideas?

Locke: Sensation and reflection.

Objector: How do you derive the idea of substance from these two faculties?

Locke: It cannot be deduced. Therefore it does not exist.

Objector: Look, friend, in your argument you certainly start from two facts, from the existence of sensation and reflection, but you then exclude a third fact, the idea of substance (and others like it) because you are unable to derive it from the primal facts alone.[49] Do you feel justified in denying a fact merely because it is not derived from the facts that you had previously selected. The way to prove or disprove facts is by *observation*, not by *argument*. You start from argument, and exclude a fact. This is not the way to apply the method you have so carefully devised. To say: the idea of substance does not exist because *it cannot exist*, and it cannot exist because it does not originate from sensation and reflection, is to talk irrationally, quite contrary to the right method. If you are to follow this method, you must first of all assure yourself whether the idea of substance exists or not. If this fact is found to be true, you must say: therefore it can exist. But you begin by inquiring whether it can exist, that is, whether it can be fitted in with some of your arbitrary principles. Because you cannot harmonise it with the theory you have initially adopted, you deny it completely. This means abusing some facts to the detriment of others. Every system, however theoretical it may be, is based on facts. But it is wrong to pick out certain particular facts from the full range, and try to reduce everything to these alone. The real advantage of a method that starts from facts consists not in establishing *some* isolated facts as the basis of one's own teachings, but in acknowledging them *all* and rejecting none. In short, it consists in a thorough-going, impartial observation, unprejudiced by any blind, pet hypothesis.

I do not see how the devotees of Locke's philosophy can answer these observations.

[49] Such systematic exclusion is certainly not a fact; it is a principle. That is why I said earlier that Locke begins with principles and from them explains facts. To state, 'Only these two facts, sensation and reflection, exist', is not a fact; it is a principle that includes certain facts and arbitrarily excludes others.

Article 3

Our spirit cannot do without the idea of substance

51. If Locke, instead of observing whether the idea of substance truly exists, had also been willing to ask whether it can exist, he would have seen immediately that it could not possibly not exist.

Without it, we can reason neither in thought nor speech. Locke himself admits that it provides the general structure of human reasoning. Without such a concept, it is impossible to conceive the existence of anything, corporal or spiritual. Yet we do conceive these things. The idea of substance is therefore grasped, is possessed by mankind.

A prominent Italian philosopher makes the same comment as myself.

> The concept of substance would have been a real problem for the ideologues if they had given it some honest thought. They taught that we perceive only modifications of ourselves. From this principle, they infer either that we have no idea of substance or that such an idea must exist within us independently of our feelings. The first assumption is belied by the innermost feeling and by the very language of Locke and Condillac who admit that we are obliged to imagine an unknown support for qualities, which is equivalent to admitting the existence in the mind of some notion of substance, whatever its nature may be, independent of feelings. A person may say as often as he likes that such an idea is vague and unclear, but he still has to admit that it constitutes the central core to which qualities refer and that, without it, we cannot form the idea of a sensible object.[50]

Article 4

Why the idea of substance cannot originate from sensations alone

52. But what is the source of the insuperable difficulty Locke

[50] Pasquale Galluppi, *Lettere filosofiche ecc.* from *Tropea*. Messina, 1827.

himself encountered in attempting to explain how the idea of substance originates purely from external or internal sensations?

I regret that almost at the start of these investigations I am obliged to subject the idea of substance to analysis. I would much prefer to have dealt with this difficult issue towards the end of the work, and begun from easier matters. However, as I have to deal with substance here, I shall attempt to do so as clearly as I can.

The nub of the problem is as follows: any sensation we experience, whether within or without us, becomes an integral part of us. It is merely a modification of our natural feeling which itself is a passive experience. Our understanding has no part in receiving sensations. On the other hand, we cannot think of a substance without considering it as something that subsists in itself, which is itself subject to modifications without being a modification. It is, therefore, something which cannot be perceived by the external senses. The idea of substance is thus completely different from any sensation. It has other qualities that have no connection with sensations. It cannot therefore be confined within sensation nor encountered in it. Here are some essential differences between the idea of sensation and that of substance.

53. *First difference*: sensation is an accident that does not subsist in itself but in us; substance subsists in itself.

Second difference: sensation is something experienced by the subject; whereas substance can be the sentient subject itself.

Third difference: sensation is the effect of what stimulates our sensories; the substance of bodies remains in thought, even when all sensible qualities have been removed. This substance, therefore, is something which is not in the sensible element of bodies because everything which is external and transitory is assumed to have been removed by our mind.[51]

54. In short, when referring to bodies, we think of substance through the following reasoning: 'Sensible qualities could not

[51] We can also say that the *merely sensible element* (whatever it may be) is not a substance, without the addition of intellectual perception. As yet, it is not an ens, as we shall see shortly; the word 'substance' comprises the idea of 'ens'.

be without some support. Yet there are sensible qualities; sensation is what informs us of them. It follows that there is also some support, the subject of these sensible qualities, which is called substance.'

Sensation does nothing more than inform us of the existence of sensible qualities. It goes no further.

Deducing the need for a substance from such qualities is the work of thought, which carries out the deduction from the following principle: 'Sensible qualities *cannot exist* without a support.'

But our thought does not derive such a principle from the experience of sensible qualities because experience has never demonstrated such a totally non-sensible support. But if this support has never fallen under the senses, and cannot do so, how can we argue that it exists? How can we say that it must exist?

Our understanding cannot judge categorically that it exists and must exist unless 1. it has the idea of this support; 2. it has within itself some rule whereby it can discern what cannot exist without the support of something, from that which can so exist; 3. it applies this rule to sensible qualities and realises that they belong to a class of things that cannot exist without a support, a subject to which they belong.

The whole problem encountered in explaining the origin of the idea of substance (a problem that Locke felt unable to solve) consists in the failure to grasp how our understanding *makes a judgment*, that is, the following judgment: 'Sensible qualities need a support.'

If we examine the three things which, I said, are required by the mind to enable it to make such a judgment, we shall see that they can be reduced to one alone, that which is not provided by the senses.

In fact, the third thing to which I pointed was the act whereby the mind applies the rule to sensible qualities and judges that they require a support. Now the mind makes this judgment as soon as it has accepted 1. the above mentioned rule; 2. the idea of a support.

However, the notion of a support, a general and undetermined notion, is already included in the rule.

Let us assume that our mind has within it some principle

whereby it understands that sensible qualities cannot subsist on their own. From this principle, it has no difficulty in deriving immediately the idea of a support, that is, of some other thing, whatever it may be, which is united to the sensible qualities and gives them the possibility of subsistence.

The entire operation, therefore, hinges on discovering how our understanding can have or form for itself a rule or principle by means of which it is empowered to judge that sensible qualities cannot exist on their own.

Such a rule constitutes the major premiss of a syllogism which may be expressed as follows: 'Accidents cannot exist on their own'. This rule is equivalent to discovering fundamental repugnance between the idea of a certain species of perceived things called accidents, considered on their own, and the idea of *existence*.

Analysis of such a rule, therefore, yields two things: 1. accidents; 2. the idea of existence.

Sensations provide only accidents, that is, sensible qualities. What we certainly do not receive from sensations is the universal, pure idea of *existence* which, in fact, is involved in all our acts of reasoning — the idea of *existence* to which accidents, considered in themselves as isolated, are repugnant.

Let me sum up:

The idea of the substance of external bodies can be obtained only by means of a judgment proper to the understanding. This judgment is formed by means of a rule.

When analysed, this rule is found to consist and be the result of two elements 1. accidents, and 2. the idea of existence.

Accidents are obtained from sensations.

The idea of *existence*, however, is a universal idea that cannot come to us in any way through the senses. The idea of substance remains inexplicable, therefore, if we assert that all our ideas come to us from sensations alone.

Article 5

How the difficulty of assigning the origin of the idea of substance is the same as the difficulty I proposed under a different form

55. The difficulty posed by the attempt to deduce the idea of substance arises from the need of a judgment by which to deduce it. To do so, we must possess a universal idea, the idea of existence, that cannot be derived from the senses.

Now, the difficulty which I noted in explaining the origin of ideas, if one thinks carefully about it, comes down to this: how is our first judgment possible if we assume that we do not previously have an innate, universal idea?

We cannot begin to make judgments without possessing a universal idea because every judgment is an activity of the understanding that requires the use of a universal idea. We must, therefore, assume such an idea, granted the impossibility of using something we do not have.

Before we have universal ideas we cannot therefore form any judgment about sensations or about any cause of sensations.

But if our spirit is completely lacking in universal ideas and cannot make any judgment either about its sensations or their causes, it cannot, in such a state, take any step forward and move even a fraction beyond sensations themselves. If you deprive the spirit of its act of judgment, you deprive it of its entire activity and oblige it to remain completely inert. Thus, the human spirit, unable to make any judgment about its sensations or the entia which correspond to them, cannot form any universal idea. Such an idea, when formed by the spirit for itself, is only produced by a judgment.

For example, let us assume that some sensible agent — a tree, a rock, an animal — strikes my senses. First, I have all the sensations of colour, size, shape, movement, etc. which that sensible agent produces on my senses. But as long as I experience all these sensations in a passive way as alterations to my sensitivity, without any involvement on the part of my understanding, my intellect will still not have perceived any ens. To perceive something intellectually, my spirit must pronounce a judgment, that is, say to itself, 'Something exists which is endowed with such and such

[55]

sensible qualities' (that is, qualities perceived by my senses). In forming such a judgment, I am simply attributing existence to something real whose sensible qualities alone have been grasped by my senses. Thus, I perceive the ens itself intellectually. The universal idea which I make use of in this judgment is the idea of existence which, if I did not possess it previously, I would be quite unable to apply to my sensations. Consequently, I would be unable to pronounce the inner judgment: 'The ens endowed with the sensible qualities which I perceive exists.' My understanding could perceive nothing, because perceiving something intellectually is the same as judging that something exists.

This universal idea of existence or being, however, cannot come to me from sensations alone because they do not contain such an idea. They are merely modifications of being, without having being within themselves. Consequently, they cannot be perceived in isolation by the intellect. They have to be perceived in something else, that is, in an ens (substance) completely different from them. Here lies the whole problem which Locke, on his own admission, encountered when he sought to deduce the idea of substance from sensations.

56. However the difficulty, in the way I formulated it, does not end here. The argument needs further development.

Observation certainly assures us that the understanding perceives nothing except by an inner judgment whereby it says to itself: 'Such a thing exists.' It is indisputable that to pronounce such a judgment, the understanding must already be endowed with the idea of *existence* which it adds to the sensible qualities perceived by the senses.

This by itself is already an insoluble difficulty for those who wish to deduce all ideas from the senses. It arises with the formation of any idea, be it the idea of a tree, a rock, an animal — in a word, however determined the idea may be. In the formation of these ideas, and consequently of intellective perceptions, a judgment is needed which always involves the use of the universal idea of *existence* because these ideas are used to posit something existent. But the idea of *existence* cannot be derived from sensible qualities. These cannot be considered as existent without thinking of existence, which cannot be predicated of sensible qualities, unless they are conceived in some other thing which does not fall under the senses.

Thus, even the formation of particular ideas, or more accurately, of perceptions, is inexplicable unless we assume the pre-existence in us of the universal idea of existence, with which alone we can form them.

57. We are justified, therefore, in saying that Locke's school of philosophers did not carry out a sufficiently detailed analysis of ideas to enable them to know the truth which I have indicated, that is, there is no idea, even relative to something particular, that does not contain within itself some universal idea or at least the idea of existence. Having the idea of a tree, and referring it to a particular tree is the same as intellectually perceiving a tree, and intellectually perceiving a tree is the same as judging that a tree exists, or as classifying a tree among existent things. It follows that perception on the part of the senses is not an *idea* until the felt element is classified, so to speak, among existing or possible things. To do this, we need the idea of existence, that is, of the class in which it rests. This truth, however, completely eluded the philosophers of whom I am speaking. They supposed that there actually were particular ideas without any universal, common notion.

58. In arguing, therefore, with such philosophers, I maintain that, by starting from their assumption that particular ideas do not contain any universal and common element, it is impossible to deduce universal ideas from particular ideas by abstraction.

It is impossible to draw universal ideas from strictly particular ideas which are assumed not to contain any universal element. It is a glaring contradiction to say that we can find something where it is not.

But our philosophers have little difficulty in teaching us how to do this. They say that universal ideas are derived from particular ideas by abstraction. When you have the idea of a tree, a rock, an animal or any other individual thing, you observe what is common to them all and what is proper to each. By fixing your attention on the common element and totally disregarding anything proper, you form the idea of the common quality alone; this is the universal idea. If you want to form the idea of existence for yourself, ignore all the other qualities, and concentrate solely on that quality which you have found is commonest of all in the objects you know. Thus, you form for yourself the perfect idea of existence.

[57–58]

I do not wish to spend precious time enumerating the multiple mistakes contained in this statement. I shall deal solely with the points required to highlight the difficulty of which I spoke.

My answer, therefore, is as follows: you want me to reflect upon my particular ideas of a tree, a stone, and so on, by concentrating on their common qualities and isolating them from the qualities proper to them. You are assuming, therefore, that the idea of a tree, etc. which I have in my mind, is a composite of 1. ideas of common qualities and of 2. ideas of proper qualities. In fact, if the idea did not contain these two elements, I could neither divide the idea as you want me to, nor find the elements there, nor concentrate on one element rather than another. In other words, you are contradicting yourself. You began from the assumption that *particular ideas* did not contain *universal ideas*, and that my mind, although totally bereft of universal ideas, could form them for itself with the assistance of particular ideas.

These philosophers, therefore, make the following mistake. They say that it is very easy to form particular ideas, which are furnished through sensations. They conclude that it is easy precisely because they assume that particular ideas do not contain any universal, common element. Having done this, they next go on to deduce common, universal ideas from particular ideas in the way I have described. However, it is equally easy to answer them. When you deduce common, universal ideas from particular ideas, you assume that the former are a part, an element, of the latter. On the other hand, when you deduced particular ideas from sensations, you assumed the contrary. If, in fact, you had assumed that particular ideas contained some common, universal notion, you would have had to assign to them an origin different from sensation, which contains only entirely particular elements.

59. Seeking at a deeper level the cause of the illusion entertained by Locke's disciples, I think it is to be found in their not having perceived clearly enough how sensations and sensible elements, in themselves, independently of our mind, are so particular that in reality they contain particular qualities only. A common, universal quality has no existence except in our mind. But Locke's disciples, who did not realise this — I shall take the

opportunity to explain in greater detail later — attributed to things something which was merely in their mind, that is, common qualities. After this first mistake, which affected the whole system, other errors occurred automatically.

60. The error which occurred in the initial notion was communicated from one notion to the next by a series of links, as follows.

The first erroneous notion involved things perceived by the senses. The unnoticed error stated: 'Corporeal beings actually contain *something in common* independently of the way they are perceived.' Now if what is *common* does exist in real things themselves and not in the intellect, we waste time searching the human intellect for the origin of what is *common*; it is a real quality of things.

Stage two: the elements of which things are composed, that is, 1. what is *common* and 2. what is *particular*, pass into the sensations as soon as things are perceived by the senses. If we accept as a fact 1. that our senses perceive the sensible qualities of bodies and 2. that what is *common* exists in the sensible qualities because some sensible qualities are *common* and others *individual*, it follows that sensation also perceives what is common and what is proper.

Stage three: if sense receives within itself and perceives what is *common* in things, it is easy to explain the origin of *particular* ideas since, although these ideas are made up of 1. common notions and 2. proper notions, they are nevertheless furnished by sensations. Consequently, there is no need to resort to any other principle to explain the origin of particular ideas because all the elements of which these are made up are furnished by the senses.[52]

Finally: (and this represents the fourth stage of Locke's argument) it is extremely easy to abstract universal ideas from particular ideas containing 1. what is common and 2. what is proper. All we have to do is to analyse these ideas closely and concentrate solely upon what is common while disregarding proper qualities.

---

[52] Yet the contradiction already mentioned would never be entirely absent amongst Locke's followers, even if the whole argument which they erect upon such an unreliable basis were sound.

All the conclusions of this argument are without doubt correctly deducted provided the principle is true. If the first notion we have of external things is composed of 1. a common element and 2. a proper element, all the other deductions are correct. There is no doubt that *universal ideas* can be derived from *particular ideas* by analysis if it is true that the former are contained in the latter.

Particular ideas derived from 1. what is common and 2. what is proper can undoubtedly be obtained from sensations alone if it is true that sensations themselves are derived from both common and proper elements.

Finally, there is no doubt that sense perceives what is *common* and what is *proper* if it is true that these are two real elements that go to make up external *things* and their sensible qualities.

The error in this entire argument is to be found in the first proposition.

What is *common* has no existence outside the intellect; it is an element of our ideas, not a real element of external things. External things have, in fact, only an individual, proper existence; they have only particular qualities; the word *common* implies a *relationship* between a number of objects observed by the mind. A *relationship*, however, is not a quality of any species in such a way that it can exist in a real entity; it lies completely outside existing real things and exists only in thought.

61. If, therefore, the notion of what is *common* is present only in ideas, and everything has a merely *particular* and *proper* existence in external things, we have to ask about the origin of this notion of common quality. Sense, when perceiving external things, cannot perceive anything that is not present. Not having what is *common* in its perceptions, sense cannot transmit what is common to ideas. Yet the concept of a common quality is found in ideas. It follows that it must be something found in the intellect itself, independently of sensations. This argument admits of no reply.

The difficulty I set forth amounted to this: how can the intellect have the idea of what is common?

It is a fact, as I said, that an intellectually developed person makes judgments.

Therefore this person has begun to judge.

There is no middle way here. The attempt to discover a

middle way is a pipe-dream. There can be no conceivable intermediate stage between my stating, when something strikes my
sensories, 'This is an ens', and my not stating it.

Let us go back to our first judgment. In this judgment, we
already have to possess some common notion. This common or
universal idea, which is necessary in forming a judgment, can be
derived by reflection only from 1. sensations or 2. from particular ideas. We cannot derive it from sensations because they contain no concept of what is common; it must be derived,
therefore, from particular ideas. It is to be assumed, then, that
we begin to make judgments after the acquisition of some particular ideas. However, these particular ideas either contain or
do not contain a common notion. If the concept is contained in
such ideas, it still remains to be explained how we have formed
these particular ideas which cannot subsist without a common
notion. If it is not contained in them, the difficulty arises once
again. There is, therefore, no means of avoiding this difficulty
unless we assume that the intellect itself furnishes the common
notion and has in itself something that has not been received
from the senses.

62. The first part of the inquiry which I introduced in this
work, 'Whether the human mind has within it an innate element?' is now complete. That leaves us with the second part: 'If
there is an innate element, what exactly is it?' which has already
been clarified, although dimly, when I showed that the *idea of
being* is the universal notion from which every universal concept
originates. However, before developing this statement, I feel I
must keep the promise I made about examining the main philosophical systems relative to the first part of my investigation.

Article 6

Conclusion about the shortcoming of Locke's system

63. A brief summary of what has been said so far.

1. Particular ideas always contain at least one common or
universal idea, the idea of *existence*. There is no *idea* of anything until the mind has pronounced the inner judgment: 'Such
a thing is.'

2. Particular ideas are initially formed by the human spirit's combining what is sensible with the common notion of existence, as though placing it in the class of existent things. The particular idea is thus the perception by the intellect of something sensible which the intellect considers as belonging to the class of existent things. In other words: 'It is something sensible to which is attributed the universal quality of existence which then becomes proper.'[53]

3. Hence, the particular idea cannot be formed unless the intellect introduce the notion of existence. If we call this operation 'synthesis', the particular notion cannot occur without a *synthesis* on the part of the intellect.

4. The intellect cannot derive a *common notion* from sensations because it is not contained in them. It must therefore derive this notion from within itself.

5. A *universal* idea can be derived by abstraction from a particular idea when the universal, common idea is already contained in the particular idea. This operation is called *analysis*.

6. Locke, who did not suspect the existence of any problem in explaining the formation of *particular ideas*, supposed that they came directly from sensations in the way I have described. Consequently, he thought that *universal, general ideas* could be derived by analysing the particular ideas. In fact, *common* ideas are contained in particular ideas.

64. The flaw in Locke's system consists in his supposition that a *common element* actually exists in sensible things. He did not appreciate the difficulty that arises in seeking the origin of such a notion.

This flaw resulted in his failure to see the need for a *synthesis* prior to *analysis*, that is, for an intellectual operation in which what is felt is united with the *common idea* of existence pre-existing in the intellect. This is how judgments are made from which particular ideas are formed.

Locke assumed the formation of the *synthesis* in the nature of external things, and thus posited from the beginning the theory

---

[53] I shall point out elsewhere, however, that I make a distinction between *perception* and *particular idea*; the latter is the intuited *object* embedded in the affirmation which the spirit makes about the subsistence of the object. Perception is the *affirmation* itself.

of the *analysis* of ideas. From this, merely by separating them out, he deduced *universal* ideas in the guise of *abstractions*. He did not explain how these ideas were formed. He took the process for granted.

I shall finish the present section by quoting a passage from an Italian philosopher who pointed out most clearly and accurately the flaw in Locke's philosophy:

> We have to distinguish two ages in human knowledge. First, synthesis which forms the objects of experience and produces the great book of sensible nature. In the age to which I refer, the intellect's first operation must be a synthesis. — The second age begins when we read from the book of nature. In this second age, the spirit examines its own operations; analysis is its primary activity. Locke concerns himself with the second age: he assumes that the great book of nature has already been formed, and suggests the spirit in which it is to be read and understood. He starts from the fact that the senses give us complete ideas of individual things, which are objects of experience. He takes for granted the external character of our sensations and their union in an object (*and, I would add, the common notion of existence*). Consequently, he makes use of analysis to derive all simple ideas from experience.

Further on, the same philosopher adds:

> The English philosopher, by opening up the great book of nature for study by the human spirit, enables the spirit to use analysis to infer all simple concepts.[54] Now we cannot conclude from this that all simple concepts derived in this way are given by sensibility or are feelings, distinct and developed from other feelings. If, among these simple notions, some subjective elements are found,[55] these may well

[54] Talking of *simple notions* does not bring out the difficulty as clearly as talking of *common or universal notions* because initially it would be necessary to prove that what is simple cannot be found by resolution of what is composite. Only then could we grasp the difficulty of deriving simple notions from the phenomena of sensation. On the other hand, it is clear, when we speak of *common notions*, that they cannot be found in what is particular because this intrinsically excludes common notions. What is particular essentially excludes as its contrary what is common.

[55] *Subjective*, that is, introduced by the intelligent subject and therefore innate in the intelligent subject, at least virtually. However, the expression

be deduced analytically from experience, but only because
the spirit has introduced them by means of the synthesis
with which it formed the objects of experience. The fundamental question consists in deciding whether the primal
activity of thought is analysis or synthesis.[56]

subjective, is not accurate. As we shall see, this inaccuracy led to error in
Kant's philosophy. The fact is that the spirit may have within itself innate
common notions without its having derived them from within itself, but by
receiving them from outside itself. This remark is highly important for a clear
understanding of the theory I shall be expounding in its proper place.

[56] Galluppi, *Lettere filosofiche, etc.*, Letter 7. Actually, it is not sufficient to
know that the primary activity of thought is synthesis; we also need to know
what kind of synthesis is involved. This is the crucial question.

CHAPTER 2
Condillac

Article 1
D'Alembert raises objections to Locke's system

65. The first ideas to come under analysis are those of physical entia. Locke's modern philosophy concentrates upon these. Locke scarcely sees the difficulty arising from a desire to explain the origin of the idea of substance. Indeed, he went further, setting aside the idea of substance and even denying its existence. It did not fit his system and therefore was not.

He was unaware that, without it, we would have no way of forming for ourselves the idea of external bodies; nor did he grasp that every idea we have of a body inevitably includes the idea of substance, that is, of an existence proper to itself and not to anything else; in short, of a subject of sensible qualities.

However, Locke's remark about the impossibility of deriving the idea of substance from the senses was shrewd, although as an isolated remark, it took considerable time to come to fruition.

Because the idea of substance had occurred to him in abstract form, Locke was unable to see its connection with many other, more limited ideas. Consequently he spoke of it theoretically, as if it were an imaginary ens which philosophy could perhaps do without.

The philosophers who came after Locke were also unaware of the full impact of Locke's remark, and failed to give it due importance.

Instead they concerned themselves particularly with the way in which Locke deduced the ideas of bodies. In so doing, they discovered that some of his arguments were arbitrary and that he skirted around difficulties which should have caused him thought.

Locke was unaware of the need to pause and offer a more satisfactory explanation than that available to the ordinary person of the way we can form the ideas of things outside ourselves. He took as his starting point the following principle, which for him was a basic fact: 'Sensations give us immediately the ideas of bodies outside ourselves.' He did not think there was any need to spend time explaining such a primal fact.

D'Alembert noted that this could not be accepted as a primal fact; it presented difficulties requiring a solution. These were the problems d'Alembert saw:[57]

1. Sensations are only modifications of our spirit. They exist purely in ourselves. How, then, can we go out of ourselves and form the idea of something outside us if we have no other source for our ideas than sensations which are wholly present within us?

66. 2. Sensations are all separate and independent of each other. Our sensation of smell, for example, has nothing to do with our sensation of colour; that of colour has no correspondence with that of taste or sound, nor with that of touch. Our idea of body, however, is a complex of all these sensible, yet intrinsically distinct qualities which, in our idea, are combined and assigned to a single subject, that is, to the body of which we have the idea. How does our soul happen to combine these sensations and assign them to a single subject? If the senses alone provide us with the ideas of bodies, it is not clear how this can come about.

67. The difficulties which d'Alembert noted as rising from Locke's theory were the very difficulties that Locke had seen in attempting to explain the idea of substance. Locke however was considering the idea of substance in general, while d'Alembert, adopting a more partial approach, was considering the idea of substance in bodies.

In fact, thinking of a body outside us as a single subject to which the sensible qualities perceived by our senses are referred is merely the equivalent of thinking of a support, of a necessary centre for sensible qualities, in short, of bodily substance.

D'Alembert, however, did not realise that the two difficulties

---

[57] Yet d'Alembert speaks of Locke's *An Essay concerning Human Understanding* as a complete treatise of metaphysics! At the time, it was the book to read. We cannot now accept the way in which people of the time overrated Locke. The human spirit has since moved on.

were only one.[58] In fact he showed that he concurred fully with Locke in denying the idea of substance[59] while, without realising it, raising the question: 'Whence do we derive the substantial idea we have of bodies?' Such is the indolence of the human spirit! Even the sharpest minds grope after the truth in a dim twilight.

Article 2

Condillac's criticism of Locke

68. D'Alembert indicates the two difficulties I have mentioned, but without solving them. Condillac followed him and attempted a solution.

To highlight a question in any way is always a step forward for philosophy, and d'Alembert deserves credit for what he did. However, he remained faithful to Locke's principle that all ideas come from the senses. At the time, such a principle, affirmed obstinately, was impossible to abandon.

[58] One way to simplify philosophical questions is to clarify one's ideas and reduce the difficulties and questions to a minimum. The forms in which the difficulties occur are too numerous, and each new form is taken for a new question, although it may be the same. This is the result of the nature of language which furnishes thought with countless variations and forms. Those who wish to make a vain, ostentatious and useless display of their learning try to introduce problems, arguments and objections in their hundreds. Such pathetic ostentation can only impress morons. It is worse than the ostentation of the lunatic who broke everything that came his way into tiny pieces and claimed that this multiplied the number of objects he possessed.

[59] In my view, the *idea of substance* was repudiated as a result of a misunderstanding. In other words, it was thought that having the idea of substance required more than was actually the case. In fact, it was sufficient to know that *modification requires a modified subject*. This subject is the idea of substance. If you say to me: 'But I do not know what this subject is,' you may well be right. What is more, I grant that it is essentially an unknown for you, an 'x'. You do know, however, that it is the subject of certain modifications, that it is the cause of certain effects. But, what more do you wish to know? If you strip it of its modifications, its properties, its effects, it still remains an 'x' for you. You still have an idea of it, therefore, because you know how this unknown is related to what you know. This is our knowledge of substance in general, nor can we expect any more; this is sufficient for us to have the idea of substance.

Asking how we can pass from sensations, which are within our spirit, to form our ideas of bodies is the same as asking: 'How can we form a judgment before being supplied with ideas?' Actually, to have the concept of something outside ourselves, we have to form the following judgments: 1. some thing exists; 2. this thing which exists is outside me; 3. this thing which exists is the subject of the sensible qualities which I perceive. To form all these judgments, I must possess universal ideas. The formation of ideas, therefore, requires previous ideas: the first ideas that I form (such as those relating to bodies) are inexplicable unless I assume a first idea given to me by nature.

69. This is the question expressed to its fullest extent. Condillac however saw only the first part of it. He realised that judgments were necessary for the formation of ideas of bodies, but did not realise that these judgments presupposed prior universal ideas. This second step was short and easy after the first. Nevertheless, he failed to take it; such is the slow, protracted progress of the human spirit.

Condillac, therefore, with the benefit of hindsight was able to see things more extensively, and could reproach Locke with not having noticed how judgments are mixed with our sensations.

Condillac refers to Locke at the beginning of his *Treatise on Sensations* when he says:

> Most of the judgments mixed with all our sensations eluded him.

And a little later:

> He was so far from understanding the full scope of the human system that, had it not been for Molineux, he would not perhaps have seen that judgments are involved in visual sensations. He expressly denies that this is the case with sensations from the other senses. He held that we use them through a kind of instinct, and that reflection plays no part in enabling our use of them.

Article 3

Condillac's system

70. This passage perhaps gives the impression that Condillac had thoroughly grasped the difference, which had eluded Locke, between external sensations and the *judgments* associated with them. It would seem to follow, therefore, that he had to posit two essentially distinct faculties, one enabling us to experience sensations, the other enabling us to make judgments upon them. His fondness for systems, however, leads him to do the opposite, that is, to reduce them all to a single faculty, to *sensation* alone. Thus, instead of adding to Locke's two *principles*, *sensation* and *reflection*, he attempts to reduce them to *sensation* alone. This systematic error is similar to that already indicated where a person tries to explain all kinds of sensations by means of a single sense. Anyone setting out to show that the faculty of sight, which enables us to perceive colours, is the same as that enabling us to perceive sounds and tastes, makes an assumption as difficult and absurd as that which forms the whole essence of Condillac's system:

> The sense which perceives the sensation of touch is the same as that which forms a judgment about it.[60]

71. In order to grasp more clearly Condillac's errors, let us follow him step by step. First, this is how he states the argument in the second part of the *Treatise on Sensations*:

> The second part deals with touch, the only sense which of itself judges external objects.

A single faculty, a single sense, performs two different

---

[60] St. Augustine accurately defines the difference between *feeling* and *judging* in a number of passages in his works and sees a vast distance between these two operations of the spirit. He adds that the *mind*, strictly speaking, consists in the faculty of judgment: *Servat aliquid quo libere de specie talium imaginum judicet, et hoc est magis mens, id est rationalis intelligentia,* QUAE SERVATUR UT JUDICET [(The mind) contains something with which it may freely judge about the species of such images (of corporeal things). And this much more is the mind, that is, rational intelligence, which IS CONTAINED SO THAT IT MAY JUDGE] (*De Trinit.*, bk. 9, c. 5).

operations called by different names and recognised as distinct by Condillac himself: 1. it feels external things and 2. makes judgments about them.[61]

Condillac also attributes two distinct kinds of operation, feeling and judgment, to the other senses. He claims, however, that the senses do not receive the power of judging from themselves; rather, a power is *communicated* to them by the sense of touch (a very mysterious communication!) which is also sole judge. This is what he proposes to show in the third part:

> The third part shows how the sense of touch teaches the other senses to judge external objects.[62]

Article 4

Inaccuracy of Condillac's analysis

72. Condillac, read carefully, appears as someone who intends to explain the progressive development of our faculties in a careful, analytical way, without any unwarranted step. He seems convinced that he can succeed where all his predecessors have failed. At the same time, it is obvious that his approach to rigorous, reliable argument is still at an infantile stage. As we ourselves try to retrace his steps with accuracy and skill (observation is more refined now, and we are less tolerant of unjustified argument), the crudity of his analysis of the operations of the spirit becomes more obvious. He interposes and assumes

[61] Both Aristotle and the scholastics teach that the sense *judges*. But it would appear that the word *judge* was understood at that time metaphorically as conveying any similarity noted between the effects of the senses and those of judgment. I am led to this conclusion by passages in Aristotle where he explains the judgment he attributes to the intellect very differently from that attributed to sense. I find it difficult, however, to absolve Aristotle from the error I attribute to Condillac without accusing the former of inaccuracy and impropriety in his expressions.

[62] When I am told that one person communicates knowledge to another by instruction, I understand perfectly well what *communicate* means. However, I am baffled when told that one sense *communicates* the faculty of judgment, which it does not possess of itself, to another. Here *communicate* becomes unintelligible and inexplicable to me.

the most telling facts without explanation and without accurate observation — or at least without realising that they require justification and explanation.

To show this more clearly and to reveal how he was quite unaware of the difficulty involved in explaining the act of judgment without presupposing the existence within us of something innate, let us see how he crudely and artlessly reduces all other faculties to sensation alone.[63]

Article 5

Intellectual attention is not the same as sensitivity

73. First of all, Condillac attempts to reduce attention to sensation in the following way:

> If a man has a great number of sensations, simultaneously, with more or less the same degree of intensity, he is still merely an animal which feels. However, if we discard all but one sensation or, without removing the others, reduce their power, the spirit is immediately seized more particularly by the sensation, which retains all its intensity. This sensation is transformed into *attention* without the need to assume anything else in the mind.

However, it was easy to see that the action of external agents on our sense organs and the accompanying sensation is distinct from the activity of the intellective spirit which particularly handles this sensation.[64]

[63] Further remarks on the system of transformed sensation are to be found in the short work *Breve Esposizione della filosofia di M. Gioia*, included in the two volumes of *Opuscoli filosofici* and especially in the notes to pp. 358–365 in which I have endeavoured to set out briefly the absurdities of such a philosophy.

[64] Condillac himself distinguishes in the human spirit *passivity* and *activity*. But these two terms must be different if they produce opposing concepts. It is impossible to reduce to a single passive principle, such as mere sensation, all the most active powers of the soul. No one saw this error of Condillac more perspicaciously than Baron Galluppi in his *Elementi di filosofia* (Messina, 1820), vol. 2, pp.192 ss. In Condillac's native France, we find the following: 'Either Condillac was deluded for thirty years, or never expressed his thought clearly enough, or perhaps did not have the required insight to grasp it.

74. We can experience pure sensation without any act of will on the part of our spirit provided the spirit is ready to welcome the sensation passively. But attention to a sensation is an activity subject to our will; it is not mere passivity. Let us imagine that we receive four sensations simultaneously. Let us also imagine that we are in a state of passivity or inertia, and that all the sensations are of more or less the same intensity. Now if, instead of displaying the same equanimity and indifference to these four sensations, we concentrate as hard as we can on one, there is no doubt that, as a result of this concentration, we shall experience more keenly the sensation in question. Nevertheless, we cannot fail to perceive the others as well, although less forcefully. There is in our spirit, therefore, an operation of the will, a power enabling us to focus (where four similar sensations are involved) on any one we wish and thereby make its impact upon us more intense. This observation clearly shows that the power of our spirit, when activated by our will as it concentrates on sensations and chooses one rather than another, is something entirely different from the sensations themselves which exist even when such power does not come into play.

This can be experienced when we listen to a quartet. In allowing the music to pervade our hearing without our spirit's making use of any particular activity, we take in the playing and we experience all the sensations which the four instruments produce in us. However, it will soon be obvious that there is in our mind an operation of will quite different from this passive feeling. We deliberately compose the spirit either to take in more fully the entire range of harmony or to focus on a single instrument and enjoy its variation of tone or admire the player's virtuosity. *Sensation*, therefore, is a passive faculty for which the spirit has no need of any special, autonomous operation. *Attention*, on the other hand, is an active faculty whereby a person frequently and willingly brings into play the power of his spirit.

Whatever the reason, I have always found it impossible to understand not how sensation is prior to attentiveness, but how sensation can be transformed into attention; not how an active state can occur immediately after a passive state, but how these two states can be identical in nature in such a way that activity is a transformation of passivity. I am so far from agreeing with this proposition that I scarcely know what is meant by the juxtaposition of the terms of which it is composed' (Laromiguière, Part 1, Lecture 5).

[74]

In this sense, it is true that if engaged in sensation alone 'a human being is still no more than an animal that feels.' However, human beings never engage with sensation alone; besides the capacity for feeling, they have another power, whether they actually use it or not, of focusing their intellective activity upon one thing rather than another. From the very first moments of their existence, this marks them off from other animals and places them in an essentially higher class.[65]

Article 6

Memory and sensitivity are not the same

75. Condillac is no more successful when he endeavours to show that *memory* also is a sensation.

> Our ability to feel is divided between the sensation we have had and the one we experience at present. We perceive them simultaneously, but differently; one appears past, the other present.
>
> To perceive or feel these two sensations is one and the same thing.[66] This feeling is called sensation when the impression is actually made upon the senses; when it comes to us as a sensation that has already occurred, it is called *memory*.

It seems impossible for someone to be so wrong as to state that perceiving present and past sensations are acts of the same nature. Can a past sensation be perceived or felt?

76. A sensation, when past, no longer exists. Its existence in

[65] What I have written in this article about attention as the faculty which directs intellective force does not exclude in any way the *sensitive activity* required for feeling. I accept that this *sensitive activity* is 1. almost always active in living persons who sense their own body and 2. modified by external sensation. At one moment, it expands quietly; at another it focuses on one of the sensations in accordance with certain instinctive laws.

[66] Can we imagine a more gratuitous statement than this? Condillac offers no evidence for it. Evidence, in the eyes of the philosophers of this school, is nothing but a forthright assertion of their own opinions. Strong assertions have an impact on the unwary reader, and serve as principles of knowledge, from which conclusions can be drawn that are easily reconcilable with their authors' preconceived systems.

our memory cannot be said to exist in the same way as a real sensation. Its reality is over and done with, as the saying goes: 'We remember past sensations.' To exist in the form of a real sensation implies that our sensories are currently affected. Sensation really begins when our sensories are affected in the way necessary for feeling. The actual sensation remains as long as the sensories continue to be affected. As soon as the impression has ceased, the reality of the sensation has also ceased. On the other hand, the *memory* remains or, more exactly, begins precisely when the sensation has ceased. It is not therefore a sensation.

77. The expression: 'Past sensations are retained in the memory' seems to have led Condillac astray. He would not have erred if he had realised that, strictly speaking, the expression is inaccurate. The word *sensation* in the statement: 'Sensations are retained in the memory', has a different meaning when actual sensations are under discussion. It is not in fact *real sensations* which are retained in our memory, but their remembrance, which creates the memory. Anyone can see that *remembering* a pain is different from *feeling* a pain, and that calling to mind a pleasant feeling is different from feeling the actual sensation.

The mistake arising from the double meaning of the word 'sensation' applied to sense organs and to memory is in a way similar to the mistake of those who, when shown a portrait and told 'This is Manzoni', take the portrait as the real, living Manzoni! In fact the picture of Manzoni is intrinsically different from Manzoni himself, who is not a meagre canvas daubed with oils and colours, but a grown man of flesh and bone. Nor would it be correct to claim that the portrait was Alessandro Manzoni transformed. Manzoni, who would certainly deny having been transformed into a canvas and plastered with colours, would think we were mad. The sensation said to be in me when I recall it is not the actual sensation which, for example, caused me such an acute pain when my arm or leg was pierced. This can be felt only in the arm or leg, not in the memory where it is pure recollection, assisted perhaps by some residual or revived image but always something distinct and entirely disparate from the reality of sensation.[67] Hence *sensation* and *memory of sensation*

---

[67] Strictly speaking, an idea cannot be called an *image*; the expression may be applied to the phantasms of bodies when we imagine them to be present

cannot be confused even if they are both called 'sensation'. Whatever their interdependence or relationship, one can never be called a transformation of the other. Sense and memory are essentially different faculties which cannot be treated as one for the sake of some systematic, unnatural simplicity.[68]

Article 7

Attention is different from memory

78. Condillac, after imagining that he had shown the non-essential difference between the faculty of memory and the faculty of sensation, continues in the following forthright vein:

> As a result of this, we are capable of two forms of attention: one exercised by memory, the other by the senses.
>
> As there are two forms of attention here, a comparison is involved; paying attention to two ideas is the same as comparing them. But they cannot be compared unless one perceives some difference or similarity between them. To perceive such relationships is to judge.

This is a rapid bird's eye view of a vast area; obstacles magically disappear as Condillac takes flight.

79. First, it requires little thought to understand that the act whereby we focus our attention either on the objects of memory or on the terms of sense is neither memory nor sense.

Attention is a power directed by our spirit or rather, it is the deliberative activity itself of our spirit (cf. 73–74). We focus our attention by an act of will, and can vary the intensity of such attention to suit ourselves.

just as our senses experienced them, but not to the idea. To understand what an idea is, we must accustom ourselves to consider it as it is in itself without introducing comparisons and metaphors drawn from material things. The idea has its own proper being which is intellectual and superior to bodily sensation.

[68] Condillac himself distinguishes the *attention of memory* (*active*) from *attention of the senses* (*passive*). This difference, which regards the two as contraries, is the most fundamental of all.

We have already seen how sensation is distinguished from attention by its passivity, and from memory by its different term (cf. 75–77).

It is also easy to see that attention is distinct from memory, which is formed from remembrance of things past. This is its very nature. The act whereby we focus our attention can be applied to things past and things present. It is therefore different from the act of remembrance.

80. Consequently we have three essentially different faculties: 1. that whereby we feel present impressions; 2. that whereby we *retain our memory of them* when they are over; finally 3. that whereby we focus the *intellective activity* of our spirit at will on present or past sensations (this can be done with varying degrees of intensity).

Article 8

Judgment must not be confused with simple attention

81. Let us press on:

> Where attention is twofold, you have a comparison,[69] because focusing attention on two ideas and comparing them is one and the same thing.

This method of argument is utterly wrong. It requires only a moment's thought to realise that focusing on two ideas does not constitute a comparison. I can restrict my attention perfectly well first on a single idea, then on another, without comparing them and seeing how they differ.

82. Even if focusing attention on two ideas inevitably involved comparing them and seeing how they differ, we would still have to distinguish three contemporary effects in our spirit: 1. attention focused upon one idea; 2. attention focused upon the other idea; 3. attention focused upon the difference between the two ideas. It would remain to be seen whether these three

[69] Comparison does not imply twofold attention, but a twofold object: in other words, comparison arises only when a single act of attention is focused on two objects at one time.

effects were of the same nature, and could be attributed to the same faculty. They could be contemporaneous, but dependent on different powers. Simultaneity is not sufficient to attribute them to the same power if they are not of the same nature.

83. Moreover, these three effects are not necessarily simultaneous. The fact is that I can first focus on one idea, then on another, without having focused my attention on the difference between them.

To realise more clearly that focusing one's attention on two ideas is not the same as comparing them and discovering how they differ, and that not even the attention focused on both ideas leads me inevitably to compare them and work out their difference, we have only to look at what occurs in the case of ideas involving numbers.

Let us assume I have the idea of the number *thirty-five* and that of the number *forty-nine*. Can I not concentrate on both without having to compare them and see how they differ? My knowledge of these two numbers is altogether different from my knowledge of the difference between them. The difference in this case is *fourteen*, that is, a third number which is neither *thirty-five* nor *forty-nine*. It is a third object of my thought, different from the first two, which I myself produce by means of a particular operation proper to my spirit and carry out on the two numbers given to me and kept before my spirit.

I can focus my attention on both numbers without performing that operation or act of the spirit by means of which I notice their difference, but I am also able to keep both numbers present at the same time and carry out numerous different operations on them without any need to carry out that which shows their difference.

84. The reason why Condillac was persuaded that attention could not be fixed on two things without discovering their difference seems to depend on his having observed solely that which usually and most frequently occurs when we think about things which are easily compared and whose difference is easily grasped.

85. However, it is quite remarkable that he did not observe how the act of the spirit whereby we compare two ideas for the sake of discovering their difference is of its nature quite distinct from merely fixing our attention on the two of them. Even if,

every time we focused on two ideas, we were induced to compare them and discover their difference by an inherent law of our nature, we would still have to say that the act of comparison and the discovery of the difference is intrinsically distinct from merely focusing one's attention on both. Furthermore, it is an act of the spirit worthy of separate analysis. It should not be skipped over casually.

When I simply focus my attention on two ideas, I do not create a new object of my attention, but I engage my attention with two objects already existing in my spirit. On the other hand, when I compare two ideas and distinguish what is proper from what is common to them, I form for myself a new object of consideration, that is, their difference, which previously I had never thought of as separate and distinct from the objects (cf. 95).

Article 9

Condillac does not see the problem and comes to grief:
he explains how ideas are formed by assuming
that we possesses some ready-formed ideas
which he uses to deduce all others

86. Condillac should not have skipped so casually over the act of comparison and differentiation without analysing it. This is the duty of any philosopher who proposes to explain the inner working of the human spirit, and would perhaps have enabled him to see the difficulty of which I have spoken. It is, I think, insuperable, unless we first admit something innate in our spirits.

> In fact, we cannot compare two ideas without perceiving some difference or similarity between them: to observe such relationships is to judge.

This passage, in which the philosopher discusses the comparison of ideas, would imply a prior explanation of the word *idea*.

Condillac, however, does not define 'idea' until much later. As a result, it was natural, when undertaking the explanation of the formation of judgments through the comparison of ideas, that he should encounter no difficulties. Without a definition of the nature of ideas, it is impossible to grasp what he is saying. But it is precisely when the argument is formally correct that readers are more indulgent to error, even though the meaning of the words used in the argument remains unspecified.

87. To avoid the same fate, let us first examine what Condillac means by the word *idea*, and then see whether his argument is free from difficulty.

He distinguishes sensations from ideas in the following way:

> A sensation is not an idea until it is seen as a feeling which is limited solely to modifying the state of the spirit. If I am experiencing pain at the moment, I do not say that I have the idea of the pain but that I feel it.
>
> If I remember a pain I have had, the remembrance and the idea are therefore one and the same thing.

It would appear from this passage that Condillac does not attribute the word 'idea' to the sensation we experience here and now. On the other hand, he does assign 'idea' to the sensation which is retained solely in the memory. I have pointed out that sensation, when present in our memory, even though given the same name, is nevertheless something entirely different from actual sensation. Essentially, the nature of sensation consists in the passive modification which our spirit undergoes when our sensories (cf. 75–77) receive impressions from exterior things. It follows that the meaning of idea is essentially different from the meaning of sensation precisely because idea is applied to the remembrance of sensations, which is not a sensation but arises when a sensation no longer exists.

It is helpful to see how Condillac is led to such a distinction.

His following remarks show that he does not give the name 'idea' to sensation properly speaking but to our memories of it. Sensation does not represent anything outside itself. Memory on the other hand represents, or rather recalls, something different from itself, that is, sensation, of which it is the remembrance. According to our philosopher, what makes some apprehension by our spirit an idea is its capacity to *represent* something different from itself. This is why he attributes to the sense of touch the power to change sensations into ideas. He imagines that touch alone of all the senses is that which has the power to *make our sensations representative*. He says:

Existing sensations of hearing, taste, sight and smell are only feelings as long as such senses have not been taught by touch. Until this moment, the soul can consider them only as modifications of itself.[70] But if these feelings exist only in the memory that recalls them, they become ideas. We do not say in that case: *I have the feeling of what I have been*, but: *I have the remembrance of the idea.*

The present — or past — sensation of solidity is the only one which is *per se* simultaneously feeling and idea. It is feeling relative to the soul which it modifies, and idea relative to something external.

This sensation compels us very soon to judge all the modifications which the soul receives from touch as something external to us. That is why any tactile modification is representative of the objects which the hand touches.

Touch, accustomed to assign its sensations to an external source, causes the other senses to do likewise. All our sensations appear to us as qualities of the objects around them. They represent them, therefore; they are ideas.

Note that, in this passage, the abbé de Condillac bestows the power to transform sensations into ideas (that is, to make sensations represent something external to themselves) upon the very sense to which he had attributed the power to judge external objects (cf. 70–71).

His entire theory of sensations is devoted, we may say, to demonstrating 'that touch alone judges of itself external objects, and teaches the other senses to judge them'. In the same way, touch is that faculty whose sensations are simultaneously ideas, and which transforms the sensations of the other senses into ideas.

According to Condillac, sensations are transformed into ideas by means of a judgment. In the passage I have quoted, he teaches that touch has the capacity to transform sensations into ideas only because it has the capacity of judging external objects. Touch, therefore, transforms sensations into ideas by means of judgment whereby it judges that such sensations are external to us.

---

[70] This statement is gratuitous; Condillac advances not the slightest evidence for it. But whatever the case — and this is not the place to discuss it — it should be pointed out that it is statements like this, accepted without any evidence, which often stealthily introduce errors into philosophical systems.

88. I have already shown that it is as absurd to attribute to touch the ability to judge as it is to grant the eye the faculty of both seeing colours and hearing sounds. What is more, it requires only a moment's attention to recognise that the act of judgment is essentially internal, and proper to the spirit alone.[71] It does not require any external, actual impression on the organs. The action of touch, on the other hand, originates from an actual modification of the external, bodily organs. For the moment, however, I do not intend to take this distinction into account. Based solely upon Condillac's principles, my argument is as follows:

89. You say that the act of judgment consists in comparing two ideas and discovering how they differ.

In a different passage, you explain what you mean by the word *idea*. You teach that ideas are such that no one can have them without some judgment. You conclude that only the sense of touch is able to transform sensations into ideas because it alone has *per se* the ability to judge concerning sensations.

Now this is just where the difficulty lies. The problem consists in reconciling these two propositions: 1. a judgment is made by comparing ideas; 2. ideas are formed by means of a judgment. Which is the first, then, to be formed in our spirit, the judgment or the idea?

If every idea needs a judgment in order to be formed, it would seem that judgment is prior to the formation of ideas; but if judgment originates only by comparison between ideas, it would seem that ideas should be present before we can form judgments.[72]

---

[71] The senses provide only the matter of judgment. The act of judgment takes place entirely within the spirit, and does not refer to any point of our body or of the space outside us.

[72] Fortunato da Brescia made a pathetic attempt to evade the difficulty when he thought of adding to Heineccio's definition of idea (*a true image of an object which the spirit immediately contemplates*) the words: *without our affirming or denying anything about the thing itself*. Nevertheless, the addition shows that he had at least glimpsed the difficulty. If, through the *particular idea*, I perceive that real things are outside me, can I realise this without having internally affirmed it to myself? But telling myself that real things are outside me means affirming something, judging that they exist outside me. I think it useful to mention here these obstacles, encountered by all authors who have attempted to explain the origin of ideas, and the various

Article 10

Every representative apprehension is universal:
as a result, Condillac, involved in ever greater difficulty,
finds no solution

90. This is precisely the difficulty which I outlined above and which requires a solution; it emerges here in all its generality.

It no longer involves a particular class of ideas, that is, common or universal ideas, but all ideas without distinction. It does not say: 'In order to make a judgment, some abstract element is necessary; but to produce an abstract, a judgment is necessary. Which of the two will be first, the abstract or the judgment?' It says: 'To make a judgment we need ideas which require comparison with each other. However, to produce ideas a judgment is needed. Which will be first in the human spirit, judgment or idea?'

This inquiry, when transposed into the form of a philosophical problem, may be expressed as follows: 'To assign origins to ideas and judgments so that neither takes the existence of the other for granted and, as a result, to avoid the absurd situation whereby an effect is taken to be the cause of its own cause.' This would be the case if all ideas were the result of judgments and all judgments the result of ideas.

91. Before attempting to see whether any other philosopher managed to extricate himself from this embarassing difficulty by solving the problem, it will help if I consider Condillac's theory more at length.

The concept of idea that Condillac offers us is that of a perception representative of something different from itself. It seems obvious that a judgment is required to realise that a

makeshift solutions which they have devised. Such explanations show universal agreement about the existence of the problem. Those who at first tried manfully to hide the difficulty, later disclosed it by the confusion, uncertainty and incoherence of their statements and the poverty of their painful efforts to hide it from themselves and their readers. Elsewhere (Section Five), I shall illustrate the ingenuity displayed by Wolff in extricating himself from this difficulty, and how poorly he succeeded.

perception has a relationship with something different from itself, and is thus able to represent it.[73]

A mere modification affecting the soul, such as a pain, a pleasure, is certainly felt without the need for any judgment. However, in order to understand how a modification may represent something else, the soul must make a judgment about the modification. This explains why Condillac attributes the formation of ideas to touch; as I said, he bestows on this sense the faculty of judging that its own or others' sensations are representative of external agents.

The difference between us, as I see it, for the moment, is simply that for me, but not for him, *touch* and *judgment* are two distinct powers. Touch consists in the impression of external agents felt by the soul; judgment is proper to the spirit, independently of any actual modification of the bodily organs. Judgment is not the prerogative of the sense of touch, which merely has the task of furnishing the spirit with the occasion and matter for making a judgment.

92. This difference between Condillac and myself has no bearing upon the objection which I am bringing against him. Whether judgment and touch are identical, as he claims, or are separate faculties, as I maintain, we both agree that a judgment is needed to form ideas.

Here the truth to which I referred in my exposé of the difficulty will become much more apparent: every idea, however particular it may be, contains within itself a universal or common element (cf. 43). Where ideas are involved, even when they are applied to particular things, we can always separate what is common from what is proper and thus find in particular things the common element. This would be impossible if it were not there. This truth flows, as we can see, from Condillac's views themselves.

---

[73] As we have seen (cf. 70), St. Augustine expressed extremely well the distinction between the faculties of feeling and judging. In a number of places he points out that if we were endowed with senses alone and lacked any faculty of judgment, we would be unable to use signs because we would lack any means of distinguishing the *sign* from the *thing the sign stands for*. This remark is most apposite here and, if philosophers paid due attention to it, could take them a long way towards understanding the way in which our spirit operates. Cf. St. Augustine, *The Book of 83 Questions*, q. 9 (amongst other works).

As Condillac sees it, having an idea or a representative conception[74] is equivalent to having a model to which he can refer the objects which the model presents or expresses.[75]

A portrait is a representation of the person whom the artist has painted. However, as I said earlier, the painting in this image or portrait is merely a resemblance; it is not the nature or common substance of the person depicted. Consequently, persons other than the one the artist has painted may resemble the same portrait. The person depicted does not have such an exclusive relationship with the painted image that he can monopolise, so to speak, the resemblance and prevent others resembling the portrait in some way. Likewise, the moment a perception has become representative of something other than itself, it has become *universal* in the sense that, besides representing the thing from which it derived, it can, like the portrait of a specific individual, also represent and express everything resembling it. Being representative of something means bearing its likeness; this does not exclude but rather includes similar relationships with countless things that are or can be like it. A relationship of resemblance between two things does not pervade them equally; it does not endow them with the same nature; it does not wed them, so to speak, with a lasting bond. It leaves them free to resemble as many things as possible which they resemble. One similarity does not prevent or interfere with another but embodies and presupposes it. That is why, as soon as Condillac states that all ideas are perceptions representing things, he also has to state that there is in all of them a universal element which alone can make them representative. There must be a common feature because several things are not similar unless they have something in common. It is this *common essence* which, when viewed in isolation, can be considered as being typical of everything it refers to. A type therefore is

[74] I say 'conception'; Condillac would say 'sensation'. But, as we have seen, he stretches the word 'sensation' to mean 'remembrance of a sensation'. This is a dangerous interpretation, an error arising from the inaccuracy of everyday speech. Strictly speaking, a real sensation represents nothing, as I pointed out. What *is* representative is the remembrance, in the spirit, of the sensation. It is this mental remembrance that should be called 'conception'.

[75] I have already indicated the restricted sense in which one must take the words *models, types, images* as applied to ideas (cf. 77).

always universal. If, however, we want to particularise by referring it to an individual thing, that is, to the thing from which it has been extracted, we have a merely arbitrary, positive particularisation, not a natural, necessary one.

If Condillac had noticed this, he would not have spoken in one place about ideas and in another, much further on, of universal ideas. He would not have spoken about ideas without indicating the universality they all contain. He could then have spoken elsewhere about the different kinds of universality.

It is highly important to remove any doubt about the truth which I have demonstrated, that is, that every perception, from the moment it represents something, is universal. Let us see once more, therefore, how Condillac explains the universalisation of a particular idea.

> We have no general idea which has not been particular. Any first object which we have had occasion to observe is a MODEL to which we refer anything which resembles it. This idea, which initially was merely singular, is as general as our discernment is untutored.[76]

93. As a result, we mean that an idea, when said to be general and universal, is a model for many objects, or rather for many real individuals. This is tantamount to saying that its function is to represent them. But every idea is a perception possessing the faculty of representation; every idea is a model. Every idea, therefore, has within it a universal element. Now, in my view, Condillac was prevented from grasping this truth because he confused the capacity of an idea for representing an infinite

[76] Condillac is alluding here to a factual experience. 'Precisely when the understanding is less informed, people tend to generalise their ideas more readily.' This fact spells the ruin of Condillac's system. If the *universality* of ideas is an operation of our spirit, will those who are less educated, the most uncouth, be more suited to carry out such an operation? If in universalising ideas, we move from the *particular* to the *universal*, how can those who are least experienced scale this ladder faster? Is it easier to universalise much or little? Why is it that this is the sole instance in man's initial development when steps are skipped? The philosophy of Locke and Condillac allows no explanation of this fact which will prove perfectly simple after I have shown that the most universal idea of all (that of being) is bestowed by nature on every person coming into the world.

number of individual real entities with its use, that is, with the act whereby we explicitly recognise such an aptitude in the idea.

People who have an ancestor's portrait at home probably think only of the connection between the portrait and the ancestor on which it is based. This particular relationship gives the portrait a definite status as representative of the forefather of the family.

It remains to be seen, however, whether this fixed representation is derived from the nature of the picture and its exclusive relationship with the person depicted, or whether it depends on the accidental attitude of those who look at the picture not in its purely natural relationships but in a formal relationship, so to speak, whereby they know and remember that it was painted to bring out the desired features of this person alone, not of anyone else. It is clear that the issue involves a formal, not a natural relationship. Although fortuitous causes lead the family members to think constantly about the particular resemblance of the picture to the ancestor, this does not alter the nature of the image, nor prevent it from truly resembling and representing all those whom it resembles and represents, as well as the infinite number of people whom one can imagine endowed with the same features.

Similarly, as soon as a perception of ours is representative, it has a necessary, universal relationship with everything that it can represent. This is independent of the use we make of it and of the attention we bestow on different individuals whom it expresses and represents. It may be that we consider it as representative of a single individual, or two or three. This does not rule out its natural capacity to represent an infinite number of others even though we are not paying any attention to them. Moreover, because these individuals whom it represents can be multiplied indefinitely by our imagination, it is impossible for us to go through them all and apply it to all. Consequently, whenever we have a representative conception, we still have the task of applying it to individuals. This becomes almost an art which we learn step by step; we study, as it were, how to use our conception. But whether we do this well or ill, the nature of the concept always remains what it is. As such, it is capable of representing an infinite number of individuals even when we ignore this. True, we may tend to believe that this conception represents a single individual, just as the members of a family are accustomed to think that the ancestor's portrait represents one ancestor alone. The portrait, however, does not thereby cease to resemble those whose likeness it depicts. In the same way, our representative conception truly represents everything it stands for, and we conceive it as such. We think of it as endowed also with its representative character.

Condillac, as we know, requires his statue to see, after acquiring the concept of an orange, not one orange or several similar oranges successively, but two or more simultaneously. The aim is that the statue, by referring the multiple oranges to the idea it already possesses, may recognise this idea as the model or type of all other oranges.[77] But in doing this, he does not demonstrate, as he himself notices, how the idea is converted into a model or a universal. He only shows how we set about using it as a model for a number of oranges. The idea already constitutes a model *per se*, and our application of it presupposes that it is already such in itself. If we compare the various oranges which we see simultaneously to the idea of the orange we already have, we do not alter the nature of this idea. We merely apply it as a universal type. But if we can do this, the idea is *per se* universal, and has been so from the moment it was put in our mind. If not, it could not be used as such.

Take the portrait we have mentioned and imagine that someone outside the family looks at it. Its universal relationship with all the persons who do or can resemble it is not a new relationship created by the viewer, who simply discovers something already existing in it. Similarly, if we relate more oranges to the type of orange we have in our spirit, we do not change the nature of this type which was capable of representing all oranges, even if we ourselves have not focused exclusively on its aptitude and function, or thought that it represented only one orange.

Condillac thinks he has explained how our ideas become models for many individual ideas. In fact, he has merely pointed out the way whereby we later come to use them as models and recognise in them the in-built identity which makes them what

[77] *Traité des sensations*, part 4, c. 6.

[93]

they are. This identity consists in being representative of countless individuals, that is, of making us know the qualities which are or may be common to countless individuals. So, if we presuppose our acquisition of such conceptions, we also presuppose our acquisition of universal, common ideas which have slipped furtively and unseen into our spirit. These certainly escaped the attention of Condillac who found them in his statue, without realising how they had got there. Having found them, his investigations caused him no further difficulty. He assumed, without any justification, that the difficulty had been explained. In fact, he never saw it.

94. Having an idea and knowing how to use it are different things. Our spirit, which always proceeds step by step, comes to know the uses of ideas only as a result of sustained reflection and close analysis. It thereby discovers new relationships which ideas have with one another and with external things and, as a result of these relationships, finds new applications for such ideas. However, this does not mean our spirit does not fully possess the idea on which it carries out all these different operations. Without the idea, it could not carry out such operations nor discover the relationships and applications to which I am referring.

It is a condition of the human spirit that with one act it takes in the idea of things, and with another knows how it is to be used. But, as Condillac says, our spirit normally uses ideas as models for things. Thus it uses the idea of orange to judge about all oranges. When our spirit, therefore, perceives a number of oranges and is drawn to judge them all with the same idea which it uses as their general type and model, it does not acquire a new species of idea, that is, a universal idea, as Condillac seems to claim. We have to say that his idea was universal by nature, that is, apt to serve as a model or common type for all oranges. Only when the spirit sees a number of oranges together is it moved to use such a type to judge them.

Article 11

Continuation

95. The truth of this teaching is such that occasionally even Condillac seems to have glimpsed it, although reluctantly.

Take, for example, the passage where he speaks about judgment, which he conceives simply as an operation through which a person refers the object or present sensation which he is judging to the model or type of the sensation he has already stored in his memory.

As we have seen, he distinguishes two forms of attention: one proper to memory, the other to the senses. The former is active, the latter passive. He believes that these two kinds of attention (that enabling us to recall things previously seen which are retained in the memory, and that enabling us to perceive an individual object by means of our senses at any given moment) enable him to explain what a judgment is. We form a judgment when we compare the object which we presently perceive with the object which we have previously perceived, the image of which is retained in our memory. Now this is merely to refer what is real and actually felt to the type or model which we have already lodged in our memory. He says:

> If, after smelling a rose and a carnation a number of times, it (the statue) smells a rose for a second time, the passive attention created by what we smell will be fully activated in the present scent of the rose. The active attention which memory provides will be apportioned between the memories that remain of the scents of the rose and the carnation. Now, modes of being cannot be distinguished from one another when a capacity for smell draws them to itself unless comparisons are made between them;[78] the act of

[78] I have already shown the difference between feeling two things at the same time and comparing them (cf. 81–85). Each claims part of our attention and struggles to attain it all. On the other hand, the spirit, when judging, works in the other direction. It concentrates on both objects simultaneously without focusing exclusively on one. Otherwise, judgment would be impossible. This shows how absurd it is to attribute judgment to the senses. It is an act clean contrary to any action which the senses can contain or exert on our soul. Sensation tries to draw full attention to itself; the faculty of judgment tries to share attention fairly, as it were, among the different things it must

comparison is equivalent to focusing on two ideas simultaneously, and whenever comparison is present, a judgment is made — a judgment, therefore, is merely the perception of a relationship between two ideas which are being compared.[79]

When one thing is compared with another in order to make a judgment, one of the two things is used as a model. The judgment simply endeavours to ascertain whether the thing about which a judgment is to be made is like the model or not. All judgments are of this kind. According to Condillac, the model is the idea present in the memory, while the thing to be judged is actually being perceived by sense.

96. However, if the idea in my memory, with which I compare things submitted to my senses for judgment, serves as a model in such judgments, it is consequently general in the sense that Condillac attributes to this word. As we have seen, the generality of an idea consists, according to him, in its acting as a model to a great number of objects. We ask Condillac, therefore, why he deals with judgments in his works even before discussing the universality of ideas. In fact, he deals with universal ideas in the fourth part of the *Traité des sensations* and judgments in the second.[80] If universal ideas are needed to form a judgment, as Condillac's theory would lead us to believe, it is impossible to explain the nature of judgments without first explaining the nature of ideas. Condillac, however, dealt with universal ideas after judgments because he realised that ideas of this type could not be formed according to his system except by means of judgments. He says:

compare in order to derive a judgment from them. On the other hand, the expression: *sensations judge,* is so inaccurate that it would appear impossible to be formulated by a philosopher. If sensation judges or if the senses judge or if judgment is a sensation, one sensation must feel another (because no judgment can occur without some comparison), or the sense of one sensation is the very one which simultaneously senses another sensation, or the relationship felt between two ideas which is the term of the judgment is itself a judgment. All this, however, is manifestly absurd.

[79] *Traité des sensations*, p. 1, c. 2, §14 & 15.

[80] He does refer to general ideas also in the first Part when he describes how his statue, endowed with the sense of smell alone, begins to create abstract ideas. But he does this in c. 4 after discussing judgments in c. 2.

> The particular idea of a horse and of a bird will likewise take on a general character when occasion requires comparison between a number of horses and birds. The same holds true of all sensible objects.[81]

It should be noted that, in Condillac's system, there is no comparison without a judgment. If, then, a comparison is required to transform a particular idea into a general idea, a judgment is certainly required. In fact, the opposite holds good: all judgments require an idea in their formation. This implies the prior formation of general ideas, or simply ideas (because all ideas have some universal element in themselves). The opposite also holds true: the formation of general ideas presupposes judgments, according to Condillac. His theory does not meet this difficulty which he bypasses without noticing it. He discusses ideas, judgments and general ideas in three different places as though they were unrelated, despite the impossibility of discussing one without intimate knowledge of the others. Finally, having spent much time explaining general ideas, he preens himself on the ease with which he has done this: 'It can be seen from this how easy it is to form general ideas.'[82]

Article 12

Conclusion about the inherent defect of Condillac's system

97. So far, we have attempted to focus our discussion on Condillac and to bring to bear the type of arguments usually referred to as *ad hominem*. However, it would not be fair of me to overstate my last criticism of Condillac. I have myself already made a remark which mitigates Condillac's mistake, as we shall see.

In explaining the formation of universal ideas, Condillac mentions two sorts of ideas, *particular* and *general*. The former become general when our spirit, by making a comparison between general ideas and the individuals presented to it, uses them as models. In doing so, it forms a judgment about them.

[81] *Traité des sensations*, p. 4, c. 6.
[82] *Traité des sensations*, p. 4, c. 6, §6.

As I showed, however, ideas do not become universal at this stage. They already have a universal element from the time they begin to be ideas. Condillac's own system bears this out. He defines an idea as a sensation representing other things, such as those retained by our memory. He uses the term 'general' for ideas which are used as models. But a representative idea is the same as a model. Condillac himself says that 'idea' necessarily contains this universal aspect. This shows that his mistake about the formation of general ideas consists above all in the incorrect use of the phrase 'formation of general ideas'. He ought to have said: 'The recognition and application by our soul of the universality inherent in all ideas.'

If Condillac's followers were to admit the inaccuracy of the expression, I would not be justified in putting forward my argument, which states: 'You require a judgment to form universal ideas; you require universal ideas to form a judgment. This is a vicious circle from which, given the nature of your system, you will never find a way out.' They would reply: 'We admit our mistake in saying that we form universal ideas only when we recognise them and apply them as models. They were already universal as soon as they were ideas. The judgments we form with them do not make them universal; they merely enable us to recognise them as such. They are consequently universal independently of such judgments, and there is no need for us to make these judgments before the ideas.'

98. However, if Condillac's followers are able, by rectifying their expression, to shrug off the force of my argument, which is strictly *ad hominem* and based on his inaccurate statement, the problem as I stated it earlier remains unsolved because it lies at the heart of Condillac's philosophy. It is impossible to form an idea unless a judgment is involved in the operation,[83] nor can

---

[83] Anyone requiring further proof should read carefully the whole paragraph by Condillac from which I quoted. He says: 'If I recall a pain I have had, the memory and the idea are one and the same thing. If I say that I form the idea of a pain about which someone tells me and which I have never experienced, I MAKE A JUDGMENT about a pain which I have suffered or am suffering. In the first case, the idea and the remembrance are identical. In the second, the idea is the feeling of an actual pain, MODIFIED BY THE JUDGMENTS which I make in order to represent to myself someone else's pain' (*Extrait raisonné du Traité des sensations*).

judgments be made without pre-formed ideas. This leaves the problem in a state of complete ambiguity. Indeed it brands either Condillac's philosophy as false, or the formation of both judgments and ideas as inexplicable.

CHAPTER 3
Reid

Article 1
Origins of the Scottish school

99. I felt I should deal at some length with Condillac's system because of its continued popularity in Italy although it cannot be claimed as the system best suited to the kind of thought found in our nation which, compared with others, has remained free from systematic, extravagant thinking.[84]

100. Condillac's philosophy may be described as Locke's thought naturalised in France. The slight modifications undergone by Locke's thought in France after Condillac's time may be ignored. The cluster of disparate data which confuse and muddle research into the activities of the soul under the guise of medicine, anatomy and chemistry add nothing to the explanation of the origin of ideas.

101. In England, Locke's philosophy was discussed by much more acute spirits than in France. Berkeley and Hume pushed it with amazing courage to its ultimate limits, that is, to idealism

[84] In southern Italy, there is still (1829) a certain *penchant* for the thought of Descartes and Malebranche, especially in the State of Rome. This, I think, is due to the works of Gerdil and other enlightened thinkers who have modified and perfected those systems of thought. In Vico's homeland, we have a flourishing tradition of bold thinkers such as Miceli, Galluppi, etc. Moreover, it seems that a kind of eclecticism is generally predominant in Italy. In the Lombardo-Veneto kingdom, Fr. Soave, with the purest of intentions, caused a great deal of harm by disseminating Condillac's philosophy and by reducing philosophy to a tenuous thread which, although it attracts the ordinary person by its apparent simplicity, prompts others, who can never be philosophers, to imagine that they are such. It also sows seeds of contempt for great problems which far surpass the loquacious, tendentious mediocrity of these pseudo-philosophers. Nevertheless, there were a number of powerful thinkers in this part of Italy who had escaped the general malaise and, with their own particular drive, had applied themselves to the most profound issues; Fr. Ermenegildo Pini, author of the *Protologia*, is for me outstanding in this respect.

and scepticism. They shook the foundations of all branches of science and suggested to human nature that it might be content to doubt its own existence.

102. Only when the system based on sensation was seen to produce such unexpected consequences, and to open before mankind an abyss of nothingness which first swallowed the world of matter, and then the world of the spirit together with mankind itself, did people wake up and begin to have serious doubts about it. Perhaps the system, which had been so readily accepted and welcomed by the ordinary reading public, contained some deep-seated flaw which over-eagerness had obscured, leaving its unproven principles considered as obvious. It was thought wise to backtrack, to subject all the premises to rigorous analysis and to submit to a minute screening those which, though not necessarily obvious, seemed at first glance to be true. The fatal flaw which inevitably produced such dire consequences might be concealed in any one of them. In short, human nature protested against this philosophy and, having been brought to the abyss by such an untrustworthy guide, recoiled in horror simply because it was impossible to continue.

At this point, when the force of nature and prompting of common sense warned mankind that such an inhuman philosophy could not be true,[85] a new Scottish school arose which took *common sense* as its guide and resolved to use individual reason only to explain doctrines accepted by common sense.

103. These new philosophers saw that the consequences which Berkeley and Hume derived from Locke's principles by means of close and robust argument were unassailable. This meant going back to first principles to investigate the basic, hidden flaw. But the Scottish reformers, who were dealing with clever adversaries and had to be rigorous in their argument, not surprisingly relied very little on Condillac's doctrine despite its continuing popularity.

Reid, it seems, never quotes him; Dugald Stewart generally

[85] The need for this was inevitably felt more in Scotland than elsewhere because, as Stewart assures us, the idealism of Berkeley and Hume had made wide inroads into all the schools in that country and was generally accepted. *Histoire abrégée des sciences métaphysiques, etc.* [*A General View of the Progress of Metaphysical, Ethical and Political Philosophy*], 3, p. 191.

spoke of him with contempt, calling him an annotator of
Locke's work who failed to understand his master.[86] Among
other remarks, he says of his philosophical style:

> The clearness and simplicity of Condillac's style add to the
> force of this illusion, and flatter the reader with an agree-
> able idea of the power of his own understanding, when he
> finds himself so agreeably conducted through the darkest
> labyrinths of metaphysical science. It is to this cause I
> would chiefly ascribe the great popularity of his works.
> They may be read with as little exertion of thought as a
> history or a novel; and it is only when we shut the book,
> and attempt to express in our own words the substance of
> what we have gained, that we have the mortification to see
> our supposed acquisitions vanish into thin air.[87]

Article 2

Reid's theory on the distinction between faculties

104. The problem which I raised about the origin of ideas did
not occur to Dr. Reid with the generality with which I tried to
expound it. He never had the chance of viewing it in such a

---

[86] D. Stewart was extremely well-disposed towards Locke and spoke of him
fondly. He was, after all, a fellow-countryman. In a number of passages,
however, he admits the insufficiency of Locke's system, which contained
serious flaws. He says: 'With those who attach themselves to that author, as an
infallible guide in metaphysics, it is vain to argue' (*Histoire abrégée des
sciences métaphysiques, etc.*, 3, part 3). Even more remarkable, considering the
high opinion which Stewart shows for Locke in so many passages and his
contempt for Condillac, is the following open admission: 'The difference
between Locke's theory and that which derives all our ideas from sensation
alone (Condillac's) is more apparent than real' (*Éléments de la Philosophie de
l'Esprit humain* [*Elements of the Philosophy of the Human Mind*], vol. 1, part
4). Mainly for this reason, I thought that by dealing at length with Condillac,
who has had such direct influence upon us, I could examine Locke's
philosophy more quickly without repeating the same remarks. Moreover,
whatever else I needed to say about particular aspects in Locke's theory is
dealt with in discussing the work of Reid who refutes several basic
propositions of Locke, in addition to those of Berkeley and Hume.

[87] *Histoire abrégée des sciences métaphysiques, morales et politiques, etc.*,
part 3.

broad perspective. This perhaps explains why such a sound thinker did not develop the argument as we might have expected.

Yet he does see it in part, and tried very hard to solve the part he did see. It is impossible to rebut the arguments of the idealists and sceptics whom he undertook to oppose without being involved in part at least in the difficulty.

105. To enable us to discover the depth at which the Scottish philosopher dealt with the problem, we first need to know the opinions he was impugning.

As I said, Condillac, deceived by the double meaning he assigned to the word *sensation*, maintained that the objects of sense[88] and memory are essentially the same. In other words, the object of sense is a present sensation; the object of memory, a past sensation. He thought that in this way he could reduce the two faculties to a single faculty of feeling. Using a similar argument, he reduces all other faculties of the human spirit to feeling alone since, according to him, they all have essentially identical objects which are, as he puts it, *sensation transformed*.

Locke had grasped that the object of memory was essentially different from that of sense. He had posited a specific distinction between the power of feeling and that of remembrance. He stated that the immediate object of memory is not a sensation, for example, of the rose smelt yesterday, but an idea, a model, a phantasm, in short a remnant, of the sensation left behind in our spirit.

Berkeley and Hume, who had perfected Locke's system in England as Condillac had done in France, tried like Condillac to reduce the two objects of sense and memory to one. They believed they could do so by assuming that the objects of sensation and memory differ only in their degree of vivacity.

106. It is odd that Dr. Reid who applied his keen intellect to

[88] *Sense object* is not a correct term; on the contrary, the inaccuracy of this expression gave rise to a number of errors. Anyone can see that a large variety of sensations, at least all those involving mere pleasure or pain, do not have any object. They are simple and (if it can be expressed in this way) they are their own object. They have a cause outside themselves but not an object. However, until I have the chance to clarify this argument, I am compelled to use ordinary language to express my thoughts, especially when expounding the systems of others who make liberal use of such phrases.

the refutation of the idealism and scepticism of these two philosophers should have chosen to reject Locke's distinction between the object of the senses and of the idea.[89]

> In the meantime, I beg leave to think, with the vulgar, that, when I remember the smell of the rose, that very sensation which I had yesterday, and which has now no more any existence, is the immediate object of my memory; and when I imagine it present, the sensation itself, and not any idea of it, is the object of my imagination.[90]

107. I was about to say that it is difficult to understand how the human spirit can think, here and now, of something which is not in any way present to it. Not by means of an idea, because Reid rejects any idea, type or sign of the thing; not by means of the thing itself, because he assumes that the object is not

---

[89] Dr. Reid, it would seem, is not always precise in defining the opinions of the philosophers whom he is refuting. In his *Inquiry into the Human Mind on the Principles of Common Sense* (Section 3: 5), it would appear that he attributes equally to Locke, Berkeley and Hume two contradictory views: 1. the immediate object of memory is merely an idea of a sensation, an image, a model of the sensation and therefore essentially distinct from it. This essential distinction between the object of sense and memory results in an essential distinction between the two powers; 2. sensation and the object of memory differ solely in the degree of power and intensity with which the spirit perceives them. This simple distinction between different degrees of power would rule out the claim that the object of both faculties is not one and the same. Thus, it would appear that the two faculties were not fundamentally distinct.

It is possible — in fact it is the case — that these writers are not consistent in their definitions. In one passage, they distinguish sensation from the object of memory solely by the degree of intensity of the percipient spirit, in another they appear to hold that the object of memory is not a fainter sensation, but the idea of a sensation. Hume's way of expressing himself certainly leads one to believe, rightly, that he is inconsistent. For example, in his *Essay on the Origin of Ideas* he sometimes says that the idea is merely a fainter sensation, at other times, he describes it as a perception of the soul which reflects on its sensations. But *reflection* by the soul on its sensations is not merely a fainter sensation. This reflection involves more activity than in any simple sensation. Nevertheless, I have felt obliged to attribute the first view to Locke and the second to Berkeley and Hume because this seems more noticeable in their writings, their main thrust, as it were. When they express the opposite view, they seem to say it unwillingly, because they lack more precise terminology.

[90] *Recherches sur l'entendement humain* [the French translation of *Inquiry into etc.*], Section 3.

present. Nor do I believe that the ordinary person thinks about this as Dr. Reid does. It seems to me that any ordinary person who remembers something previously seen or felt, thinks he has present to his spirit what he has seen or experienced, but recognises it as such solely because he possesses the idea and trace of it in his feeling [*App.*, no. 2].

108. Dr. Reid, however, does not reduce human faculties to one alone, although he does reduce their objects to one alone. Here, his system deviates completely from Condillac's. He says, after the passage I quoted above:

> But, though the object of my sensation, memory, and imagination, be in this case the same, yet these acts or operations of the mind are as different, and as easily distinguishable, as smell, taste and sound. I am conscious of a difference in kind between sensation and memory, and between both and imagination.[91]

Elsewhere he writes:

> Indeed, if a man should maintain that a circle, a square and a triangle differ only in magnitude, and not in figure, I believe that he would find nobody either disposed to believe him or to argue against him; and yet I do not think it less shocking to common sense to maintain that sensation, memory, and imagination differ only in degree, and not in kind.[92]

Article 3

How Reid felt the difficulty I have presented

109. However, to deal with our difficulty, we have to state what Dr. Reid means by the words 'sensation', 'memory' and 'imagination'. According to him:

> A sensation such as smell, may come before the spirit under three different forms.[93] It can be experienced; it can

[91] *Recherches sur l'entendement humain*, Section 3.

[92] *Ibid.*, Section 5.

[93] Note how close this way of speaking is to the theory of *transformed sensation*. Nevertheless, Reid's view, as I mentioned, posits an intrinsic

be recalled or remembered; it can be imagined or held as an idea.[94] In the first case, it is necessarily accompanied by the persuasion we have of its actual existence. In the second, it is necessarily accompanied by the persuasion of its past existence. In the third case, it is not absolutely accompanied by any persuasion or by any idea of existence; it is precisely what the logicians call *simple apprehension*.[95]

110. Using words in one sense rather than another does not prejudice the truth of an argument provided care has previously been taken to define them, and they are then used only in the sense attributed to them. I shall not inquire, therefore, whether the meaning attributed by Dr. Reid to the three English words [*sensation, memory* and *imagination*], which I have translated as *sensazione, memoria* and *immaginazione,* is the same as that attributed to them in ordinary speech. Instead, I would beg the reader to note carefully the difference in concepts which he wishes to express by these words.

First, notice the difference between the first two and the third. For Reid, the first two, *sensation* and *memory*, do not mean only the perception of an ens, but in addition persuasion of the real existence of the ens (present existence is linked to sensation, past existence is linked to memory). On the other hand, by *imagination* he understands the faculty of perceiving only the ens without any persuasion of its present or past existence. The Schoolmen called this — more appropriately, in my view — *simple apprehension*.

111. We must now see whether *simple apprehension of an ens*, or the act of imagination, taken in Reid's sense, precedes sensation and memory, as Locke and Hume seem to maintain, or

difference between these faculties. In any event, the remark I made earlier about Condillac's expression *transformed sensation* is relevant here also. It is not a philosophical expression because the principal idea, based on a metaphor, is vague and deceptive.

[94] Imagining a sensible thing or having an idea of it are very different, although Reid confuses them here. *Image* or phantasm is characteristic of an animal, *idea* of an intelligent being. This idea is the scholastics' *simple apprehension*. Nevertheless, the image constitutes the positive, natural element of perceptions of corporeal things, which I shall explain more fully elsewhere.

[95] *Recherches sur l'entendement humain*, section 3.

whether sensation and memory precede *simple apprehension*, as Reid claims.

The real issue is to explain the conflict between Reid on the one hand and Locke and Hume on the other, a conflict which highlights the problem I have mentioned. It is always the same difficulty, although it appears under a number of different guises according to the viewpoints from which the philosophers envisaged it. Let us see whether either of the two parties manages to unravel the tangled skein and find the thread to lead them out of the labyrinth.

112. Dr. Reid describes his opponents' *system of ideas*, as he calls it, in the following terms:

> These philosophers inform us that the initial operation of the spirit is merely simple apprehension, that is, a pure concept, a naked idea devoid of any inner judgment. They also inform us that, with many such ideas occurring to our spirit, the spirit compares them with each other and, by such a comparison, senses how they resemble one another, and how they differ. We call this perception of their agreement or disagreement judgment, persuasion or knowledge.[96]

This we may take to be the final expression, in France and England, of the system of Locke and his followers.

My analysis of Condillac's system has demonstrated that this system consists essentially: in first fabricating ideas, and then comparing them to compose judgments. It was here precisely that I saw and discovered the insurmountable difficulty inherent in his system. Condillac himself provided us with the arguments which led us inevitably to conclude that no idea could be formed without the intervention of an inner judgment. Consequently, ideas cannot be discussed apart from judgments; some judgment is essential to the formation of ideas. Now, as judgments can only be formed by means of ideas, we still have to explain the possibility of a judgment prior to ideas, if we accept Locke's and Condillac's view that ideas are all constructed (cf. 86–98).

This was precisely the difficulty seen by Dr. Reid, although

[96] *Recherches sur l'entendement humain*, Section 4.

not quite so fully. As a result, he knew perfectly well how to refute the opposing systems, but according to me was himself unable to offer a system capable of resolving the difficulty.

Article 4

Reid's difficulty with Locke's system was foreseen by Locke himself

113. If writers listened carefully to their own consciences, they would probably escape much public censure, which seldom attacks their writings and castigates any true failing unless the authors themselves have already some fear deep down, some suspicion which mistakenly they have not dared to lay bare and acknowledge in their hearts.

114. I feel that Locke had an inkling of the opposition his system was to encounter, that is, of the difficulty which Reid would later raise against it. I have already pointed out the vagueness of his idea of substance. He is equally nonplussed when, in defining *knowledge*, he refuses to use the term for anything accompanied in the human mind by a judgment.[97]

I certainly do not wish to quarrel about language. However, I feel I am right in saying that either Locke is not consistent in his terminology or gives the word *idea* a sense different from that in standard use where we normally say that we *have an idea of something* and *have knowledge of something*. These are equivalent expressions because it is impossible to have the *idea* of something without having some *knowledge* of it. But it is contradictory to say in common language: 'I have an idea of something of which I have no knowledge whatsoever.' We have to accept therefore as a universally received statement that the idea of something always includes some knowledge of it. It would seem to follow that Locke, who realised that we cannot know

[97] Book 2, c. 2. Laromiguière, in his *Leçons de Philosophie*, part 2, lesson 1, lists the word *knowledge*, which he thinks barbarous in French, amongst the synonyms for *idea*. In fact, the meaning he gives to the word *idea* corresponds exactly to what Locke calls *knowledge*, as we can see by comparing the passages I have quoted earlier from the two authors.

anything without a judgment, also sensed that we cannot have an idea without a judgment. However, unable to explain to his own satisfaction the formation of our first ideas (a judgment prior to the ideas was an impossibility, as it in turn presupposes some prior idea), he resorted to the imaginary distinction between knowledge and *idea* and to the absurd notion of positing ideas without any knowledge. He had to rule out their need for any judgment.

It was Locke's fondness for systems, it seems to me, which persuaded him to think in this way. He could not have avoided such specious notions which flew in the teeth of common sense and his own good sense — which otherwise was sound and solid — without completely discarding his own system, summarised in the proposition: 'Nothing is innate in the human spirit; everything in it is acquired through sensation and reflection.'

Article 5
Reid's objection to Locke's system

115. Reid realised, therefore, that Locke's system was flawed and, although he did not clearly grasp where the flaw lay, was still able to put forward powerful arguments against the system.

He set out the entire problem of the origin of ideas in the following terms: 'Does simple apprehension of things precede judgment about their existence, as Locke's school would have it, or does judgment precede simple apprehension?'

He rejected the view of Locke and his followers that simple perception precedes the act of judgment.

> It is acknowledged by all, that sensation must go before memory and imagination;[98] and hence it necessarily follows,

[98] Note carefully the meaning that Dr. Reid gives to the expression *imagination*. He means in this instance the faculty of *simple apprehension*, that is, the power enabling us to conceive a thing as possible, apart from subsistence, unlike *sensation* and *memory*. Sensation links to the perceived thing persuasion of its present subsistence; memory links persuasion of past subsistence. Without any doubt, such expressions are not precise, as I indicated earlier. This imprecision gave Dugald Stewart the opportunity to

that apprehension, accompanied with belief and knowledge, must go before simple apprehension, at least in the
matters we are speaking of. So that here, instead of saying
that the belief or knowledge is got by putting together and
comparing the simple apprehensions, we ought rather to
say that the simple apprehension is performed by resolving
and analysing A NATURAL AND ORIGINAL JUDGMENT.[99]

Article 6

Reid places judgment before ideas

116. The passage I have quoted is very enlightening. Dr. Reid
sees that, unlike his opponents, he cannot first assume, in man,
simple perception of some thing devoid of persuasion of its
existence so that we become convinced of the existence of
something only later by means of comparison and judgments.
His opponents saw that we cannot be intimately persuaded that
a thing exists unless we make a judgment about its existence.
But they did not see how a person utterly devoid of ideas could
make a judgment, and imagined that persuasion about the existence of things perceived was not contemporaneous with the
perception of the things themselves. They held that it occurred
at a later stage when we had already perceived things and had
within ourselves the ideas of those things which we could

embark on a long discussion (Chap. 3 of his *Elements of Philosophy*) to reveal
whether *imagination* had associated with it persuasion of the existence of
anything. This shows how vagueness in the use of terms multiplies problems
to no purpose! Stewart rightly remarks that if our imagination of something is
very vivid, we conceive the thing as present even if we know speculatively that
it has no existence. Now it is precisely with this speculative knowledge of the
non-existence of the thing that we have to deal. What we are discussing is the
speculative apprehension of the thing, if one wishes to call it that, by means of
which we study the thing in itself dispassionately, without the use of any vivid
imagination in examining its nature, and without our being interested in its
existence or non-existence. This is what we call *simple apprehension* of
something. It is a faculty inappropriately called imagination. If we wish to be
precise, we cannot even say that merely by simple apprehension of the thing
we know that something does not exist. We think neither of its existence nor
non-existence. We consider it merely as something possible. Strictly speaking,
this faculty is called *intellect*.

[99] *Recherches sur l'entendement humain*, Section 4.

compare. By making the comparison, we could judge of their existence, and thus persuade ourselves of the fact.

For Dr Reid, however, this was due solely to their attachment to the system they adopted, not to careful observation of fact.

According to Reid, practical observation independent of system shows that we perceive real external things through our senses and are immediately persuaded of their subsistence BY A NATURAL AND ORIGINAL JUDGMENT. Having thus perceived real, subsistent things, we separate their present and past existence by a process of abstraction and proceed to view them as merely possible. This gives rise to what is called *pure apprehension* or pure concept of something, that is, the concept of the thing apart from the persuasion and thought of its real existence.

Article 7

As a result, Reid shows that the first operation of human understanding is synthesis and not, as Locke claimed, analysis

117. Reid maintains that this is the only possible way to arrive at the fundamentals of human cognition. Consequently, he claims that the operations of human understanding begin with synthesis rather than analysis. He adds immediately:

> And it is with the operations of the mind, in this case, as with natural bodies, which are indeed, compound of simple principles or elements. Nature does not exhibit these elements separate, to be compounded by us; she exhibits them mixed and compounded by concrete bodies, and it is only by art and chemical analysis that they can be separated.

Article 8

The system put forward by Reid is unsatisfactory

118. Dr. Reid's opponents have no answer to his scrupulous observation of facts. There is no doubt that simple apprehension of an object, that is, the concept of an object devoid of any

persuasion about its existence,[100] is not given to us before we
have perceived the body as existent and then, by an operation of
our spirit, separated from it our persuasion of its real existence
and viewed it only as possible.

119. But the opposite is also true. Reid's opponents in their
turn can require him to examine his own system more closely. It
is not without its problems.

Their objection could run as follows: 'We are willing to suppose with you that the inner persuasion of the existence of perceived entia is not subsequent to simple apprehension of such
beings. This is a kind of abstraction carried out by the judgment
we make concerning their existence. We do not, however, consider reasonable your bold claim to have thereby arrived at the
primary, fundamental fact proper to our spirit relative to the
origin of ideas, the ultimate observable fact. You hold that the
first thing we can note in our spirit is of a composite nature. You
posit the persuasion of the existence of real, external things
prior to their simple apprehension. In short, you consider the
development of the spirit as originating from judgments, not
from ideas. But we find it contradictory to affirm that the composite should be prior to the simple, and the judgment prior to
the idea. Let me explain our position in more detail.

'First, you maintain that the first operation of the spirit is a
judgment; this is the first fact that can be observed in our spirit.

'Having established this, you must also accept that this judgment has all the constituents of the essence of the operation of
the spirit that we call a judgment; in turn, these constituents are
proof that judgment is always a composite operation, that is, the
end-product of a number of elements. It is never simple.

'True, you apply the adjectives *natural* and *primal* to this
judgment. This is equivalent to saying that we perform it necessarily and by an intrinsic power of nature. As you say, it is a
kind of *suggestion* prompted by that force. This, however, does
not prevent its being a proper judgment, which is what you
yourself call it. In fact, we do not begin to be intimately persuaded of the existence of an ens before affirming to self: "This
ens exists", because the persuasion of an ens' existence is simply

---

[100] The argument hinges especially on corporeal entia which are the first
real things, different from ourselves, which we perceive externally.

an interior affirmation by which we say: "This ens exists."
Now, when we say interiorly: "This ens exists", there is no
doubt that we are making an internal judgment whereby we
attribute existence to that ens.

'Whether we say this to ourselves as a result of an internal,
natural impetus constraining us to link the judgment with sensations immediately after them, or whether we form the judgment freely, is indifferent and irrelevant as far as the nature of
the judgment is concerned. In either case, it does not cease to be
a true, complete judgment. It appears that up to this point we
agree. Moreover, we retain the same idea of a real, complete
judgment even if we alter the phrase and, instead of affirming :
"I judge that this ens exists", we say: "I feel that this ens exists"
or "I have an inner feeling of the existence of this ens whose sensation I experience" or some even more accurate phrase.[101] It is
still true that I am aware of a relationship of identity between
what is sensible and existence. But feeling a relationship is the
same as feeling a judgment, and feeling internally a judgment is
equivalent to forming a judgment. There is no way of preventing a true, complete judgment from preceding the persuasion of
existence of the external ens. This is precisely why you introduce a primal, natural judgment.

'If this is the case, you begin by describing the development of
the human spirit by means of a complex and composite operation, not a simple one. In fact, every judgment is made up of a
number of constituent parts. The concept of judgment common
to all philosophers and yourself consists of the association of a
predicate with a subject. In our example, the inner judgment we
make: "This ens exists", is merely the relationship we feel
between existence, which becomes the predicate, and the real
thing in so far as it is felt, which becomes the subject. So we may
ask: if we associate existence with sensation and thus form the
inner judgment, "A sensible ens exists", is it not inevitable that

---

[101] A more accurate expression for this primal judgment would be: 'The
sensation which I experience requires some existent thing (different from
me).' I must also point out that the phrase, 'This object exists', would involve a
twofold repetition of the idea of existence. When I say *this object*, I am already
referring to something I have perceived as existing. As a result, the phrase does
not indicate a simple, primal judgment. Merely pronouncing the phrase, *this
object*, presupposes a formed judgment.

we have to possess beforehand the two elements, that is, the sensible element and the idea of existence? How can you call *primal* the judgment which you introduce to explain how we acquire the persuasion of the existence of objects when you take *primal* to mean 'not preceded by any other information'? If, on the one hand, *sensation* is necessary to make the judgment in question and, on the other, the idea of *existence* which we connect with the sensation is also necessary, we have to say categorically that your judgment is not primal in our spirit. It is preceded by two more simple operations. Let us grant, by all means, that judgment follows these operations instantaneously. Nevertheless, it must be preceded by them.

120. 'Having established this, let us analyse the proper nature of the two elementary operations. The idea of existence is universal and you, with your judgment, offer no explanation for it; you presuppose it. It is an element that goes to form a judgment; it is simpler than the judgment and logically, at least, must precede it. You are wrong to criticise the method by which we explain the development of the human spirit which, according to us, begins from ideas. It is impossible to start, as you would, from a primal judgment without assuming the prior existence of some idea' [*App.*, no. 3].

Article 9

The failing common to Dr. Reid and his opponents

121. Reid's opponents, it must be said, offer a vigorous response as long as they have to show the impossibility of conceiving a first judgment without some prior idea. But they can never defend themselves with the same success because it is impossible to defend the proposition: 'Simple perception, that is, the pure idea of something, precedes the judgment of its real existence'.

From one point of view, this proposition does seem to be true. How can I judge that an ens exists of which I have no idea? The idea of this ens, or simple apprehension, if seen in this light, inevitably seems prior to the act of judgment which we make about its real existence.

From another point of view, experience absolutely contradicts such a tenet. Experience assures us that we first form the concrete idea of the really existent ens. Only later do we derive the abstract idea, separate from the persuasion of its real existence, which we call simple apprehension of an ens. Do we actually think of a possible horse without having first perceived a horse through our senses?

122. Neither Reid nor his opponents clearly saw this aspect of the problem. As a result, each party was able to demolish the other without being able to vindicate its own position.

Reid fused two problems into one. It is one thing to ask: 'Can we form a judgment about the existence of external things without some prior universal idea in our mind?' and another to ask: 'Does the judgment of the existence of external things need to be preceded by simple apprehension, that is, by the ideas of things themselves?'

Reid's opponents solved this second question positively and incorrectly.

In opposing them, however, Reid was not content to show that formation of the judgment about the existence of external things does not need to be preceded by the simple apprehension of things. This was sufficient to demolish their theory. It was, in fact, exactly the opposite proposition to theirs. He also set out to prove that inexplicably and mysteriously we form a primal judgment prior to any idea. This reply, which went well beyond that needed to defeat his opponents, extended the argument to a broader question. Reid was now maintaining that judgment about the existence of external objects was possible not only without the ideas of the things themselves but also without any pre-existent, universal idea in our spirit.

This undue enlargement of the original problem was Reid's undoing. After overcoming his opponents, he voluntarily chose to venture, so to speak, into the domain of error. His adversaries, unable to defend themselves, could now successfully attack him.

In fact, it is fairly evident that a judgment can only be formed if we possess some universal idea. The proposition defended by Reid was, despite his righteous zeal, exaggerated and unsustainable.

Moreover, it was easy to show his opponents that a judgment

about the real existence of external things inevitably preceded their simple idea. An appeal to experience was sufficient. But it was not so easy to find a satisfactory reply to the fearful objection: 'How can I judge that something of which I have no idea really exists?'

The reply to this objection would have led the Scottish philosopher into the depths of his research. But he either despaired of finding it or felt he did not have the strength to do so. He did not in fact pursue it, but was happy enough to wreathe his primal judgment in a mysterious cloud where he attempted to conceal it from human curiosity.

123. There was only one way to solve the objection. It was necessary to devise a system in which the object considered as existing was an effect of the judgment itself, that is, the object was only present in virtue of the judgment made about it. The entire problem, therefore, was to find a kind of judgment which provided its object, that is, our idea of the thing judged, with existence, or (and this amounts to the same thing) which would produce within us the specific ideas of things.

124. Now, when we examine in turn all the species of judgments we form about things, we see clearly that as long as the judgment alights upon some quality possessed by the thing, this thing necessarily exists in our spirit prior to the judgment, and to the quality which our judgment attributes to it. However, when the judgment is such that it alights upon the very *existence* of the thing, the thing judged does not exist in our thought prior to this judgment, but in virtue of it. In fact, unless we think of the thing as existing (that is, as having a possible or real existence) it is nothing, it is not an object of our thought, it is not an idea. Unlike all other judgments, judgment about the existence of things produces its own object. It has a dynamic of its own, almost a creative drive which requires the philosopher's deepest intellectual meditation.[102] This *object*, which does not exist prior

---

[102] St. Thomas's view was somewhat similar; he recognised that there is always a primal operation by our spirit which produces for itself its own object. He says: *Prima ejus actio (intellectus) per speciem est formatio sui objecti, quo formato, intelligit; simul tamen tempore ipse format et formatum est, et simul intelligit* [The intellect's first action is to form through a species its object; then it understands. At one and the same time, it forms and the object is formed, and it understands] (*De natura verbi intellectus*).

to such a judgment about it, exists in virtue of, and at least simultaneously with, the judgment itself. Such a judgment is a singular power of our understanding which focuses on something currently existing.

125. Three questions may be asked about this power: 1. how is it moved to think about something actually existing? 2. whence does it derive the universal idea of existence which it requires for such thought? 3. how does it confine the idea of existence, which is a universal idea, to some determined thing and thus focus on this rather than the determined, existent object.

126. The first and third questions are easily answered on the basis of our experience.

We are stimulated to think about an existing object by means of sensations. Moreover, sensations determine this object existing in our thinking. We experience sensations, and under the stimulus of this modification our spirit says to itself: this felt element exists.

The difficulty, therefore, consists only in knowing whence we derive the idea of existence which is essential to the first of our judgments, to the judgment by which we know that something external exists. This is the great epistemological problem.

127. To sum up in different words. To the difficulty, 'How can I judge that a thing exists of which I have no idea?', I answer: 'The judgment that a determined thing exists involves two parts: 1. I think about some thing which can exist universally; 2. I think about this thing as present and as determined by all its properties.'

As long as I think about universal, completely undetermined being, I am not judging anything. My judgment begins when I apply or determine the thought of being or of existence by means of particular qualities.

Assume now that I already have the thought of being in all its universality. In this case, I need only sensations to form the judgment, 'Such a thing exists'. They provide me with the determination of being — that universal being which I am already presumed to possess. The whole problem then comes down to explaining the origin of the idea of being which must necessarily precede every primal judgment.

128. However we come to have the idea of being, let us

continue for the moment to speak on the basis of our assumption that we have it prior to every judgment we make about the actual existence of some determined, sensible thing.

In this case, judgment about the existence of one thing or another determined by our sensations, about this body which is at present sensibly perceived, can be very easily explained, and analysed as follows.

We have a spirit which is both sensitive and intellective, that is, we are endowed with sense and understanding. Sense is the power to perceive sensible things; understanding is the faculty to perceive things as existing in themselves.

Now, anything that falls under our senses becomes an *object* of our understanding because we who feel are the very same as we who are endowed with understanding.

What operation will our spirit carry out upon sensible qualities when we have perceived them?

Understanding, as I said, consists in seeing things as existing in themselves. Our understanding, therefore, will now perceive sensible things existing in themselves, not in the intimate relationship they have with us in so far as they are sensations.[103]

But the act of perceiving sensible things as existing in themselves independently of us is equivalent to judging them as existing in themselves. This is tantamount to judging that there exists outside us an *ens* in which the sensible qualities are

---

[103] I use the word *sensation* to express the modification that our spirit undergoes in perceiving *sensible qualities*; I use the phrase *sensible qualities* when I consider such qualities in their relationship to the bodies to which they refer.

This distinction is based on the analysis of *sensation*. In fact, when our sensory power undergoes some modification and, consequently, our spirit experiences a sensation, we are aware of two things: 1. that which we are experiencing: pleasure, pain, etc.; 2. our passivity. To be aware of our passivity necessarily implies the idea of an action done in us without us. Such an action encompasses something distinct from us. Its presence occurs within us but is neither ourselves nor an effect of our activity. Granted this, and granted that we conceive a determined action, we also conceive all that is necessary to conceive an action. Consequently we also conceive an agent distinct from ourselves. This agent which we conceive does not remain undetermined for us, but is determined by the effect which it produces in us. This effect, this action within us, are the *sensible qualities* which we call *sensations*, in so far as they are within us and modify us.

present, whatever form they may take, but certainly in the mode that they can be. Our primal judgment plays no part in determining this mode.

Let us focus, therefore, on the difference between the two species of judgment which we make.

Sometimes, in using our judgment, we merely think of a *quality* as existing in an ens which we have already conceived. Thus, when I say, 'This man is blind', I think of blindness as existing in the man, of whom I already have the idea, the man who is the subject of my judgment.

On the other hand, we sometimes use our judgment to think of an ens as adhering to certain *sensible qualities*. For example, we judge: 'There exists an ens determined by these specific qualities which I am presently perceiving through my senses.'

In the first species of judgment, the object of judgment is prior to the judgment itself. In the second, the object of judgment is not prior to judgment; only the elements of the judgment are prior, that is, 1. the sensations which have not yet become cognitions; 2. the idea of existence which casts its light upon them by adding being to them, and makes them become known in being and through being.

I conclude, therefore, that judgment is not always an operation exercised on some object as thought, but sometimes on the sensible elements which, through judgment itself, become objects of our thought.

129. All this enables us to solve without difficulty the two problems constituting the matter of dispute between Dr Reid and his opponents.

I. Question 1: 'Is it necessary that the simple apprehension of external objects should pre-exist the judgment made on their actual existence?'

This is not necessary; only the pre-existence of the perception of sensible qualities is necessary.

Reid's opponents arrived at their view — that the idea of a thing comes first in us and that we afterwards form the judgment of its real existence — because they had not succeeded in distinguishing clearly between *sensation* and *idea*. They confused the two processes. Realising that *sensation* was necessarily prior if we were to think of the existence of a body, they decided that the *idea* of that body should pre-exist. If they had realised that *sensation* only furnishes our mind with particular sensible qualities of a thing, and that the idea of the thing, on the contrary, implies the thought of an ens furnished with sensible qualities, they would easily have recognised also that the idea of a body is unattainable without a prior judgment which links the concept of being to the particular sensible qualities furnished by sensation, and thereby forms the notion of the body determined by the sensible qualities actually perceived. This concept of body is the *object* of the understanding formed by our judgment itself which subsequently abstracts from this object the persuasion of its existence, leaving it as simple possibility. This species of abstraction is called *simple apprehension* by the scholastics.

II. Question 2: 'Is it necessary that some universal idea should pre-exist in us prior to the primal judgment about existsence?'

Certainly, because a judgment not preceded by a universal idea is impossible. Reid's mistake was to overlook this idea. He accepted what he called a primal, mysterious, inexplicable judgment. Of course, a philosopher cannot be forbidden to accept a mysterious and completely inexplicable principle, if he so wishes, but it is not fitting that he should accept an absurd principle. In fact, a judgment without any universal idea is a contradiction in terms. It is no less contrary to the status of a philosopher that a person should accept a principle without studying and analysing the conditions which make it possible. In this case, although the principle is not shown to be absurd, at least it will remain doubtful until some study of it has been undertaken. The existence of a universal idea in us prior to the primal judgment whereby we affirm to ourselves the existence of some body, is a necessary condition for Reid's judgment.

It was therefore inadvisable to suspend the study of the fact to be analysed, that is, of the judgment whereby we judge whether something exists different from ourselves. It should have been extended to everything presupposed by this judgment, if it is to be made possible and capable of being conceived and thought.

Article 10

Reid's solid arguments against that of his opponents

130. Nevertheless, it is clear from what has been said that Reid's system contains sound, conclusive features relative to his opponents.

Let us suppose that Reid, advised by a friend that he was taking his supposition too far, had corrected himself on this point. His reasonable attitude would have entitled him to address his opponents fairly vigorously: 'I willingly grant that the internal judgment which we make upon the real existence of things impinging upon our senses comprises two basic elements, that is, sensation and the idea of existence. However you must admit that as soon as we experience sensations, our intelligent nature compels us to admit the presence of an ens. In other words, we have to make what I call the primary, natural judgment which although not prior to all ideas (this would be contradictory) is at least prior to all other judgments.'

In fact, the very core of Reid's system consists in the emphasis he puts on the way the human spirit, as soon as it receives sensations from external agents, inevitably forms a judgment about their existence 'by a simple act' as he says, but not, as he goes on to say, 'by a completely indefinable act.'[104]

The argument I have put forward in the previous article shows that there is no need to resort to any distinctive, inexplicable principle, a kind of arcane power, a philosophical mystery.

131. If Reid had clearly seen the basic failings of earlier philosophical systems, he would not have insisted that ideas should precede judgments. He could have ventured further and, in his own phrase, used a more refined chemistry to analyse the simple apprehension of the object which, according to his opponents' supposition, is prior to persuasion and judgment of its existence.

He would also have placed them in difficulty with a much stronger line of argument. 'You claim', he could have said to them, 'that the simple apprehension of an object is prior to the

---

[104] *Recherches sur l'entendement humain*, Section 5.

judgment we form about its real existence. You therefore describe the development of the human spirit by supposing that the ideas of things exist first. Judgments are then formed from them.

'This behaviour of our intelligence is a real problem since, in my view, you cannot have an idea of anything except by means of a judgment.

'To discover whether my statement is true, let us get down to details. Let us take the idea or simple apprehension of a horse. How can I think of a horse independently of its present or past? Or to put it another way: how can I have a simple apprehension of it, how can I think about it? If you tell me that I form the idea of the horse distinct from its actual or past existence by the mental act called abstraction, you presuppose that I have previously had a perception of some actually existing horse and have performed the act of abstraction on this perception of the concrete object. You grant, therefore, that I have the persuasion of the horse's actual existence before the basic apprehension. So you grant that before I have the simple apprehension of the horse, I have already judged for myself that it subsists. In fact, what you have written shows how you resort to abstractions when you attempt to explain the simple ideas of things. You contradict yourself when you say, on the one hand, that we form our simple ideas of things by means of abstraction and, on the other, that our ideas of things precede all judgments about them. In fact, abstraction can only be exercised on the perception of an individual, existing idea for whose formation a judgment is required, that is, the judgment that the thing exists.'

132. He could further strengthen his argument by adding: 'You say that a simple idea precedes our judgments.' I reply that analysis of the simple idea of a thing shows that the idea contains a judgment. Let us stay with the idea of a horse. When you think of a horse, even if you exclude completely its present or past existence, what does your mind think about? Does it think of something so basic that it cannot be broken down into a number of other ideas, or does the idea of the horse derive from several ideas which can be distinguished from one another? Certainly, if I think of the idea of a horse, I am thinking of 1. an ens and 2. of all the constitutive elements of this ens which make the idea of this ens less vague and undetermined for me. In

fact, they make it more precise and assign it to the particular ens called horse.

On analysis, therefore, I discover that my idea of the horse is the result of two sets of ideas: 1. the universal idea of ens; 2. the ideas constituting the horse which together form the idea of the *nature* of the horse. This idea is less extensive than the universal idea. The idea of the horse, therefore, derives both from a universal, totally extended idea, and from another that is more limited.

Let us see how these two ideas are associated in our idea of the horse, that is, how together they form a single idea.

A moment's thought shows that the less extensive idea is conceived by us as existing in the more extensive. In other words, the idea of the horse's nature is conceived by us in the idea of ens, or again (which amounts to the same thing), we conceive the horse in the class of entia; or, again, having the idea of a horse is the same as thinking of an ens endowed with those determinations which make it a horse.

This analysis of the idea of a horse shows that it includes and comprises everything needed for a complete judgment.

Two terms are required for a judgment, one more extensive, the other less. In the concept of a horse, we have in fact found the universal idea of ens, the more extensive term, and the idea of the constitutive of the horse, the less extensive term.

A further requirement is that the less extensive term be conceived in the more extensive. We have seen, in fact, that we conceive the nature of the horse, the less extensive idea, in the idea of ens, the more extensive.

The simple apprehension of a finite thing is itself therefore a complex idea which conceals a judgment. It is one of those ideas that we can only make present to our mind by comparing and linking them with other ideas or perceptions.

The proposition: 'The simple apprehension of things is prior to judgments about them because the apprehension itself is only the product of a judgment' is thus untenable.

Article 11

Conclusion

133. It is obvious that the participants in the controversy which I have outlined are as incapable of building as they are expert at destroying.

Their problem can be reduced to the following ultimate terms:

Locke says to Reid: 'Ideas must be prior to judgments. It is absurd to admit a comparison between two things before these things exist.' His reason seems obvious. Reid answers Locke: 'Judgments are prior to ideas because it is impossible to form the idea of a thing before judging that it exists' and his reason, too, seems obvious. How can these two statements, which together seem both correct and contradictory, be reconciled.

We saw earlier that the problem to which they gave rise was, in the last analysis, that of discovering the origin of the idea of existence. Let us hope that the system which I shall explain more fully below may solve the important question which forms the subject of this *Essay*.

CHAPTER 4
Dugald Stewart

Article 1
Various aspects of the difficulty

134. I have already dealt briefly with it; all major philosophers have come up against the difficulty, a kind of reef encountered on their philosophical voyage.

This is how great problems are always solved; a great problem is merely a great difficulty to overcome. However, we should not think that philosophers freely set themselves difficulties as though they already knew or had an inkling of them all, and could choose to deal with one rather than another, and to make one problem the subject of their thinking rather than another. If difficult problems were not resolved for many centuries, this was due not to their intrinsic complexity but to ignorance of it. When a problem is put forward for investigation by the human mind, we can say that it is already half solved. At times, it is brought to the attention of thinkers purely by chance. Mathematics, for example, owes the theory of isochronal arcs to Galileo's observation of a swinging lamp, and the theory of universal gravity to the falling of an apple on Newton's head.

However, merely to submit difficulties to human attention is not in itself enough to ensure a solution; they have to be properly presented. The length of time taken to solve them is to be attributed in the main to the time that has to elapse before the state of the question is outlined simply, fully and directly to the mind. Difficulties cannot be pondered directly while the mind is thinking about something else.

Our difficulty is a case in point. Almost every philosopher came across it, almost every one of them passed over it because it was not the direct object of their consideration. Most of them saw it only by chance and under an accidental form.

I say this because it offers a legitimate excuse and defence for them. If they had been able to formulate the difficulty as clearly as we can, thanks to their work, they would have solved it as easily as we can.

135. Let me sum up the various accidental occasions, already dealt with, which brought our difficulty to the attention of modern philosophers.

Locke came up against it when he was obliged to deal with the idea of substance and when, in trying to define the term *knowledge,* he realised that he had to bring judgments into play. Condillac came very close to it when he had to distinguish between ideas and sensations, and deal with general ideas. Reid, in his attempt to explain our persuasion about the existence of bodies, realised that Locke was wrong in taking our acquired ideas as the starting point of the development of our spirit; before we acquire ideas, we have to posit a primal, natural judgment. How did Dugald Stewart, until recently a pillar of the very worthy Scottish school, see the problem? He too gets close to it, but does not see it clearly, when he tries to explain how we can form general ideas when naming things. Let us see what happens to him.

Article 2

Stewart bases his theory on a passage from Smith

136. Stewart, in the chapter of his *Elements of the Philosophy of the Human Mind* where he deals with the faculty of abstraction, quotes a passage from Adam Smith's essay, *Considerations concerning the first Formation of Languages.* As it contains the main argument of his theory of abstraction, I shall quote it here.

> The coining of certain particular nouns to designate particular objects, that is, the creation of nouns, must have been one of the first steps in the formation of language. The particular cave which enabled the savage to shelter from bad weather; the particular tree whose fruit satisfied his hunger; the particular spring whose water quenched his thirst were *without any doubt* the first objects to which he referred with the words *cave, tree, spring* or any other

term which he cared to use in his primal jargon to express those ideas. As the savage subsequently gained more experience and had occasion to observe and especially to name other caves, other trees, other springs, he *naturally*[105] had to attribute to each of those new objects the same name which he had been wont to assign to a similar object with which he had long been familiar. Thus it came about that those words which were originally proper names indicating individual objects imperceptibly became common names each referring to a group of individual objects.

Smith adds:

This allocation of the name of an individual to a large number of similar items must have initially suggested the idea of these classes or groups which are designated as *genera* and *species* whose origin Rousseau, despite his ability, had such difficulty in conceiving. A *species* is made up simply of a certain number of objects linked by a common

---

[105] The whole of Smith's discourse — whether true or false — is not a factual account: it is a piece of pure *imagination* whereby he attempts to discover what seems the most likely explanation in the *hypothesis* of the savage. We should not believe that the philosophies of Smith, Stewart and similar modern philosophers are based solely on *observation* and facts. Imagination also has its part to play in their work where it occupies a prominent place. We have an example here. The subject is crucial in philosophy, and deals with a problem on which the whole of philosophy hinges. How do Smith and Stewart go about solving this important question? They begin by laying the foundations of their whole argument, and these foundations are based on imagination! So they begin by using their imagination to discover what they think the most likely way for a savage — assuming the *theory* that he was devoid from the beginning of ideas and words — to form words and ideas. The charming fiction of this savage enables them to draw their conclusions. And they call this 'philosophical method'! It is true that their account contains heartening phrases such as: *there can be no doubt* and *of course this was how it had to happen* and similar expressions. And you still do not believe them? Have you no faith in the authority of their imagination?

However, I do not think that we are dispensed from examining: 1. whether what might *inevitably* occur in the *natural* course of events (according to their imagination) corresponds to fact, to what has actually been seen to occur in similar cases; 2. whether, as a consequence, their 'hypothesis' of a savage completely devoid of words and ideas, on which the whole of their system is ultimately based, is sustainable. This is what I shall attempt to do with the observations that follow on the passage from Smith's work and on Stewart's theories.

likeness and, as a result, indicated by an identical name which applies equally to all.[106]

137. At first sight, it would seem that the explanation given for the formation of the ideas of genera and species is extremely easy and natural. Actually, the error and insufficiency in this explanation are impossible to find without careful examination. On thorough examination, however, the explanation is found to be deceptive and misleading, unsound and false. In my view, it is one of those explanations which offer undiscerning readers an attractive argument distracting them from the study of the individual sections comprising it. The readers to whom I refer, considering the whole approach to be fair and honest, accept the truth of its contents. They do not bother to distinguish the ideas which their favourable disposition leads them to accept on trust as reliable and accurate. Previous experience, however, has often shown me willy-nilly that arguments which seem plausible conceal disastrous errors leading to a long series of similarly disastrous results. I feel justified, therefore, and even obliged to investigate the argument fully before accepting it.

Article 3

First flaw in the passage from Smith's work: he does not distinguish the different species of nouns referring to groups of individuals

138. I note first in the passage quoted from Smith, that common nouns are mentioned as though they were all of the same type. There are, however, many types of common noun, and I

---

[106] Stewart admits that Condillac mentions under the same heading the development of the human spirit in the formation of genera and species. Condillac's achievement in bringing the interdependence of speech and thought to the attention of philosophers is widely acknowledged. When dealing with Condillac's theories, I could therefore have made some of the comments which I am now making on Stewart's system and his explanation of the formation of genera and species. However, I thought it better to reserve it for this article rather than speak for too long about Condillac. Readers can themselves apply to Condillac's theory several of my remarks on the views of Smith and Stewart.

need to investigate whether it is exact to refer to them without specifying their various species and whether the argument holds good for all species or for one particular species.

The concept of common noun which the passage puts forward is that of a group of individuals. Let us first see, therefore, whether this applies to all species of common noun or whether, strictly speaking, all the nouns referring to a group of individuals are common.

The first species of nouns used to refer to a group of individuals consists of numerals, two, three, four, five, and so on. Ignoring the abstraction involved whereby they cannot refer to a species of individuals without some mention of the group referred to — for example, two, three, four, five men — let us consider them in so far as they have the power to represent for us a group of individuals.

When I speak of ten men, ten towns, and so on, I am certainly referring to a group of individuals, but cannot say that the number ten is *common* to each town or each man. It is not true, therefore, that all nouns referring to a group of individuals can be called common. This is used only when it can be applied to each one of a number of individuals.[107]

Numerical *nouns*, therefore, are a species which express not only a group, but in addition the number of members contained by the group. They express its size in numerical terms. A number does not express an undetermined group of individuals but determines the group by establishing its number.

139. A second species of nouns, referring to a group of individuals, are those which, in naming a group, do not accurately determine its limits but indicate its extent in a general way. Examples are *few, some, many, too many*, and so on, which are all applied to groups of individuals although they cannot be called *common* because they cannot be associated with each individual member of the group.

A third species of nouns represents groups but without

---

[107] The word *ten* is common to all species of things of which there are ten. This commonality, however, does not invalidate my remark that it is not a noun common to each individual member of the group referred to. If it is common to all things of which there are ten, then it contains another abstraction and is used in a different mode; it no longer expresses the group but a qualification of the groups themselves.

expressing the number of their individual members or their quality relative to many or few. This quality is, however, associated with some idea such as *people, tribe, assembly, family*, and so on, all of which are nouns referring to groups of individuals. These nouns, although they do not express the numbers contained in the groups, do nevertheless indicate a relative numerical size by the various ideas which they join and to which they refer. Thus, although *family* tells us neither the exact number of its constituent members nor whether they are few or many, the term refers to a group of individuals smaller than the one suggested by the word *nation*. Nor can these nouns, although they indicate a group of individuals, be called *common* because they are not applicable to the individual members which make up the group.

140. All plural nouns are nouns referring to groups of individuals. They form a fourth class which in no way specifies their numerical character. Thus, in saying *men, animals, houses* etc., we are referring rather to a group of these different species of things but without indicating the number of individuals contained in the groups. Nor are these nouns *common* to a number of individuals; they merely express groups of totally undetermined number.

We ought to dwell for a while on this lack of determination, but to avoid breaking the series of nouns, let us at this stage continue to list their different classes and see which can easily be confused with the genus of common nouns.

Article 4

Second flaw: Smith does not distinguish between nouns referring to groups of individuals and nouns referring to abstract qualities

141. Some nouns do not refer to individuals but to their essential or accidental qualities considered in isolation from the other features making up the individual. This is an indisputable and glaringly obvious fact. For example: *humanity, animality*, and so on, refer to essential qualities; *whiteness, hardness, fluidity*, and so on, refer to accidental qualities.

[140–141]

These nouns may be called *general* because they refer not to individuals but to qualities common to many individuals. Nevertheless, they still cannot be called *common* because they are nouns indicating single qualities found in many individuals, not nouns common to several individuals.

This becomes very evident when we consider the singular characteristic which distinguishes and separates them from all other nouns: they may never be used in the plural. Each of these nouns expresses a single, abstract, entirely simple thing[108] which because it cannot be confused with any other, is unique and indivisible. Thus it would be incorrect and imprecise to say *humanities*, *animalities*, *whitenesses*, and so on, in the plural. These nouns are not used for a number of individuals but solely for a single characteristic of a number of individuals. Consequently, they do not stand for any group of individuals, nor can they be called *common* but merely general or abstract.

Article 5

Third flaw: Smith confuses nouns referring to groups of individuals with common nouns referring to general features

142. From these nouns or — to put it more accurately — from the *idea* to which these nouns refer,[109] we derive the nouns

---

[108] In saying this, I do not mean to assert that these *abstract ideas* cannot be analysed and broken down into *simpler* ideas. In fact, all abstract ideas which express species of things, such as *tree*, and so on, are merely a *complex* of simple qualities gathered into one. However, I maintain that we unite them (this is not the place to deal with how we unite them) and consider them as a single, indivisible thing. We need this operation by which we unite a number of qualities in a single concept if subsequently we have to invent common nouns.

[109] In fact, the existence of the noun which refers to the abstract idea is not strictly necessary for the existence of the *common* noun which refers to the *ens* possessing the abstract characteristic. There are many nouns in our language without a corresponding abstract. For example, we say *tree*, *cave*, *spring* and so on, but not *treeness*, *caveness*, etc.

The existence of such nouns, like that of all the rest, depends on whether humans have needed to use them. Only the need of a word ensures its creation. However, while languages do not always register the entire process

which we can rightly refer to as *common* because they relate to a number of individuals. Examples of these are: *man, animal, plant, cave, tree, spring,* and so on, and adjectives such as *white, hard,* etc., which may be taken purely as adjectives or used elliptically to stand for nouns understood implicitly.

In analysing the value of these nouns, we have to take great care not to be led astray by the subtlety of modern languages. We are always inclined to think that a single idea has a corresponding single word, which is not the case. Words which express a single idea rather than a complex of ideas are exceedingly rare. The nature of language, and especially of modern languages, is such that we can with one word express an extremely complex idea, that is, an idea made up of a number of others. Not only do we express all those ideas but, at the same time, the link between them which binds them into a single unit. Hence, when we have analysed the meaning of a word, we can often break it down into one and even a number of propositions.

The same applies to the nouns to which I am referring; the noun 'man', for example, is equivalent to this proposition, 'an *ens* with humanity'; the noun 'tree': 'an *ens* having the characteristics which make up a tree. (If this had to be associated with a word not found in our language, we would speak of *treeness*)'. The same thing can be said about all other nouns of a similar genus. These nouns attribute to *entia* qualities which belong to them. They contain, therefore, a covert judgment by means of which, in uttering them or thinking of them, we attribute a

of ideas (it is not always necessary to use language to express concepts), it does not follow that the process of ideas in the mind is *discontinuous* and incomplete. If the process of ideas in the mind were interrupted, the mind would work by fits and starts, without any coherent inner argument, which is absurd. Even more absurd is the assumption that composite ideas can exist without thought of their constitutive elements. It is necessary therefore to accept that, where a common name has been invented, for example, *tree*, the corresponding thought has also occurred in the mind. This, expressed in isolation in the example I gave, would be *treeness*. The fact that this idea is not expressed by a noun does not mean that such a noun is not essential to form the term *tree*. This concept, reduced to its elements, merely indicates 'something endowed with those characteristics which, expressed in one word, would be called *treeness.*' However, this does not prove that these qualities have been thought abstractly, apart from their subjects. They have been thought together with the specific subject to which they belong.

predicate to a subject and for the sake of brevity express our operation in a single word which provides us with the result of the operation. It explicitly presents us with the connection we have discovered between predicate and subject. These are, properly speaking, the only *common* nouns because they apply to each individual member of a certain class. Thus, the word *man* applies to each man; *tree* applies to any one of all existing trees; *cave* applies to any cave regardless of type. The same can be said about all other nouns of this kind.

143. However, if the common being of a noun merely means its characteristic for expressing one individual at a time, the individual can be anyone of those possessing the quality indicated by the noun. Smith's assertion that each of these common nouns refers to a group of individuals is totally untrue and inaccurate. On the contrary, every common noun refers in every case to a single individual, but by means of a characteristic common to a number of individuals. This explains how the same noun can be applied first to one individual, then to another, and another, and thus in succession to each of those individuals which have the quality referred to in the noun. If it were true that the word *tree* referred to a group of trees, we would, by using it in the plural (by saying *trees*), have to express many groups of trees. This, however, is unheard of; no one has ever thought of expressing a number of groups of trees with this kind of plural, but only several individual trees.

Article 6

Fourth flaw: Smith does not know the true distinction between common and proper nouns

144. Note how cautious we should be about Smith's argument when we are faced with so many mistakes in such a few sentences.[110] At first sight, the argument looked so attractive,

---

[110] I choose to analyse carefully this passage of Smith, referred to by Stewart, as an outstanding example serving to disabuse so many of our youth and superficial people who imagine that the prerogative of thinking philosophically is exclusively confined to people who live north of the Alps and beyond the seas surrounding our beautiful land.

and almost compelled our assent. It seemed intended solely to describe a perfectly natural and inevitable fact.

The assertion is that common nouns merely express groups of individuals. But I listed all the four species of nouns which express groups of individuals and found not one of them common to several individuals. I then examined general and abstract nouns which refer to either essential or accidental single qualities. None of these can be called common. They are proper nouns with a common quality.

Finally, from such abstract nouns or, to put it more accurately, from the ideas they represent, I showed how common nouns were derived. I discovered their nature which consists entirely in expressing a judgment by which a quality is assigned to a subject, that is, in identifying an object by the quality which indicates or distinguishes it. Because this is common to many subjects, it ensures that the noun itself is suitable for each of those things possessing the same quality. But let us press on.

145. Now that we know what the nature of *common* nouns is, let us examine that of *proper* nouns.

Both refer to individuals, but with this difference: when the common noun refers to an individual, it indicates and distinguishes it by one of its qualities. On the other hand, the proper noun does not indicate and distinguish the individual by one of its qualities, but directly names the individual itself and, so to speak, its individuality which, however, cannot be communicated from one individual to another. The word 'individual' expresses what is proper and exclusive to an ens — that which makes it what it is and nothing else. Consequently, a proper noun may be applied only to a single individual because, as I said, it expresses that which makes the ens single and unique. On the other hand, a common noun, by indicating the ens by means of a quality which can be found in many other entia, does not indicate it accurately enough to distinguish and separate it from all the others. As a result, a common noun, while applying to an individual, can also apply to any other ens which possesses the same quality to which the noun refers and is related. Thus, *man* refers to an individual man, not many men. But by indicating *man* through a common quality, humanity, it does not indicate him in such a way that he is distinguished and separated by this sign alone from all other men. In fact, given the nature of

[145]

this noun, I may be led to think indiscriminately about this man or any other man. On the other hand, if I say that the man is called Peter, I have marked him off from all other men because the name, Peter, is not derived from a common quality but taken to indicate directly that individuality through which Peter has his own proper being, distinct from and incommunicable with all others.

Article 7

Fifth flaw: Smith does not realise why nouns are called common and proper

146. Having clarified the terms *proper noun* and *common noun*, let us look more closely at Smith's argument.

I assign a proper noun to an ens to indicate its individuality. However, as this noun has no necessary connection with this individuality, I can still use the noun to indicate the individuality of another ens different from that to which I first gave the name.

That, in fact, is what happens. If a father has twelve sons, he can call them all in turn by the proper name "Peter". Moreover, if all the people alive today christened Peter were to meet, we would have not twelve but hundreds of persons named Peter. But granted that the name Peter has been given to such a large number of people, it does not follow that it can be called a common noun. It has remained the proper noun it was even though, in fact, it has been attributed to so many people. The reason is obvious. The status of proper noun or common noun does not depend on the fact that the name (noun) is given by him to a single individual or a number of them. It depends on how the name is given to them. If they are named by marking them off as having a common characteristic, as for instance by the word *man*, which assigns humanity to men, it is a common noun. If, however, they are named without attributing to them a common characteristic but strictly as individuals without any other connection between the noun and the individuals than the one given arbitrarily by the person who coined the noun, the noun is a proper one. Thus, even if all men were called Peter, the only consequence of this would be that each person would have two

[146]

names, that is, the name of *man* which would be common and that of Peter which would be proper. As a matter of fact, even today, each person usually has two names, a common one and a proper one; it is purely accidental whether the proper names are different or the same, since even a single name would suffice. Actually, the number of proper nouns is very small compared to the number of people in the world.

147. This reveals another error in Smith's argument. He says that the savage changes proper into common nouns merely by applying them to a number of individuals, without giving any further explanation. The proper name, it would seem, becomes common merely through its extension to a number of individuals. But this is certainly not the case. Even if the name Peter were extended, as I said, to everyone, it would still be a proper name because it would refer to people not according to their *common quality*, but according to the individuality proper to each.

Let us assume that the savage had given a proper name to the first known cave where he had sheltered from the weather, to the first tree whose fruit he had eaten, and to the first spring which had quenched his thirst. Let us assume also that he then saw one, two, three similar caves, and one, two, three similar trees and streams and that finally he gave these new caves, trees and springs the same name as the first. We now have four caves, four trees and four springs, all bearing the same name.

At this stage, it still remains to be seen whether the savage who applies this single name to four similar things applies it to them as a proper or as a common name. In neither case can it be said that the name by which he called each of the four caves, the four trees or the four springs indicates groups of individuals, as Smith claims. The names would not, in fact, indicate anything other than one of the four, particular caves, trees or springs. It would still not be a collective noun until the nouns were made plural and one could say, caves, trees, springs instead of cave, tree, spring. There would be only one difference between the savage's giving the names as common or proper to the four individual things. If common, they would indicate the individual things by their common qualities, that is, by the qualities embodied in the concept of cave, tree, spring; if proper, they would indicate each of the four caves, trees and springs not by their qualities but in themselves as individual things. The names would be arbitrarily selected without any connection between the noun and the nature of the thing.

Article 8

Sixth flaw: Smith does not notice that the first names given to things were common

148. In my view, it is more likely that the names given by the savage to his *tree*, his *cave*, his *spring* were common from the very beginning.

Note that we do not, as a rule, give proper names to objects such as those we are discussing, that is, caves, trees, springs, and so on. Rather we are inclined to give proper names to persons, places, rivers and so on in order not to confuse them. Normally there is not the same need to bestow an individual proper name upon a tree, cave, spring. If there is, this is usually done by resorting to the surrounding circumstances.

We speak, for example, of the cave of Polyphemus, from the man who lived in it, or the cave of Hebron from the region where it is located; the cedar of Lebanon, the rose of Jericho, the palm-tree of Kadesh from the places in which such plants flourish; Jacob's well from the person who opened it up or discovered it or took it over; the fount of healing waters from the health-giving quality of the liquid, and so on. The need to devise proper nouns for all these things is never totally compelling.

149. Proper names, therefore (that is, names used to indicate the individual substance of a thing), are not in fact the most numerous. In all languages, even the richest and most elaborate, an infinite number of objects do not have them. On the other hand, everything has a common name because it is more necessary than a proper name. It would seem that people did not apply proper names until they realised that similar things could be confused without them. I mean similar things which they needed to distinguish and name individually. This could not be achieved without giving each a name indicating its proper, individual nature which alone marks off one particular thing from all others of the same species in such a way that it cannot be confused and associated with them.

150. The point in this argument that needs emphasis is this. Assigning a name to the individual property of an ens by which the ens is singled out and distinguished from all others of the same species requires much greater effort of abstraction than assigning a name which indicates it through one of its common qualities. When we are dealing with bodies, the *common qualities* of corporeal beings are the first to affect our sensories and become known to us. Consequently, it is much more likely that we would name an ens after these qualities than after its own individual substance which, when stripped of its accidental qualities, does not fall under our senses but is isolated by us from all its other qualities through a process or rather a series of processes of abstraction. For this reason, I hold it to be true that, in the development of the human spirit, a very long time elapses before we realise clearly and specifically — after considerable experience in comparing things — that beyond the common qualities which fall under senses there is something so proper in an ens, something so unique, that it can never be confused with other individuals. Indeed, it actually separates it off from everything else. This something is its very self.

Consequently, our imagined savage will not, in my view, be led to give a proper name to his tree, his cave, his spring at the outset, but only much later when, having seen many caves, trees and springs, he has first managed to distinguish the individuality of each and, more importantly, feels an urgent need to indicate their reality and individuality. This happens perhaps when he is talking to his wife or his children and wants to indicate precisely *that* cave, *that* tree, *that* spring, so that they cannot confuse it with other trees, caves and springs. I do not think that he would ever feel this need in his savage state nor for a long time after, until he had begun to be civilised and taken a number of steps towards civilisation. When the need to indicate the objects individually occurred to him, there can be no doubt that he would achieve it by another, easier method than by the extremely difficult task of devising proper names. He would, instead, use the context, or additional accidental details which I mentioned before, or some other means.

151. We cannot know, therefore, if a name is common merely by examining whether a number of individuals are called by that name. A number of individuals may be called by the same

proper name. Similarly, we cannot be certain that a name is proper merely by knowing that it indicates a single individual. Even a single individual can be assigned a common name. If, for example, there were only one survivor from the human race, he would have no need of a proper name; the common name *man* would be adequate as he could not be confused with others. Nevertheless, that noun would still be common because it would not refer to an individual by means of his own individuality but through his humanity. This quality he alone possesses, since there are no other human beings alive, but it could be possessed in the same way by many other individuals, who would be entitled to the same name. This makes the noun common by nature.

This is more than a mere imaginary conjecture on a par with Smith's account. It is a fact described in sacred Scripture which speaks to us of a time when there was only one man on the earth. Scripture tells us that this man was not given a proper name (which he did not need) but the common name *man* (in Hebrew, 'Adam' means *man*). To see more clearly how such a name was truly common, we must look at its origin. It came from the word *earth* of which, sacred Scripture tells us, man was composed, and it was intended to mean 'an ens made of earth'. The first person in the world to receive a name was not called after his individuality, but after a quality common to those who were to come after him. In other words, Adam was a common name.

152. Instead of resorting to the notion of an imaginary savage, or losing their way in following hypotheses, which all agree is an anti-philosophical approach, our shrewd philosophers could have been expected to consult the great monuments of antiquity which provide real facts.

By investigating these facts, they would have begun to doubt their opinion which, at first sight, appears so certain, that is, 'proper names were formed before common names'.

It is precisely in such seemingly obvious, but deceptive statements as these that the most pernicious, unassailable errors are concealed. Their false evidence leads otherwise cautious people, Mr. Stewart included, to embrace such statements without any evidence, and to imagine themselves dispensed from the painstaking, tedious study of the facts.

[152]

If, as I said, these worthy philosophers had examined the origin of the names actually imposed on things by the first human beings, they would undoubtedly have recognised that those ancient names were never arbitrary, as is the case with proper names. They would have realised that these names did not indicate the individual nature of the thing but always a common property. Cain, for example, meant possession, something acquired, possessed. Eve gave him the name, saying: 'I have obtained a new thing with the help of the Lord.' This name is obviously common because it applies to everything recently acquired or recently obtained. Abel means vanity, Eve, lifegiving; Seth, substitute ens; Enoch, dedicated; Lamech, poor, humiliated: all of them are common names. The same may be said of the other Hebrew names for persons and things, all of which are formed in such a way that the individual is signified by a common quality. Consequently they are true, common nouns [*App.*, no. 4]. The same can be said of Greek names and those of the whole of antiquity. There is no doubt that during this period, no one ever knew how to form truly proper names, that is, nouns indicating the very individuality of a thing. This is not the case with modern languages where we find Peter, Paul, etc., Italy, France, England, etc., Adige, Tiber, Po, etc., which became truly proper nouns when their etymology was forgotten or people no longer paid any attention to it in conversation.

Moreover, these proper nouns, handed down to us in modern languages from antiquity, are proof of what I am saying. The remaining fragments of their etymologies show that in antiquity they all had their own meaning and were not in any way arbitrary sounds.[111] This is equivalent to saying that

[111] This explains why the ancients were much more ready to note the priority of common nouns over proper nouns than we are. Aristotle did so in his *On Physics* (bk. 1, c. 1), where he clearly states that man first formed common nouns and then proper nouns. It is strange, then, to see how Aristotle bases his view on a fact very much like that mentioned by Smith to demonstrate the opposite view. This shows how facts, when not supported by good, correct understanding on the part of their user, do not on their own lead to truth, but are themselves an occasion of misuse and error. According to Smith: 'The savage calls all the caves he sees by the name assigned to his cave. He first formed the proper noun and then made it common.'
According to Aristotle: 'The child calls all the men he sees *father* until he has learned to tell the difference between *father* and other men. It follows that

antiquity had given to these individual persons, countries, rivers, names which marked them off not by means of their own proper features, but by the features common to a number of other beings of the same species.

Article 9

Seventh flaw: Smith is unaware that it is easier to know what is common in things than what is proper

153. Antiquity shows us, therefore, that common nouns were discovered much earlier than proper nouns, and that ancient languages normally used common nouns even when they needed to name particular individuals. Truly proper nouns are found only in modern languages.

Behind this fact, as we examine it more carefully, we find that such a process in the formation of languages, though strange at first sight is, in fact, natural to the human spirit and the only one it can adopt. A greater power of abstraction is required of us to perceive and name the individuality of entia than to focus on their common features and assign names to them. It is, moreover, natural and necessary that man's first need is to call entia by their most general features. The need to call them by more special qualities arises only later when confusion caused by lack of specification causes harm and trouble. As human experience and expertise developed, human beings felt the need to distinguish things into smaller classes and give them progressively less common names. Finally, at the ultimate stage of more advanced society, we experience the need to indicate individuals themselves by proper names. These names, the last to be formed, endow speech with its ultimate, perfect completion.

This also explains why everything has a common but not a generic name. An even smaller number have a specific name

the name he gives his father is common for the child who does not restrict the meaning of this common noun to indicate his father alone until he notices the differences and his mistake in taking his father for any ordinary man. His understanding therefore proceeds from the general to the particular, from the genus to the differences allowing him to know the species'.

[153]

and, finally, less than one in a thousand — and only in modern languages — are called by a proper name.

It is clear that the worthy philosophers of whom I am speaking, by rejecting the facts to pursue their hypothetical speculation, began their description of the progress of the human mind in the formation of languages and thought at the exact point where they should have ended. They assumed that the first step of the human spirit was the last, and that the first operation was the attribution of proper names, although this occurs only at the final stage because it implies the most highly developed social culture. This is so true that even in modern European languages, which are so advanced and the fruit of thousands of happy years under the influence of Christianity, we can still see in proper names their origin and earlier state as common names.

Article 10

Eighth flaw: Smith does not realise how common names become proper

154. When Smith stated with such assurance that the particular cave, tree, spring which his savage came to know for the first time were *without doubt* the first objects designated by proper nouns which then became common nouns associated with other individual objects, he was describing exactly the opposite of what occurred. He said that all nouns which are common, were originally proper, and all proper nouns were originally common ones.

This error was due to an inexact concept of proper and common nouns. He believed — and at first sight it does seem true — that a proper noun is one by which a single individual is named and a common noun one by which several individuals are named. In this concept, however, he took what accidentally happens to proper and common nouns for what properly constitutes their nature. A common noun is sometimes applied to a number of individuals and a proper noun to one alone. This, however, occurs accidentally and, as we have seen, the opposite may be the case. Sometimes a common noun is applied to a single individual without ceasing to be common and, conversely, a proper noun is applied to a number of individuals without ceasing to be proper. In fact both proper and common nouns are never applied to more than one individual at a time. The only difference between them is that the individual, when called by a common name, is called and designated by possession of a certain quality in which a number of other individuals share or can share; when called by a proper name, the individual is designated by its own individuality, that is, by aspects that are proper or incommunicable to any other.

It is better, therefore, to say that common nouns have been taken and made to serve as proper nouns rather than say that proper nouns have gone on to be common nouns. Common nouns come to express the individuality of entia which previously was not expressed but implied.

To better clarify how this may have occurred, we need to reflect that a common noun indicating an individual by means of a quality possessed in common with other individuals does not define the individual so completely that it is set apart from all others which share the same quality. Such a noun is not therefore by nature proper, that is, applicable to a determined individual. It becomes a proper noun only as a result of a tacit convention [*App.*, no. 5], or to put it better, by a convention expressed by the fact of assigning that name, which by nature is common, to designate a particular ens. A common name is thus capable of nominating an individual although this aptitude for indicating and naming an individual is not expressed within the name itself, but lies implicit and latent in the spirit of those who use that particular name to refer to the individual. This fact — that individuality is not expressed directly but only implied in the use of common names applied to individuals — comes about precisely because of the difficulty the human mind has in abstracting individuality, one of the last and the most awkward tasks of all.

155. By way of summary, then, we should remember that the first step which the human spirit takes towards a knowledge of individuality consists in perceiving it associated and enveloped with all its other common qualities, and focusing on it less distinctly than on these qualities.

The spirit initially indicates the common qualities by nouns; it then makes use of them to indicate individuality whose idea, however, has not yet been distinctly perceived and cannot yet be expressed on its own by a proper noun. As I said, this is so difficult that only modern languages offer a few examples of it. So, let us return to our savage. If we wish to claim him as the discoverer of the name of his cave, his tree or spring, we have to say that he most likely observed the following procedure in his operations.

He observes straightaway in his cave, tree or spring some more striking features that have a stronger, more immediate impact on his senses: he sees the cave as hollow, the tree as gnarled and stout, or emerging from the ground to form a tall canopy over his head; the spring as deep or gushing or something similar. Then, by means of these features, he forms truly common names which in his spirit stand for the propositions: 'that which is hollow, stout, high, deep or conspicuous.'

He then appropriates these common nouns to refer to his particular cave, tree and spring. The common noun is to be applied, like the proper noun, to individual objects and does not differ, as I said, from the proper noun except in its capacity for being applied to all objects possessing the qualities the savage notes and mentions. This communality, if I may put it this way, is restricted and removed by the user's attention and by the circumstances in which he uses it.

Let me grant, therefore, with Smith, since he presents us with these assumptions, that originally the savage knew only one cave, one tree, one spring. Given this, he can only apply the nouns he invented to this cave, this tree, this spring, which are all he knows. However, when he comes to discover other caves, other trees and other springs, I maintain that he immediately grasps that these hollow, stout, conspicuous things are not alone in the world; there are a great many hollow, stout and gushing things. It follows that the names he has made up to express whatever corresponds to these qualities already indicate on their own and express each one of the caves, trees and springs, as well as the first.

Our savage would therefore apply — and this would represent a second stage — his common names to a number of caves, trees and springs. Thus the noun which was common from the start, but used initially for only one individual, would not undergo any further modification. It would simply be used to name several individuals, each taken singly.

However, our savage, if he recognised the need to distinguish his cave from all the others, would be taking a third step but without yet forming proper nouns. He would probably distinguish the various caves in his forest by adding such possessive pronouns as *mine*, *yours*, *his*: *my* cave, *your* cave, *his* cave, and so on.[112] But whatever the formation of this phrase, it would always be such as to indicate the cave belonging to him, or to his interlocutor or to a third person.

He still had a very long way to go, therefore, before arriving at the formation of proper nouns. He would have to cease being a savage and to join with others in society. This domestic society, created in his forests but initially restricted and domestic, would then have to broaden out, make great strides in cultural and civil fields, and finally reach the stage of perfection. This would be a level of high civilisation where people become capable of the most subtle and sustained abstractions and of focusing on them, a level at which the need for artefacts increases enormously, at which moral needs develop, extend, become more sophisticated. These needs continually drive people to distinguish things [*App.*, no. 6], to divide major categories into minor ones, to designate more limited species closer to individual status, to arrange them in every necessary and arbitrary way, and finally — as the last and most refined operation — to allocate to individuals themselves names which are used exclusively to indicate their individuality.

Article 11

Ninth flaw: Smith's paragraph in which he attempts
to explain abstract ideas is totally inadequate

156. So far, I have merely studied the development of language which we assume to have been formed by human beings. I have examined only the external product of the inner

---

[112] Consider this fact: in ancient languages there are many names which are actually made up of a common noun and a possessive pronoun joined to it. For example, in Hebrew *Sarai* means *my lady*. The same can be said of many other words ending with the letter *i* indicating the possessive pronoun *my*.

workings of the spirit without penetrating into the spirit; I have not seen how and with which faculties it is possible to obtain this external product of language. If I were to describe and demonstrate the presence within us of the faculties required for such an operation, developments in the formation of language would be explained. We would have a sufficient reason for these developments and the causes likely to produce them.

Most people are content when they are given an external description of the development of the spirit, because they dwell on what is actually said. Even Stewart, in his attempt to explain how people formed genera and species, is happy with Smith's passage and says that the explanation seems to him as simple as it is satisfactory.

Now, I am also willing to accept for the moment that what Smith tells us in the passage is perfectly true: that people actually did make the transition from proper nouns to common, appellative nouns. Even so, I have to confess that I do not see how Smith's paragraph explains the formation by the human spirit of the classes of individuals which he then calls genera and species. Telling me that people move from proper to common nouns still does not explain what takes place in the spirit during this process. It does not constitute a study of the internal operation of spirit which corresponds to the transition from one type of noun to the other. Nor is it an investigation of the faculties which must be posited for such an operation, or an attempt to solve the problems which, as Stewart himself says, some philosophers have considered one of the most intractable metaphysical quandaries: the formation of genera and species.

Article 12

Tenth flaw: Smith carefully conceals his difficulty in explaining the origin of abstract ideas

157. First of all, it should be noted how Smith somehow shrouds and conceals from himself and his readers the difficulties which arise in seeking to explain the formation of genera and species or, more generally, of abstract ideas.

[157]

He does so by feeding the reader with inexact concepts which lead the spirit astray and prevent it from getting to the heart of the problem.

First, he has led us to assume that common nouns refer solely to a group of individuals. As we have seen, these nouns do not apply to a group but to each individual member of a given group or species.

Then, his use of the word *group* instead of *species* harbours another error. A group of individuals is always a determined number or, at least, a finite number of individuals. On the other hand, the noun *species* does not refer to a determined number but to all possible individual members endowed with the characteristic or quality deemed to determine the species. This distinction is extremely germane to our problem for the following reason.

If I am explaining how a person, having assigned a name to an individual, allots the same name to five others and if I assume that with the name he intends to refer to only one single individual at a time, without reference to any similarity they all share, I need assume in that person only the following faculties: 1. of perceiving individuals; 2. of assigning to each of them an arbitrary sign. The person had five individuals and five signs. As the signs were independent of each other in the same way as the individuals were, he was able to use the same word five times in reference to each of the five individuals. If, however, it is a question of explaining the transition from a proper to a common one or, generally speaking, how we come to create common nouns, the problem comes down to this: 'How were people able to name objects by means of a common quality?' To answer this question we have to assume the following faculties in man: the faculty 1. to conceive individuals; 2. to focus his attention on their common qualities, that is, to form abstract ideas; 3. to consider individuals in so far as they are endowed with these common qualities; 4. to express in sounds all these three known things, that is, individuals as such, the common qualities of the individuals, and the individuals in so far as they are endowed with common qualities. This final mode of naming individuals corresponds to the invention of common nouns.

When we form a common noun, therefore, we are not actually assigning a proper name to a *determined* number of individuals but designating all the individuals which have a common quality.

We are not inquiring how many individuals possess this common quality; we assign the name universally to all individuals having this quality, whether they be few or many, or to put it more accurately, to all individuals that can possibly possess it — an infinite number. On the other hand, when we assign the same proper noun to several individuals, we need to know in a particular way all the individuals to which we assign the name one after another. In this second case, none of the individual objects — which are not actually present to the person assigning the name — can be said to be designated by the name itself. The common noun however comprises all those objects which are not only not individually present to the person inventing the name, but are merely possible.

Let us assume that a father gives the name 'Peter' to nine children in turn. It does not follow that the tenth son should be called Peter. To name the child, the father has to take another decision, and can either repeat the name or use another. This situation arises whenever he has a new child. He can assign the name 'Paul', 'Anthony' or 'Andrew', or any other name he pleases. On the other hand, when someone invents a common noun, for example, the noun *man*, he does not name one man or only those men whom he knows and specifically intends to name, but all those who possess or may possess *humanity*, that is, those common qualities which together make up the human being. He achieves this, not by a number of decisions but by one alone, by the mere imposition of a name. Such an imposition is a general decision which tacitly states: 'I call *man* all those people who have or will have these qualities.'

To make such a decision, a universal, abstract idea is necessary, that is, not determined to a particular number, such as the idea used in assigning proper names.

Finally, if it is claimed that a proper noun becomes common merely by being applied to a number of individuals in turn, I make the following distinction: either the noun is used to refer to a number of individuals and thus becomes a proper noun standing for each of them (if such is the case, a common noun is not thereby formed, and consequently the formation of common nouns has not yet been explained); or the proper noun, when applied to a number of individuals, has changed its meaning. Instead of referring to the individual itself, as it did from the start, it has moved to indicate the species, that is, individuals by means of a common quality. In this case, we still have to explain how this transition has occurred. How has the human spirit altered the meaning it originally bestowed on the word, and replaced the individual with the idea of a quality common to many individuals? Moreover, how does the spirit discover the common quality? What is the nature of this quality which is first observed by the mind, then detached from the rest and given a name? In other words, all the problems of ancient ideology reappear, though somewhat veiled thanks to Smith's and Stewart's stylish narrative. These problems are not picked up by the younger reading public although their solution and the consequent explanation of ideas is not thereby rendered less urgent, or less difficult.

This approach, by assuming that the only faculty in man consists in our perception of individuals, renders impossible any explanation of common nouns, and of ideas of genus and species, although this is what Smith and Stewart attempt to do. In their zeal, they would have us believe that a proper noun, when applied in turn to a certain number of individuals, is automatically changed to a common one. According to them, a proper noun represents simply a group of individuals although they do not say how many are sufficient to form the group. In fact, a common noun is applicable to all possible individuals in a given species. These individuals are infinite in number.

158. In order to understand better the unreliability of the assumption made by Smith when he accepts that a proper noun becomes common as soon as it is applied to a number of individuals,[113] we should also note the absurdity to which it leads. If

---

[113] The philosophers in question make no attempt to prove this statement: they assume their readers take it as true. Their argument is as follows: 'A common noun is one applied to a number of individuals. Therefore, to invent a common noun requires only that a proper noun be attributed to a number of individuals; this is a basic fact.' The first assumption in this argument is taken as certain; the remainder is completely correct, *if the major premiss is true.* With this method of theirs, you can go a long way; in fact, you get wherever you wish. If you wish to prove some strange theory, you begin by carefully

a proper noun becomes common by its attribution to a number of individuals, it becomes more common each time it is attributed to an additional individual. In other words, it will then refer to a more extensive species of thing — something which, as we can see straightaway, is utterly untrue. Thus, the name Peter, if given to two sons, has in Smith's view already become a common noun; if it is given to three or four, it will be even more common, and if to five, six, seven and so on, more common still.

Obviously, we can use the meaning of *common* noun improperly, if we want. A *proper noun* can certainly be called *common* in one sense when it is referred to a group of individuals taken as individuals, that is, to the three, four or more people called Peter. But it is not *common* either in the grammarian's meaning of the term or in the philosopher's because it does not refer to a *species* or *genus* of things. We are trying, however, to explain how the ideas of species and genus are formed. The noun certainly becomes more common in the first sense, as it is successively applied to more individuals. But a common noun, taken in the sense of our argument is common right from the beginning; it does not become more common when applied to a larger number of individuals. Of its nature it refers intrinsically to all possible individuals of a species, neither more nor less. Take the noun *man*, and apply it in turn to one, two, three, ten, a hundred, a thousand human beings. Is it now more common than it was? Previously, it already indicated not a restricted group, but all possible human beings taken individually, that is, all those entia referred to by the word *mankind* —wherever and whenever they may be, even when conceived solely in the mind.

159. I appeal from the philosophers' theories to the common sense of any ordinary person; the former, when they hold firmly to some opinion, deny that they see what everyone else sees. They fear that a frank avowal of this nature would lead to the rebuttal of their statements. But even the most ordinary person, using his common sense, is able to express his opinion on a

forming a proposition which implicitly contains your theory. Then you either declare it to be true, or assume that it is accepted, or if you prefer, imply it in your argument. Next, you analyse it and draw from it precisely the finding which it already contains. You will have proved your point easily since you have skilfully assumed as true what you were required to prove. This is a most useful method.

subject, such as the meaning of words, which falls within his right and competence. Such meaning is not the exclusive property of philosophers and, fortunately, cannot readily be altered by their quibbles. Take the word *man* or any other common noun. Does it refer to a determined number of individuals? Or has it some value that can be applied to an unspecified and undefined number of individuals, that is, to all entia possessing human nature or thought to be able to possess it?

But, if the common noun, in its usually accepted sense, involves the notion of the possibility of other individuals, we still have to explain the nature of this undetermined *possibility* attached to common nouns. How does such an idea, which extends the meaning of the word as far as the concept of possibility, originate in us?

It is an undeniable fact that everyone who speaks, adds to the meaning of common nouns the idea of the possibility of other individuals of the species represented by the noun. This idea of possibility is universal; indeed it is the most universal idea of all. It bears no relationship with individuals, although it enables us to think of an ever greater number of them.

Let us imagine the case of entia who lack the power to think this possibility and who, as a result, are able to perceive only a given number of individuals. In this singular species of entia, we can imagine a wide variation in perceptive powers because we could assume that some would be capable of perceiving five individuals, others ten but no more, others a hundred, a thousand, a thousand million and so on. All of them, nevertheless, would be determined to perceive a determined number of existing individuals, but none would be able to extend itself to the possibility of other individuals above that number. Now compare human intelligence with such a species of entia. We do not perceive merely a determined number of existing individuals, five, ten, a thousand, and so on. Using our innate intelligence, we can always add the concept of all possible individuals, something indefinitely greater, to the number of individuals perceived by us. Now, the species of our imaginary entia could never form anything but proper nouns. Only human beings can form common nouns because we can think universally of purely possible individuals. If our imagined entia also wished to designate with a separate name each of the specified number of individuals which they perceive (although this is in fact impossible, we can still assume it), they would not assign the same proper name to many individuals. No common noun would have been formed. Humans, on the other hand, are able to formulate a common noun because they can give a name to entia in so far as they recognise them as endowed with a common quality. We can assign such a name because 1. we have the faculty, as I have said above, of focusing upon a quality possessed by one individual which can be shared by other individuals; and 2. we have the faculty of knowing this possibility; that is, the possibility that this quality is shared by other individuals, regardless of number, place and time.

160. The following ideas are added, therefore, to the common noun: 1. the idea of some *quality*; 2. the idea of the quality's *aptitude* for being shared by an individual; 3. the idea of the *possibility* that this quality may be shared by an indefinite number of individuals. All these ideas are comprised in the idea of *species* and *genus* which is presupposed by the common noun. In fact, the common noun expresses the *species* or *genus* which is obtained by means of a quality known to be potentially common to an infinite number of individuals.

What more can we say? Smith's argument offers no explanation about the way in which we form the ideas of genus and species. To put it briefly and clearly, his argument is summed up as follows: 'We turn proper nouns into common nouns by assigning them successively to a number of individuals. These nouns, when applied to a number of individuals, are those which form species and genera in our mind.'

My reply can be summed up as follows: 'The mere assignment of a proper noun to several individuals does not make it common. To become common, that noun must change its value; in other words it must no longer indicate individuals through that which forms their individuality, but begin to indicate them by some common quality. For this to happen, an internal operation of the spirit is needed, as only the spirit can change the meaning of a word. But the spirit cannot alter the meaning of a word except 1. by using it to indicate a common quality in place of the previously indicated individuality; and 2. by adding to this quality the concept that the possibility may be shared indefinitely by individuals.

[160]

'The common noun, therefore, does not replace such ideas in our mind; these ideas give the noun its value. In other words, these ideas are the means whereby the spirit transforms proper nouns into common nouns.

'Consequently, although it has been stated — falsely, it must be said — that we acquire proper nouns first, which later become common, we still have no explanation of how we form genera and species. The spirit cannot in fact devise common nouns unless it has formed, previously or simultaneously, the genera and species of things.'

Article 13

The form taken by the difficulty I have pointed to in Smith's and Stewart's arguments

161. If my argument so far is true, the difficulty which I mentioned at the start in Smith's and Stewart's theory has not been solved.

At present, as we inquire how the spirit conceives the ideas of species and genera, the argument runs as follows: 'We are unable to form a genus or species without the idea of some common quality which, in turn, cannot be formed without a judgment. But a judgment presupposes the idea of a common quality, that is, the idea of one of those classes called genera or species. How is it possible, then, for us to form an *a priori* judgment if all the ideas of common qualities — which is another way of saying universal ideas — are acquired, and there is nothing innate in our spirit?'

Article 14

Nominalism does not meet this difficulty

162. Smith and Stewart, like all nominalists, resort to denying the existence of universal ideas which, they maintain, are merely *words*. They are incapable of disentangling this complex issue because they cannot define what else these mysterious ideas

may be, and how the spirit forms or discovers them. The difficulty is present in any attempt to explain their formation. Many contemporary philosophers cannot see how to extricate themselves from such a philosophical quicksand and, as a result, have tried to convince themselves that the difficulty is merely an illusion. In Stewart's view, for instance, 'what the ancients' — poor unfortunates — 'had considered one of the most difficult problems in metaphysics, had a simple solution such as Smith's.'

However, this way of underestimating the problem does not constitute a successful solution; words cannot replace things, nor common nouns supply for universal ideas. On the contrary, the human spirit cannot form a common noun unless it possesses the universal idea corresponding to the noun in question.

Nothing would seem more obvious. But is there anything so obvious that is not openly denied by philosophers who find it distasteful?

Today, nominalists are on the increase because people imagine they have found a very easy solution to such a serious difficulty. The following argument, showing more clearly the fallacy of the reasons advanced by Stewart to confirm his view — all of which assume what has to be proved — will not therefore be wasted.

Article 15

The cause of Stewart's blunder

163. Words without any meaning whatsoever are merely useless sounds and cannot be used to help forward an argument; this statement seems as clear as daylight.

But words with a universal meaning, such as common nouns, do not refer to determined individuals, and are therefore either meaningless or indicate universal ideas.

This reason alone might have led Mr. Stewart to see how impossible it is to assume the non-existence of universal ideas whose place is taken by mere words. In other words, what is usually termed a universal idea is merely a word. This argument is so simple and so conclusive that it is difficult to understand how the Scottish professor did not think of it.

164. He may have reached his conclusion, however, by his success, without ever mentioning the terms *genera*, *species*, *general ideas*, in describing how we make use of universal words. Having eliminated these words from the discussion, he was led to believe that he had succeeded in making their corresponding ideas superfluous and useless.

This is how he explains the use of universal terms:

> When we talk of conceiving or grasping a general proposition, we simply mean that by habitual use of language we know that the general terms of a proposition can be replaced by the names of certain individuals to which the terms refer.[114]

He seems to mean that we do not need to have connected universal ideas to words. It is enough to have acquired the habit of mentally replacing them with given individuals. All we need to explain the formation of universal arguments is 1. to know how to conceive individuals; and 2. to have words for which we normally substitute certain individuals at our choice. According to him, this is the way words represent so-called universal ideas.

Article 16

The *petitio principii* in Stewart's theory

165. His argument, however, contains a *petitio principii* as the following shows. First, how can such a habit be acquired? How do we acquire the habit of replacing a given universal term not merely by some random individual but by certain, designated and determined individuals? For example, the term *man* is never given the meaning 'animals' or 'rocks' but always and only, 'individuals of the human species'. Why is the habit of using the word *man* restricted to that class of things and not to others? Is there some power, intrinsic to the material word which forces us to apply it only to certain, specific individuals? Not at all. There is no necessary connection between the physical word and the individuals which it signifies. A word is pure

---

[114] *Eléments de la Philosophie de l'esprit humain*, chap. 4, section 3.

sound; it frequently draws our attention to things which are not sounds and have nothing to do with sounds. The only possible relationship between the sound which forms the word man and the ens to which it refers is that made by our spirit between the word and the thing.

166. This is an arbitrary connection, you will say. Here we agree on one point: if any society wished to use the noun *man* to refer to animals as a genus and agreed as a body to give it this meaning, the members of the society would understand by the word *man* what we now call *animal*, just as we understand one another when we use the word in a more restricted sense.

It is the will which decides and determines that certain individuals, and not others, can be replaced by a given common noun. This is the crux of the matter: how can the will determine that these, rather than those, particular individuals replace a given term in such a way that others cannot? Is a fixed number of individuals determined and assigned to the term? This would be possible if it were agreed that three men, Peter, Paul and Andrew should be called by a certain noun which could be replaced only by one of these three individuals. In this case, however, either this noun would not be universal but a merely proper noun given arbitrarily to each of the three or, if it were a common noun — for example, if it were agreed that *friend* should be reserved only for any one of these three — this noun would be usurped by agreement in place of the proper noun. In this case, two things rather than one would have to be explained: 1. how did it come to be a common noun, and 2. how could it be used instead of a proper noun? In short, the issue is to show how the human spirit links a certain individual to a common noun. Whatever assumption one makes, this difficulty can never be avoided. As I said, it is not a question of replacing certain enumerated, determined individuals by common nouns.

If this were the whole matter under discussion, we would need only some association of ideas or a mere power of recall which, upon hearing the sound, would awaken in us one of the two, three, five, ten determined individuals to whom we had designated the noun. But the exact opposite is present in common nouns. It is not a question of our mentally replacing a common noun by a known individual which we specially discern and target, that is, an individual previously selected from a determined number of known things. On the contrary, the issue is to replace an individual taken from an indefinite number of individuals that are unknown to us from experience. These individuals may not even exist; they may only be possible.

Think for a moment. We do not have to substitute the universal term *horse* by one of the horses we have seen or even by an existing horse. We can, if we wish, substitute a non-existent horse. The word alone does not refer to an existing horse. But even if we were obliged to substitute an existent horse for the word *horse*, it would not matter which existent horse we substituted. It could be one seen years earlier or one seen for the first time. But if this does not matter, why does it not matter? We certainly have not seen, one by one, every horse that exists and decided in every case to call each one a *horse*. Assigning names to so many beasts would have been impossible. Nor would other persons have had the time or patience to make such a pact with us. They would need not only the word *horse* but countless other nouns required by human conversation which refer to different species of things. It would be far too tedious and tiring to have to name individuals one by one to obtain a common noun so that, on hearing it we could mentally substitute one of the individuals already designated singularly. Moreover, it would be a disaster not to be able to name newly born or formed individuals with names already given to their predecessors. We could do nothing more than name individual things which would be extremely difficult and tedious to enumerate.

167. This is tantamount to saying that common nouns are not formed in this way. The human spirit does not attach to them a given number of individuals examined one by one. It attaches a *species* of individuals to them, that is, all the possible individuals having a common quality. Thus individuals are substituted for the common noun, if it is used. These individuals, however, are 1. not selected at random (there would be no distinction between species and genera); and 2. not selected as a result of conventions governing particular individuals (this would mean going on *ad infinitum*). On the contrary, certain individuals are substituted for a common noun: 1. on the basis of a universal rule which ascertains whether individuals possess the *common quality* to which the common noun refers; 2. these are not known or existing individuals but *possible* individuals, that is,

any individual whatsoever that can be thought of as endowed with the common quality.

Consequently, although we may never have seen the individual previously, its mere appearance suddenly reminds us that its name had been determined and set by human beings even before it had come to exist. It has the quality which places it in the class of individuals to which the name has been assigned.

168. Stewart's habit of resorting to the expedient of substitution is thus of no avail. The habit of replacing certain things by such nouns is useless for merely possible things and for things which, although not yet known individually, can be grasped by the human mind.

This explains why Stewart, when he states that there is no need for universal ideas and that we only need to know how to replace given individuals for the common nouns which express them, contradicts himself by asserting what he has already denied. Being able to replace the given individuals for common nouns means possessing universal ideas. The substitution cannot be made without these ideas because without them we would not know which individuals were to replace the common nouns. The mind needs first to distinguish the *species* and *genera* of individuals so that it can link to a given term the individuals of a given species, not others — and, of course, individuals of another species to another term. Then it must know how to distinguish these individuals of different species as belonging to one species rather than another, and be able to do this before naming them. It will know what to call them only when it knows the species to which they belong. If a flower is covered by grass, I can't apply the word flower to it, but as soon as I can see it I recognise it as belonging to the species of things called flowers.

Article 17

Another of Stewart's mistakes

169. Stewart makes a mistake similar to that noted above when he expounds his views in another way:

> According to this view the process of the mind, in carrying on general speculations, that *idea* which the ancient

philosophers considered as the essence of an individual, is nothing more than the particular quality or qualities in which it resembles other individuals of the same class, and in consequence of which, a generic name is applied to it. It is the possession of this quality that entitles the individual to the generic application, and which, therefore, may be said to be essential to its classification with that particular genus; but as all classifications are to a certain degree arbitrary, it does not necessarily follow that it is more essential to its existence as an individual, than various other qualities which we are accustomed to regard as accidental. In other words, (if I may borrow the language of modern philosophy)[115] this quality forms its nominal, but not its real essence.[116]

170. Anyone studying this passage can easily recognise the uncertainty and hesitancy of its author. Having no clear proof for his system, he tries to support it with a line of argument full of *approximations* intended to suggest a link between ideas where, in fact, there is none.

Look at the final words of the passage just quoted. The statement, 'This quality constitutes its nominal essence but not its real essence', implies the presence of two essences rather than one, and therefore admits more than he intends to deny.

171. But I shall not be over-critical of Stewart's use of words. Rather, let me ask whether by *nominal essence* he means a word. This would seem to follow from what he says in other passages and from the aim of his argument which is to show that universal ideas are nothing.

If by the term *nominal essence* he does not mean a mere word but something more, his whole argument is invalid. In that case, the general terms would express something objective, and would not be mere words.

172. In the passage I quoted, Stewart himself admits this. He calls *nominal essence* a quality actually possessed by the individual, and adds:

It is the possession of this quality that entitles the individual to the generic application.

---

[115] How poor modern philosophy is to use such language!

[116] *Eléments de la Philosophie de l'esprit humain*, chap. 4, section 2.

If this quality were nothing, the individual could neither possess it nor receive from it the generic name. Moreover, Stewart himself attributes to the human spirit the faculty of thinking of a quality of an individual without conceiving the other qualities which go to make up the individual. He says:

> The classification of different objects supposes a power of attending to some of their qualities or attributes, without attending to the rest.[117]

Thus he accepts that 1. the single characteristics of individuals are real; 2. we have a faculty for considering them on their own, separate from the individuals themselves (considering them on their own is the same thing as considering them while prescinding from everything with which they coexist); 3. when our spirit considers these qualities on their own and in isolation, it has a true object before itself because these qualities are true.

Let us consider the qualities of bodies: colour, taste, smell, sound, extension, hardness, fluidity, and so on. Setting aside for the moment the question of the existence of bodies and assuming with Stewart himself that they are real, we have here, according to Stewart's own principles, as many qualities, as many mental objects, as there are bodies.

The names therefore of these qualities, that is, the words *colour*, *taste*, and so on, which are all abstract nouns, also express something effective. They are not merely names, but have something which actually corresponds to them, that is, they have these qualities, whatever these may be in things. If abstract words such as the colour, taste, etc. of bodies are not merely names but have something beyond what they signify, it follows that common nouns and appellatives such as *coloured*, *tasty*, and so on, *body*, *man*, and so on, also have some effective meaning. In fact, they are simply nouns meaning *that which has colour, taste*, and so on, *that which has corporality, humanity* and so on. Common nouns, therefore, are not mere words without any corresponding object but, in accordance with Stewart's own principles, signify some object proper to them.

---

[117] *Eléments de la Philosophie de l'esprit humain*, chap. 4, section 1.

Article 18

Further mistakes by Stewart, and further examples of
the inadequacy of his system in solving the difficulty raised

173. At this point, Stewart may reply: 'I cannot deny that
abstracts and common nouns indicate something. If I have
denied it anywhere, this was merely an inaccurate expression.
However, I maintain what they indicate is merely "the particular quality or a group of qualities by which an individual resembles other individuals." Consequently, it is in no way universal,
but entirely particular. This quality is only in the individuals
where it is always individual.'

I shall certainly not bring up again Plato's question: do
abstract qualities have an existence outside spirit and distinct
from *entia* themselves? This would contribute nothing to my
purpose. I am perfectly willing to grant Mr. Stewart the right
to his view that the qualities to which we are referring do not
have an existence outside a spirit except in the individuals
themselves. But he likewise accepted, with me, that our spirit
can and does consider them in isolation from individuals, and
as if these qualities existed alone. This is a fact which cannot
be disputed.

From this I conclude: our spirit, if it considers qualities in isolation from individuals, has an immediate, universal object for
its focus, that is, a quality distinct from an individual is a universal object completely independent of the word used to express
it.

174. If I show conclusively the truth of this last assertion, I
believe that these consequences will follow: 1. our spirit can
have a universal object; 2. it can give this object a name, and consequently 3. there are nouns which express universal ideas.
These are not mere words devoid of meaning nor words for
which, by a blind habit, we substitute certain individuals.

When I say that a quality, considered in the way in which our
spirit can view it, that is, apart from an ens, is universal, I simply
mean that I can conceive it in an indefinite number of individuals. That it can be thought in an indefinite number of individuals, or be universal or common, is synonymous in the sense
normally given to these words.

The particular being corresponds to the universal being of a quality. This simply means that it cannot be thought of as common to a number of individuals, but as fixed and proper to one individual. The individuality of the ens to which it is applied makes the common quality particular. This explains why qualities remain common for us as long as we do not think of them as existing in determined individuals. In other words, we think of them in such a way that we retain the option of imagining them as connected with any individual, until we have linked them to one individual. Once they are linked to this individual, they too are individualised by it and are called *particular*. In this case, the whiteness, size, and so on, of one body is not the whiteness or size of another body.

If a quality is particular only in so far as it exists in an individual and if, as I have said, our spirit has the faculty of considering it without considering the individual to which it belongs (which Stewart himself concedes), I conclude that our spirit has the faculty of considering it as merely possible without thinking that it has a real existence in some individual. Dr. Reid calls this *simple apprehension*; Professor Stewart seems to call it *conception*. If this cannot be disputed, and our spirit can think of whiteness not as something really existing but as merely possible, I maintain that in such a case the object of our spirit is universal in the sense in which the ideologues use the word. This whiteness is not linked to any individual; it is whiteness which we conceive as capable of being received by an indefinite number of individuals. We think it in such a way that, if we had the faculty to create, we would be able to realise it, from the idea we had of it, in an indefinite number of white bodies.

175. This whiteness conceived by our mind is not therefore merely a name, as Stewart would seem to maintain, nor is it any of the whitenesses we have seen really existing in the white bodies under our gaze.

It is not any of these really existing whitenesses all of which are particular whitenesses, as I have said, in the individual in such a way that they cannot be transferred from one individual to another nor joined with a number of individuals even by thought.

How could I conceive a way of transferring the whiteness of one white body to another without depriving the former of its whiteness? The white body in question either has a white surface and the rest of a different colour, or it is completely white like chalk which, as friable, leaves its own whiteness on bodies it touches. Let us now consider the difference between making bodies white by means of the whiteness really existing in an individual, and making them white by means of the idea of general whiteness which is, I maintain, in our mind.

1. In the first place, a body cannot transfer its own whiteness to another, however white it is, unless it is friable. But at the same time its parts are so hard that they cannot easily release the tiny fragments that will cover and whiten the surface of the other body. On the other hand, anyone who has the power to create, creates bodies endowed with whiteness by giving them this quality, but does this by drawing the whiteness only from the idea of whiteness present in his spirit. This idea has no need to be friable nor possess any other quality in order to be communicated to bodies.

2. If a white body which will pass some of its whiteness to another body has only a slight surface area of white, it will deprive itself of a slight covering of colour when it whitens the other body. On the other hand, the intelligent spirit to which I am referring is able to create white bodies at a stroke, as it conceives them possible, without reducing or destroying the notion it has of general whiteness.

3. When the colouring body, such as chalk, is friable and completely white, it cannot make another body white without losing a thin white coating which is attached to the whitened body. In losing this thin coating, the whitening body, although still seen as white, does not present the same previous whiteness. The white surface previously seen has been transferred to the other body; the first body now reveals another surface, white like the first, but not the first.

We can infer, therefore, that it is not strictly accurate to say that the whiteness really existing in an individual is transferred to another. When a white body whitens another body upon contact, it is not the same whiteness communicated to two bodies, nor one whiteness transferred from one body to another. The first body is an amalgam of many particles or tiny white bodies which detach themselves or are taken from the walls of the first body and settle on the walls of the second. In this way they whiten the other body but do not communicate their own whiteness; the particles simply change position. The second body, despite appearances, does not in fact change colour.

Indeed the whiteness really existing in individuals is so particular to them that it is wholly incommunicable. Although the bodies possessing it may be minced and pulverised, and the powder derived from them change position, nevertheless, the whiteness alone is never transferred in exactly the same way from one body to another.

On the other hand, if we were to imagine a spirit able to create white bodies, we certainly cannot imagine it as removing and erasing the real whiteness of the bodies and transferring it to other bodies which it wished to produce. That particular whiteness is incommunicable. However, we can think and imagine the spirit as giving existence to particular whitenesses on the basis of the standard, general whiteness which it contemplates in its mind.

4. Finally, even if we supposed that a white body communicated its whiteness to another, it could not communicate it to an infinite number of bodies. In this self-communication, it would become increasingly weaker by losing a thin coating of its substance to each body that it whitened. Eventually, it would vanish completely.

On the other hand, the quality of whiteness conceived in a universal manner by the intelligent mind, makes this spirit, which we imagine endowed with creative power, capable of creating an infinite series of white bodies without any diminution to the whiteness, or without its becoming less apt for renewed realisation in countless other bodies.

It is, therefore, this quality of whiteness, not the particular quality received in an individual, which enables a creative spirit to realise whiteness in an indefinite number of white bodies. The particular quality is of its nature incommunicable to other individuals.

176. Nor can we say that a spirit, which we imagine endowed with the faculty to create, imparts whiteness to the bodies it creates without needing to possess the idea of whiteness in addition to creative force. Such a force does not determine the creator to create bodies of one colour rather than another. This power cannot be thought as determined to create anything

unless the understanding puts forward the objects which it creates.

It would also be unreasonable to reply that, in the hypothesis of a creating ens, we can no longer propose any argument because the idea of creation transcends both the way we conceive mentally and the rules governing our thought. The idea of a creative spirit was only introduced into the discussion to make the matter clearer; it does not mean that my argument relies on such an assumption. All that is needed for my argument is to take the example of a man who imagines as many white bodies as he likes. I can also ask him whether the whiteness he imagines is the whiteness he sees in individuals. It seems obvious to me that it is not, just as it is obvious that the whiteness which a creating ens would transmit to created bodies is not. The whiteness seen in individuals is inseparable from them; it is individual and incommunicable by nature. But the whiteness which our imagination bestows on possible bodies is indefinitely communicable.

The obvious reason why these two whitenesses are not identical is this. On the one hand, we know we perceive the whiteness of the white bodies each time we see them, and we realise that the whiteness related to those bodies is inseparable from them. On the other hand, we are aware that we can imagine many other white bodies similar to those we have seen.

Let us assume that we imagine all the white bodies we have seen during our life. Now, using our imagination, we could add a similar number of possible bodies as white as those we have seen. Is the whiteness of this imagined and thought-out array of bodies, together with that of the bodies we have actually seen, the whiteness of the seen bodies or some other whiteness? It cannot be the whiteness of the actually seen bodies because this is individual, and we have already assumed that all the bodies we have seen are present to our inner gaze. In addition to all the whiteness it has seen, our spirit can endlessly conceive another whiteness and a whiteness which is not real but purely imaginary, or rather purely thought. In fact, we are dealing here — and this must be noted — solely with the object of thought.

177. If our spirit were restricted to conceiving or recalling the whiteness it had seen in bodies, its only faculty, apart from sense, would be that of recalling phantasms. But all agree that in

addition we possess conception and imagination. If we consider only the imagination, we see that we are able at will to multiply infinitely entia similar to those we have seen. It is this faculty which needs explanation. It cannot, however, be explained in any way by assuming, with Stewart, that our spirit is bereft of universal ideas, that is, of ideas which stand for qualities in isolation from individuals and without the faculty of attributing these qualities to an indefinite number of possible or thinkable individuals [*App.*, no. 7].

Now, if our spirit can conceive whiteness only in an indefinite number of possible individuals and is not obliged to think also of the determined individual in which it exists, and if this possible whiteness is not the whiteness existing in single entities which we can see (since the definition of whiteness is whiteness as thought, after removal from the thought of the individuals to which it really belongs) it follows, I maintain, that this whiteness is not by any means a mere name. What I said earlier about common nouns would seem a sufficient demonstration of this. Nevertheless, I think it worthwhile proving it once more, granted the propensity of modern philosophy to nominalism.

If whiteness, as thought and not existent in any of the entia we see, were merely a name, we would be doing precisely nothing whenever we imagined white objects but did not name them. But no-one will allow himself to be persuaded that his mind, in imagining things he has never seen, experienced or named individually, is doing nothing. We have all found relief at times from our woes in pleasant, though vain and imaginary images. At times we all enjoy pursuing pleasant dreams presented at happier moments by the wondrous power of intellective imagination when we are fully awake. The lover will never be persuaded that his daydreams are merely pleasant illusions, without reality, and non-existent in his spirit or soul. The poet will not be persuaded that his lovely verses are vain and wasted words when he expresses in them individual objects he has never seen, touched and felt. If these words, which have no reference to actually existing objects, are empty, meaningless sounds, how can a sublime poet enchant all his contemporaries by his almost divine art and astound later ages? Does he alone have the gift of discovering magical, powerful sounds, devoid of meaning? Where does he derive such sounds? What God inspires him to utter them? What spirit moves his lips mechanically to utter them? Before uttering them, has he no concept, no thought, no imaginative representation present in his spirit as his whole song deserts the sensible world and takes flight beyond the afflictions of these individual things to range over the interminable fields of endless imagination?

Finally, what would a person, known for his new discoveries and enterprises, say to a philosopher who dryly insisted: 'Listen, you cannot conceive anything except already existing individuals. You are wasting your time if you are thinking of helping the world with beautiful, new discoveries, or some original writing or some magnanimous enterprise. When you think about such things which do not yet exist, you are just like the idiot who does nothing and thinks of nothing. When you talk about these things, you are nothing more than a trickster. In fact, you are not even that, because your words and sounds are purely empty, like the noise of a collection of stones rubbed or knocked against each other. They express nothing existent, no particular individual, without which there is no thought.'

Anyone stipulating that we have no ideas of the individual qualities of entia unless they are observed in the individuals we have seen, and that such qualities, when considered in isolation from the individuals as being merely possible, are mere names — this is Stewart's case — unwittingly and unwillingly renounces and disowns all arts and sciences. He has no means of explaining intellectual imagination. According to such philosophers, human beings can have only the threadbare remembrance of things they have seen (and even this remains unexplained) [*App.*, no. 8]; they cannot imagine possible entia. This blocks the wellspring of all rational and human activity, which has its source in the power to carry out and obtain possible, future good. To imagine possible things, their qualities must first be considered in the mind as possible, that is, as qualities shareable by indefinite, but as yet non-subsistent entia.

Article 19
Stewart's nominalism derives from Reid's principles

178. What I have been saying so far has particular force

[178]

against Stewart's system thanks to his dependence upon Dr. Reid's principles on the nature of ideas.

Reid denies the existence of ideas considered as an intermediary between the real objects of the spirit and the spirit itself. Locke, like the ancients, distinguished between ideas and things. He considered ideas, not things, as the proximate *term* of the intellect. Reid, however, did not want any intermediary between the real, perceived ens and the perceiving spirit. This is also Stewart's view.

Now, as far as individuals are concerned, the real object truly exists because real individuals exist. However, Reid's system had no way of explaining universal ideas which have no existence outside the spirit. As a result, Stewart decided to deny them completely; for him, they are names, and nothing more [*App.*, no. 9].

179. I shall not enquire here if this part of Reid's system is true or false. I have already dealt with it. Nor shall I examine if Stewart understood it correctly, and if the refusal to accept universals completely while supposing that mere names may take their place is an inevitable consequence of the system.

I need only point out that Stewart thought he was obliged to do so by the strict necessity of the system. His acceptance of the principle that there are no intermediate ideas between objects really existing outside us and ourselves who perceive them led him to deny completely the existence of universal ideas in which the spirit has no really existing object.

But I have proved that: 1. names are not sufficient to explain the act whereby the spirit imagines possible entia, and in greater number than all the individuals it perceives by the senses; 2. the ideas of qualities perceived in individuals themselves (in so far as qualities adhere to them) are not sufficient either; 3. it is moreover necessary for our mind to conceive these qualities in themselves, that is, in isolation from the individuals and hence simply as possible. It seems obvious, therefore, that Stewart's system is defective and inadequate; it provides no explanation of this final mode of conception by which universal ideas are formed and are present.

Article 20

In explaining how likeness between objects is conceived,
we have the same difficulty under a different aspect

180. There are still a number of reflections to be made on the
passage quoted from Stewart.

First, the reader should consider the phrase Stewart uses
when he states what he understands by the essence of an individual. He says:

> The essence of an individual lies solely in the particular
> quality through which it resembles other individuals of
> the same class and by virtue of which its generic name is at-
> tributed to it.

The odd thing about this passage is that nobody can disagree
with this definition. I am quite certain that Plato himself would
have had nothing to add to it. This means that Stewart's passage
leaves untouched the question it was meant to deal with.

181. It is true that in the passage he does not mention the
words *universals* and *general ideas* and similar terms. What I
maintain, however, is that the passage contains the meaning of
those very words which have been studiously avoided. Consequently, by the use of such terms, universals have not been
banished from metaphysics although it would seem that fear
has prevented the use of their proper names.

182. To see how this comes about, I would ask the reader how
he would interpret our philosopher's phrase, 'the quality by
which an individual resembles other individuals.'

He may answer that he does not feel it necessary to enquire
about the likeness one thing has to another. Everybody understands the expression: one individual is like another. I too
believe that everybody can understand it, and I believe that it
can be easily defined.

'Two or more individuals resemble one another,' obviously
states less than: 'Two or more individuals are the same.' One
cannot say that a number of individuals are the same unless they
are the same in all their parts and qualities. For them to be similar, on the other hand, all that is needed is that they be the same in
some particular quality. There is no similarity between a number of objects except that under some aspect they have an equal,

common quality. But I do not wish to break off at this point to work out what follows from this relative to the nature of the identical or common quality. I would rather point out that I can never know the likeness or identical nature of a number of objects if in my mind I have only their individual idea or the idea of their individual qualities. In fact, the qualities of two objects, in so far as they are individual, that is, adhering to an individual, cannot be compared with each other in any way because the qualities found in one individual are found in a different place from those in some other individual. Two things to be compared can never be put together for comparison as long as they are found in different places. Comparing a number of things or qualities to discover how they are alike and how they differ requires an intellective spirit which possesses not only the faculty of perceiving them individually, but that of mentally isolating them[118] from the individuals and linking them together. Through this comparison, we discover what they have in common and what is proper to them.

The surveyor wishes to discover whether two triangles are equal; he mentally superimposes one upon the other and observes if they meet exactly. Similarly, the carpenter superimposes one table upon another when he needs to see whether two tables are the same size. Yet the carpenter's action is quite different from the surveyor's. Note that merely placing the tables close up to one another would be useless. Mere physical collocation would not enable the carpenter to see if the two tables were equal unless he possessed in addition within himself an intelligent spirit, capable of conceiving them interpenetrating each other, that is, both occupying the same space. If the spirit wishes to compare two lines, it must put one line in the place of the other. If it wishes to compare two surfaces, it has to conceive them one inside the other. If it wishes to compare two solids, it is obliged to conceive them as mingled in all their dimensions. Thus the spirit sees if they are equal or unequal, and which of

---

[118] To reply: 'Isolating mentally is not genuine isolation. The argument, therefore, is false' would show that the question at issue had not been understood. I am referring to intellectual operations of the human spirit, to what occurs in the mind, and not outside it. Relative to the mind, isolating and uniting means conceiving, separately or as a whole, the object which we are thinking of.

the two is greater, which smaller. However close and coherent the two physical solids become, they still remain apart and are not, therefore, truly compared with each other. One exists and has no relationship whatever to the existence of the other.

Someone may say: If, in placing side by side two solids to see which is greater, the carpenter does not produce any comparison except in his spirit, why does he bother to place them side by side? He does so, not in order to make a comparison outside his spirit, but because, by this external action, he enables his spirit, and his imagination also, to carry out a true interior comparison. Moreover, there seems no possible doubt about this to anyone who tries to discover how our spirit makes a comparison between two or more things.

183. I must simply point out that what I have said about bodies and extension in the example also applies to any two individuals whatsoever. Two individuals can never be entirely intermingled. As individuals, they have two distinct, independent existences. It can therefore be affirmed that if there were only individuals, they could never be compared because they could not be lodged in the same place or, to put it in a more general way, in one and the same existence.

184. What does the spirit need to enable it to compare two or more individuals and ascertain how they are equal and unequal, how they are alike and how they differ? According to Stewart, and Reid before him, the spirit has only strictly individual ideas which do not differ from the individuals themselves which are enveloped by thought. However, these individual ideas are insufficient to set up a comparison, just as the individuals, from which these ideas do not differ relative to their distinctiveness and independence, are insufficient. In fact, the idea of a quality would cease to be individual if this quality which we think about could, by virtue of our thought, be passed on from one individual to another. A quality is particular or individual solely when it is conceived as adhering to a single individual. Thus, just as there is no comparison established between two individuals in isolation from the spirit which compares them, so there is no comparison between two individual ideas, one of which can never (precisely on the assumption that they are merely individuals) be confused or identified with the other. For the spirit to find that two individuals are similar or dissimilar, it

must also possess some universal idea in addition to the individual ideas as I shall explain.

185. The issue here is to ascertain how two white surfaces are like each other, where one is whiter than the other.

Neither the surfaces themselves nor the individual whiteness of the surfaces can be transferred from one to the other. If it were possible, the two whitenesses would produce a third, which would still not furnish the intended comparison between the first two whitenesses. Nor can the idea of the individual whiteness of one surface be compared with the idea of the individual whiteness of the other surface without some intermediary aid. When I say individual whiteness, I mean whiteness which has such a proper existence that it cannot be externalised, nor transferred to another surface, nor take any other into itself; it is alien to any other, unaware of it, and excludes it. The means by which our spirit is able to compare the two forms of whiteness of which we are speaking has to be a potency through which we have a universal notion of whiteness, not the mere sight of some individual, existing whiteness. Only to the universal notion can we directly compare the individual whitenesses perceived by the senses and see to what extent they share in the notion of white.

Indeed, let us suppose that we have formed in our mind the idea of universal whiteness (how does not matter for the moment). This whiteness has not been received in any existing individual, but stands on its own so that we view it as capable of being actualised in an infinite number of individuals.

Such an idea, untrammelled, so to speak, by the individual in our spirit, is by nature a type, an example, a rule we use to judge rapidly the resemblance of the sensible individuals which come under our gaze. We do this as follows. As we see a white surface, we have in our spirit 1. the perception of the surface in question; 2. the universal idea of possible whiteness. We then compare this second whiteness with the first, and thus judge it. Such a comparison is possible because the universal idea of whiteness, unrestricted to any individual, can be conceived by us in all possible individuals and, therefore, in the individual whose whiteness we intend to judge. Thus the individual, felt whiteness and the mentally conceived universal whiteness become involved with one another, that is, are found together without being confused because it is impossible to confuse the general with the particular. Nevertheless, the particular is received in the general where it can be seen without losing the determination which makes it particular.

When we make a similar judgment about another surface, we have two individual surfaces, both judged to a certain degree of white.

Consequently, in accordance with the axiom that two things similar to a third are similar to each other, we discover the similarity of the two white surfaces.

In order to discover whether two or more individuals resemble one another we must suppose that in our spirit there is a common type or example of that quality which makes those individuals similar. This type or example, then, is simply the same quality considered by our spirit, but in isolation from all individuals and consequently in a universal manner. In short, it is the same quality, no longer as really existing but as *possible*, and capable of being *received* in an indefinite number of individuals.

186. If anyone finds this method of explaining how we discover the similarities between things unsatisfactory, I would be pleased were he to offer a more satisfying explanation.

It seems odd to me, though, that in a study of the difficulty of the nature of universal ideas formed by the spirit, anyone is happy to state that such an idea is merely 'the particular quality which renders an individual similar to other individuals of the same class.' He shows in this way that it is useless and superfluous to explain how the similarities in individuals are known. If it is useless to explain how the spirit comes to know similarities and differences, it is equally useless to undertake a study of universal ideas. These are not two questions, but a single, identical question expressed in different words. As I said, I cannot conceive how it is possible to make a judgment on equality or similarity between two objects, without some common yardstick which, precisely because it is common, cannot be individual, but must be universal.

187. If these yardsticks, these common qualities, these universals (such words are synonymous in our discussion) cannot be properly understood, or perhaps contain something mysterious and recondite, it does not follow that they can be rejected. That

unfortunately is what human philosophy tends to do. If something cannot be understood, or is found mysterious, philosophy is quite prepared to deny it or maintain that it is an illusion, a dream of our backward, ancient world. At best, it describes the difficulty as inexplicable. Each thinker judges human ingenuity on the basis of his own mental forces, and makes this the limit of his philosophical modesty.

However, whatever present or past writers may say, the true lover of wisdom will think it imperative never to deny the existence of anything well-proven simply because he cannot grasp it. He prefers rather to confess ingenuously that he still does not understand its nature rather than declare that it is unintelligible and outside the scope of human investigation. Such statements can be left to the encyclopedists.

Article 21

The same difficulty is found in explaining the classification of individuals

188. I should like to make one further remark on the passage from Stewart to which I referred. He writes:

> It is this quality, therefore, which may be said to be essential to an individual in its classification under a particular genus. However, as every classification is to a certain degree arbitrary, we cannot conclude that this generic quality is more essential to the individual's existence than a host of other accidental qualities.

In setting out to explain a fact which is the subject of great controversy, it is necessary, I think, to avoid the use of ambiguous terms which may generate doubt and uncertainty. Great care is needed also to ensure that ideas relating to all the words are scrupulously examined. Stewart, however, does not seem to have examined the idea of *classification in a genus*. If he had done, he would easily have seen that this classification can be carried out only by means of a *common idea*, that is, by means of the quality which makes the individuals resemble one another precisely because it is common to them. But Stewart, in

[188]

his use of the word *classification*, falls into the logical error of *petitio principii* just as he did when using the word *likeness*. To explain a fact, he assumes the fact as explained. He claims that there is no difficulty in *classifying* objects and uncovering their *likeness*. But this is the very difficulty that thinkers were seeking to explain. In other words, he has defined something by itself, *idem per idem*.

Article 22

Stewart's uncertain expressions

189. The expression he uses, 'as every classification is to a certain degree arbitrary', is also odd. Is this a strictly philosophical expression?

My objection would run as follows: 'When you state that every classification is *to a certain degree* arbitrary, you clearly admit that it is not arbitrary in all respects. So why not examine what is arbitrary and what is not in these classifications? Your reluctance to carry out this inquiry entitles your reader to suspect that the non-arbitrary aspect of classification is precisely the nub of the question. He will say that classifications are only based upon qualities which make things similar, or upon qualities they have in common (the two expressions are synonymous). Consequently, we have to accept that not all classifications called *genera and species* are arbitrary. The common qualities are neither arbitrary, nor mere names, but qualities actually existing in individuals. Your perfunctory admission that the formation of such classes of possible individuals (classes designated as genera and species) involves a non-arbitrary element — but one that is necessary and real — is tantamount to casting doubt on your whole system. It enables careful readers to discover for themselves, by a process of reasoning, the ruinous defect of the system.'

Article 23

Stewart confuses two distinct questions

190. Lastly, I would point out that, in the short passage I have

quoted, Stewart runs together and confuses two entirely different questions.

First: Are there universal ideas in the human spirit, that is,
does a person think of the common qualities of things as merely
possible?

Second: What are these universal ideas or common qualities
of things outside the human spirit?

These two questions should not be confused and treated as
one; the second, as I shall subsequently maintain, must be broken down into others.

191. The question about the existence of a common quality
outside the spirit is an inquiry which has no bearing on my
argument.

We all agree that outside the mind common qualities of themselves have no separate existence. They do not really exist unless
they are made individual, that is, in the individuals to which
they belong. However, despite this agreement, we still need to
answer the first question: do common qualities exist in our
spirit? Are they an object of knowledge?

This final inquiry, of course, is certainly very easy and obvious, provided our spirit is free from the sophistry into which
present-day masters have led us. Over-reliance on their intellectual ability causes them to lay traps to catch their fellows rather
than attain the truth.

192. Good sense tells us that the qualities of things are objects
of thought not only as individual, but as common. A moment's
reflection upon self makes us realise that 1. our spirit can know
these qualities as they are present in this or that individual
(knowledge of individual qualities); 2. we can consider them
prescinding from the individual in which they are seen and perceived (we think of them as common); 3. consequently, we can
grasp that certain qualities are simultaneously shared by a number of individuals and can also be shared by an infinite number
of possible individuals. If this were not the case, I would be
quite unable to think and express in words what I have thought
here.

Article 24

Stewart ignores the teachings of ancient philosophers which he criticises relative to the formation of genera and species

193. I do not wish to move on without first pointing out how Stewart introduces the other difficulty about common qualities considered as the essences of things although it has not the slightest bearing on his argument. Other philosophers regularly do the same:[119] they confuse the platonic question with our present problem. Moreover, they present it in an extremely inaccurate, false manner.

Where, for instance, did Stewart find that ancient philosophers made the essences of things consist in their common, universal qualities? As far as I can see, they too distinguished common qualities into essential and accidental qualities; and they formed genera and species from both. In fact, every common quality, accidental or essential, can be the basis for the formation of a genus or a species. But, if I speak about species of white and of black men, or like Aristotle, classify animals by the number of their legs, I have taken as the basis of those species an accidental quality, that is, the colours white or black and the number of legs. It seems to me that this twofold way of forming genera and species has always been distinct. Moreover the property of containing the true essence of individuals was attributed to genera and species formed in the first way, that is, on the basis of an essential quality.[120] On the other hand, genera and species formed in the second way on the basis of accidental qualities, were never thought to contain the true essence of individuals, but only their essence in so far as they belonged to that accidental, arbitrary species.

---

[119] Such confusion is, I think, common among modern philosophers. Unable to solve the first question, they introduce the second and unload its absurdities on the first.

[120] Thus, it is the essence of a thing which forms the genus or the species, not the genus or the species which forms the essence. The idea of genus or species presents us with a group — although undetermined and indefinite — of at least possible individuals. The essence of a thing is utterly simple and unitary.

[193]

194. This second species could be called *nominal*[121] in a rather improper sense, but Stewart can never, strictly speaking, call the first nominal. The second species has an arbitrary element in it: if the issue is the formation of species based upon common accidental qualities, I decide which accidental quality to select. In the first sort of species, based upon an essential quality, there is nothing arbitrary. The essence of a determined ens is unique, and must be used either to form the genus or abandon it.

However, as I said, the term 'nominal' would not be correct either. Calling this quality a nominal essence could lead people to think that it was merely a name. This, as I have shown, is false. The common qualities of things, whether accidental or essential, have an existence at least as objects of our spirit.

Article 25

Stewart does not understand the question debated by realists, conceptualists and nominalists

195. Stewart finds it impossible to imagine that an object can exist in our spirit without there being some corresponding thing outside. Consequently, after expounding the views of the two schools, the realists and nominalists, and coming down on the side of the nominalists, he goes on to mention the intermediate group of conceptualists and frankly admits that he is unable to form a clear idea of their teaching. He then sets about speculating on or rather guessing at the nature of their hypothesis.

He finds it only in two propositions which he puts forward as follows:

> From the indistinctness and inaccuracy of their (conceptualists) language on the subject, it is not a very easy matter to ascertain precisely what was their opinion on the point in question; but, on the whole, I am inclined to

---

[121] Strictly speaking, *nominal essence* should be applied to an essence in which the name alone forms the genus, e.g. 'the genus of those called Peter, Paul, etc.' would be a genus based solely on a thing's name. Comparing this nominal essence with other essences, this genus with other genera, we can easily see how it differs from all other essences and how this genus differs from all other genera. These things cannot therefore be rolled into one as Stewart would wish.

162   *A New Essay concerning the Origin of Ideas*

think, that it amounted to the two following propositions:
first, that we have no reason to believe the existence of any
essences or universal ideas corresponding to general
terms; and, secondly, that the mind has the power of reasoning concerning *genera*, or classes of individuals *without
the mediation of language.*[122]

Immediately after this, he adds:

Indeed, I cannot think of any other hypothesis which it is
possible to form on the subject, distinct from those of the
two celebrated sects already mentioned. In denying the
existence of universals, we know that the conceptualists
agreed with the nominalists. But on what basis could we
suppose they differ from the opinions of the nominalists
except about the need for language as an instrument of
thought and as a means of pursuing every species of meditation or reasoning on general objects?[123]

196. The conceptualists agreed with the nominalists in denying the subsistence of *universal essences* in themselves, but did
not agree with them in denying the existence of *universal ideas*
in the mind [*App.*, no. 10]. In other words, they admitted that
our spirit certainly did have universal concepts but that these
concepts or ideas had no real existence outside our spirit. In
short, they were ideas produced by the spirit at the moment of
particular perceptions of things received by the senses.

197. In this system, the spirit came to possess 1. particular
perceptions; 2. the faculty of working upon particular perceptions and adding to them a new form making them *universal*.

In fact, our spirit has the power to carry out operations on its
own ideas and alter their form.[124] All the idols of our fantasy are
simply aspects of the activity of our spirit which, as such, that is,
in their very form, have no reality outside the spirit. They are
tasks undertaken by the spirit through the operation of sensible
things upon sensations and ideas.

[122] *Eléments de la Philosophie de l'esprit humain*, chap. 4, section 3.

[123] *Ibid.*

[124] It is absurd to say that a sensation is altered: it is extremely particular and
would first have to be destroyed in order to be altered. Thought, on the other
hand, has an object, or idea provided with universal and particular elements.
The idea, in so far as it is universal, can be determined and particularised in
various ways, and this perhaps could be called 'taking on another form.'

Article 26

Stewart confuses the question of the need for language with that of the existence of universal ideas

198. On the other hand, Stewart considers the question of the need for language as the essential element in characterising the opinions of the three schools of which we are speaking, realists, conceptualists and nominalists. He considers this question as an essential part of the problem of universals to which these philosophers offer different solutions. He assumes that the realists are obliged by their system to think that words are not necessary to conceive universals. After stating that the difference between individuals and genera relative to the use of language consists in our capacity for reasoning about individuals without language, but not about genera, he goes on to say:

> This remark is so important that, if I am not mistaken, it has caused the realists to go astray. They thought that words, which are not necessary for thinking of individuals, are not necessary for thinking of universals.[125]

199. However, the question of the need for language is completely independent of the question which divided the three philosophical schools. Confusing them can only serve to make the main question extremely difficult and inextricable.

Although I have no intention whatsoever of being a *nominalist*, I am convinced, on the other hand, of the need for words if we are to be drawn from the first to reflect upon universals (*Theodicy*, 100–102).

There is a great difference between supposing that universals are mere names to which neither things nor ideas correspond, and supposing that universals are things existing in themselves or, at least, ideas existing in our spirit, but in such a way that we can neither know these things nor possess these ideas for the first time without the aid of words.

Both those who hold the first opinion and those who hold either of the second opinions (that is, nominalists as well as realists and conceptualists) may consider language necessary to enable mankind to start to think of universals. On this issue,

---

125 *Eléments de la Philosophie de l'esprit humain,* chap. 4, section 2.

164 A New Essay concerning the Origin of Ideas

there is only one difference between them. Nominalists *are bound* to believe language necessary. The other two schools *may* think so, but are not bound to do so in virtue of their opinion about the nature of universals. Nominalists are bound to consider language necessary to attain universals because, according to them, universals are only words. On the other hand, conceptualists and realists, if they consider language necessary, hold this opinion not by considering words as taking the place of ideas,[126] but as a suitable and necessary means of rousing and directing the attention of our spirit (which in itself is inert) towards the common qualities or of carrying out the operations on our perceptions by which we have universals.

Article 27

Another *petitio principii*: Stewart's attempt to explain how the intellect conceives the ideas of genera and species starts by assuming the formation of these ideas

200. I have purposely reserved for the end of these observations on Stewart's teaching on universals the author's most powerful passage in support of his case. This makes it easier to grasp its force and the force of the refutation which I am about to set out. Moreover, the ideas which I have been explaining

[126] If we isolate the question of the necessity of language from that of the nature of universals, it is not as difficult as Professor Stewart appears to believe to discover Locke's opinion on this subject. Stewart accuses Locke of employing *odd and seldom used expressions* in this matter and thus allowing himself to be saddled with contradictory views. This is true, but I do not think that the contradiction lies where Stewart says it does. Stewart finds it contradictory that, in certain passages, Locke does not judge language indispensable to the workings of the intelligence, although he is not a realist. Locke admits that universals are something in the spirit of the thinker, a view which is independent of that relating to the necessity for language. In fact, we may hold that universals are objects of the mind (*entia rationis*) and at the same time hold, if we wish, both that language is necessary and not necessary for the spirit to form these objects, that is, these ideas which have a nature all of their own. What can rightly be said about Locke is, I think, that he did not get to the root of either question, and that the ridicule heaped on his philosophy by Doria, Martino Scriblero and many subsequent critics is fully justified.

[200]

while studying other passages of our philosopher could be helpful to readers.

In the following passage, Stewart attempts to determine how we can reason about universal truths with the help of words only and without permanently adding ideas to words. I shall quote the whole passage, despite its length, so that there can be no suspicion of my distorting his views. According to Stewart, these are the steps by which we attain universal truths.

> It is further evident, that there are two ways in which such general truths may be obtained; either by fixing the attention on one individual, in such a manner that our reasoning may involve no circumstances but those which are common to the whole genus, or, (laying aside entirely the consideration of things) by means of the general terms with which language supplies us.

He thinks, therefore, that we can reason about general truths by simply placing before ourselves either individuals or words. He explains his idea as follows:

> In the first case, our attention being limited to those circumstances in which the subject of our reasoning resembles all other individuals of the same genus, whatever we demonstrate with respect to this subject must be true of every other one to which the same attributes belong.[127]
> In the second case, the subject of our reasoning being expressed by a generic word, which applies in common to a number of individuals, the conclusion we form must be as extensive as its application, as the name of the subject is in its meaning.[128]

201. Here I feel I must interrupt Mr. Stewart's argument for a moment to ask him what exactly he is seeking to achieve by it.

He is trying, he says, to explain universal truths, that is, trying to explain the formation of genera and species. In this case, I feel I have to ask him to examine the following phrases used by him in his argument: *The circumstances common to the genus — the circumstances whereby the subject of our argument resembles the other individuals of the same genus.* These two phrases (I want to concentrate solely upon them) naturally presuppose

---

[127] But what if these same attributes are merely a word?

[128] *Eléments de la Philosophie de l'esprit humain*, chap. 4, section 2.

formed genera and presuppose that we make use of them. But how can he introduce already established genera and species into an argument whose aim is precisely to explain the formation of genera and species? This is another example of a blatant *petitio principii*.

Article 28

Another *petitio principii*: Stewart assumes that general ideas are something in the very argument he uses to prove that they are merely names

202. Stewart goes on:

> The former process is analogous to the practice of geometers, who, in their general reasonings, direct the attention to a particular diagram; the latter of the algebraists, who carry on their investigations by means of symbols.

I raise no objections to this statement: it is in fact correct. However, it remains to be seen whether, if it is correct, universals are to be considered simply as names or whether the opposite is the case. This will become clear as soon as our author's theory is explained.

Stewart's own comment about the two ways he established for the attainment of general truths, is I think, attractive and perspicuous, and seems to throw light on the subject.

> These two methods of obtaining general truths proceed on the same principles, and are, in fact, much less different from each other than they appear to be at first view. When we carry on a process of general reasoning, by fixing our attention on a particular individual of a genus, this individual is to be considered merely as a sign or representative, and differs from any other sign only in this, that it bears a certain resemblance[129] to the things it denotes. The straight lines which are employed in the fifth book of Euclid to represent magnitudes in general, differ from the algebraical expressions of these magnitudes, in the same respects in which picture writing differs from arbitrary characters.

[129] Does this amount to nothing? Explaining which resemblance is precisely the nub of the question (cf. 180–187).

[202]

This is perfectly true; this excellent remark reduces the two methods of attaining universal truths to only one. The human spirit attains its aim by means of signs, which may exist in two forms: signs exhibiting similarity with the thing signified, and purely arbitrary signs totally without any similarity to what is signified. The picture depicting things has the first form, the letters of our alphabet have the second form. Geometry, which uses figures, has signs similar to the thing signified; algebra, which uses letters, has signs totally unconnected with what is signified.

203. I maintain that the very use of such signs implies the existence of universals and that there is no way, as Stewart claims, in which these signs are of themselves sufficient to explain how we use universal truths.

According to Stewart these signs enable us to *attain general truths*. But if these truths were nothing and did not differ from the signs themselves, what sense is there in speaking in this way? It would mean: 'By means of signs we attain signs; and not different signs but precisely those we make use of.' This is an odd, useless kind of philosophy, seemingly of little importance. My question to Stewart — and to anyone else in their right mind — is this: Surely the mere word sign directs our mind immediately to the thing signified? Could anyone possibly grasp the meaning of the word *sign* or *things signified* without immediately conceiving the idea of both of these things, related in such a way that one inescapably calls for the other?

Article 29

Signs alone cannot explain universals

204. Consequently, signs on their own cannot explain how we attain universal truths unless these truths are, in fact, something.

Saying that these signs direct our spirit to thinking of individuals is still not sufficient, as I have shown (cf. 198–199).

And, indeed, when I am told that a sign must focus my attention on a single, determined individual, I understand perhaps how, for such a requirement, I need only to grasp two things, the sign and the individual signified. However, if I am told that a sign must lead me to think not about a single, determined individual but about any individual whatsoever of a given genus or species (and no other individual outside this genus or species), I cannot understand, unless I conceive three things: 1. the sign; 2. the individual signified; 3. something which determines me to discover the genus or species of the individual of which I must think — in other words, the idea of the genus or species to which the individual signed with the sign belongs.

205. Moreover, with the words, or more generally with the signs which express universals, I do two things:

1. By means of these signs I am led and induced to think of any individual of the given genus and species. For example, with the word *man*, which indicates for me an individual of the human species, I can mentally concentrate on any particular man, true or imaginary, or I can apply the word *man* to any particular human being I wish.

This is the first benefit afforded by universals, the first step taken by the spirit as it descends from the species or genus to the individual. But what I have said so far shows perfectly well that I cannot make first use of these names by employing a single idea, that is, the idea of individuals. I need two ideas, that of individuals and that of the species or of the genus to which they belong. Consequently, these ideas of species and genus cannot be mere names. The same is shown by considering the second use we make of universal terms.

2. I also form theories for myself with universal names, that is, I reason in an abstract, universal way without referring to individuals.

In this second use, individuals are either completely excluded and abandoned or act only as signs to assist my spirit in reasoning, but without their constituting in any way the subject about which I reason. Stewart refers to this with an example connected with the use geometricians make of shapes. When a geometrician draws a triangle on the blackboard to demonstrate a universal proposition — for example, the sum of the three internal angles is equal to 180° or two right angles — he uses the individual triangle only as a sign to assist his abstract argument. The proof he gives is not more applicable to the individual triangle than to any other, but it is applicable to all triangles in general.

[205]

The object of the geometrician's thought is not the specific individual, which is merely a sign, an example, an aid to his thinking. He is thinking of something else, that is, the universal truth he intends to discover and which he does discover with the help of signs, although its nature is totally different from that of signs.

206. Stewart gets close to the truth, yet skirts it, like Horace's charioteer who rounds the half-way mark without touching it. Certainly, if Stewart had hit that half-way mark, his system would have been ruined. He says that individuals have no part in universal reasoning; if they are present, they often do nothing more than hinder and disrupt the flow of the argument. He states all this in the same section of his works in which he discusses universals, but without realising that one single fact of this nature is sufficient to disprove his basic theories. In referring to cases where arbitrary signs are used to support arguments, as in algebra, he says:

> In cases of this last sort, it may frequently happen from the association of ideas, that a general word may recall some one individual to which it is applicable, but this is so far from being necessary to the accuracy of our reasoning, that excepting in some cases, it always has a tendency more or less to mislead us from the truth.[130]

He had made the same remark in repeating his opinion about universals:

> When we reason, therefore, concerning classes or genera, the objects of or attention are merely signs; or if, in any instance, the generic word should recall some individual, this circumstance is to be regarded only as a consequence of an accidental association, which has a tendency to disturb rather than to assist us in our reasoning.[131]

When an author has committed himself to a false teaching, it is incredible how many contradictions he is obliged to accept, how many mistakes he will pardon himself to ensure that his argument has some sort of appeal. The more intelligent he is, the more his mistakes lead him astray. At this stage, it is worth following his errors carefully and closely examining the track of his tortuous way through the huge labyrinth. There is so much to learn

[130] *Eléments de la Philosophie de l'esprit humain*, chap. 4, section 2.
[131] *Ibid.* section 3.

from others' dangers. This is why I take the liberty of pointing out yet again an odd fallacy of reason in a passage of Stewart.

Article 30

Another fallacy in Stewart's argument

207. Stewart maintains: 'Only individuals can be the object of our thought; what we call general ideas are pure words or signs.' However, in formulating the difficulty for himself, he writes: 'How, in the light of what has been said, are general arguments possible?' To avoid the quandary, he attempts to prove the strange proposition 'that we are able to reason using words, regardless of what the words stand for.'

If his theory is true, such a proposition is, in fact, required. As he did not make use of words expressing individuals in universal reasoning, he had to maintain one of these two statements: either universal words have no meaning or there is something universal, the object of our thought, which these words signify. If the second statement is excluded, the first must be upheld.

To demonstrate this with an example, it was necessary, in my view, to take a universal argument and replace the universal terms which composed it with other random universal terms and see if it still retained some meaning. If the universal terms of an argument are merely valueless signs for us, as Stewart claims, our use of some rather than other signs is totally irrelevant because we pay no heed to their relationships with the things signified.

208. Stewart, however, does not attempt this because it would have been impossible. Instead he offers the following advice about reasoning (I leave it to any common-sense person to say if he is right). He takes some particular reasoning, removes from it the names of the individuals, and replaces these with other names or signs of individuals. He then turns round and says: 'Look, I have changed the names but the reasoning retains its original meaning.' He then infers that we can reason simply by using signs without attributing any value to them. But the only correct conclusion that can be drawn is that in one particular reasoning the names of the individuals may be changed at will,

and can also be replaced by common nouns. Stewart's proposition proves nothing more than this.

This is his example.

> As the decision of a judge must necessarily be impartial, when he is only acquainted with the relations in which the parties stand to each other, and when their names are supplied by letters of the alphabet, or by the fictitious names of Titus, Caius, Sempronius; so, in every process of reasoning, the conclusion we form is most likely to be logically just, when the attention is confined solely to signs, and when the imagination does not present to it those individual objects which may warp the judgment by casual associations.[132]

First, I deny Stewart's assertion that our attention, in the case he proposes, is focused upon simple signs.

I accept that the parties who bring a case before a judge may be designated either by real or fictitious names or by letters of the alphabet. But this merely means that, when dealing with arbitrary names such as proper nouns, we can use whichever we wish. This indifference however is relevant to the signs, not to the ideas. The judge's thinking is directed and focused on the idea signified and does not dwell on the sign itself with which he is not concerned in any way provided that altering the sign does not mean altering the idea and that the first sign is replaced by another which is capable of representing the same idea. This is much easier in the case of proper nouns which have a purely arbitrary connection with the thing designated. Thus, a thing can be designated by any word, by a letter, a syllable, a word of a number of syllables, or by any sign. This is not the case with common nouns or universal terms — or at least the fact does not take place to the same extent. It occurs, however, whenever different synonyms can be found to express the same common notion. This proves that one sign can be substituted for another, but only when ideas do not change as a result. Reasoning is based upon ideas, not upon signs, which have value only to the degree that they signify and suggest ideas. This rules out the possibility of reasoning by simple signs unconnected to any idea. Signs are in fact arbitrary; ideas cannot be arbitrary. Signs

---

[132] *Eléments de la Philisophie de l'esprit humain*, chap. 4, section 2.

may alter provided ideas remain the same. Stewart's example, therefore, proves the exact opposite of what he intended.

209. This will become more obvious the more we study his example. The judge does not need to know the real names of the contending parties, because he does not need to know the *individuals* themselves in their private relationships outside the case. It is sufficient if he knows them in relationship to the case in hand. The real names allow him to know them as individuals; the fictitious names, or the letters of the alphabet that stand for them, allows him to know them as belonging to a *genus* of things, that is, as 'persons who have the kind of relations that arise from the case they are bringing, nothing more'. To know them in this second way, the judge must possess universal, abstract ideas; relationships between individuals are merely universal ideas abstracted from real individuality. People who possess some rather than other relationships belong to an accidental species formed from such relationships. Consequently, in replacing the real names of the parties by fictitious names, the only alteration that has taken place in the judge's idea is that an individual idea has been replaced by a *generic* idea. Stewart was trying to prove with his example that there is no need for ideas of *genus*, but he has, in fact, given us the best demonstration of the opposite. He intended to show that reasoning can be constructed without the need for general ideas. Instead, he has succeeded in showing us that it is possible to reason without individual ideas, but not without general ideas which may stand alone. This is the outcome of his argument.

Individuals, therefore, are not the only object of human thought nor can signs take the place of universal ideas. The mind, if it is to reason, needs universal much more than individual ideas. It is possible to carry forward an argument which contains no individuals (as in Stewart's earlier example [*App.*, no. 11]) but impossible to conceive how any reasoning can be constructed without universal ideas. Even where reasoning is concerned solely with individuals, they must be considered as endowed with common qualities or common relationships.

[209]

Article 31

Conclusion: Scottish philosophy, aware of its own inability to
overcome the difficulty, tried in vain to eliminate it
from philosophy

210. It is impossible, therefore, despite the application and
ingenuity of Scottish philosophy, to eradicate universal ideas
which could not even be discussed if they had never existed.
This school cannot be praised for eradicating this problem (as it
wrongly thought) which Stewart admits as having always been
one of the most difficult in metaphysics, that is, the problem of
the origin of universal ideas: the problem which, to express it as
succinctly as possible, states: 'The human mind cannot form
universal ideas for itself without a judgment. But it cannot form
a judgment unless it already has universal ideas. It is necessary,
therefore, to grant the presence in us of some innate universal
idea prior to all our judgments. If nothing innate is acceptable,
some other explanation of the difficulty must be found.'

Either way, philosophy is obliged to solve this problem. But
the study I have so far undertaken of systems in which an
attempt has been made to explain the workings of the spirit
without accepting any or almost any[133] innate element in it,
shows that they are unable to solve the core issue and that their
authors have not even understood it sufficiently.

[133] I say *almost any* because, in conceding that we come to know bodies,
not because sensations offer images of them, but by a kind of *inspiration* (a
faculty *sui generis* which enables us to perceive bodies when sensations occur),
the Scottish school accepts rather more of what is innate than the schools of
Locke and Condillac. It admits a *new*, although obscure and completely
mysterious power.

[210]

CHAPTER 5

Steps taken by philosophy through the works of the philosophers we have studied

211. I am not asking whether Locke and the philosophers who followed him, the object of our study so far, contributed to progress in philosophy.

This is a futile question because, in the great design of Providence, even mistakes further the progress of the human spirit. Errors offer an opportunity of clarifying important truths; they stimulate the love of truth in mankind which, though disturbed over long periods by error, finally recognises truth as the most precious and most beneficial boon of all. Consequently, even if the philosophers whom I have discussed fell into serious error, they would still have been helpful to mankind which, precisely because of philosophers' irresolution and flawed doctrines, feels the need for the inestimable value of sound, true philosophy.

It will be helpful therefore, at the end of this Section, to review the ground I have covered in expounding modern philosophical thought. Let us examine the state of philosophy when Locke was writing. This was my starting point. I also need to examine the changes undergone by the main doctrines under discussion at the hands of this new School.

212. To do this, let me recommend a brief, elementary work by one of Locke's contemporaries. This contains a simple exposition of the main ideas of the philosophy of the period, and will enable us to grasp the changes suffered by these ideas since then. The booklet is the *Traité de la Connaissance de Dieu et de soi-même* by Bossuet[134] written for the Dauphin of France who would not have had much leisure to penetrate the deep mysteries of metaphysics, but who needed as simple an explanation as possible of the substance of metaphysical teaching.

Let us see what was known at the time of this booklet, and compare the main truths held then with the opinions, noted

---

[134] Bossuet was born in 1627, Locke in 1632. Both died in 1704.

throughout this Section, of the new school of philosophers, dependent for its origin and impetus on Locke.

213. First we saw that from Locke's time to the present a considerable number of philosophers have tried everything to merge sense and intellect by making the two faculties one (cf. 70–85). Today, the writings of these authors are so widespread, so widely read and so cluttered with gross sophisms that it is extremely difficult to explain the distinction between these faculties to persons entangled and confused by what they have read.

Locke's contemporaries were fully aware of the distinction between sense and intellect, which they accepted without hesitation. Bossuet, in the work mentioned above, spelled it out at length in defining the intellect as 'the faculty for knowing truth and error.' This is totally alien to sense.[135]

214. Condillac confused feeling and judgment even more than Locke (cf. 81–89). At Bossuet's time, these two operations of the spirit were perfectly distinct; in addition, thinkers had come to see the importance of judgment in knowledge. As Bossuet says:

> The senses merely provide us with their own sensations and leave the understanding to judge the dispositions which they find in objects.
> The true perfection of the understanding lies in good judgment.
> Judgment is an internal pronouncement about truth and error; good judgment means pronouncing on truth and error rightly and knowingly.[136]

215. Reid and Stewart occasionally confused imagination and intellect (cf. 117–135). Although these faculties were so distinct before their time that such confusion was impossible, Bossuet writes:

---

135 Chap. 1: 7 [*App.*, no. 12].

136 Chap. 1: 7. How easy it was to pass from this teaching of Bossuet to show that all ideas are acquired through a judgment unless they are innate. The first operation of the intellect, therefore, has to be a judgment. On the other hand, this judgment has to be preceded by a universal idea which we know naturally. Without a universal, no judgment is forthcoming! This development, which at that time arose spontaneously from current ideas, will perhaps be difficult to achieve now, and I am writing this volume to assist it. Cf. especially 41–45, 117–135.

Confusion between imagination and intellect is greatly to be feared. To avoid it, the characteristics proper to each faculty should be noted.

There is, for example, a great difference between imagining and understanding a triangle. Imagining a triangle means picturing a triangle, of a determined size, with specific angles and sides. To understand 'triangle' means knowing its nature and understanding in general that it is a three-sided figure, but without any particular size or proportion. Understanding 'triangle' means that its ideas are relevant to all equilateral, isosceles or other triangles of any size. But the image of a triangle is restricted to a certain type of triangle, and to a set size.

The essential distinction, however, between imagining and understanding is expressed in the definition: understanding is knowing and discerning what is true and what is false. Imagination, which takes its lead from the senses, cannot do this.[137]

216. Some of the philosophers who reduced intelligence to sense and imagination reasoned in this way: 'That which cannot be felt by our senses or cannot be imagined, cannot be thought or understood.'[138] In this way, they branded as unknowable to the human spirit all knowledge referring to spiritual beings.

The teaching current at Bossuet's time, on the other hand, was this:

> Another difference between imagining and understanding is that understanding embraces a much wider span than imagining. Thus, although only bodily, sensible things can be imagined, bodily and spiritual things can be understood as well as sensible and non-sensible things such as God and the soul.
>
> Those wishing to imagine God and the soul commit a serious mistake because they want to imagine what is

[137] Chap. 1: 9. The development possible to Bossuet's teaching at this point would have shown how the intellect, the faculty for discerning what is true from what is false, is from that very fact the only faculty for dealing with universals. Sense and imagination, on the contrary, could perceive only sensible individuals and, consequently, individuals without any universal relation between them, etc. (cf. 156–159).

[138] This is substantially the argument used by present-day nominalists to deny the existence of universals (cf. 177–179).

unimaginable, that is, what is devoid of body or shape. In other words, without anything sensible.[139]

The substance and nature of external things cannot be felt because they do not fall under the senses or the imagination. Consequently, philosophers who reduced the intellect to sense stated that we had no ideas of such things (cf. 48–64). In fact, it was well-known prior to them that we possessed the ideas of such things but not their images or sensations. This resulted from the distinction made between feeling and imagining, on the one hand, and understanding on the other. According to Bossuet, the distinctive feature of the intellect consists 'in knowing the nature of things.'[140]

217. We saw earlier how d'Alembert realised that Locke's philosophy had omitted two important inquiries: 1. how we think something external to us; 2. how we unite in a single subject the various sensible qualities which we perceive (cf. 65–67). Indicating the lacunae in Locke's philosophy represented a step forward and, in going back to the earliest period [of philosophy], d'Alembert deserves great credit for identifying these questions.

Before d'Alembert and Locke, however, Descartes had addressed, for good or evil, two issues ignored by Locke. This means that the issues were known. Bossuet, brought up in Cartesian thought, was aware of them and expounded the second inquiry as follows:

> Although sensations differ from one another, there is in the spirit a faculty which unites them. Experience shows that only one sensible object is produced from experiences which we receive together, even when different senses are affected, but especially when the impression comes from the same source. When I see a certain coloured type of fire, and feel the heat it produces, and hear the rushing of the air, I do not merely see the colour, feel the heat, hear the sound, but I feel all these different sensations as emanating from a single fire.
>
> This faculty of the soul, which unites sensations, is either a mere after-effect of the sensations which form a natural unity when they come together, or a constituent

[139] Chap. 1: 9.

[140] Chap. 1: 7.

part of the imagination. I maintain that this faculty —
whatever it may be — is called *common sense* to the extent
that it forms a single object of everything experienced at
one particular time through our senses. The phrase, 'common sense', is connected with the workings of the spirit,
although its real meaning is the one I have just indicated.[141]

218. Stewart did not realise that the conception of relationships between things, like that of their similarity, were merely
universal ideas which cannot pertain to the senses — these do
not extend beyond bodily, individual sensations — but belong
to the understanding (cf. 180–188). On the other hand, in
Bossuet's time, it was already well understood that knowledge
of the relationships and order of things could be only intellectual operations. Bossuet says:

> There are intellectual acts which follow so closely upon
> sensations that we confuse one with the other, unless we
> pay great attention to ourselves.
> The judgment which we naturally form about proposi-
> tions and their resultant order is of this type.
> To know the propositions and their order is the work of
> reason, which compares one thing with another or
> discerns their relationships.[142]

219. What, then, is positive in the views of the post-Lockean
philosophers examined in this Section? Is there any genuine
addition to the store of philosophical knowledge already held at
Locke's time?

I cannot think of anything worth considering as progress (if
we are to confine ourselves solely to the subject at hand) except
the doubts raised by Reid about the views of those thinkers who
accepted simple apprehension as the first operation of the spirit.
Bossuet also had no difficulty in accepting it. He says, for example about the propositions: God is eternal, man is not eternal:

> Understanding the terms means understanding that
> God means First Cause, that man means rational animal,

---

[141] Chap. 1: 4. This section is susceptible of extraordinary development and
it is right to say that present-day philosophers have made great efforts in this
matter which I shall put to good use in the second volume of this work.

[142] Chap. 1: 8.

that eternal means that which has neither beginning nor end; this is what we call conception, *simple apprehension*; it is the first operation of the spirit.

It may be that it never appears entirely on its own, and this is perhaps why some people say it is not the first operation.[143] But they do not realise that understanding terms is an operation which naturally precedes any attempt to link them; otherwise, no one would know what to link.[144]

220. At Locke's time, therefore, cognitions were available which were insufficiently esteemed by the new School, and consequently neglected. When new teaching carried the day, such cognitions were increasingly lost and erased from human memory. At the moment, the task of rediscovering them, and persuading others about them, requires considerable effort, although what seems new is in fact very old.

How are we to explain the growth of modern philosophy and the neglect of truths which were then known?

The principal cause is negligence on the part of the Cartesians, who held such truths but did not pay enough attention to the spread of the new philosophy and initially derided it. Descartes' followers alone were in a position to assess Locke's philosophy but, proclaiming their own teaching in a narrow, systematic way, they paid no heed to the spread of Locke's thought. This led to its steady dissemination. It did in fact present many enticements to self-love by its superficial approach, and to passions by its appeal to the senses. It exerted a powerful effect upon high society which at that time was beginning to dabble in philosophy, and had great influence on the young who were taking over from an older generation which had lost influence, just as ancient teachings were also losing influence.

I am not the only one to relate this history of the downfall of Cartesianism, which affected many of the beneficial things it taught and, even worse, many of its fine aims. We are now beginning to see what occurred. In France itself, they describe the transformation that philosophy underwent and how Locke's thought, once it appeared, was worked into an ancient

---

[143] One can see from this passage that, even before Reid's time, there was some inkling of this problem.

[144] Chap. 1: 13.

philosophy of the senses. This movement, although earlier routed by Cartesianism, had retained and still retains in society far too many practitioners. We find in *The Globe*:

> In the struggle which ensued between materialism and spiritualism at the time of Descartes and Gassendi, spiritualism was victorious in the sense that Descartes' thought continued to be represented in France by an unbroken sequence of philosophers until the middle of the eighteenth century. Gassendi's, however, was abandoned by metaphysicians although he[145] retained some support in high society and, after Beriner, Molière and Chapelle, can be followed down to Voltaire. In this school of charming, pleasure-loving men, the traditions of practical Epicurism and religious unbelief were better preserved than the metaphysical dogmas of materialism. No notice was taken of the principle of sensation in Ninon de l'Enclos, and Gassendi's philosophy had long been dead in France even among his own disciples when the translation of Locke's book brought about its revival. At that time, in this country, only Cartesians were able to understand *An Essay concerning Human Understanding*. They, however, were so preoccupied with their own old ideas that they were the only people unwilling to study the book. Those who welcomed the new teaching were unused to metaphysical problems, and misinterpreted its true spirit. In England, Berkeley and Hume, arguing logically, saw it as a spiritualist work; Condillac in France considered it materialist.[146]

The contempt Locke displayed for Descartes was the same as displayed by Descartes towards his predecessors.[147] By a display

---

[145] The same could have been said of the philosophy of Hobbes who was born before and died after Gassendi, and lived for a long time in France.

[146] 3 January, 1829. — I would not be so bold as to accuse Condillac of *materialism*. He stops at *sensism*; Berkeley and Hume do not abandon sensism, but build upon it. Locke's philosophy, however, contains the seeds both of materialism and of idealism. *Reflection*, a faculty admitted by Locke, which could have rescued his system from out-and-out sensism, is dealt with too summarily. Locke introduces it without understanding its nature, as I showed earlier.

[147] It has to be admitted that Italy was the nation in which the thread of traditional ideas suffered least damage, thanks to great and deep-rooted

of arrogance and contempt, philosophers are able to deprive mankind of its precious store of knowledge, drag it back to its infancy and resume operations already undertaken and carried forward. The result is an infinity of wasted time; patience is exhausted, and people become bored with the very philosophy which philosophers represent.

The true spirit of philosophy can never be exclusive and individual. It is a conservative spirit, impartial and comprehensive, which treats the traditions of mankind and of individual scholars with respect. It is not, in short, the vain spirit of the world, but that of Christianity applied to the study and consideration of natural truths.

Christian principles. As a result, we see Locke's innovations come up against worthy opposition in Italy in the person of PAOLO DORIA, while Descartes' ideas were similarly combated by GIOVAMBATTISTA VICO. These two great men would have saved Italy from many mistakes if the nation had fallen not so much for new as for foreign ideas. It was a party, not a philosophy, which prevailed. Unfortunately, the party was anti-social and anti-religious. But the 18th century is now over, and the present century has begun to judge it sternly.

SECTION FOUR

False Theories Assigning a Superfluous
Cause of Ideas

221. So far, I have been dealing with the systems of philosophers who were unable to suggest a sufficient cause to explain
the fact of ideas. I now have to discuss those who put forward a
superfluous cause of this fact. By offering over-facile explanations for the existence of ideas, the first group clearly showed
that they had not really got to the heart of the difficulty of this
arduous philosophical problem (cf. 41–45). The others produced tortuous explanations to solve the problem, of which
they were certainly aware, but failed to find the simplest and
most natural solution. Both groups were deficient in method;
each rejected one of the two principles which I assigned for the
purpose of method (cf. 26–28). The first group failed by defect;
the second through excess. Amongst the second, head and
shoulders above them all, stood the outstanding genius of Plato.

CHAPTER 1
Plato and Aristotle

Article 1
Plato's view of the difficulty present in the problem
of the origin of ideas

222. Plato grasped with real insight the problem faced by
those who seek to explain coherently the origin of our ideas.
To see this, it is sufficient to refer to any one of the many passages in his fine dialogues where the problem I raise about the

origin of ideas is expounded with genuine clarity and in substantially the same way as I have presented it.

Here is one of the most famous passages on the subject.

Meno of Thessaly, a friend of Aristippos of Larissa, and a disciple of the overbearing philosophy of the Thessalian sophists,
begins to argue with Socrates, who professed to know nothing
apart perhaps from his capacity for pointing out to others the
difficulties contained in even the most obvious philosophical
issues. Very soon, they come to the core of our problem. In the
dialogue, which I transcribe below, Socrates says that although
he could not define virtue, he would like to investigate it. Meno
then puts forward the following objection:

> Socrates, how do you intend to look for something com-
> pletely unknown to you? How can you have a picture of
> what you are seeking if you have no knowledge of it? And
> if, by chance, you come across the thing you seek, how
> will you recognise that it is, in fact, what you are looking
> for if you are totally ignorant of it?

In his reply, Socrates brings out the full force of the objection
which Meno himself had probably not realised:

> I understand, Meno, what you are saying, but are you
> aware of the intractable nature of the statement which you
> have just made? You are saying that we cannot investigate
> either what we know or what we do not know. The fact is
> that if we know it already, no investigation is needed. If we
> do not know it, we can never investigate it, since we can-
> not, in fact, know what we intend to investigate.[148]

---

[148] St. Augustine deals with this problem in an ingenious way in Book 10 of
his *De Trinitate* and concludes: *Quilibet igitur studiosus, quilibet curiosus non
amat incognita, etiamsi cum ardentissimo appetitu instat scire quod nescit. Aut
enim jam genere notum habet quod amat, idque nosse expetit etiam in aliqua
re singula; vel in singulis rebus quae illi nondum notae forte laudantur,
fingitque animo imaginariam formam qua excitetur in amorem.* [No studious
or inquisitive person loves what is unknown, even though he is most ardent
and persistent in his quest to know things unknown to him. For he either
knows in general what he loves, and desires to know it in an individual, or he
forms — in individual things which he does not yet know, yet whose merits he
has heard praised — an imaginary picture in his mind to stimulate his love].
The second way, by means of which we occasionally wish to know something
unknown to us, assumes some development of faculties and acquired

This difficulty was formidable. Anyone giving it careful thought must have grasped the need, in any investigation, to know something, but not everything, of what he is seeking. Total ignorance would make investigation impossible. It is clearly absurd for anyone to be seeking while totally ignorant of what he is seeking. Our desire cannot be focused upon an object of which we know absolutely nothing nor can our action be directed towards a type of object which, as totally unknown, does not exist for us. On the other hand, if we had full knowledge of the truth we were seeking, we would no longer seek it; our mind would already possess it.

Meno's observation, therefore — the full impact of which Socrates astutely tried to indicate — was sound and produced the following conclusion: 'We cannot mentally investigate anything unless it is partly unknown and partly known.'

223. First, note the distinction between seeking something real in order to possess it and seeking some truth in order to know it.

When we are looking for a friend lost in a crowd of people, or a household item mislaid in some corner of the house, the difficulty does not arise. The friend or the item can be known perfectly and still be looked for. Meno's argument refers to the investigation of truths which are being sought so that they may be known. In this case, possessing them is not distinct from knowing them, but is one with knowing them. The source of the difficulty lies here: how can we seek truths without knowing them or, if we know them, why are we looking for them?.

In short, an argument of this kind implies that there is an intermediate stage between knowing something perfectly and being totally ignorant of it, and that the solution to the problem must lie in this state of intermediate *chiaroscuro* knowledge of the thing under investigation. This stage provides just enough light to enable us to *recognise* what we are seeking and to identify it when we encounter it, and enough obscurity to oblige us to seek it in order to be able to say we really *know it*.

knowledge. The first way, by means of which we wish to know in particular what we know *in general*, can lead us to the source of all our cognitions, as we shall see later.

Article 2

Plato's solution to the difficulty

224. To overcome the dilemma, Socrates resorted to an inter-mediate form of knowledge which he located in knowledge for-gotten at our birth.

To lend greater credence to his view, he took his stand on the fact that we sometimes possess knowledge which we do not remember — a kind of soporific knowledge roused and brought into play as soon as its objects come once more to our attention. We then remember having known the objects previously; in other words, we recognise them as objects which we had for-gotten despite their being previously lodged in our memory. Socrates applied his observation of this phenomenon, which happens daily to us all, to the difficulty he was faced with; he thought that it offered an adequate explanation of the problem. His argument comes down to the following: 'I note that, in man, there exists knowledge expunged from the memory and knowledge present in the memory. Present knowledge cannot be investigated because we already possess it. But we can cer-tainly investigate expunged knowledge because we retain a gen-eral memory of it. Although this general memory is unsatis-fying, it is enough to lead us to investigate more fully what has been cancelled in our memory and to resurrect its lost traces. If this happens to us daily, we can now presume that from birth we possess some potential, not actual knowledge of things. This knowledge is comparable to that which we have when, after learning something, we do indeed forget it, but not so finally that, when it is put before the mind, we cannot recall that we have had it previously. This single assumption, based upon a commonly experienced phenomenon, clearly explains how, from our very first movements, we manifest a burning desire goading us to seek truths and how, when we discover them, we recognise them as those we are eagerly seeking and satiate our-selves with the object of our desire.'

225. Socrates' theory was an ingenious discovery and gave a complete answer to the difficulty raised by Meno. However, Socrates, the great logician, did not stop there. The explanation he offered was bolstered by other observations and facts.

One of these observations concerned a youth who had not yet received instruction on some subject. Socrates questioned him so deftly that the interrelated sequence of questions elicited quite naturally from the youth geometrical truths, first easy and then difficult. This method, entirely made up of questions, ensured that Socrates could truthfully affirm that he was not teaching the youth anything. In fact, he never said: 'This is how it is' but let the youth tell him. Socrates was quite happy merely asking questions. From this experiment he concluded that the youth, by enunciating truths which he had never heard from anyone, already had such truths within him. Initially, they had lain dormant. All that was needed was someone to rouse him and re-focus his attention upon truths which had as it were been abandoned and forgotten. This helped him to recall them.

The fact that Socrates proposed to explain was incontrovertible because 1. it was perfectly true that the youth had not learnt from anyone the truths he was uttering; and 2. it was also true that when he was questioned in a suitable way he was able to discover those truths for himself without his being told them by anyone.

Anyone who carefully considers Socrates' solution will see that it can be expressed alternatively as follows.

When I ask the youth a series of appropriate questions, he answers correctly even on things that no living person has told him. Consequently, the young man has a faculty for judging (this is the only strict consequence that can be inferred from the fact). Socrates has to explain how, therefore, human beings possess the faculty of judgment, that is, the capacity to form judgments even about something previously unperceived by the senses and unknown.

To explain this fact, we have to say either that the judgments upon such things have been conveyed to us by other persons — which is excluded by our hypothesis — or that, from birth, we have possessed some inner faculty enabling us to attain such judgments.[149] In short, to use St. Augustine's expression, we have an in-built *faculty for judging*,[150] a norm guiding us to judge in one way rather than another. To explain this fact,

---

[149] A judgment is merely an inner word, an affirmation.

[150] *De libero arbitrio* 2,10.

Socrates posits that such judgments or truths are themselves innate, but have been obliterated. Thus, by accepting as innate the ideas to which these judgments refer, he offers a complete explanation of such a singular fact.

Article 3

The difficulty seen by Plato is substantially the same as the one I have indicated

226. Note carefully how Plato's difficulty in attempting to explain the origin of ideas is the same as the one I put forward. Reduced to its final terms, it asks: 'How can there be in us a faculty for *judgment* which must be present granted that acquired ideas are acquired only by means of a judgment?'

The only difference between my way of formulating the problem and Plato's lies in my confining the inquiry to an explanation of the first judgment which we form when we use our intellectual faculties for the first time. Plato, who thinks that the difficulty occurs in the case of all judgments, even after the first, formulates the problem far too widely.

He did not in fact grasp adequately the way in which ideas or truths — and therefore judgments — are inter-linked. I point out that this interconnection is such that when the first judgment has been explained, all other judgments, which depend on it entirely, raise no further difficulty. The nub of the question consists wholly in knowing how the first judgment, with which the first idea is acquired, can be made (granted that every acquired idea is the effect of a judgment), if no prior, non-acquired idea is possible. But if we presuppose a single, prior idea, the possibility of the first judgment is explained. Similarly, the possibility of acquiring further ideas which are then used to form further judgments, and so on, is explained. In short, it is now clear how the faculty of judgment, which is the same as the faculty of reasoning, exists in human beings.

227. Later, I shall deal more fully with the defect in Plato's argument. At present, I am concerned that readers should recognise how clearly Plato realised that the whole difficulty of indicating the origin of ideas consists ultimately in explaining

the existence within us of a potency capable of producing them, which is impossible if reason is devoid of ideas.

If we require further persuasion that Plato was highly aware of the difficulty, we could examine his success in discovering the nature of thought which for him consisted in making interior judgments, or reasoning: 'As I see it,' he says in *Theaetetus*, 'thought is the discourse which the spirit carries out with itself.' This explains why Plato also called reason, or the faculty of thought, *discourse* or *word*. This was not the case for Plato alone. The meaning of the word λόγος was deeply rooted in the Greek language. Such a conception of human thought seems to be based upon a common-sense feeling. If necessary, it would not be difficult to show that such a manner of conceiving it did not, in fact, originate with the Greek peoples when they began to philosophise but sprang from an ancient tradition shared by all oriental nations. Nothing is truer and more natural than to conceive a thinker as someone who says something to himself, who pronounces a word. Saying something to oneself, uttering an interior word merely means affirming or denying something. But every affirmation and negation may be reduced to a judgment. Thought, therefore, begins with a judgment; judgment is the first act of the faculty of thought in humans. Our use of reason begins with a judgment, and the basic error of modern systems of logic and psychology is to start with acquired ideas and to speak of the formation of ideas as prior to, and independent of, the faculty of judgment [*App*., no. 13].

228. If judgment is the first operation of our spirit and if, therefore, this operation is not preceded by any other enabling us to acquire ideas, we are forced to accept as necessarily prior to judgment some innate element which makes judgment possible as the first operation of our spirit.

Article 4

Plato's theory offers a valid but too general solution
to the problem

229. Plato, then, had presented the difficulty in question in too extensive a form.

He should have been satisfied with showing that the first act of our reasoning faculty was a judgment. The acquisition of any idea whatsoever is not merely a sense experience on our part, but a mental act, a word we address to ourselves. In short, it is the judgment which we form upon our sensations by which we state, at least implicitly, what the felt element, the term of the sensation we have experienced, is. If he had done this, he would then have been able to prove that some prior notion was needed enabling us to carry out the act by which we acquire the first idea. This notion would serve as a rule for the judgment in question; judging is merely the application of some rule to the thing we judge.

230. But Plato pushed the difficulty too far. Instead of working backwards to the first judgment which a person makes as his intellective faculties develop, and seeking its explanation (all other judgments are easily explained after the first), he thought that the same difficulty necessarily arose with every judgment. He reasoned: 'When a human being judges something by himself, he learns through his judgment alone a truth of which previously he was ignorant. Now, if he discovers, of himself, this truth which previously he did not know, how does he recognise it as true? How does he distinguish it from falsity? This can only occur if he already possesses within himself the type of the truth he is seeking. Comparing the truth which he finds with its type, he recognises it as the truth which he is seeking!' Thus, he admitted the existence of innate types of all truths. In other words, he admitted the existence of innate but shadowy ideas in us, as I said. These ideas are then revised and clarified by means of the senses which perceive external things as a copy and likeness of the ideas in question.

The flaws in such an argument, as I said — these are different words though it amounts to the same thing — consisted in this: Plato did not notice that although I acquire a new truth when I make a judgment about something, I do not need to have within me the *specific type* of the truth which I acquire by my judgment. All I need is a *general type* with which to compare the various propositions I may formulate about a thing, and distinguish from among them which is true and which false. I do not need to recognise this new truth, which I discover by a judgment, as a particular truth already noted by me, but merely as truth. In fact, in any individual thing, I am seeking only to judge what is true [*App.*, no. 14]. I do not need to have within me as many innate types as there are ideas obtained through judgment. All I need is the *type of truth* so that, in comparing any opinion about things with this, I can distinguish error in them all from truth which, I maintain, has the same appearance everywhere. Thus Plato was led to put forward a fuller solution than necessary, and posit the existence in us of something more innate than required to explain the fact of the origin of ideas. This is contrary to the second rule already established (cf. 27) [*App.*, no. 15].

Article 5
Aristotle reveals the inaccuracy of Plato's argument

231. This inaccuracy in Plato's argument seems to have been the reason for Aristotle's defection from his master's school.

In very many passages of his works Aristotle points out that Plato is guilty of linguistic impropriety when he attributes *knowledge* to the boy who, under questioning from Socrates, gives an answer which he has never learnt, and produces interiorly the solution to some mathematical problem. The youth certainly knew the principles of reasoning on which the solution was based. However, strictly speaking, he did not yet know the solution, which he deduced as conclusions are deduced from known principles. It is true, says Aristotle, that if one wishes, conclusions may be said to be virtually contained in the principles and that anyone who knows the principles, *potentially* knows the conclusions. But what do we mean by 'knowing something potentially'? Simply 'being able to know'. But being able to know something does not yet mean knowing it truly. We should not say therefore that the young man knew the mathematical truths. Saying that he knew them *sic et simpliciter* would imply that he had known the truths in themselves, and not only in the principles in which they are contained as in a fountain. If we want to say that the young man knew these truths, we have to add 'in a certain respect', that is, potentially, in so far as they are virtually contained in what he already knew. This eliminates Plato's apparent contradiction that we learn what we already know. Stated correctly, and in unsophisticated language, we should say: We do indeed learn what was previously unknown; our previous knowledge was only virtual knowledge, in other words, the knowledge necessary to lead us to proper, actual knowledge.'[151]

Article 6

Nevertheless Plato's argument retains something solid

232. Aristotle's comment, although true, demolished only the inexact part of Plato's argument, without destroying the fundamentally sound element.

It would appear that Aristotle experienced what normally happens to many thinkers of lesser status than himself. When we discover something erroneous in a theory, we do not bother to carry out a deeper investigation, but reject it *a priori*, assuming it to be wholly false. We fail to realise that the error found in it is perhaps only a small part of the teaching, due perhaps to poor presentation or a defect in some part of the concept. Consequently, when I examine the criticism to which Aristotle subjects Plato and see how he appears not to have penetrated Plato's teaching, I can easily understand how the Platonists maintained that the teaching on ideas was much too elevated for Aristotle to understand, pursue and make his own.[152] They felt that a fundamental core of truth remained in Plato's teaching, though even they were unable to purify it and indicate it clearly — thanks to the opposite error of accepting Plato's teaching en bloc.

233. Certainly, Plato's argument was flawed by its application to consequential truths, such as the solution to a mathematical problem. Its force and strength, however, is shown when it is applied to indemonstrable principles, and to these alone.

[151] *Posterior*, 1.
[152] See Atticus' remark, quoted by Eusebius, *Praep. Ev.*, 15: 13.

When Plato applied his mode of argument to a deduced truth, that is, in showing how the mathematical truth which Socrates was able to extract from a person unversed in mathematics must have been known to the youth previously, he was leaving himself open to Aristotle's reply: 'It was not necessary for the young man to have prior knowledge of such a truth. All he needed was prior knowledge of the principles from which such a truth might be deduced, and reason, that is, the faculty for making a similar deduction.' Such a reply was unanswerable: the particular instance put forward by Plato was disproved because it was restricted to proving only that the geometrical truth extracted from the young man was known to him before he was questioned. But Aristotle's reply showed that the geometrical truth was unknown to the young man; what he knew beforehand were universal principles from which the geometrical truth was derived.

However, even if the particular instance cited by Plato was disproved in this way, the general argument remained intact. The spirit of this argument was not shattered; it retained its power. Everything depended on making that power felt, and it is felt immediately when, instead of applying it to derived truths, it is applied to the first, indemonstrable truth, that which contains all the others in itself and, as the first, and most universal truth, is not contained by any previous truths.

Article 7

It seems that Aristotle does not offer an adequate explanation of universals

234. At this point Aristotle sins by omission, or at least is obscure.

He was clearly able to distinguish first truths from derived truths, and appears even to have reduced first truths to one alone, the principle of contradiction.[153]

As I have shown, he explains the origins of derived ideas by

---

[153] *Metaphy*, 4.

means of *demonstration* or deduction from *first* truths and proves — against Plato — that they are not innate.

However, in endeavouring to explain the origin of *first* truths, Aristotle shows that he no longer feels the strength of Plato's argument, doubtless because Plato himself did not apply it more to first truths than to others and, when Plato was refuted about derived truths, Aristotle took it that Plato's whole cause was in ruins.

According to Aristotle, therefore, first truths arise in the following way.

They are such, he argued, that they cannot be deduced from other, prior truths. Otherwise, they would not be first truths. It follows also that they are indemonstrable. Consequently, they have to be BELIEVED without any demonstration.[154] In fact,

---

[154] By *demonstration* is meant the deduction of one truth from another which is already accepted as indubitable.

Now, if we believe in first truths without any *demonstration*, that is, without any *deduction* from other truths, does this mean that we believe them without any *reason*? If we answer affirmatively, we destroy human intelligence and sow deep scepticism. This is the dismal fate of the system of those who take as their criterion of truth *blind common sense*, that is, an *authority* lacking any reason to justify it. The most fatal of all the new types of scepticism was that sown involuntarily by Reid; it would reach its full development in Kant. If, on the other hand, we answer that we do not believe in first truths out of *blind necessity* but because they themselves are *reasons*, a shining light which overcomes and almost creates our assent, we shall have great difficulty in reconciling Aristotle's system (at least as it is commonly understood) with the *belief* which Aristotle claims we give without demur to first truths. In fact, if these first truths are *reasons*, how can they ever be deduced from the external senses? Such reasons are not to be found in external things which we perceive through our senses; external things are not *reasons* but *facts*. And facts are specific; reasons universal.

These reasons or first truths in which we believe must therefore either be imparted to us instantaneously along with sensations, as the Arabs said, or they must somehow exist independently within us. If the Arab philosophers are correct, first truths are not posited innate within us but placed innate in intelligences other than ours — which does not explain how we acquire such truths from the senses. In the second case, they must somehow exist of themselves within us so that, by first believing in them, we may subsequently believe in all other derived ideas which have their motive for their credibility in first truths. In other words, we recognise first truths as *innate*. In short, we either have to accept scepticism or admit that there is in us some *per se* visible light bestowed by nature.

everyone BELIEVES them. It is therefore necessary to accept the presence in us of a certain potency which enables us to have an immediate intuition of these truths and to assent to them.[155]

235. This, in substance, is the way in which Aristotle explains the formation of first notions. He accepts that we have a faculty enabling us to form them. In many ways, this faculty is similar to reflection in Locke's system.

As I said, such thinkers seem to argue like this: 'How does our explanation of the origin of ideas prove inadequate? What more do you want us to admit in man? We admit the presence of a *potency* capable of forming such ideas; isn't that enough for you? If we have the potency for forming these ideas, aren't they fully explained?' The argument is perfectly correct. However, it cannot satisfy anyone because it does not answer the question arousing our curiosity about the origin of ideas. We all agree that, if we assume in the mind a potency enabling us to form ideas, no further explanation is required if our assumption is true. The difficulty lies in knowing how this potency must be made if it is to be put to such use, that is, to form, or rather to intuit first ideas. Aristotle, after saying that the mind forms a universal idea from the remembrance of a number of sensations, immediately adds: *But the mind is such that it is able to suffer this internally.*[156] It is obvious that every difficulty can easily be resolved in this way. We are asked if there is any possibility of resolving a problem and we claim that, by positing SOMETHING unknown, we have solved the problem.

---

[155] *Posterior*, bk. 1.

[156] *Posterior*, bk. 2, final chapter. The term *suffer*, used repeatedly by Aristotle to indicate intellectual intuition, shows that he conceived intellectual intuition as a *passive experience* totally similar to that of sense. In fact, he accepts as a principle that, to explain the workings of the intellect, it is helpful to proceed on the analogy of sense operation. See *De Anima*, particularly book 3. Conversely, to explain sense operations, he often resorts to the operations of the intellect. Thus, he occasionally attributes to the senses what is proper solely to the mind (such as judgment), and attributes to the intellect what is proper to the senses (such as passive perception of the impressions of particulars). Or, to put it more clearly, he associates the operation of both faculties to both these distinct potencies. It is no longer difficult therefore to explain intellectual acts. Sense, in which intellectual operations are supposed, is used to explain them and, in sense, intellectual acts themselves are taken as presuppositions. This is an obvious *petitio principii*.

As I see it, both Aristotle and Locke still have to propose a rational solution: 'You accept the existence of an intellectual potency, that is, something in the human soul from which its cognitions can arise. So far, we agree perfectly. But let us take the investigation further and see whether such a faculty of thought can exist without any primal notion, or whether this faculty of thought is nothing more than *the potency for using some concept or first idea* which the human spirit bears within. In short, is it possible to conceive any thought whatsoever which differs from the seeing or applying a standard, an idea?' At this point, if our two philosophers refuse to let us broaden our investigations, they show themselves very narrow-minded and, in their intolerance, sow the seeds of their own error. But it seems unlikely that the parameters laid down by Aristotle and Locke will be generally accepted as the limits of perfect wisdom.

Article 8

In some passages in his work Aristotle does not seem to have emphasised sufficiently the difference between sense and intellect

236. Aristotle, therefore, focused solely on the refutation of Plato's innate ideas in relation to deduced and obviously acquired ideas. He was also convinced that he had easily settled the issue in respect of first, immediate ideas (as he calls them) by saying that they owe their origin to the senses through a particular *potency* designed for that purpose and possessing all that is needed for its fulfilment. This potency he calls *intellect*. These assertions of his provide reasonable grounds for suspecting that he had not got to the heart of the problem of the origin of ideas. This becomes perfectly clear when he sets about explaining the origin of the primal, most universal ideas, which cannot be deduced syllogistically from previous ideas simply because there are no ideas from which all others are deduced.

My opinion is confirmed when I see how, in some passages in his works, he appears not to emphasise sufficiently the distinction between the operation of sense which receives sensations, and the operation of the intellect which thinks.

237. Clearly, he saw that they are distinct potencies, and does not confuse them as Condillac and others do nowadays[157] but he distinguished them solely by their objects without realising that the *terms* of the senses are not *objects* and without noticing an essential difference in their *mode* of operation. He assigned *particulars* as objects to the external senses, and *universals* to the intellect.[158] He also assigned to the intellect the power of

[157] The distinction made by Aristotle between sense and intellect is correctly noted by Sextus Empiricus in Book 7, *Against the Logicians*, §217 ss. In explaining the teaching of Aristotle and Theophrastus, he maintains that we receive into our spirit from the senses the *likenesses* of external things. These likenesses, however, do not constitute the soul's *thinking*. For thinking to arise, we must suppose that the soul is endowed with a certain personal *energy* or force entirely its own through which it can, *by an act of will*, derive from the fantasy of singular things the concept, say, of *man in general*. Without this internal power of the soul, an ens could receive sensations, even have memory and imagination, but would still be devoid of *thought*. The term *by an act of will* used to describe the operation of the mind in forming ideas, shows that Aristotle did not assume this to be a *blind* operation but one carried out by means of an inner light, as is the case with all acts of will. Anyone doubting this, only needs to see how Sextus Empiricus had a little earlier expressed the same concept. He said that, in forming ideas, the intellect operates by virtue of a *judgment* and by *our choice*. This shows also that Aristotle had at least glimpsed the extremely important truth that we cannot form an *idea* of anything *determined* (we cannot begin to carry out particular cognitive acts) except through a *judgment*; forming ideas simply means judging about sensations. Although it seems that elsewhere Aristotle describes the formation of ideas differently, we have to put this down either to lack of consistency or to his having seen truth on one occasion without realising its importance and applying it consistently.

[158] In the passage above, Sextus Empiricus whilst expounding Aristotle's thought states: 'Generally speaking, things are twofold by nature; some are *sensible things*, some perceived by the mind.' Such expressions are often to be found in Aristotle's work. But if these things are different in nature, how do we pass from one nature to the other? Aristotle locates this transition in the fact that *phantasms* of singular things, as he calls them, are *universal in potency* (*De Anima*, bk. 2, Lect. 12).

But what is meant by these expressions? How do you know that singular phantasms are universal *in potency*? Obviously, from the fact that you suppose that the intellect derives *universals* from them. Consequently you say: 'If the intellect derives universals from them, it is inevitable that phantasms are suitable recipients of an operation. But being suitable for handling by the intellect so

abstracting universals from particulars (the acting intellect, *intellectus agens*) and of intuiting them after abstracting them (possible intellect, *intellectus possibilis*). This, however, still does not clearly explain the intrinsic difference between the operation of intellect and sense which we are dealing with here.

238. What makes this difference difficult to see is the continual use of our understanding. Its operations and those of sense are constantly mingled and closely united. Consequently, it is really difficult to distinguish between them. Without our realising it, we assign to sense what belongs solely to the understanding, of which we never form a rigorous, precise concept.

239. This also explains how we tend to endow animals with our reasoning power. We imagine that their behaviour follows the same pattern as our own. We also tend to attribute our feelings and thoughts to inanimate entia. We find it exceedingly hard to form a pure, wholly separate idea of a completely *inanimate ens* or of a strictly *sensitive ens*, because we ourselves are neither solely material nor solely sensitive, but made in such a way that at one and the same time we share in matter, sense and intellect.

240. As a result, on this issue Aristotle seems to commit the same mistake as Condillac (cf. 81–85) by endowing *sense* with the faculty of judgment[159] — a totally absurd notion because this faculty can only be present in the intellect.

I argue thus: either *judging* is identical with *feeling* or judging is different from feeling. If the former, the statement, 'The faculty of feeling is capable of judging', simply means 'The faculty

that universals are derived from them is precisely the meaning of the expression, 'to be *universal in potency*.' In that case, however, being *universal in potency* cannot explain how the intellect's operation on them takes place. This operation is merely stated, not explained by the expression. Claiming to explain how *singular phantasms* communicate with *ideas*, or *universals*, by saying that ideas are derived from phantasms which are *universal in potency*, is a vicious circle. It is exactly the same as saying: 'Universals are derived from phantasms because universals *can* be derived from phantasms.' In fact, saying that phantasms are *universal in potency* simply means asserting that ideas (a synonym for universals) can be derived from them; it asserts what we are trying to explain: it affirms in mysterious and obscure language what we propose, in clear, common words, to explain and demonstrate.

[159] *De Anima*, bk. 3, c. 9; *Metaphysics* 1, and in many other passages in his works.

of feeling is capable of feeling'. If the latter, how can we attribute essentially different acts to a single faculty and say, 'Sense judges'? As I said, this is as absurd as saying, 'The ears speak, or the nose sees or the hands sneeze', or as affirming any wild notion in which a potency is associated with acts not its own.

241. In fact, as soon as the external sense is divested of whatever does not pertain to it, and therefore of any judgment whatsoever, it remains a passive potency whereby the sentient subject receives certain modifications. In other words, it *feels* differently from the way it did before and feels something different from itself. At this stage, there is no thought, no act drawing the subject to say to himself: 'Such a thing exists'. The subject has not yet attributed existence (an extremely universal concept) either to itself or to anything outside itself.

As I said, we find it extremely difficult to imagine an ens endowed with sense alone because we neither have nor can have experience of this state. Our experience is of a subject, ourselves, endowed simultaneously with sense and intellect. We should need to imagine, by an act of abstraction, a subject which truly exists and feels but has no concept of *existence*, and has not attributed it to its own feeling. This attribution gives rise to a judgment; it is thought itself thinking. As human beings, we are accustomed to feeling and, simultaneously, to attributing existence to ourselves with thought. Hence, *thinking* that we exist, and *feeling* are so connected, granted our constant habit, that we fuse them. We need a finely tuned intellectual act to separate them. Reflecting constantly on this, we come to see clearly how mere feeling and judgment about existence are two very different things. Equally far removed from one another are the act in which *myself* in its entirety is experienced strictly as feeling (and hence feels the mode in which it exists) and the act whereby not *myself* in its entirety but in one of its potencies, the understanding, reflects on its own feeling of *myself* and, having the idea of existence built into it by nature, unites this feeling with the idea of existence. It then declares: '*Myself* has EXISTENCE'. In this affirmation, '*Myself* has EXISTENCE', *myself* is judged; it is the OBJECT of the judgment. On the other hand, *myself* even though modified by sensation, is not judged; it is not the OBJECT of any judgment. It is simply a single, undivided SUBJECT, without any composition or analysis of ideas, in a motionless and inactive state except for the act whereby it is and motionlessly feels. In this state, it can hardly be called *myself*. Consequently, to attribute judgment to the senses in this way as Aristotle seems to do in certain passages is to confuse two very distinct potencies and to bestow upon sense what pertains to understanding alone.

242. Aristotle's distinction, therefore, between sense and understanding seems inadequate. 'In Aristotle's view' (writes an author who had studied his work in depth), 'the sole difference between sense and understanding is that a thing is *felt* in its particularity with the same disposition which it exhibits outside our soul; the nature of the thing which is *understood*, on the other hand, is indeed outside the soul but does not have the mode of being outside the soul according to which common nature is understood. In other words, anything understood, without the principles individuating it, does not have this manner of being outside the soul.'

This amounts to saying that sense and intellect differ only as regards their immediate terms. Sense perceives the external thing with its particularities; intellect only perceives what is common in the external thing since it has within itself the power to focus exclusively on this issue by setting aside all the rest.[160]

243. In the first place, granted what has been said, the difficulty would always be to discover how the understanding can perform such abstractions without first possessing a universal to guide its operation. When a person sets out to divide a number of objects into two classes, he has to have the distinctive idea constituting these two classes; he has to know in advance the universal quality which differentiates them. Thus, to enable the acting intellect to differentiate and separate what is common

---

[160] What kind of power would this be? Sense would be much more powerful, because it would perceive both the universal and what is proper to itself. Understanding in this case would be simply a limited sense. In so many passages, Aristotle shows a genuinely deep awareness of the superiority of the understanding over sense but we have to say either that he does not realise the consequences of his theory (and was thus inconsistent in his thought), or that his entire teaching must be interpreted by adopting a different, more profound and more learned approach. At this point, I wish the reader to note that I do not intend to condemn Aristotle's thinking directly, but the more obvious interpretation of some of his terms or, at least, the meaning put upon them by so many commentators.

from what is particular, it is absolutely necessary that it has within itself some idea which acts as a norm for such a separation. This idea enables the intellect to know the various degrees of universality exhibited by the parts of the object which it endeavours to purify, if I may use this metaphor employed by the Ancients.

244. But leaving this issue and turning to our aim, it was not enough to point out that it is proper to sense to perceive the external, individualised thing with all its particularities just as it stands. We also had to ask whether, in such a perception, we address some message to ourselves, such as: 'That which I feel, exists.' If so, if we assent to this proposition, we express an internal judgment. But if we express it, is this judgment merely simultaneous with sensation, or is it the sensation itself? This is the nub of the question.

It does not take much thought on our part to realise that we experience sensation in some external part of our body; on the other hand, the judgment we form as a result of a sensation is an internal word spoken to ourselves. It does not relate to any point of the body, to a hand, a foot or to any other part, as it does in the case of a sensation. We are therefore forced to state that a *judgment* has nothing to do with *organic sensation*. Only sense feels, but it does not add any judgment to its sensations.[161] This act, completely different from feeling, is added by our understanding. Consequently, the difference between sense and understanding does not consist solely in perceiving what is particular and what is universal but also and above all in simply perceiving, and judging this perception. Sense perceives what it feels but the understanding judges what is felt, and thus *understands* it. To perceive is simply to feel; to understand is to judge.

---

[161] The *instinct* to pursue one thing and flee from another has its origin in the senses. This is not a judgment; it is a passive tendency, a *spontaneous*, *involuntary* fact. We are always inclined to assume, however, that animals act instinctively as a result of some knowledge or judgment. The precise reason for this is that we are accustomed never to act consciously without adding a judgment to our actions; we are rational beings. But sometimes we react so quickly that we do not avert to the judgment.

Article 9

According to Themistius' paraphrase, Aristotle was not fully conversant with the nature of universals

245. Aristotle, therefore, did not distinguish clearly enough between simple, passive *feeling* and *judgment*, which is active and embraces two distinct terms, one at least of which is universal. From the union of these two, another composite apprehension is formed which is the product of the judgment. Consequently, he thought that, to explain the origin of *first ideas*, it was sufficient to posit an intellect which was a kind of sense. When acted upon by universals, this sense inevitably perceived them as a passion[162] similar to that by which sense perceives sensible things. Noting that these natural universals did not exist outside the mind, he pictured an inner faculty which he endowed with the potency of making particulars into universals, by a process of abstraction, that is, by removing from particulars any common features they had (as though *common* were not the same as *universal*) and leaving the rest. He took no care to see how this was done, or even if it were possible without supposing some innate element in the human spirit.

It would seem from a passage in Themistius' work that

---

[162] As I have already pointed out, Aristotle attributed judgment to sense as he attributed feeling to the understanding. Thus in Aristotle's work, two intrinsically distinct operations, *perception* and *judgment*, are bestowed on each of these faculties (cf. *De Anima*, bk. 3, lect. 11). At this point, I should like to show how he overlooked a fertile truth about the understanding. This, however, would take too long, and I shall merely point out how in the process Aristotle bypasses the difficulty of the origin of ideas which we are trying to solve. As soon as one assumes that *judgment* is always associated with sensation, sense becomes a miniature intellect and there is no longer any difficulty about explaining the communication between sense and intellect, the only difficult step. Actually, the difficulty consists entirely in the transition from sensation to judgment. But as soon as these two things are combined to form a single potency, there is no question of a transition. The whole question is displaced from the transition between feeling and judgment to the transition between judgments. A really difficult problem has become the easiest in the world, and scarcely worthy of consideration as a serious issue. This would-be solution to the origin of ideas is like someone answering, when asked how to swim across a river, 'It's easy, you only need a boat.' The answer is quite irrelevant to the issue.

[245]

Aristotle reduced the operation which he attributed to the acting intellect to finding in particulars what was already there, that is, the common elements, without adding anything of its own. If this were true, we would have to believe that Aristotle had not grasped the nature of the universal which, as universal or common, is not in particular things. They contain only the act of the universal, if I may put it like that, which is not in any way common. The passage to which I am referring runs as follows:

> Such vigour of the soul consists in the fact that even when genera, which are experienced by the senses, suddenly are no longer there, the soul can still portray and remember their likenesses, and discover and note the common and universal elements in particulars, because SENSE ALSO PERCEIVES THIS. Whenever anyone *knows* Socrates through sense, he also *knows* the man in Socrates. And anyone who sees a red or white thing, also sees red and white. Nobody believes that Callia and man are one and the same. Otherwise, as there is only one Callia, only one man could be seen. But whoever sees Socrates, sees in Socrates what is similar and common in other men also. It follows that THE UNIVERSAL IS SOMEHOW PERCEIVED BY SENSE, not separated however from the singular, but one with it and as a consequence of it.[163]

Article 10

Judging is more than the apprehension of universals

246. It is no surprise that Aristotle should allocate to sense the power to perceive even the *common nature* in singular things; he had endowed it with the ability to *judge*.

It is impossible to judge in the absence of any common

---

[163] Themistius: *Paraphrasis in Aristotelis Posteriorum*, bk. 2, c. 35. The truth is that sense does not perceive universals either in association with, or separate from particulars; consequently, it is absurd to say that they perceive it. In fact, the word *universal* refers to the end-product of the operation of the intellect, even in Aristotle's system. How, then, can sense perceive something not yet in existence? The *universal* has no existence prescinding from the intellect in which it acquires existence.

notion, because judging means placing some objects or qualities in a class. A class, however, is formed only by means of something common to the classified individuals.

To attribute judgment to sense, therefore, seems to go beyond endowing it with the apprehension of what is common in particulars, as Themistius claims Aristotle does. According to Themistius, apprehension for Aristotle is never alone, but always united with particulars. But judgment requires in addition the idea of what is common, distinct from the particular, so that this idea may be applied to different particulars and enable them to be classified and judged [*App.*, no. 16].

Article 11

Absurdity of the teaching set out by Themistius

247. Let us look once more at the statement: 'Sense perceives what is common but united with particulars.' This is either a contradiction or makes no sense.

What is *common* in *particulars*! This can only mean: 'The common element of that which is not common.' Can what is *common* be contained in *particulars*? *Common* merely means not being particularised, not being limited to a real individual. If ten thousand individuals were to come before my senses one after the other, I should, of course, register the impression of so many particulars but I would still not have perceived anything common. Briefly, what is *common* is merely a *relationship* of a several individuals with what is in my mind. After perceiving them I compare them with each other and note their differences, always, of course, as far as I perceive them within me. This means that in *perceiving* a number of individuals, I note what goes to make up one idea and what goes to make up different ideas in me. What is similar in them, this relationship of likeness, is called their *common* nature (cf. 180–187). But no relationship between a number of individuals and my ideas is to be found in any way in each one considered in itself and, therefore, outside my mind. They have to be seen in a single conception proper to my mind. The senses have no place here as they perceive only real individuals one at a time, in isolation from the

[247]

rest [*App.*, no. 17]. In short, what is required is an inner faculty entirely distinct from the bodily senses. This faculty, by comparing individuals after conceiving them intellectually, assigns something common to each of them. In other words, it finds an idea suitable to a number of them which allows them to be thought under this concept. Only after this operation does the word *common* begin to have meaning and be used correctly. To say that the senses perceive what is *common* means supposing the completion of the operation with which we find something *common* in things that have acquired an existence in the mind. It also means supposing that this thing discovered by the understanding and *in the understanding* is the object of the senses.

248. Thus, we find ourselves in the odd and absurd situation of accepting that the matter proper to sense is a product of the understanding, and that sense no longer furnishes the understanding with the matter for thought, but the understanding furnishes the senses! Aristotle's misuse of the word *common* propels him from one extreme to another and causes him to accept a proposition directly contrary to the basic principle of his system on which his whole argument hinges, that is, that sense furnishes matter to the understanding.

Article 12

Contradictions in two of Aristotle's opinions

249. Aristotle says that what is *common*, abstracted from what is particular, is the object of the intellect alone.

Let us see more closely if this statement harmonises with the previous teaching of our philosopher.

What is *common* cannot exist before it is abstracted; it is abstraction which brings it into existence (assuming it is not innate). The word *common* merely means what is similar in a number of individuals and separate from what is dissimilar, as one nature is separate from another and especially from its opposite.

Aristotle, in affirming that what is *common* is the object of the intellect alone, or asserting that universals exist only in the soul, or contradicting Plato in the statement: 'The universal animal is either nothing or subsequent to the individual animal — and the same can be said of every *common element*,[164] comes close to feeling the whole difficulty of explaining how we form *universals* or *common elements*. In doing this, he moves away from his own views. To say on the one hand: the object of the intellect is what is *common* in so far as it is common, or — to put it in another way — the object of the intellect are the relationships of subsistent *entia* with possible *entia*; and to say on the other hand: what is *common* in so far as it is *common* does not exist in individual acts but only in the mind, is to say one and the same thing.

But, if this is true, and if it is true that sense perceives individuals and not universals as such, it follows that sense does not perceive the object of the intellect, but that the term of sense and the term of the intellect are completely different. The first is essentially singular, and the second universal and common. However, if the *singular* is the opposite of the *universal* and in the singular as such there can be no universal or common element because they are essentially mutually exclusive notions, how can the intellect receive its object from sense? All that sense can give is of an essentially different and contrary nature to that which the mind can intuit.

This is where the difficulty lies and, as anyone examining it carefully will see, it is the same as that which forms the object of our discussion, and keeps reappearing in a new guise.[165]

---

[164] *De Anima*, bk. 1, c. 1.

[165] I say that it is the same because the problem posed above was this: 'How can we begin to judge without an idea or a universal if the senses provide us only with mere particular sensations?' The difficulty is this: 'The intellect has only ideas as object, that is, universals. But the senses provide it only with sensations, which are solely particular. Will it shape these ideas for itself, that is, will the intellect make these individual perceptions universal? If so, it needs to have some universal element in itself; otherwise it can never add to sense perceptions the universality of which they are totally devoid.' These are merely two ways of putting forward the same difficulty. In the first, the problem consists in explaining how the understanding can *judge* without some concept with which it is naturally endowed. In the second, the problem lies in explaining how the understanding can begin to *perceive* something without itself possessing any idea. It will clearly be seen that the problem is the same if we notice carefully that *perception* for the understanding is the same as *judgment* when we are dealing with real things such as the existence of bodies.

Article 13

The scholastics were aware of the difficulty;
they formulated a distinction intended to evade it.
An examination of the distinction

250. The scholastics, aware of the embarrassing difficulty in
this area of Aristotle's philosophy, endeavoured to present his
thought in a more favourable light.

They offered the following subtle distinction. The word *universal* has two meanings: either it indicates common nature
itself in so far as it is subject to being understood as universal, or
it indicates the universal in itself [*App.*, no. 18].

Consequently, *universal* in its first meaning, that is, *nature
itself* which is not actually universal but is to be subjected to the
intention of universality — in other words, is *apt* to be considered *common* — was the term of sense. On the other hand, *universal* in its second meaning, that is, as actually universal, is
merely the object of the intellect. In this way, it seemed possible
to explain the transition from sense to intellect, that is, to show
how the term of sense became the object of the intellect.
Although the mind grasped only the *universal*, there seemed to
be a way in which sense itself administered it to the intellect. By
applying this distinction, it could be said that sense too perceived the universal provided the word *universal* was taken in a
somewhat different sense from that in which it was attributed to
the intellect, that is, as universal in potency, not in act. This condition, however, removes the whole impact and value of the
distinction.

If we are really accurate in our examination, we find that the
same difficulties keep recurring.

First of all, let us dwell a moment on this phrase: 'Common
nature itself is called universal in so far as it is subject to the
intention of universality.'

What the understanding *perceives* is a term which it *judges*. This term as
judged is the *object* of the understanding, which makes a judgment about it,
and thus makes an object of something that was not its object. I cannot stop to
show how this judgment may be more or less explicit, or more or less adverted
to. For our present purposes, it is sufficient to understand that the understanding perceives by judging.

[250]

Everyone will agree that nature cannot be called *common* if no account is taken of the universality to which it is subject. Without *universality*, nature is singular and cannot be predicated as common. Only when we compare this singular nature *in our thought* with other singular natures, themselves existent in our minds and not in themselves, do we find the similarity. Then, wanting to show that we see nature from this point of view, we add the predicate *common*. This nature, with the addition of the standpoint from which we view it, we call the *universal* or *that which is common*.

No *nature*, therefore, can be called *common* until the understanding has completed this operation and the relationship between a number of individuals perceived by us has been discovered. This *relationship* only occurs in an intellectual concept because it does not consist in either of the single terms, that is, in the individuals between whom the relationship falls, but solely in their union and comparison. This union is found only in the understanding where two or more things find a species, a common idea.

If some *nature* always remains *singular*, that is, remains as it is in itself before it was conceived and examined by the understanding, it would be misleading to call it *common* or universal as long as it is considered independently of the relationship it has with the common idea in the intellect. If we propose to exclude the intellect entirely, and wish to consider external things only in relation to sense, we cannot call them *common*. This predicate is attributed to them *subsequently*, that is, only from the moment when we suppose them to be conceived by the intellect where the ideas showing their similarities and differences are found. However, all this must be completely excluded when we propose to examine the powers of sense alone. At this point, we must consider external things without adding to them any contribution from the intellect as it perceives and compares them. If it is true, as Aristotle himself grants, that the *intention of universality* is added to them by the mind, we are obliged to exclude this aspect completely. We do this by adding to nature the predicate *common*. Consequently we are not entitled to say that sense perceives common nature or the universal, which gives rise to the *common* element in things.

[250]

What therefore is meant by: 'Sense perceives common nature'?

It would seem to mean: 'Sense perceives a *singular* nature which, later on, when it is perceived by the intellect acquires from a certain point of view the predicate *common* because it is united to the idea, which is always endowed with universality. This predicate is attributed to nature to express the way in which the intellect perceives it by means of the idea.'

If the predicate *common* expresses only what the understanding adds to the nature it perceives, it is easy to see that the scholastic distinction does not contribute in any way to the task of explaining how the term of sense can become an object of the intellect. The aim of this distinction was to show that even the term of sense can, like the term of the *intellect*, be called *universal* in some way. In this case, it would not be strange to find that the intellect can be provided with its objects by sense, although only the intellect is capable of perceiving universals. But, as we have seen, the term of sense can be called *universal* only to the extent that it is considered in relationship with the future act of the intellect. But if we prescind from this future act and try to define the sensible term solely in its relationship to sense, we must call it *singular*; and it does not contain within it anything that is, or can be, *common*. Where does the intellect discover the universal which makes it common? The problem remains unsolved, and untouched, as though it had never been discussed.

Article 14

How Aristotle's acting intellect explains
the origin of universals

251. The term of sense and the object of the intellect are different and essentially opposite. Sense perceives only *singulars*; the intellect adds *what is universal* [*App.*, no. 19].

If we suppose, therefore, with Aristotle, that all ideas have their origin in the senses, we still have to face the difficulty of discovering how sense can put before the understanding an object adapted and proportionate to it. Sense, as we know, has no common or universal element.

As we have seen, Aristotle in such a difficulty establishes an *acting intellect* which he designates as mediator between *sense* and the *intellect*. This mediator is responsible for taking sensible, singular phantasms and transforming them into universals. Aristotle assigns this duty as proper to the acting intellect which however is also responsible for discovering how to carry out the important, awesome duty which the philosopher has entrusted to it. Fortunately the mysterious power which we call intellect continues its work with complete disregard for philosophical speculation and for the laws which we want to lay down for it.

I confess that I would really be at a loss were I charged with the task of teaching the *acting intellect* how to fulfil the role which our philosopher prescribes for it, granted his explicit condition that it should not bring any idea whatsoever to the task, but derive all ideas from sensible phantasms.

252. First, must this intellect perceive sensible, singular phantasms or not?

If it does not perceive them, it would seem that it cannot operate upon them or distinguish within them what is proper from what is common.

If it does perceive them, as sense does, it is a faculty [*App.*, no. 20]. But if it perceives singulars in the way sense does, how can it find, in singulars, universals which are not there?

We have already remarked that *singulars*, as long as they remain such, contain no *universal*. We also saw that the word *universal* merely expresses a relationship which a thing has with other *possible* similar things. It is, therefore, the kind of object which only the intellect apprehends: sense knows nothing of it. But, if the intellect alone is responsible for adding the *universal* attribute which is not present in the terms of sense, where does the intellect find it?

253. Plato presumed this attribute was innate. According to him, the soul added the *universal* idea of singulars when sense perceived them; the soul was called *intellect* in so far as it bore this concept within itself. Or he assumed — this comes down to the same thing — that the intellect bore in itself the exemplars of things. These are possible things, and dictate, as distinctive norms, the classification of sensible realities. The problem, Plato thought, was solved.

Avicenna resorted to an *intellect* completely *separate* from human beings. We receive from this intellect fully formed ideas from which we then isolate the realities perceived by the senses. This system also met the difficulties to a certain extent.

In Aristotle, however — at least according to later commentators — there is nothing like this.[166] According to him, the *acting intellect* adds the idea of universality to singulars perceived by the senses — this is what the mind does in every system of thought — though the senses do not have such an idea within them, and the acting intellect itself does not bring it to them!

Article 15

According to Aristotle the intellect bestows its own form on what it perceives. This, together with the rejection of every innate idea in the intellect, is the basis of modern scepticism

254. Occasionally, Aristotle puts every effort into solving a difficulty forcefully put to him, though it seems present more to his feeling than to his intellect.

He will say, for example, 'What is received, is received as though by a receptacle. And just as liquid takes on different shapes in different shaped vessels, so what is received by our sense and spirit must be different. They are like two vases which give a different form to the same thing. The form bestowed by sense allows the thing to remain singular; the form bestowed by the intellect is the *universality* of the thing, because this alone is the way the intellect can conceive mentally.'

It is easy to see traces of kantian thought in such teaching. This would require us to accept, without knowing why, the presence in the human spirit of a certain *form* to which perceived entia would conform.

Now, either this form is the type of truth and, in this case, the type, that is, the essence of truth, must be innate in us (this is my position), or nothing of this kind is admitted in the spirit. In this case, the spirit, limited and determined as it is, will endow what

---

[166] In Aristotle's works we come across passages which show him dissatisfied with his own system and only a step from another, as the reader will see in the following article.

it perceives with a purely subjective form. This is the foundation on which modern scepticism and critical philosophy is founded.

255. However, it is easy to see that in this supposition all the immense work of critical philosophy would be based upon the material analogy of a receptacle.

I see perfectly well how a liquid can be placed into a vase without its initially having the form which it receives as it is gradually poured in. But I do not understand how *singulars* can enter the intellect if we accept the principle that the intellect apprehends only *universals*. And if they do enter, why do they inevitably have to be transformed there into universals?

If *singulars* do not enter the mind, they cannot receive the form which the intellect would give them, just as the liquid, unless it enters the vase, cannot take on the shape of the vase.

If they *do* enter, the intellect is no longer constituted so that it can apprehend only under a *universal* form. If the intellect has this form, necessarily, it is conditioned by it and the *singular* is inconceivable in it.

In the example of the vase, two stages stand out: the liquid prior to its introduction and the liquid already poured in. Here again, the liquid is distinguished from its accidental form: the former can exist without the latter.

On the other hand, *common nature* has nothing singular about it; it is a completely different object from that perceived by sense. The object does not exist for us before the intellect apprehends it; it begins to exist with the act whereby the intellect knows it.

On the other hand, if the *object* of the intellect had such a form because the subjective intellect bestowed that form upon the object, scepticism — as I have indicated — would be inescapable. There would only be subjective truth, that is, non-truth (truth is essentially objective and absolute). This is the case in Kant's system which is, in fact, merely the Aristotelian analogy of the receptacle, developed and ingeniously sustained.

[255]

Article 16

An Aristotelian contradiction

256. To avoid this rock of scepticism, Aristotle occasionally refrains from using the image of the receptacle which receives everything and arranges it in its own likeness.

According to him, the *acting intellect* does not alter anything; it simply separates what is *common* from what is *proper* in things. Once this separation has taken place, the *passive intellect* perceives only what is *common* in things. *Apprehending* only part of something does not mean perceiving it in an altered, false way, but apprehending it partially, though at the same time unerringly.

Aristotle, expounding his theory in this way, appears to present his *acting intellect* as a kind of prism which breaks up light and separates colours. This suggests that it does not separate them by an act of will, but by a kind of *blind* necessity.

257. If we compare the acting intellect to the senses, we could say that it separates *what is common* in things from *what is proper*, as the eye and the ear distinguish light and sound by taking what is appropriate to each. But this way of explaining such a separation, however ingenious it may appear, is as unjustified and ineffectual as all the others.

First, it is based upon an obviously false premiss; it assumes that *proper* and *common* are two elements which go to make up the external thing as colours combine to form a single cluster of light, or as light and sound, in striking both sensories, arouse feeling only in the relevant sense organ. On the other hand, as I said, *what is common* does not exist in things before the mind puts it there; the word 'common' expresses only a relationship with an idea, and an intellectual view of things.

To state that the mind apprehends the *universal*, that is, *what is common* by separating it from what is proper is to posit that the *universal*, or *what is common*, pre-exists the act of intellect. But the whole question consists in knowing how the *universal* appears to the intellect when it is not to be found in the nature of things which contain only singular individuals.

My question is about the origin of *universals*, and you tell me that I separate them from *what is proper*. But this does not explain them; it supposes their existence, and assumes what is to be proved.

Article 17

In Aristotle's system, the intellect would be operating blindly, which is absurd

258. Next, is it possible to imagine a blind operation in the intellect, as in physical actions such as the choice of canals in digestion or the separation of colours by a prism?

Some momentary credence might be possible as long as the discussion is abstract and universal, and does not consider the intimate nature of the intellect. But such credence is impossible when we think and reflect about this nature.

The intellect is the cognitive faculty, whose acts cannot be blind. They are essentially knowing acts. We are in fact discussing the source of our light and knowledge.

To press the matter further, let me ask: Does the *acting intellect*, when it operates this so-called separation between what is proper and what is common in things, know *what is proper* and *what is common* in such a way that it can reject the former and choose the latter? If it grasps the difference between them, it does not operate blindly but knowingly sets what is proper to one side and what is common to the other. In such a case (the only case in which we can conceive a similar distinction made by the intellect), it must possess ideas prior to this separation, which serve as guides. The thought, 'This nature is common' is the same as the thought, 'There can exist an infinite number of natures similar to this one.' But thought of this kind supposes the *idea*, that is, the *simple apprehension of that nature*, which is not determined by time, place or any other individual circumstances. It is mere possibility; in short, it is a universal.

I have to conclude that I am quite unable to find any evidence for the role which Aristotle assigned to the *acting intellect* by which it converts single sensations into ideas without itself possessing anything innate.

[258]

Article 18

A trace of the true teaching in Aristotle

259. Aristotle himself, however, in happier moments when he was less concerned with combating Plato, suspected or glimpsed that the conditions which he imposed on his acting intellect were harsh and unjust, and that it would have carried on just as before even if he had not relaxed them.

Consequently, he seems at times inclined to attribute some kind of universal to the intellect and by referring sense percep-tions to this universal converted them into universals. As I have often said, this universality consists solely in their relationship with a *universal*, that is, with an intellectual idea through which they are called *common*. However, he touches upon this matter so elusively that I do not know if we can form a really clear pic-ture of his views, which he puts in two words.[167]

These words show that the acting intellect, in drawing univer-sals from particular things perceived by the senses, must have an act within itself. This *act* must be substantial to the intellect which otherwise would be unable to carry out the operation referred to, that is, drawing the ideas of things from sensations.

Aristotle's concept, if we follow his usual principles, seems to come down finally to the following argument:

The sensations, or more accurately the phantasms which sen-sations leave in our souls, are not, as such, objects of the intel-lect. In other words, they are not true ideas except *in potency*. They are particulars, and the intellect can apprehend only uni-versals. We must, therefore, accept the presence in the soul of a faculty (whatever it may later turn out to be) which has the power to convert these phantasms, that is, ideas in potency, into ideas in act. This faculty is called the *acting intellect*. However, for one thing to change another from potency into an act, it has to be itself to be in act. According to Aristotle's principles, for example, one body cannot move another unless it is itself already in motion. Therefore this acting intellect, Aristotle con-cludes, must be, of its nature, in act in order to reduce into actual knowledge the phantasms received by the senses.[168]

---

[167] He says that the acting intellect *est ACTU ENS.*

[168] *De Anima*, bk. 3, lect. 10.

Aristotle goes no further and I am not aware that he gives any clearer explanation elsewhere of what he understands by the *act* of this intellect.

260. One can, however, state that by firmly establishing this proposition (if indeed he concedes that this intellect in act is primordial and innate in us, and does not become active only on the occasion of phantasms), he went a step further than Locke and the modern sensists brought up in Locke's school who, although admitting a cognitive faculty in us, do not get near the thorny issue of the nature of this faculty. They are content to assume that it fulfils its purpose. On the other hand, Aristotle maintained that 'there is in us a faculty enabling us to abstract universals from particulars', and adds that this faculty has to be in act. He arrives at least at the threshold of the great and difficult question of the innate element in the human mind. According to this teaching of Aristotle, we must have in our potency for knowledge a *substantial* and consequently *innate act*. However mysterious this expression is, and however vague and brief it may be, it is nevertheless true that it indicates progress in Aristotle's thinking and justifies the belief that he had at least touched upon the difficult problem we have been discussing, that is, the origin of ideas.

Article 19

Explanation of the trace of the true teaching in Aristotle

261. If we wish to offer a rational explanation of Aristotle's cryptic, reserved manner of writing, we may perhaps approximate to the truth.

What can the *act* of a cognitive faculty be? First, it is inconceivable unless it conveys some information.

Consequently, when Aristotle says that the acting intellect has itself to be in act in order to form universals, that is, intellective cognitions, he seems to mean that this intellect possesses by nature some species of notion enabling it to produce other actual notions when sensible phantasms provide the opportunity. It also seems that he went no further with his examination of this species of *innate knowledge* because he was afraid either of the difficulty of self-contradiction in determining the problem, or of uncovering something too favourable to the platonic system he was opposing.

It could also be, as occasionally happens, that Aristotle, after having this fleeting vision leading him to recognise the need for an innate *act* in the cognitive faculty (which is the same as the need for some innate species), was distracted by other thoughts from his pursuit of such a felicitous idea that could have elicited marvellous fruit in his incomparable mind.

Article 20

Aristotle recognises that intellect entails an innate light,
as his 'common sense' witnesses

262. Commentators have shown little interest in this passage from Aristotle which, though brief, is nevertheless one of the most significant.

Nevertheless, St. Thomas's remarks on it confirm me in my views.

Aquinas, seeking to discover how Aristotle grants in us a substantially *actuated* intellect, first points out that Aristotle could not have meant that the intellect had innate ideas of all things. This would, in fact, be the platonic theory which Aristotle had refuted in so many passages. Moreover, the intellect, if it were predetermined to know all things of itself, would ruin another principle constantly taught by Aristotle and confirmed by experience: in order to think, our intellect needs to acquire phantasms of external things from the senses.

Discarding this interpretation, Aquinas asks about the nature of an intellective faculty which is in act, but does not contain the ideas of all things.

It seems that this is possible only as an intermediate state between being in act and possessing the ideas of all things, and being in act and possessing one of these ideas.

St. Thomas, the most acute of all critics, says:

> The acting intellect is considered as act relative to things which are still to be understood in so far as it is an immaterial, active power, able to render other things immaterial like itself. In this way, it renders intelligible in act things which are intelligible only in potency.[169]

This is the metaphor he uses to explain it:

> ... as light makes colours active, not because it already contains within itself all separate colours.[170]

263. This aristotelian metaphor is remarkably apposite to the argument.

In fact light, although it does not already have colours divided and separated in itself, is nevertheless capable of such division by means of a body able to refract and reflect the cluster of white light.

According to this likeness, therefore, we should affirm exactly the opposite to what has previously been stated about the theory of ideas when it was said that the action of the acting intellect consisted in separating what is proper from what is common in things. This theory falsely assumed that there was something common *per se* in things independently of the operation of the intellect. In this hypothesis, we have compared 1. external things to a cluster of light containing a number of colours, that is, what is common and what is proper, and 2. the intellect to a prism able to separate one from another. Here, however, we are no longer comparing sensible things to light, but the acting intellect to light. In other words, we are comparing to light the act in which the acting intellect terminates. The prism, that which divides this light into its elementary rays and determines the various colours, are sensible things. *What is common*, therefore, would be in the mind, not in things, and would become particular and individuated by

---

[169] It should be noted that, in St. Thomas's view, anything *immaterial* is *per se* knowable. It follows that the word *intellect* is to be understood here in the objective sense of *understood* rather than of *understanding*. Otherwise the argument would not be valid.

[170] This metaphor of light, which is so appropriate when explaining what is innate in our intellect, is a term used in all schools, a word used in all languages.

means of the things to which it is applied. These particularisations and individuations would in fact correspond to the colours; what is *common* would correspond to the *light* which pre-exists in the intellect.

In this supposition, many difficulties would be overcome and the intellect, although it would not see any separate colour without the external prism of sensible bodies which break up and determine its light, would nevertheless still possess an innate light. It would have no knowledge of anything particular and determined,[171] but would be granted the *most common* of all ideas, a form quite undetermined prior to sensations. In a word, although it would not possess any derived ideas, as Plato, Aristotle's rival claimed, it would have the primal, most universal idea as innate. Only the principle would be innate, not the consequences. The idea of what is most common is that which is called *principle* (as we shall see in the proper place), when applied to less common things. And Aristotle holds that principles are to be taken as undemonstrable.

264. St. Thomas, therefore, when he comes to explain the source from which the intellect receives its ungenerated light, concludes:

> Such an active power is a kind of participation in the intellectual light from separate substances,[172]

that is, (according to Aquinas) from God himself.[173]

---

[171] A careful reading of St. Thomas reveals that his denial of the existence of innate ideas refers solely to determined ideas or species. *Anima intellectiva est quidem actu immaterialis, sed est in potentia ad DETERMINATAS SPECIES rerum* [The intellective soul is indeed immaterial in act, but is in potency to DETERMINED SPECIES of things] (*S.T.*, I, q. 79, art. 4, *ad* 4). This is precisely my teaching. I deny that the human soul is endowed at birth with *determined* ideas or species. I attribute to it only one absolutely *undetermined* idea. St. Thomas calls this *light*, not idea, and says that it makes the soul *immaterial in act*.

[172] *De Anima*, bk. 3, lect. 10.

[173] *Intellectus separatus secundum nostrae fidei documenta est ipse Deus* [According to the documents of our faith, God himself is separate intellect] (*S.T.*, I, q. 79, art. 4, *ad* 4).

Article 21

The Arab philosophers, who were firmly intent on denying
any innate element in man, made the mistake of locating
the acting intellect outside the human mind

265. A passage such as the one we have examined is directed
against other commentators on Aristotle's work who, when
they read in some passages in Aristotle that we have no innate
knowledge and that our intellect is a mere potency, are unable to
harmonise this with other passages when the master says that
the acting intellect is not merely a cognitive potency, but is in act
substantially. If it were not, it would be unable to convert into
actual cognitions the things perceived by the senses. In other
words, it could not supply *ideas*, all of which are by nature universal, to the possible intellect. As a result, they chose to assume
that Aristotle, when speaking of the *acting intellect*, was referring to some intellect separate from man. This would be either
the divine intellect or the intellect of some angel which, in act
(that is, actually possessing the ideas of all things), could exert
some influence on the *possible intellect*, that is, on our intellect, a
mere cognitive potency. Whenever sensations occurred, this
separate intellect would communicate to them the universality
which, united with the phantasms provided by the senses, furnishes the *ideas* of external things.

266. St. Thomas, however, rejects and dismisses this interpretation as intrinsically wrong and as contrary to the mind of
Aristotle. He maintains that Aristotle, in referring to the human
intellect as a merely potential faculty of thought, is to be understood as speaking of the *possible intellect*. When he maintains
that the intellect is not merely in potency, but in act, he would
be speaking of another intellective faculty also found in us and
called the *acting intellect*. This acts continuously, not prompted
by phantasms, but of its own active nature. Certainly, if I
viewed Aristotle in a more favourable light by concentrating
solely on some of his more felicitous passages, I think that I
could fairly express what he saw in passing as follows: 'Experience shows that we do not have the ideas of external things
before receiving sensations. We must not therefore gratuitously

admit that such ideas are innate in our spirit; if we possessed them as innate, we would also know that we possessed them.[174] On the other hand, it is true that sensations, which are essentially particular and relate to the single individual producing them, are not ideas. Ideas, as essentially universal, are types of all similar individuals. Consequently, we have to assume that human beings, who receive particular sensations, have within themselves a potency for universalisation. Universality, however, which is not to be found in sensations, must be attributed to them by a universalising potency already in possession of universality. This universal view, added to things experienced by our senses, makes them actual ideas. Previously they were ideas only in potency.[175] Making the phantasms received with the bodily senses *actual ideas* means universalising them, and nothing more, because universalisation bestows upon them the *act* through which they can be called *ideas*. But nothing can be reduced to act except by something which is itself in act. This potency, therefore, which is able to place our cognitions in act must have this act in itself. In other words, it must possess that

---

[174] This is not a correct inference; it is possible for a person to have ideas without being aware of having them, as Leibniz so correctly observed. This, however, is the standard line of argument of those who deny innate ideas; Aristotle uses it (*Poster.*, bk. 2, final chapter).

[175] He calls *phantasms* cognitions *in potency* in *De Anima*, bk. 2, lect. 12. This means that they are not cognitions. Consequently we have to explain the intellectual operation by which they become cognitions, universal concepts, ideas. In the same passage, however, Aristotle comes very close to the truth because, in his desire to bring out the difference between senses and intellect, he locates this difference in the fact that 'the active part of sensitive activity is outside the soul while the active part of intellectual activity is in the soul itself'. He means that sensations occur as a result of the action upon us of bodies external to us; intellective perceptions, which contain ideas, occur as a result of the inner, essential activity of our soul. Aristotle's remark could be taken further by reasoning as follows: 'This universality of intellectual conceptions is either *created* by the intellect or merely *added* to the phantasms by the intellect which already possesses them. Granting the intellect the force to create universality is clearly greater than granting the power to add it; this reason alone would be sufficient for us to opt for the second alternative. Moreover, observation and analysis show that intellectual activity does not produce anything; it is simply a vision of what has already been produced. Understanding means only seeing interiorly, and seeing is not producing. Consequently, the intellect does not create the universal species of things; it sees them.'

which constitutes universality and then add it to the phantasms.'[176]

Article 22

St. Thomas refutes the error of the Arab philosophers

267. Returning to Aquinas, we see that he proves the impossibility inherent in supposing that the *acting intellect* may be an ens external to us. For him, it is absurd to suppose that human nature should lack whatever it needs in order to know, that is, to perform the act for which it is essentially destined.
According to St. Thomas:

> Man would not have been adequately constituted by nature unless he had within him the principles enabling him to carry out his own proper activity, that is, understanding. Nor could he carry out this activity except through the two intellects, *possible* and *acting intellect*,[177]

that is, an intellect in potency and an intellect in act.

268. Next, to show that Aristotle speaks of the *acting intellect* as a faculty found in the human spirit, St. Thomas points out that the philosopher calls his acting intellect 'as it were a habit or a light.' This term, according to Aquinas, would not be appropriate to the acting intellect if it were some substance separate from human beings. St. Thomas, while he concedes that the power of actuation essential to the *acting intellect* comes from the influence of some higher intelligence, never states that the acting intellect is, like some separate substance, external to us.

---

[176] Pondering Aristotle's views on the history of our thoughts, it seems fairly clear that, in dealing with ideas in the human intellect, he often confined his attention to the ideas of external things. Consequently, he could not acknowledge any idea in us before sensible things steered his thought to something real. It was inconceivable for him that the idea of *undetermined being* could exist in the human mind. For him, it was a light, not yet an idea. Moreover, even if the word *idea* were restricted to meaning some universal conception determined in some way, I too would say that only a *light*, not an innate idea, is to be found in the human mind. We ought not to cavil over words; things alone should be our concern.

[177] *De Anima*, bk. 3, lect. 10.

Article 23

Aristotle's achievement in realising that a primal innate act in our intellect is necessary

269. Aristotle's discovery of a cognitive faculty in us which is not simply in potency, but essentially in *act*, is, I think, of great importance even though he did not subsequently venture to investigate the nature and extension of this act.

It is possible that Aristotle, who initially refused to subscribe to the Platonic system because he saw, or thought he saw, its errors, later adopted a stance directly contrary to it. His first hope, perhaps — as is often the case with someone who has not yet investigated questions with the profundity they require — was to explain acts of the mind while resolutely denying that the mind has anything innate in it. However, when he later investigated this thorny problem in greater depth, he realised for himself that some compromise was necessary and admitted that the very faculty which produces ideas contains some connatural and innate *light*, that is, some primal idea which can serve as the faculty's benchmark and rule for forming all other ideas.

270. I am persuaded of this because, in so many passages in his works, Aristotle's language shows constant signs of hesitation. Moreover, the little phrases often introduced to condition his argument are significant. These half expressions, while saying nothing determined and forthright on the one hand, tell us only too clearly what he would rather conceal. They show that the writer, as though suspended between two opinions, does not wish, or dare, to come out with a full, absolute statement, for fear of the consequences. Or at least they show that in his conscience there remains some doubt or obscure, undetermined exception opposed to his teaching.

For example, in the passage to which I was referring, he clearly states, when speaking of the act of the agent, that the intellect in act is not at all like the intellect in potency 'which sometimes understands and sometimes does not understand'. But he continues by saying that it is 'as it were a habit and a light',[178] without daring to say outright that it is a habit, a light.

---

[178] *De Anima*, bk. 3, lect. 10.

271. As further confirmation of this view, I point to another passage in which Aristotle's diffident treatment of this matter is very clear.

Towards the end of the second of the *Posterior Analytics*, Aristotle asks how we come to know *first principles*. After establishing that we cannot deduce them by demonstration, and do not possess them as innate, he sets out to explain their origin from the senses. He says that the *phantasms* obtained from *sensations* remain and form *memory*. Then, from a number of these memories, we come to *test* what is constant and common in them. This becomes the *principle* of knowledge and skill [*App.*, no. 21].

Such an easy explanation of the knowledge of the first, most universal principles would lead, apparently, to the exclusion of innate, habitual knowledge. This is not the case. Aristotle hesitates and shows that his previous explanation does not banish all doubt from his spirit. He does not conclude absolutely that there are in us no innate habits, but merely says that there are no innate DETERMINED habits in us.[179]

272. The reader should note how this expression, which excludes from the innate elements in man only *determined* habits, fits exactly my own thinking and language.[180]

---

[179] *Posterior.*, bk. 2, in f.

[180] Where two opposing systems are restrained, they can come quite close to one another. Here Aristotle rejects innate ideas, yet does accept some species of innate *habits*. Some Cartesians also accept innate ideas, but when explaining what they mean say that they are like innate *habits*. Here the two systems are extremely close. Galluppi expounds the thought of the Cartesians in this way: 'Some of them compared (innate ideas) to *habits* of the will. Whenever a dominant passion is lodged in the human heart, even when we are totally unaware of its effects, it is still real in the spirit, according to the philosophers to whom we refer. An ambitious man, for example, who has conceived an overwhelming desire to obtain a position, still has the same passion in his mind and heart even when he is not consciously thinking of the position. We may truthfully say of him, therefore, that he is still coveting the position. The Cartesians ask what exactly is the habitual love existing in the heart of the ambitious man even at times when he is quite unaware of any ambitious act. It would appear, they maintain, that this habitual love is the very act of prolonged, lasting love which, however, is unconscious. Absence of feeling of this love marks it off, in fact, from the actual love of which the ambitious man is aware. Similarly, *a priori* and innate notions are real, lasting notions in our mind, but dissociated from the act of consciousness before

Plato's mistake, according to me, lies in his supposition that we possess innate ideas of special entia, that is, *determined ideas* wholly in conformity with subsistent things. Against this, I maintain that his system is partly true if he admits the presence in us of innate ideas not of ultimate entia, such as real things, but only of some universal essences, some completely *undetermined* ideas. Moreover, these universal, undetermined ideas are not to be more than are necessary to explain the formation of other ideas.[181] Aristotle also seems to have felt the need for this. He was not bold enough to exclude innate, *undetermined habits* but only innate, *determined habits*. Nor did he exclude light, but light already divided into colours.

Article 24

Aegidius' explanation of the undetermined habits mentioned by Aristotle as innate in human beings

273. I shall conclude these observations upon Aristotle by referring to a remarkable passage by Aegidius, *doctor fundatissimus*, on the extract from Aristotle.

I find it a remarkable passage because it shows how this shrewd commentator recognised that Aristotle did indeed acknowledge (willingly or unwillingly) *innate*, though *undetermined habits* in the human spirit. These undetermined, innate habits in us constitute the acting intellect and help to explain what passed through Aristotle's mind when he was confronted by the *act* with which the human spirit must be essentially endowed if it is to acquire habits or determined ideas. The *undetermined* habits or ideas are this act.

Aegidius writes:

sensible notions can render them present to consciousness. This is how, among others, the anonymous author of the treatise on the human mind against Locke and his followers, determines the nature of innate ideas' (*Saggio Filosofico sulla Critica della Conoscenza*, vol. 4, pp. 2 and 3).

181 In fact, only one idea is needed to explain the generation of all others, as I shall show. Similarly, there is and can be only one perfectly undetermined idea.

We must also bear in mind that the habits of principles are not *determined*, that is, *completely innate* in us. 'determined' is used of that which is finished and that which comes to its perfect term. But knowledge of the principles is not naturally and formally instilled into us in a complete state. We have, nevertheless, something which is effectively, finally and dispositively related to the knowledge of principles in so far as the *light* of the acting intellect has been inserted into us naturally. By virtue of this intellect, such principles are known to us immediately, once we know the terms of the proposition.[182]

Article 25

Conclusion upon Aristotle's thought

274. The favourable interpretation of some of Aristotle's passages which I have endeavoured to present could be taken still further.

Although Aristotle has for so long been held and acclaimed as 'the master of those who know', I could not show how close he came to what I believe is the true teaching on the origin of ideas, without expounding the whole system concerning this origin.

At the same time, bearing in mind other passages of Aristotle's work, we would have to admit that it contains a number of defects even more serious than those already noted. Taking everything into account, we would perhaps have to conclude that Aristotle, despite his amazing *subtlety*, lacks the *sublimity* of Plato.

Article 26

Two types of teaching in Plato

275. It is time to return to Plato.

In my previous remarks, I tried to show how Aristotle's

---

[182] This passage is mentioned by Dominic of Flanders in the questions which he wrote upon the *Commentaries* of St. Thomas on the *Posterior Analytics* of Aristotle.

defection from the school of Plato was caused by several factors. One of these was the unsatisfactory way in which Plato himself expounded the reasons which led him to accept ideas as natural to man, and the unjustified lengths to which he pushed his teaching or at least the lack of scientific precision with which he expounded it.

I will now present another cause for the constant opposition which Plato's system has encountered in every age, though such a long and obdurate opposition has never been able to weaken and banish it from human memory in the way that other opinions, now shown to be completely false and empty, have been set aside.

This aspect of Platonism involves two considerations: on the one hand, a sustained, intense opposition to Platonism that seemed on the verge of overwhelming it and, on the other, a continual reaction on the part of this philosophy that revealed a tenacious and inextinguishable vitality. Even in periods when anti-Platonism was at its most rabid, the Platonic corpus of teaching could never be considered unanimously condemned by mankind. Although many condemned it, there was obvious hesitation in their judgment which was never entirely free from the seed of doubt or laid down with absolute security. Even those who were intellectually convinced of its absurdity exhibited some uncertainty. When least expected, enthusiastic champions of the derided theory came to the fore only to be met with indignation by others who believed that society, by not following them, was going backwards rather than forwards. Such constant protest by a few against the multitude who derided Platonism is inexplicable unless we presuppose that it contains a core of truth. Similarly, we cannot explain the constant opposition unless we presuppose that Platonism contains some false or inaccurate parts, or at least some obscurity, or lack of precise expression.

Plato was reproached for being obscure,[183] and many, while

---

183 Laertius says of Plato: 'He is wont to use a variety of terms so that his works may not be understood by the ignorant and the uncouth.' I do not think, however, that Laertius' other remark is equally true, although it is not entirely false either. He says that Plato 'uses the same terms with different meanings and also uses incompatible terms to refer to the same thing.' This is more apparent than real when we investigate the hidden recesses of Platonism.

asserting that his system is false, earnestly assure you that they do not understand it.

What is certain is that the major opposition Plato encountered was from a crowd of pseudo-philosophers who portrayed him to a crowd of readers in the way their poor minds mentally imagined him.

However, Aristotle is not to be numbered amongst these common or garden philosophers, hundreds of whom were produced by France alone in the last century. Though he joined forces with the opposition to his master, partly out of ambition and emulation, his mind was, as I have said, great enough to identify inaccuracies in Plato's teaching.

276. But even if we ignore this imperfect and erroneous aspect of Plato's system, the following observation helps explain its various vicissitudes.

Two sets of teaching are found side by side in Plato's works: one *practical and traditional*, the other *rational*.

The distinction between these two sets of teaching is recognised throughout antiquity and it is a key as it were which unlocks knowledge of ancient philosophy. Aristotle himself notes it clearly enough and refers to a twofold division of scholars as though it were generally accepted. Some were called *theologians*, others *philosophers*.[184] Theologians must have been those who undertook to collect truths which, communicated by God in the earliest ages of the world, were never completely lost but handed down by tradition from one generation to the next. Philosophers, on the other hand, must have been those who were not satisfied with tradition and authority, and often expected little from them, applying themselves instead to the study of truth with their own individual reason as companion.

---

[184] *Metaphysics*, bk. 3, c. 2. — Aristotle usually had little time for *traditional* philosophy, and poked fun at its teachers, as we can see from this passage of his *Metaphysics*. He was partly right because theology was represented by poets who had tricked it out with innumerable fables. It can safely be affirmed that rational philosophy from Anaxagoras to Plato tended to co-mingle with the traditional philosophy which was very evident in Socrates and found its final fulfilment in Plato. Aristotle took the opposite direction, going back a step toward Thales but retaining the influence of tradition which had been accepted as a guest by philosophy. Aristotle's *De Caelo* is sufficient evidence of this.

[276]

Examination of the distinctive features of the two famous schools of the ancient world, the Italic and the Ionian, shows, I think, the fundamental difference between them: Pythagoras, the founder of the Italic school, posited *traditional and symbolic teaching* as the basis of his philosophy; Thales, the founder of the Ionic school, grounded all his research on reasoning alone and offered it as *rational teaching*. As a result, the Italic school favoured analysis, the Ionians synthesis. The former started from the whole, broke it down to arrive at its parts, and invariably returned to the whole, the object of its thinking; the latter, starting from the parts, wanted to assemble them to arrive at the whole but, on its infinite journey, was forever falling back on the parts, the sole focus of its attention. The Italic school began from God, and journeyed in the pure regions of the spirit; the Ionians started from Nature and struggled in vain to escape from matter.

Plato, a descendant of Pythagoras through Archytas and of Thales through Socrates, combined both types of teaching.

The positive feature of the trend of the Pythagorean school was its resolve to gather together the sound teaching preserved by society which God had originally entrusted to mankind;[185] the positive feature of the school of Thales was its active exercise of human reason.

Plato's travels to collect Pythagorean teachings are very well known; Socrates, on the other hand, had taught him how to philosophise, that is, to use his own reasoning powers. In fact, it can be said that the whole of Socrates' teaching is, in the last resort, merely a method of reasoning on all things presented for

---

[185] In the *Theodicy* (94–124), I pointed out that God gave two things to the recently created human race: 1. some positive truths; 2. activation, through speech, of their reason which, unable to act freely by itself, required to be moved by some principle, stimulus or external need. From these two things, given to us from the first moments of our existence, the two doctrines which I have distinguished came forth as from their own sources. *Traditional teaching* which human beings were to preserve faithfully in their memory, emerged from *positive* truth; *rational science*, which we were to develop by using our reason, or by applying abstract principles received in speech to the positive facts of revelation and the sensations which the entia composing the material universe produced in us, emerged from the movement proper to reason. Thus both branches of human knowledge are eventually reduced to the first cause: they come from God. Often we add only our own aberrations to knowledge.

our consideration. Socrates perfected the aim of Thales, the first thinker in Greece to think for himself without reference to a school.[186]

Socrates, however, was not content to perfect Thales' method:[187] he took a step forward in applying it. Until the time of Archelaus, Socrates' teacher, formal philosophical reasoning was concerned almost solely with physical entities.[188] It took more than a century (the time-span between Thales and Socrates) before Socrates changed the focus from physical objects to ethical issues. However, when Socrates said: 'Things above us

---

[186] In other words, Thales endowed philosophical reasoning with a passion similar to that shown in our modern age by Descartes with his self-imposed *methodical* law of refusing to accept from others any truth before he had subjected it to rigorous, philosophical investigation. This accounted also for his failures, and the flaws in his philosophy. What a catastrophe for mankind! The most noble venture undertaken by reason, which made mankind ruler of the universe, served only to lead us into error or obliged us to admit our infinite ignorance!

[187] Note that the Socratic method is, in fact, the one appropriate to the investigation of truth, the aim of all Ionian philosophy, that is, of a philosophy which is essentially investigative and intelligent. Such a method starts from observation, and rises from particulars to universals. Those who from childhood have imbibed prejudiced views inimical to Plato's philosophy — which has been attacked in recent times not because it is false, but because it was thought to be accompanied by some sublime, spiritual element — imagine that it adopts a totally different method of argument and, beginning from hypotheses, descends to explaining facts. This is precisely what the sensists tell us not to do. But it is these people who, prior to any reasoning upon facts, show they have formed a mental hypothesis which they use to direct their mind in their examination of facts. I dare to say without fear of error that the method of reasoning used in Plato's dialogues is infinitely more rigorous and precise than that used by Aristotle. Why therefore do sensists think that they alone are privileged to observe nature and to reason correctly? The reason could be this: they have already targeted the results of the two philosophies. Their philosophy does not rise above matter; the opposite philosophy arrives at the spirit. But the hypothesis previously established in the sensists' minds states that spirit is purely a dream or, at least, that it is impossible to attain by reasoning. This is enough: anyone who arrives at the spirit must be wrong because he uses an inadequate method of reasoning.

[188] Nevertheless, progress was visible. Although Thales' followers taught only natural science, Anaxagoras, the third in line, abandoned the materialism of his master Anaximenes, and felt the need to posit a spirit with an existence of its own. As a youth, Socrates had listened to the aged Anaxagoras.

do not concern us'[189] he revealed the source of his ideas. His statement bore the imprint of the Ionian school which, by compelling human beings to discover truth purely by their own thinking, obliged them to shift their gaze from the consideration of sensible, natural phenomena, and presented them with a slow, laborious journey bristling with dangers. The transition from physical to moral considerations was itself seen as a miracle, and taken as the foundation of a new school. This transition was not, in fact, accomplished in stages, nor could it be; it was achieved in one leap by Socrates, a most extraordinary man who came to it not as a result of his own prompting, but swayed by the obvious needs of a more mature society. From that moment Ionian philosophy showed its insufficiency. The more society grows, the more it exhibits the need of ethical truths to survive. Socrates himself, after his tremendous endeavour to make the transition into the realm of ethical teaching, halted weary and exhausted, despite his great ability. To avoid forming a philosophy too onerous for humanity, he thought it better to throw out physical investigation, and as far as possible to banish metaphysical speculations which he considered superfluous to our human needs.

[189] Socrates himself complained about Plato's importing alien teachings (that is, those of Pythagoras) into his philosophy. See Brucker *Hist. Philos.*, part 2, c. 2. Xenophantes also accused Plato 'because, having abandoned the sober philosophy of Socrates and investigated too keenly the nature of the gods, he aspired after glory on the basis of much unsuitable, useless knowledge. Captivated by τερατολογία [marvellous tales] and the astounding wisdom of Egypt and Pythagoras, this gloomy teacher of wisdom lapsed into ridiculous views.'

Such was the admission of decadent mankind's total impotence — and it came from the greatest philosophers of the ancient world, such as Socrates and Xenophantes. The supreme endowment of mankind was intelligence which, after attaining the peak of its perfection, imposed limits upon itself which forbade the investigation of what was outstanding and sublime. Why such a limit? Because intelligence foresaw that the result of such investigation would probably have been much more dire than ignorance itself. Error is worse than ignorance. But Xenophantes, when he spoke about the *sobriety* of Socrates' philosophy, indicated a great humiliation for mankind! Man's rebellion against the Creator reduced not only the individual, but the species, so much that the entire achievement of human genius when abandoned to itself throughout antiquity consisted in transforming ignorance into virtue and encapsulating universal wisdom in the saying: 'This I know, that I know nothing.'

277. Plato, therefore, presented in his works philosophical arguments to which he added positive, traditional teachings. These, however, were inevitably altered because the people, amongst whom they circulate, are never faithful guardians of a teaching. People cannot tell the same story twice without adding or removing, exaggerating or diminishing elements according to the state of their extraordinarily fickle fancy and their ever unreliable passions.

Nevertheless, these popular doctrines, rendered strange and wonderful by absurdities, helped Plato to adorn his incomparable eloquence, to which he devoted so much care, and to use it to insinuate himself more easily into the minds and hearts of the multitude. But the fables, mixed with philosophical arguments and unwisely used to support them, were a cause of the war waged against Platonism. It was thought that the whole system would be ruined if it could be shown that the peripheral attractions with which Plato, another deceitful human being, bedecked and furnished it were absurd and false. Plato was sure he could achieve the impossible, that is, please at one and the same time both the sages and the corrupt society in which he lived.

The difference between these two species of teaching is obvious enough in the *Meno* and in my discussion of the origin of ideas. Having stated the difficulty of the origin of ideas to which I referred (that is, in order to discover some truth which we seek, we need some preconceived notion of it — otherwise we could not recognise what we are seeking if we bumped into it). Plato was not content to solve the problem by rational argument, but sought the assistance of positive, fable-like teaching. The distinction between the second and first type of teaching is evident in Plato's own words. When he expounds the first type of teaching, he argues in his usual vein; when he deals with the second, he suddenly halts rational argument and resorts to authorities of a higher order.

> *Socrates*: I have heard this from certain wise men and women skilled in divine things.
> *Meno*: What did they say?
> *Socrates*: They spoke what was true in a wonderful way.
> *Meno*: What was it? and who were they?
> *Socrates*: They were men and women devoted to sacred

things, and all those who took care to give adequate reasons for what they held. Moreover, Pindar and all the divine poets handed on things of this nature. See for yourself if these things are not true. According to our witnesses, the human spirit is immortal. Sometimes it leaves this world; it dies. Sometimes it returns. But it never perishes. This, they say, is why we should live as holy a life as possible. Those who have paid the penalty of ancient wretchedness to Proserpine are given their soul back by her every nine years and sent up to the sun until they become strong kings renowned for their glory, sagacity and wisdom, and are later known as saintly heroes amongst men. So the immortal spirit goes from one life to another repeatedly, and perceives everything in this world and the next until there is nothing more to be learned. No wonder that we can recall everything that pertains to virtue and about other things. Time was when we conceived them all. In fact, because all nature is intimately united and consistent with itself, the spirit's knowledge of all things enables it, once it has remembered something (we call this 'discipline'), to recall all other things if it unwearyingly perseveres in its researches. This explains why seeking and learning is recollection.[190]

In this passage, it is clear that Plato summoned traditional science, disfigured as it was by popular and poetic fables, to buttress his theory of ideas. But the mass of people just could not conceive how these innate ideas of Plato were able to exist in our minds prior to sense experience, or where they came from. It was in order to stimulate the minds of ordinary people that Plato used a story adapted to the popular mind to make his system more acceptable. In fact, it had the opposite effect, and later did great harm to the system. Time destroys falsehoods and often, along with them, the truths mistakenly associated with them. This goes on until such truths are completely detached

[190] I remarked earlier that Plato considered it necessary to accept all ideas in man as innate because he had not clearly seen how one arises and flows from the other. In this passage by Plato, it appears that he saw a connection between ideas and their mutual dependence. But although he realised there was a certain connection between ideas, which enabled him to explain their *association* and *recollection*, he did not understand the connection well enough to be able to infer the formation of them all from a single, first *mother-idea.*

from the falsehoods and made to stand on their own. Truth, when bereft of all other forms of support, remains unshakeable.

The story-like explanation which Plato gives of the introduction of ideas into the human soul is one thing; his philosophical system, worked out and established by purely rational arguments, is another. Yet Plato's greatest opponents usually take issue with the fabulous part of the system. They show that the theory by which human souls had existed in the stars before their incarnation, and then gone up and down several times as the body dies and frees them, was unwarranted, untrue and vile. They then go on to argue that Plato's system is an empty dream, a profane religion to be shunned,[191] as if the system consisted in the embellishment which Plato thought he could add to make it more attractive to popular imagination, and especially to the collective phantasy which served as the background to his writing.

---

[191] This was not the case with the early Fathers of the Church, especially St. Augustine. He distinguishes what is false and fictitious in Plato from what is philosophical and also true and attacks only the first part with the authority of Christian faith. He argues rationally in the case of the philosophical part. He uses the same weapons as his opponent: he overcomes the fictitious stories by means of revelation and deals with the rational part by the use of reason.

CHAPTER 2
Leibniz

Article 1
Leibniz saw the difficulty involved in explaining the origin of ideas

278. Leibniz was of an admirable, reasonable and conciliatory nature. Finding himself in disagreement with Locke, he adopted an extremely friendly and magnanimous approach, instead of intensifying and exaggerating the difference in their views. He was as accommodating as possible and adopted an approach which should always characterise two men of dissenting views when they are not imbued with a spirit of hostility and vanity but motivated by a genuine desire to understand one another and to pursue the truth together.

I have already pointed out that no reasonable person can dissent (unless motivated by a sense of pique or a desire to contradict) (cf. 235) when Locke states: 'I accept that man possesses a faculty of thought, a faculty for passing from sensations to ideas and thus forming judgments and rational arguments.' Consequently, this view needs to be taken as a common starting point from which to lead one's opponent to a deeper investigation. In other words, one should inquire how this faculty of thought is formed so that it can carry out the operations which Locke himself attributes to it. The aim is to see whether it is necessary to accept some innate element as essential in such a way that the being of the faculty depends upon it. Locke is not refuted over the general principle underpinning his system, but simply invited to deepen his inquiry into the human understanding. This was Leibniz's attitude, which he displayed with a spirit of magnanimity on a par with truth and power.

279. In the *New Essays* which Leibniz wrote on *Human Understanding* (published posthumously), Philalete, who defends Locke's position, accepts the view of Theophilus — a

pseudonym for Leibniz himself — that our potency for thought is innate. Theophilus raises no objection but merely points out to him that 'true faculties are never simple possibilities', and that 'they always contain both tendency and action'.[192]

Because Locke identified the potency for thought as a faculty for reflection upon one's own sensations and on the operations of the soul, Leibniz goes along with him and happily sets about analysing this faculty of reflection. In doing so, he finds that its acceptance does not necessarily imply contradiction of the theory of innate ideas properly understood, but rather an approach to it.

Leibniz writes of Locke:

> Perhaps the views of our gifted author and my own are not all that different. After spending the whole of the first volume of his work rejecting innate lights taken in one sense, he later admits (at the beginning of the second volume and from then on), that ideas, which do not have their origin in sensation, must come from reflection. But reflection simply means focusing upon what is already in us; the senses, however, do not furnish us with what we bear within us. If we accept this, we can surely affirm that our spirit contains a great deal that is innate, since we are innate to ourselves, so to speak. We can affirm the presence within us of being, unity, substance, duration, change, action, perception, pleasure and a thousand other objects pertaining to our intellectual ideas. Moreover, these objects are immediately and always present to our intellect, although they cannot be apperceived all the time[193] because of our various needs. We should not be astonished, therefore, when we say that these ideas are innate within us, along with everything else that depends on them.[194] I also

---

[192] Bk. 2, c. 1. This remark of Leibniz is fairly important but is not the whole picture; the *tendency to action* does not originate in the *subject*; the great man did not get as far as the *object*.

[193] Leibniz distinguished between perception and apperception; the former indicates a modification of our soul of which we are not conscious; the latter, a modification of which we are aware.

[194] In this passage, I merely wish to reveal the German philosopher's stance relative to his opponent. In fact, my impression is that Leibniz's argument falls down because he uses the phrase *innate ideas* in different senses. In the passage I am quoting here, he would seem to mean purely the matter of ideas

used the comparison of a piece of veined marble rather than that of marble pure and simple, or of clean tablets or *tabula rasa* as the philosophers say. If our minds were like *tabulae rasae*, truth would be present in us just as the statue of Hercules is present in a piece of marble which could in fact be given any shape. However, if the marble contained veins which outlined the shape of Hercules better than other shapes, it would be determined to that shape and Hercules could be said to be in some way innate in it. Work would still be needed, of course, to bring out those veins, to clean them and to chip away all the excess marble which prevents the statue from emerging. In the same way, ideas and truths are innate in us, as tendencies, dispositions, habits or natural possibilities, but not as actions at this stage. These possibilities, however, are always accompanied by some corresponding, but often insensible action.[195]

Further on, he touches on this feeling of his in other words:

The axiom handed down by philosophers: *there is nothing in the mind that does not come from the senses*, will be used as an objection to what I am saying. However, an exception has to be made of the soul and its affections: *Nihil est in intellectu quod non fuerit in sensu; excipe: nisi ipse*

or ideas acquired from the first moment of our existence. What he says is: 1. we bear within us the matter of our ideas; 2. from the very first moment of our existence we bear within us our intellect; 3. our intellect cannot be inactive because it obviously has its matter to hand. It is inevitable then that it continues to receive all these ideas from the first moment of its existence. However, in many other passages, *innate ideas* for Leibniz seem to mean ideas so essential to the intellect itself that without them there could be no concept of intellect. It is at these points that he describes ideas as virtually active in the intellect. It is essential not to change these senses which are inevitably confused if words are used in different ways. It is, in fact, quite different to inquire whether there are *innate ideas* in one sense, or whether there are *innate ideas* in another sense. To inquire whether our understanding, as soon as it exists, has matter on which to operate and thus to form ideas immediately, is more a question of fact than anything else. It is not absurd to imagine it without these ideas, at least by some abstraction. On the other hand, to enquire whether the intellect itself is the intuition of some idea and a potency for using that idea to reason — so that denial of the idea is denial of the intellect, — is a question which involves the nature of the understanding, not fact.

[195] *Nouveaux Essais, etc.*, Preface.

intellectus [There is nothing in the intellect that was not first in the senses, except the intellect itself]. Now, the soul contains being, substance, oneness, identity, cause, perception, reasoning and many other notions which the senses could not have provided.[196] This concurs substantially with Locke's *Essay* which attempts to infer many of the ideas from the reflection which the mind undertakes upon its own nature.[197]

From these passages, it is perfectly obvious that Leibniz felt, although somewhat confusedly, the difficulty we have been examining. He realised that a faculty for thought, shorn completely of any notion, was inevitably a contradiction. It would mean speaking of a faculty without a faculty, of a potency that is not a potency. The simple acceptance of an innate potency of thought in an innate intellect (he says to Locke) means acceptance of some innate notion or idea through which the intellective soul can exert its power on the sensations it has received and on itself[198] — provided, of course, that 'intellect' has been thoroughly understood.

Article 2

The analysis of potencies in general, not the particular analysis of the intellective potency, led Leibniz to the difficulty

280. However Leibniz, although shrewd enough to realise that it was impossible to explain how the soul could think without some innate element, did not come to a knowledge of this truth by a close analysis of the nature of the power of the intellectual potency. He deduced it from a highly speculative

[196] Even this argument of Leibniz is not sufficiently precise. If he is speaking here universally about the idea of *being*, of substance, etc. our soul could not furnish it to our understanding better than the senses can because the soul, too, is a particular ens, substance, etc., like bodies. *Substance, as universal*, the object of our mind, possesses something not found in bodies or in the soul. This 'something' is its *universality*.

[197] *Nouveaux Essais, etc.*, bk. 2, c. 1.

[198] This sentiment, too, is expressed in the previous quotations from Leibniz, although not so clearly because it is mixed up with other things.

principle, that is, from the common nature of all the potencies which he realised he knew well.

In one passage, he says

> It will be objected that this *tabula rasa* of the philoso-phers implies that the soul has naturally and initially only 'raw' faculties. But faculties without any acts are, in a word, pure potencies in the scholastic sense, mere fictions unknown to nature which result from abstractions made by the mind. After all, where in the universe can we find a faculty which enjoys mere potentiality without exercising any act [*App.*, no. 22]. There is always some particular dis-position to action and to one type of action rather than an-other. In addition to this disposition, there is a tendency to action, indeed, an infinite number of tendencies at every moment in each subject. All these tendencies produce some effect. Experience is necessary, I admit, for the soul to be determined to one thought rather than another and to become aware of the ideas within us. But I do not see how experience and the senses can furnish us with ideas. Does the soul have windows? Is it like a *tabula rasa*? Is it like wax? Clearly, all who think of the soul along these lines see it fundamentally as corporeal.[199]

281. Thus Leibniz recognises the danger of all these analogies when discussing the soul. It is precisely by the use of such im-agery that the followers of Locke endeavour to explain their system although they then go on to claim in all earnestness that only their method of argument is strict and rigorous. According to them, all their opponents are guilty of resorting to imagina-tion rather than reasoning, merely because they disagree with them and are unhappy with the sense-based analogies to which Locke's followers contentedly resort. In fact, if we rule out such gross analogies (this is the force of Leibniz's argument) as win-dows of the soul, of wax, of the *tabula rasa*, and consider the soul as it is, as a mere potency for thought, we will see, if we look carefully, that we must inevitably attribute to it some act because there is no potency of any kind without its particular act. Now, if this act is to correspond to the potency to which it belongs, the act of the faculty of knowledge must contain some

---

[199] *Nouveaux Essais*, etc., bk. 2, c. 1.

type of knowledge, some innate notion or idea which forms the term and object of the act. In this way, the argument Leibniz uses to recognise the need to accept an innate element in the human spirit was similar to Aristotle's proof that the origin of human knowledge could not be explained without positing an *acting intellect*, that is, an intellect which would be originally and naturally in act. 'A perception is only produced from another perception, as movement arises naturally only from movement.' Brucker expounds the Leibnizian theory in words which would appear to have come from the mouth of Aristotle himself.[200]

Article 3

Leibniz sees the difficulty imperfectly because he deduces it from over-general principles

282. Nevertheless, there is a difference between Aristotle and Leibniz. Aristotle realised the need of his acting intellect from a study of the particular potency of knowledge. He saw that the actual ideas of this potency could not be explained unless it was in act from the beginning. Leibniz, on the other hand, realised the need to allocate some primal act to the intellect from his examination of the nature of potencies in general. According to him, they were inevitably endowed with some act in order to be potencies.

However, to infer the need to accept some innate notion from the nature of potency in general, as Leibniz did, is to take too rarefied a view and fail to grasp the question: 'Does the formation of human cognitions require something innate for its conception and explanation?' Leibniz does not get to the very heart of the matter, but tries to explain it by means of some extrinsic principle. This is a thoroughly risky approach which, as we shall see, produces some flaws in Leibniz's system. Leibniz saw the difficulty, therefore, but only in a general way. He saw that the formation of ideas demanded some preceding idea, but did not see the proper, particular approach in which I outlined this

[200] *Period* 3, part 2, bk. 1, c. 8.

[282]

need. At least, he did not see clearly that the faculty for forming ideas was inevitably a faculty which presupposed some idea by means of which it formed judgments and, through judgments, all other ideas.

Article 4

Leibniz's solution to the difficulty

283. Here then are Leibniz's conclusions:

The senses cannot produce the soul's primal perceptions; the body cannot exercise any activity on the soul;[201] no created ens can truly act upon another; nor can the potency of these entia go outside its own sphere, that is, move out of itself by its action and enter other entia; all changes undergone by an ens, therefore, only proceed from some principle within itself which has the ability to develop according to a determined pattern of changes; these changes, harmonised by God through certain fixed laws compatible with the changes in other entia, make us believe that some, which stably precede others, are causes of the others, although they are, in fact, merely co-existent. This was the theory of Leibniz's famous *pre-established harmony.*

The principle that all changes undergone by an ens proceed solely from an inner force of that ens, which develops and unfolds in a determined series of movements, was used by Leibniz to express the origin of ideas which are represented to our mind successively as a series of alterations or changes occurring in it.

Leibniz, therefore, imagined that all ideas were already in our

[201] This is not due to the intrinsically distinct natures of body and soul. For Leibniz, the body was merely a union of simple monads, each with its perceptions, so that, in one sense, he calls them souls. He ruled out any physical impulse because of his general principle: 'No created ens can exercise a real action upon some other ens and effect a change in it.' All changes in every ens were due inevitably to a principle within the ens itself. This was the concept of the *potency* for action which Leibniz had formed for himself. Nevertheless, he sometimes appears to forget his general principle, which underpins his whole system, and halts before the disparate nature of body and spirit.

mind from the beginning because of the nature of the mind. However, they would be present insensibly without our being aware of them. He called these ideas *perceptions*, to distinguish them from *apperceptions* which also were ideas, but ideas of which we had already become conscious.

284. He maintains, therefore, that ideas are different from thought. Consequently, they may be found in the soul without any actual thought, that is, without any act of attention by the soul on the idea itself:

> For cognitive facts, ideas or truths to be in our spirit we do not need to have actually thought about them. They are merely natural *habits*, that is, active and passive dispositions and attitudes and something more than a *tabula rasa*.[202]

Philalete, Locke's disciple offers the usual objection to this:

> But is it not true that the idea is the object of thought?

Theophilus answers:

> I grant you that, provided you add that it is an immediate, internal object, and that this object is an expression of the nature or qualities of things. If the idea were the form of thought, it would originate and cease with the actual thought corresponding to it. But because it is the object of thought, the idea can be prior or subsequent to thoughts.[203] Sensible, external objects are mediated only because they are unable to act immediately upon the soul. We would say that the soul itself is its own inner immediate object, but only in so far as it contains ideas which correspond to things. The soul is a little world in which distinct ideas are a representation of God, and indistinct ideas a representation of the Universe.[204]

---

[202] *Nouveaux Essais*, etc., bk. 1.

[203] If the word *thought* is reserved to indicate a reflective act, I agree; but I cannot conceive *idea* without *intuition*.

[204] *Nouveaux Essais*, etc., bk. 2, c. 1. In this passage, Leibniz says that the soul is the object of the intellect in so far as it contains ideas, because ideas are the proximate object of the intellect. Agreed: but this is quite different from saying, as he does elsewhere, that the intellect forms the ideas of being, substance, etc. because the soul perceives that it is all these things. In this

285. Thus, Leibniz admitted two innate elements in the mind: 1. the non-sensible ideas of all things; 2. certain instincts by means of which we are moved to reflect upon the ideas themselves, actually to think of them and thus to acquire consciousness or apperception of them. Because these instincts differ in each person from birth, they produce a series of different thoughts in each, and serve to prompt each person to reflect upon some rather than other innate ideas found in the depth of the spirit.

> It is essential that in this welter of cognitions, we should be determined by something to recall one idea rather than another. In fact, it is impossible to think distinctly at any given moment about everything we know.[205]

In short, Leibniz pictured each idea as a kind of tiny potency on its own, as an *ens* having power to incline the mind to itself. Because of this, he often calls ideas instincts, attitudes, dispositions, and so on, as though they were vying to acquire a higher degree of enlightenment in the mind and to arouse themselves by producing actual consciousness of themselves in us. Because the activity of these instincts differs from person to person, people are internally stimulated to one thought rather than others, that is, to reflect actually upon certain ideas rather than upon them all.[206]

Leibniz, therefore, made ideas emerge from the depths of our spirit. But let us see once more how he explained that some ideas were contained in others, and how we are able to come to a distinct awareness of new ideas solely by the development of a single idea.

second case, the soul is the real object of the intellect just as its object is all the physical things it knows. Confusing these quite different things is a frequent mistake in our philosopher.

[205] *Nouveaux Essais*, etc., bk. 1, c. 1.

[206] 'Every feeling is the perception of a truth and a natural feeling is the perception of an innate truth which is very often indistinct' (*Nouveaux Essais*, etc., bk. 1, c. 2).

Article 5

How Leibniz's innate ideas can all successively attain an enlightened state

286. First, we should recall another Leibnizian principle derived from his meditations on the nature of potencies in general. He was unable to conceive of potencies and entia other than purely simple ones, that is, without parts.

But because these were all inevitably different from one another, he could not picture any difference other than that of perceptions in simple entia.

He therefore attributed perceptions to all his simple entities, called *monads*, although he did not attribute consciousness of perceptions to them all.

287 On this assumption, the original connection between ideas in the human soul is the following.

First, the soul has the ideas of those simple entia or monads of which its body is composed and from which it is derived. These ideas we can call *A, B, C, D*, etc. But the soul cannot have the idea *A* except by picturing to itself all *A*'s perceptions, which determine and individualise *A*. The soul, therefore, in perceiving *A* perceives all *A*'s perceptions.

Let us now assume that *A*'s perceptions are the perceptions of the monads *a, b, c, d*, etc. The soul which has *A* represented in itself, necessarily has a representation of the other series of monads *a, b, c, d*, etc. The same argument may be applied to *B, C, D*, etc. in particular, and then to *a, b, c, d*, etc. in particular. Indeed, each of these monads also has the perception of other monads so that, in perceiving *a, b, c, d*, etc. the monads whose representations they possess are also perceived as enclosed within them.

It is now easy to see that such an argument enables us to scan successfully all the monads in the universe and observe that the perceptions of these monads are enclosed in each other just as seeds seem to be indefinitely enfolded in one other. Consequently, the mind which perceives *A, B, C*, etc. perceives in them the whole universe. This is the representation of the universe which Leibniz attributed to all his monads. In this representation, the perceptions which had more instinctive impact, or greater power to attract the soul's attention as individuals, were given greater prominence.[207] Such a picture of the universe which Leibniz called the *Scheme* of the monad was — as we might gather from our previous discussion — necessarily different in each monad, because the first perceptions in each were completely different, together with the order in which the first monads enclosed and enfolded the others.

> Just as the same town, when seen from different viewpoints, does not seem the same and takes multiple forms, so to speak, according to the different viewpoints, so the infinite number of simple substances somehow causes the same number of universes which are only different representations of the same universe according to the different viewpoints of each monad.

Article 6

Leibniz's merit in dealing with this problem

288. One issue which escaped Locke's notice was that of tiny perceptions or, to put it more correctly, of unreflected perceptions.

This phenomenon was carefully observed by Leibniz whose lofty intellect found in it a rich philosophical seam; here, I think, lies his greatest merit in our difficulty.

Locke so radically ignores the existence within us of feeling experiences and information which remain in us untouched by reflection that he would exclude from the soul any kind of virtual knowledge. Leibniz observes:

> This is such a paradox that Locke cannot have wanted us to take his words literally. After all, it is an everyday occurrence for us to casually recall things which we have forgotten. This proves that those ideas were already virtually in our minds.[208]

---

[207] See the *Theses for Prince Eugene* published by Leibniz in 1714.

[208] *Nouveaux Essais*, etc., bk. 1, c. 1.

289. The German philosopher establishes the fact of unreflected perceptions when he says:

> Moreover, while our opponents, although highly able, offer not the slightest proof of what they assert so often and with so much conviction, it is also easy to demonstrate to them that the contrary is true, that is, that we could not possibly reflect on every individual thought; otherwise the spirit would reflect upon each thought *ad infinitum* without ever producing a new thought. For example, if I become aware of some present feeling — in other words, I am thinking about it — I would always have to think that I am thinking of the feeling, and so on *ad infinitum*. But it is also necessary for me to stop reflecting on all these reflections. In the end, I have to possess some thought which I let pass in me without reflecting on it. Otherwise, we would continually be returning to the same thought.[209]

290. This argument proves not only the fact, but the need for the fact, to ensure that some thought of ours is completed. Leibniz makes the same point in confirmation of his theory and bolsters it by reflections which I consider worthy of attention. Such a fact is easily lost sight of and it is of the utmost importance in the history of philosophy. It cannot be over-emphasised.
Leibniz says in one passage:[210]

> There are many instances which show that we have within us at any given moment an infinite number of perceptions[211] though without apperceptions and without reflection upon them. These changes in the soul remain undetected because the impressions are too slight,[212] or too numerous, or too closely connected. In other words, they have nothing distinctive which makes them stand out individually. Each of them is linked to others and, as a

---

[209] *Nouveaux Essais*, etc., bk. 2, c. 1.

[210] *Nouveaux Essais*, etc., bk. 1, c. 1.

[211] The word *perception* has an extremely wide connotation in Leibniz's philosophy, and comprises all thoughts.

[212] Not because they are too *slight* (if we are speaking of ideas) but because they are not subjected to reflection. Sensations may be *slight*; ideas cannot be slight, though they can be *unobserved* or not considered closely and with concentration by the mind.

result, does not produce its own effect or make even an indistinct impact on the whole. This explains why we pay no attention to the operation of a mill or a waterfall to which we are accustomed because we have lived close to them for a long time.

In another passage, he adds:

To illustrate more graphically the presence in us of such slight perceptions which we are unable to distinguish from one another because of their profusion, I usually use the example of the roaring of the sea, or of the roar which assails us when we are standing on its shores. For us to be able to hear this roar — and we do indeed hear it — we have to hear the different elements[213] which make up the roar as a whole. In other words, we have to hear the murmur of each wave, although each of these tiny murmurings can only be heard in the overall confused roaring with all the others, and would not be noted if the wave causing it were the only one. We have to be affected in some small way by the movement of such a wave and have some perception of each of these murmurs, however tiny they may be. If not, we would never have the perception of a hundred thousand waves; one hundred thousand nothings could not add up to something [*App.*, no. 23]. On the other hand, one never sleeps so deeply as to banish all faint, confused feeling. In fact, some individuals would not be woken by the greatest din in the world if they had no perception of its initial, faint beginning, just as a string would never snap by being pulled with maximum force if it had not first been stretched and lengthened by a less powerful

---

[213] Leibniz therefore assumes that the slight sounds, by means of which we acquire an *apperception* of the complex of many sounds, are heard. If so, he would seem to be in clear contradiction with himself here and in other places where he describes *perception* as a true *sensation*. However, assuming that we do actually feel the perception without reflecting on it, I would maintain that occasionally this *perception* may be produced perfectly well by a great number of lesser perceptions but not by an infinite number, as will be seen from the comments I make in the next note. If such were the case, the act of the spirit would be simple, but would terminate in what is multiple, or the multiple would be perceived in what is simple, and again, many would be perceived by one. This fact cannot be more difficult to accept than that of the union of two terms in judgment.

force, although this tension and successive extension may
remain unobserved.[214]

291. Locke's objection to innate ideas, that is, if they existed,
we would be aware of them from the very first days of our existence because things of which we are unaware can have no virtual existence in our spirit, is utterly frivolous. This is belied by
the extremely obvious fact noted and exploited by Leibniz, that
is, the existence of some perceptions of which we are not actually aware. Examples of this are ideas which, although not actually present to the spirit, can be recalled at will, or present
themselves to us through association with fortuitous incidents
to which they are bound and referred. Similarly, we continually
receive perceptions which because of their faintness or weakness, or of their number, or some other cause, elude our attention as they come and go within us without our noticing them.
In a word, it is one thing for some idea or perception to exist in
our spirit and quite another for us to be actually thinking about
it. It can be present without our thinking of it. We have it, therefore, but we do not know we have it. Not knowing that we have
it, we cannot talk about it. We can, in fact, think and assert that
we do not have an idea while we do, in fact, possess it.

This, says Leibniz, is the way I assume that all ideas of things
exist in the human soul: they are present within us as *non-
sensible perceptions*[215] like the statue already faintly designed in
white marble by slender reddish, yellowish or other coloured
veins which can be used as a guide by the stone-cutter to extract
it. The artist uses this trick of nature in the marble to design the
statue. In Leibniz's view, therefore, the development of the
intellectual faculties would consist entirely in the soul's efforts
to ensure that the ideas it contained in outline were rendered

---

[214] *Nouveaux Essais*, etc., Preface.

[215] The phrase, *non-sensible perceptions*, indicates that in this passage
Leibniz is not self-consistent. As I remarked earlier, he sometimes describes
perceptions as *felt* by us, though devoid of *apperception*. However, it should be
noted that *sensation* is quite different from the *thought* which we have of
sensation. We are aware of having *sensation* only because we think about it.
Without thought, we would have *sensations* in the soul (quite distinct from the
external *impression* upon our body), but not know that it was taking place.
Animals have sensation unaccompanied by thought.

[291]

more noticeable and strong by reflection, which enables us to become aware of them, actually to intuit them, and to be able to discuss them with others.

292. Leibniz makes great play of this multitude of slight perceptions originating within us; he uses them to explain almost all facts of the spirit.

> It is these which make up these mysterious elements, these tastes, these images of sensible qualities clear in their overall form, but indistinct in their parts. They produce the impressions which bodies around us have upon us and which contain the infinite; they link each ens to the rest of the universe. We could also say that, as a result of these tiny perceptions, the present is pregnant with the future and full with the past: that everything conspires together, σμπνοια πάντα, as Hippocrates said; that in the tiniest substances, the whole series of things in the universe — *Quae sunt, quae fuerint, quae mox futura trahantur* [which now are, which once were and which the future will shortly bring forth] — is open to the penetrating gaze of God.[216]

Article 7

Leibniz posited fewer innate elements than Plato

293. Leibniz tells us in certain passages that he posits in the spirit more that is innate than Plato did. He admits not only *remembrance*, but *presentiment*.

However, we do not have to take this statement of Leibniz as literally true. Presentiment of the future comes as much from Plato's ideas as from Leibniz's tiny perceptions; and there were several Platonists who deduced from ideas not only presentiment but prophecy, divination and enthusiasm.

294. If, therefore, we consider the two systems in themselves, and ignore their consequences, I think we can say that Leibniz posited less that was innate in the human mind than Plato did.

Plato claimed that, here below, our mind bears within it all ideas. We are like people who learn, but then forget. We have all

---

[216] *Nouveaux Essais, etc.*, Preface.

ideas, completely formed, but have forgotten them. All we need do is recall them. On the other hand, Leibniz describes them as the tiniest vestiges of ideas, like veins in marble or the delicate fissuring in a wooden board. Leibniz's innate ideas are the outlines of ideas rather than fully finished ideas; it is the instinctive activity of the mind which brings them into existence and perfects them. To do this, it requires more than the mere act of remembrance.[217]

Article 8

Leibniz posits more that is innate than is required to explain the fact of ideas

295. I have no doubt that Leibniz, if he focused upon the fact of ideas and had been content to explain it, would have inevitably been led to the correct solution by his perceptive mind.

However, instead of concentrating directly on the acts of the intellective potency, he focused, as I said, on potencies in general. This led him to accept the presence in the mind of more that is innate than is actually required. What happened was this.

Because he had not established sufficiently the nature of the intellective potency and of ideas, he was unable to avail himself of the intimate link between ideas which enables one to generate another. One consequence of this is that the vestiges of all ideas need not be admitted as innate. Leibniz could have accepted as innate the one, single idea which gives birth to all others.

As I said, the problem consists in explaining how we first begin to form judgments. If there is only one innate idea, we already have enough, because use of this one idea enables us to have, at our convenience, a series of judgments. These judgments can produce other ideas with which we form further

[217] Philalete, in the work already quoted, objects to Theophilus that proofs derived from sense experience are needed if we are to grant the existence of innate ideas. Theophilus replies: 'This question is decided in the way we prove we have imperceptible bodies and invisible movements, although certain persons ridicule the notion. Thus there are perceptions which are so slight that they cannot be *apperceived* and recalled, but are known through certain consequences' (*N. Essais, etc.*, bk. 2, c. 1).

judgments, and so on. It is necessary, therefore, to examine closely the genealogy of ideas. This leads us to see that they all come from one stock, a first idea, *the essence of ideas*, through which alone we come to possess in its fullness the faculty of judgment. Leibniz was not greatly interested in this kind of inquiry and, as a result, was unable to reduce innate ideas to a single, primal idea, the head and origin of all others.

I do not mean that Leibniz did not see how one idea was deduced from another. I am saying that he did not make as much use of this principle as he could have done. If he had done so, a single idea, with the addition of sensations, would have been sufficient to serve as a source of all other ideas and cognitions. Instead Leibniz posited in the soul the perception of the universe and of all the individual things which the universe embraces — an infinite number, according to Leibniz [*App.*, no. 24].

Article 9

Other errors in Leibniz's theory

296. Leibniz was prevented from seeing this, I repeat, by his concentration on general metaphysical principles rather than on the human being to whom those principles were to apply.

This resulted, I feel, in his failure to grasp fully the distinction, so difficult to understand, between *sensations* and *ideas*.

Having established his principle that the body could not exercise any real action upon the spirit, he was obliged to derive ideas as well as sensations from the same internal energy of the human soul. After this, it was easy to confuse the two or to be casual about establishing their completely different natures.

297. 'Sensation,' he maintains, 'occurs in us when we *apperceive* an external object,'[218] that is, not only when we perceive it in line with the distinction he makes between perceive

---

[218] *Nouveaux Essais*, etc. bk. 2, c. 19. Leibniz's definition shows that his *perception* is something lacking *sense*. This is the opposite of what he has said elsewhere. I cannot myself agree with him: an *unthought, unadverted sensation* is a *perception* for me in so far as it apprehends a foreign term. If it is adverted to or thought, it could usefully be called *apperception*.

and apperceive, but rather when we are aware that we perceive it.

But sensation, although it has a *term*, has no *object*, which pertains to the understanding. Leibniz confuses the two orders.

298. Next, we are aware of our perception when we are thinking about it. If, therefore, *sensation* is not, in fact, perception but *being aware* of perception, it becomes *thought* itself. This confusion between *sensation* and *thought* threatens once more to confuse the *order of real things* and the *order of ideal things*.

In fact, sensation refers to something real; thought reflects upon what is real and compares it with what is ideal [*App.*, no. 25]. Consequently, every thought contains something universal. Sensation, on the other hand, contains nothing universal; all is particular and real.

299. This explains why Leibniz, in so many passages, inadvertently confuses the world of real *entia* with the world of abstractions, and in his argument moves back and forward from one to the other without noticing clearly the infinite distance between them.

The following is one example of such imprecision.[219]

Having distinguished between necessary and non-necessary truths, Leibniz is unaware that the former can be only universal truths, that is, truths which involve the mere possibility of things, if we exclude the case of God who is the only real, necessary *ens*. Consequently, wanting to prove that necessary truths cannot be deduced from the senses, he goes on as follows: 'If some happenings can be foreseen before we have any proof of them, it is obvious that we must have contributed something of our own to foresee them.[220]

Fundamentally, this argument contains a precious truth, but an error needs to be noted. Leibniz was well aware that our imagination cannot extend to anything not previously perceived by the senses. He knew it perfectly well, and immediately adds:

[219] I have quoted others earlier in the footnote to 280 [cf. *App.*, no. 22].

[220] *N. Essais, etc.*, Preface. The argument is perfectly sound if we bear in mind that even a forecast based on a mere conjecture requires universals in the human spirit, in the same way as any comparison between one thing and another. Anything common in a number of things is always a universal, an idea.

[298–299]

'The senses are necessary for all our actual cognitions although they are not sufficient to provide us with them all.'[221] But he asks: 'Among the things of which we actually have an idea when we are stimulated by the senses, is there any instance in which we can foresee with complete security and necessity that such a thing, such an occurrence, will take place?' If we can have such foresight, he says, it cannot come from the senses. They only furnish examples and instances and an argument by induction and analogy which never constitutes necessity.

Even so, he continues, there is no doubt that we *do* sometimes have the faculty to foresee events. It follows that we must also have something innate which furnishes us with this necessity which is not derived from the senses. Yes, but how does he prove to us that we have the faculty to foresee events with apodictic certainty? [*App.*, no. 26]. He cites the example of Euclid who, from the principles he lays down, induces necessary consequences. Here, Leibniz has certainly confused the world of abstractions with the world of realities. Euclid's example is valid for the world of abstractions; he simply deduced abstract truths from abstract principles. But predicting future events pertains to the world of realities, and the possibility of such prediction cannot be inferred from the possibility of deriving the truths of *pure geometry* from their principles.

Leibniz, therefore, unduly extends the potency of *a priori* reasoning. In other words, he is not content with establishing the limits of its dominion within the reign of abstract truths or of mere possibilities, all of which are immutable and necessary. He allows them to descend to the world of real things[222] where they are suitable for foreseeing some events with absolute certainty, although their necessity is merely hypothetical.

As I said, given the nature of his system, Leibniz was bound to do this. In accepting that the spirit contained the innate

---

[221] *N. Essais, etc., ibid.*

[222] Leibniz, if he had merely attributed to *a priori* reasoning the demonstration of the existence of God, would have been within proper limits. God is the *necessary reality*, and the presence in reason of a necessary principle from which to deduce the necessary reality is not absurd. But contingent things could have only *moral necessity*, which Leibniz was actually pursuing. But I shall be dealing with this issue later.

representation of all things in the universe, he presupposed in the nature of such a spirit not only *ideas* but the *perceptions* of all the real things which go to make up the entire universe. It was natural, therefore, for him to admit that the human spirit drew from itself and, as he put it, from its *own depth* concrete as well as abstract truths (concrete truths relate to real things). This is the origin of Leibnizian *presentiment*, that is, the faculty of foreseeing events by means of reasoning.

Article 10

Concluding remarks on Leibniz's theory

300. From what I have said, it can be established that Leibniz

1. Posited too much of what is innate by accepting as innate all ideas and the very perceptions of real things. A single idea is sufficient to explain the formation of all other ideas, granted the presence of sensations to the spirit,[223] as we shall see.

2. Extended unduly the force of *a priori* reasoning. He was not content with granting it the abstract fields of possibility and the real fields of probability, but attributed to it the right to descend, by necessary reasoning, to real contingent things, which it would sometimes foresee with certainty without any need for experiment. Leibniz's system therefore is excessive relative to both its heads, *remembrance* and *presentiment*.

Leibniz's *remembrance* goes too far because although it does not consist, as Plato's did, in the simple recall of ideas but rather in activity which intensifies the light perfecting and fulfilling them, it still remains a potency which does nothing except give greater prominence to what previously exists in the soul. On the other hand, it seems obvious at first glance — and emerges more clearly after analysis — that the potency for

---

[223] In Leibniz's view, organic sensation seems merely to be the occasion when we become aware of the idea, present within us, of an external *ens*. Such an occasion stimulates the act of the instinctive energy with which Leibniz endows ideas.

reasoning consists also in generating new ideas or concepts by means of the judgments which this potency first makes on sensations. It can form these judgments as soon as it is given a single, completely universal idea to use as an examplar or norm to judge whatever sensations put before it. Nothing more is required to explain such a marvellous feature of the spirit as reasoning.

Leibnizian *presentiment* goes too far because the mind can never deduce any future occurrence except by conjecture or under certain conditions. For example, if the sun rises tomorrow with nothing to impede its action, I foresee that it will shed its light near and far.

CHAPTER 3
Kant

Article 1
Kant uncritically accepts Locke's principle of experience

301. Kant came onto the philosophical scene at a time when modern philosophy had already made some headway.

He combined a thoroughly analytical mind with a profound study of previous philosophers; to some extent he opposed them all; to some extent he also agreed with them all.

Nevertheless, the outward form of his eclecticism was so original in its expression and so regular in its form that it seemed a new system, perfectly coherent and wonderfully put together.

The spirit of his age, by which he was thoroughly influenced, tended towards Locke whose philosophy had undergone various changes and met hostility from various quarters. Kant went along with his age and took a further step in the same direction.

302. In commencing this brief, obligatory exposé of his system, I wish to point out that he adhered without prior investigation to Locke's principle that all our cognitions are derived from experience [*App.*, no. 27]. 'However,' he adds, 'if all our cognitions come from our experience, it is necessary for us: 1. to investigate the nature and various species of our cognitions; 2. to see how experience can transmit all cognitions to us.'

In this he was correct: Locke had begun by explaining the origin of our cognitions. This was a departure from the sound method in philosophy, a hasty pursuit of cause before getting to know and examine facts. The facts were human cognitions which Locke should first have examined carefully. He should have obtained an intimate knowledge of their nature, analysed them, pointed out their constituent elements, classified them and sorted them into all their species. Explaining the origins of human cognitions amounts to assigning them a cause proportioned to their nature, from which they are derived or may be derived. However, before a suitable, proportioned cause can be assigned, we first need to address the issue of the qualities and parts of the effect without which the inquiry cannot begin. As a result of this procedural error, Locke, instead of beginning his inquiry at the natural starting point, plunged in 'half-way'. He attempted the impossible, that is, to explain what he did not yet know because he had failed to examine it.

Article 2

In opposing Locke, Kant adopted Leibniz's approach

303. In attacking Locke from this quarter, Kant adopted Leibniz's approach.

Leibniz had challenged Locke on the issue of the *faculties* of the spirit; Kant challenged Locke on the issue of the *cognitions* produced by these faculties. Both argued in the same way. Leibniz had stated: I am willing to agree that, in attributing to the human spirit a reflective faculty over and above sensitivity, all human cognitions are explicable. The whole issue consists in seeing whether this *reflective faculty* can exist without being endowed with innate concepts. Kant said to Locke: I am willing to concede that all human cognitions come from experience. The whole issue consists in seeing whether *experience*, which produces all the knowledge we have, is possible if it furnishes the spirit with sensations alone.

Kant was pointing out that it is one thing to say: 'All our cognitions come from experience' and another to say: 'All our cognitions come from the senses.'[224]

---

[224] Kant does not always appear consistent in his evaluation of *experience*. When he says: 'All our knowledge begins *with* experience, but not all our knowledge is derived *from* experience' (*Critique of Pure Reason*, Introduction 1), he uses the word *experience* relative to our senses. On the other hand, when he asks: 'How is experience possible?' (*ibid.*, 2), he seems to be using experience as the source of all our cognitions, and to distinguish it from the senses. In this case, he takes the word *experience* to mean the acts of our spirit, which are a combination of sensitivity and intelligence. As a rule, however, he attributes the first meaning to the word *experience*. For myself, I prefer to use it in the second way because I think that this brings out better the essential core of Kant's thinking. In doing this, I am straying somewhat from

There is no doubt, he says, that we have no knowledge at all before we have any experience, that is, before we make use of our faculties. But does this mean that our experience is obtained purely through our sensitivity? This is a quite different question; in order to answer it, we need to know what the fruit of our experience is (cognitions), and to see whether this fruit can be the product of sensitivity alone.

Article 3

Two types of knowledge, one *a priori*, the other a *posteriori*, are admitted by all philosophical schools

304. The first task to be undertaken by any philosopher is the investigation of the different species of human knowledge; the second, assuming that they all derive from experience, is to inquire into the *conditions* necessary for such experience[225] to

his habitual mode of expression, but not from the substance of his philosophy. I warn my readers of this so that they can, if necessary, make adjustments to the terms I use.

[225] As a rule, modern philosophers accept that all human knowledge comes from *experience* but without asking what experience is.

Is *experience* perhaps *facts*? Facts alone cannot constitute experience because until *facts* are known by me they are, relative to my knowledge, non-existent.

Nor can *experience* be taken to mean *facts* known to me. If this is the meaning of *experience*, we would have to inquire about the kind of *knowledge* under discussion. It would be absurd to maintain that experience is facts *known* by *sense* alone. When I say that I know a fact by sense alone, I have removed all thought from the fact. In such a case, facts are sensations and nothing more; there is no contact between them, no connection of any kind. These facts *known* by the senses alone — an incorrect expression if ever there was one — can neither be written or spoken about, because language does not have individual words suitable to express them and because, if I connect them to some sensible sign to make them speakable, I would have to reflect upon them. But this runs counter to the assumption that they are known to me through sense alone, and nothing else.

Experience, therefore, will be facts which are truly known; this inevitably brings in the *intelligence* which endows them with some universality by considering individual facts in relationship to being and, in being, in their relation to one another. Thus they form classes or species. This kind of experience can and does produce our cognitions. But if this is the *experience*

[304]

provide us with all the different types of cognitions which we have identified. I shall examine both tasks.

Prior to Kant, all philosophers without exception had realised and accepted as an obvious fact that our cognitions are of two kinds. They distinguished them by calling them *a priori* and *a posteriori* cognitions. This distinction we owe to the scholastic philosophers, who took it from the ancients. We can say, therefore, that it has the support of every age.

305. Let us confine ourselves to showing that it is accepted by modern philosophers who are otherwise deeply divided.

Descartes accepted *a priori* knowledge and in it alone found the source of certitude. Locke recognises the distinction to which I am referring. He writes:

> When ideas, whose agreement or disagreement we perceive, are abstract, our knowledge is *universal*. For what is known of such universal ideas is always true of every particular thing in which that essence,[226] the abstract idea, is found; and anything once known about these ideas has to be continually and eternally true.

Note his immediate conclusion:

> All general knowledge must be sought and found only in

we mean when we assert that all our cognitions come from experience, we first have to discover the nature of our *intellective knowledge of facts* and the nature of the *intellect* which we use to form or, at least, complete this experience. We also have to examine how such a faculty of knowledge must be constituted to be capable of having such experience. In other words, we want to know if this faculty has anything innate, and if so, what. This again amounts to discovering the *conditions* which make such experience possible.

226 Locke uses the word *essence*, but in other passages maintains that we have not the slightest knowledge of *essence*. This is the eternal contradiction to be faced by all philosophers determined to banish from the field of human knowledge something which mankind cannot forego. They specifically exclude something as foreign to philosophical inquiry, but later introduce it indirectly and unknowingly into their arguments and presuppose what they previously had stubbornly rejected. They have to do so; otherwise they could not argue or converse. *Essences* of things are elements in all human thinking; discourse, which is based upon the first principles of common sense, is mainly reduced to the expression of essences. It is impossible to speak without expressing essences or alluding to them.

our spirit; only examination of our own ideas furnishes us with it.[227]

It seems impossible that, having noted the universality of some of our ideas and noted also the impossibility of finding this universality outside our spirit, he did not subsequently perceive the need to accept that our spirit needs something other than that provided by the senses. But at times, although we are no further from the truth than a hair's breadth, we cannot bridge that tiny gap.[228]

In his *Cours d'Etudes*, Condillac asserts that this distinction between *a priori* and *experimental* truths really exists. From the former, he derives *rational evidence* and from the latter, *evidence of feeling* and factual evidence.

Leibniz agrees and also proves that the certainty of our cognitions cannot be derived in any way from sensations, but from the mind itself.

Thus, all conflicting philosophical schools seem equally to recognise as a fact that our knowledge is of two species. We can, therefore, take this as a sure starting point enabling progress to be achieved in this field.

---

[227] Bk. 4, c. 3.

[228] Locke says: 'The only place for universal ideas is in our spirit, and it is reflection which furnishes the mind with them.' But how does *reflection* furnish the mind with them? 'By *abstraction*,' replies Locke, 'to which it subjects the particular ideas derived from the senses.' But what does abstraction do? It divides up, it breaks down; it does not add or create anything. He assumes, therefore, that a component, a *common*, universal concept is present as an element in particular ideas. The origin of this universal concept, therefore, still requires an explanation. When *particular ideas* are formed in this manner, Locke's *abstraction* intervenes and breaks them down into their elements. It discovers *what is abstract* and *what is sensible*. It reconstitutes them and unites them in as many ways as it wants. But unless this *intellectual perception* is granted, Locke's *reflection* has nothing on which to operate.

Article 4

Characteristics of *a priori*[229] and *a posteriori* knowledge

306. The characteristics of *a priori* knowledge specified by Leibniz and Kant[230] are *necessity* and *universality*. The experience of our senses shows us *what is* but cannot show us *what must be*. There is absolutely no necessary reason to say that a fact which happens once, twice or a hundred times in one way, must also happen in the same way the hundred and first time. If, therefore, sense experience gives us knowledge of things which happen, such knowledge is not *necessary*. Knowledge of some contingent thing is always *a posteriori*. On the other hand, *necessary* knowledge may be *a priori*. Indeed, its necessity never comes from the senses but from an intrinsic reason seen by the mind. This seems so obvious that it cannot be doubted.[231]

Each morning we see the sun rise and we predict that the sun

---

[229] Kant took care to define exactly the meaning of this phrase, *a priori knowledge*, in order to avoid equivocations in the development of the argument.

He points out that this term is used in two senses:

1. Occasionally *a priori judgment* is applied to that which is formed before an event takes place, although this judgment depends upon a rule we acquire from experience. I see the eroding foundations of a house and I judge, before it actually collapses, that it will fall. To form such a judgment we use a rule acquired through experience: 'A building without support will fall.'

2. Occasionally *a priori judgment* is applied to a rule which is not acquired through experience but contains some *rational necessity*. For example, a fact occurs; I judge that some cause has produced it, though I do not see the cause. I make this judgment not because on other occasions I have found that those facts had a corresponding cause, but because I know that a fact cannot occur without its cause

Kant uses the term, '*a priori* knowledge' solely in this second sense.

[230] Other philosophers saw this but, among modern thinkers, these two focused more specifically upon certain characteristics and sensed their importance. The achievements of great philosophers are almost always confined to this: metaphysical truths are known but not differentiated and defined in a way that brings out their great fecundity. These ideas do not take their rightful place in the genealogical table of ideas, in the human spirit, and in the appraisal made of them.

[231] Even the sceptical Hume accepts that truths which consist of relations between ideas are *necessary*.

will rise the following day, but this is a mere conjecture based on analogy for which we can offer no intrinsic reason. In fact, there is nothing repugnant in our imagining that the sun will not rise tomorrow. God can indeed halt it in mid-course. On the other hand, to say, 'The part can be greater than the whole', is so repugnant that no one could possibly admit it as true. This is not because we have never seen a part greater than a whole, but because we feel it to be an intellectual impossibility. If we are talking of something which we have never experienced, we can say at most that we do not know whether it will happen or how it will happen. However, from the mere fact that we have never seen it happen, we do not say that it is impossible because, to say this, we have to find an intrinsic, logical repugnance to the thing.

A posteriori knowledge, then, such as that of sensible facts, is *accidental* knowledge. In addition to such knowledge, there is within us *necessary* knowledge which is called *a priori* precisely because it has as its basis an intrinsic necessity bestowed by pure reason, not in any way by the senses.

Sense experience, as well as offering us knowledge devoid of *necessity*, also offers us knowledge devoid of *universality*.

We can have experience only of a determined number of cases. If we wish to find out whether all jasmines are equally sweet-smelling, we can go into the garden, and pick one, two, three, ten, twenty, fifty flowers. If we are patient enough to smell them one by one, but do not wish to venture beyond the knowledge given us by experience, we can only learn from these tests that one, two, three, ten, twenty or fifty flowers have transmitted the same sweet, distinct fragrance to us. Further than that we cannot go. Any advance beyond this by our mind goes beyond the limits of experience.

We cannot even say from experience that the flowers we have picked, when brought up to our nose once again, will give off the same scent. We say they will, but only by a law of *analogy* which, when applied, enables our mind to transcend the narrow limits of its experience.

If, after the fifty tests, we see that the flowers left on the pergola are similar in everything to those we have picked and smelt, and we imagine and conjecture that these too, when sniffed, would transmit the same pleasant scent, we go far beyond the limits of experience, and are in fact pushing the analogy much further. A similarity proved valid by tests upon fifty flowers is applied to thousands of untried flowers. In other words, from the jasmines which we have smelt, we argue that all other jasmines even outside the garden have the same scent. In our imagination, we run through all the other gardens and all plants of the same flower in bloom throughout the world, and apply to all of them the result of our little experiment.

Nor does the mind stop here; it transcends the bounds of experience[232] much more freely because the mind also thinks of all *possible* jasmines and applies and attributes the same fragrance to them all. Books on botany, therefore, rightly assign the fragrance to the *species* of plants called jasmines.

Thus, it is clear that knowledge derived purely from sensible experience is not and can never be universal. It is only particular, and more or less extended according to my opportunity and occasion for acquiring it. It is always infinitely restricted, however, when compared to universal knowledge which, to be such, must apply and does apply to all possible examples of a species, which are infinite.

307. The universality of *a priori* knowledge is due to its *necessity*.

Indeed, what is necessary must always be what it is. On the other hand, universality obtained by applying, for example, the law of analogy to some observation of mine is not true, rigorous universality. It is merely, to use Kant's expression, 'only an arbitrary extension of validity from that which may be predicated of a proposition valid in most cases to that which is asserted of a proposition which holds good in all.'[233]

---

[232] Our experience of anything whatsoever, however many times it is repeated, is slight, even infinitely slight in relation to all possible cases. It is almost nothing in relationship to a universal, necessary idea which encompasses whatever is possible.

[233] *Critique of Pure Reason*, Introduction 2. When we render universal a particular proposition that has come to us through sensible experience, we cannot truly be certain of this universality. Let us examine experientially a part of the human body. The dissection of countless corpses offers us the following result; the liver is connected to the right part of the heart. Next, let us attempt to universalise this fact repeatedly demonstrated to us by experience by stating: 'All human bodies have the heart on the left and the liver on the right.'

308. A point which needs the greatest emphasis is that if we were to focus on the senses alone, we would never be able to furnish our cognitions even with this imperfect universality of analogy.

In fact, if we considered only what the senses give us, we would never have even the thought of any universality whatever.

Let us imagine that we have perceived six objects. We cannot extend our experience with our mind to a seventh object because we have not perceived it. Still less can we extend it to all existent beings, relative to which what we have perceived may be a tiny proportion. And it is even more impossible to extend it to absolutely all possible objects. For this final extension, we must have conceived some universality, that is, the conception of the indefinite *possibility* of objects which cannot be experienced by the senses because they do not exist, but are solely able to exist.

309. It follows that even this *universality* by analogy, although not necessary, although uncertain, presupposes in our mind some *a priori* knowledge which owes nothing to the senses. If necessity is inevitably accompanied by *de facto* universality, analogy presupposes in us the concept of some *potential universality. Necessity, de facto universality, potential universality* are concepts which transcend all sense experience and can be

But we cannot be absolutely certain of the truth of such a statement because it does not possess any intrinsic necessity. Unknown to me there may be cases where the opposite is true. On the contrary, independently of experience, I can know that I have to doubt it. Experience may confirm my doubt; thus, during a dissection of a body carried out in Paris, Leibniz relates that the heart was located on the right and the liver on the left.

However, to avoid any ambiguities, I should point out that when I universalise experience I conceive the result of it as either *accidental* or *essential* to the thing. It is *essential* when the result relates to what shapes and constitutes the *substantial concept* of the thing. For example, the statement: 'Man is a being endowed with reason' is a proposition which expresses the *essence* of man. When, therefore, I experience it, I accept it as *necessary* in so far as I form the concept of man only by means of the rational element which intervenes to form him. Consequently, I could no longer conceive him without the use of reason. *Hypothetically*, therefore, every man must possess reason. Without it, he would not be what I call *man*. Thus, *necessity* and universality are founded in the knowledge of *essences* and Locke is, yet again, in self-contradiction when he acknowledges a truly *universal* knowledge and denies that we know the essences of things. However, knowledge of essences is not given to us by the sense experience of which we have spoken.

explained only by deduction from the inner power of our mind itself [*App.*, no. 28].

Article 5

Hume eliminates a section of *a priori* cognitions and produces scepticism as a result

310. Locke had laid down the principle, 'All ideas are derived from sensations and from reflection.'

At the same time, he had recognised this fact: 'Human knowledge is of two species, *a priori* and *a posteriori*.'

He had not realised that the two propositions were incompatible, and that one must inevitably cancel out the other.

If he had noticed it, he would either have altered his principle: 'All human knowledge is derived from sensation and reflection'[234] or denied the fact that an *a priori*, necessary, universal knowledge existed, just as he denied the other fact — that we have some notion of substance[235] — because he saw that it was not easily reconcilable with his theory.

311. However, no error concealed in a philosophical theory, no matter how tiny and invisible it may be initially, can remain

[234] Locke defines reflection as the application of our attention to sensations and to the other operations of our spirit. Consequently, it merely adverts to what the spirit already has within it. This is his error. If Locke had posited *reflection* without defining it, he could have saved himself by approaching it from its more favourable side, as Leibniz tried to do.

[235] We have already seen that the problem of deducing the idea of substance from sensations arises from the idea of *existence* contained in the idea of substance. But the idea of existence is the idea of something more common than anything else. Thus, the difficulty present in explaining the origin of substance through deduction from the senses, is the same as that present in trying to deduce universal or common ideas from them. Moreover, it is universal ideas, particularly those of *essence* and *substance*, which produce *necessity* in propositions, as I have already remarked (cf. 305). But Locke, giving no thought to this, denied the idea of substance because it seemed to clash with his principle of the origin of ideas and, at the same time, recognised the existence of necessary and universal notions and of *a priori* knowledge. He did not see that the very same problem arises when we seek to explain the origin of the latter.

there for long without beginning to proliferate. Like truth, error is subject to development but, when developed and fully grown, unfolds all its ugliness and harmfulness. There is nothing hidden that will not be revealed. In this case, the revelation of error is a necessary step in overcoming and destroying it, just as tumours on the human body have to swell and burst before the body can regain health.

Hume absorbed Locke's philosophy through his studies; it had become the philosophy of his age. Even the most apparently independent thinkers feel the influence of opinions around them. Hume thus accepted critically, as an established fact handed down by tradition from his teachers, Locke's judgment: 'The only cognitions we have come from the senses.'

Having retained this principle, he began to examine Locke's other proposition, '*A priori* knowledge exists,'[236] and saw clearly that it is irreconcilable with the principle admitted by this philosophy.

312. Let us take, said Hume, one of the most famous *a priori* propositions: 'Every effect must have its cause.' The necessity of this proposition, that every effect must have its cause, cannot in any way be deduced from sense experience for the following reasons.

First, sensible experience presents us with facts alone, each completely distinct from the other. One fact may be observed to follow another repeatedly, constantly, as the feeling of heat succeeds the sensation of light when the sun rises. This, however, is simply a *conjunction* of two facts, distributed in the order of time. But there is nothing to assure me that they are *connected* as cause and effect. I cannot say that one fact is the cause of another solely because one comes before the other. It is obvious that the succession of two things gives me no right to consider them as linked together as cause and effect.[237]

Next, let us assume that my senses enable me to perceive the

---

[236] Actually, he investigated this proposition only in part, and discussed only a single part of *a priori* knowledge, that is, the principle of causation. If he had been consistent, he would have saved nothing. His argument would have demolished *a priori* knowledge completely, down to the last fragment.

[237] Any *fact* pertaining to outward experience is merely an *effect*; the *cause* does not fall under the external senses.

link of cause and effect between two facts (something utterly impossible because the senses provide a mere temporal *conjunction*). I would still have no right to conclude that the thing *had* to be so, and could not be otherwise. The senses tell me what is; they cannot tell me what must be, and do not therefore provide the *necessity* expressed in the proposition 'Every effect MUST have its cause'.

Third, if I could note through the senses 1. the causes of a number of facts I have witnessed and 2. that these facts must inevitably have their causes, I would still not know that the thing would *always* happen in the same way, even in the case of events which I have not experienced, or in the case of all possible facts. The *universality* exemplified in the proposition: 'Every effect must have its cause', could not be given me in any way by the senses because universality is not experienced; all existing occurrences are not investigated, and possible occurrences, which do not yet exist, do not fall under the senses.[238]

Hume concluded therefore that the proposition, 'Every effect must have its cause', could not be deduced in any way from sense experience.

313. However, the principle: 'All our knowledge has its origin in sensations', was already accepted as irrevocably true; on this point there could be no compromise. All that remained was to apply the method of argument which Locke had used when discussing the idea of substance. This consisted in rejecting as non-existent anything which conflicted with the principle of his system.

The idea of substance, considered to be at odds with this principle, was denied by Locke. In the same way, Hume, having discovered an identical incompatibility (overlooked by Locke) in *a priori* knowledge, found it necessary to deny that such knowledge existed.

He therefore denied that the principle: 'Every effect must have its cause', was a necessary, universal truth. In a word, he affirmed that this pronouncement of human common sense was unjustified.

---

[238] In expounding Hume's thought, I am reinforcing it with reasons which are perhaps even more powerful than his own; but the core of the argument is the same.

314. But why does mankind deceive itself in this way? Why do we always assume the pronouncement to be true, and use it continually in all our reasoning?

Hume put the mistake down to habit. It is so easy to switch from the idea of *conjunction* to that of *connection*; it is so easy to consider one item as cause and the other as effect when one constantly precedes and the other constantly follows. It is so easy for us to confuse one thing with another and call cause and effect all regularly succeeding facts. Moreover, if our erroneous judgment were confined to things we actually experienced, there could never be a universal proposition. We arbitrarily render a proposition universal by extrapolating experience beyond its set limits. Having experienced many examples of succession and the apparent interdependence of two facts, we conclude that this will always be the case, even for unexperienced facts, as well as for those non-existent but merely possible facts. We thus invent the universal proposition and believe that 'All effects have a cause.'

But this proposition, rendered *universal* by the imagination, would still not be *necessary*. We make our imagination work even harder and perfect the maxim. We imagine that the proposition cannot be otherwise than it is, and that all effects must necessarily have a cause. We then restrict the proposition to this solemn statement: 'All effects must have a cause'.

315. In this way, a necessary, universal proposition, which had always been accepted by the whole of mankind, on which all human reasoning is based, which is the foundation of all the most lofty truths, of all beliefs, of all ethical doctrines, is eliminated from modern philosophy. 'Nothing can happen without a cause' is now viewed as an illusion created by the over-hasty imagination of the whole of humanity. All mankind is convicted of error by Locke's principle that human cognitions have their origin in the senses alone. A few philosophers immediately prior to us rebelled against common sense, which they abandoned to the countless masses and schools. They discovered and proclaimed a theory so simple and profound that, in assigning to sensations alone the right to produce ideas, it declares everything rational to be empty illusion merely because it is not sensible.

[314–315]

Article 6

No aspect of *a priori* knowledge can be explained by the senses

316. It is obvious that Hume was under no obligation to stop here; he could have extended much further the consequences of Locke's theory.

The very argument that Hume devised to invalidate the proposition considered by everyone to be obvious, 'Every event must have its cause', can be used to destroy every other axiom. The universal formula to wreak such havoc runs as follows: 'An axiom is a necessary, universal proposition. It cannot be derived from the senses because they do not provide anything necessary and universal. But we have no other knowledge than that which comes to us from the senses. Therefore, we do not possess any *axiomata*; we cannot be certain of any necessary, universal proposition; in short, our arguments have no fixed principle from which to begin' [*App.*, no. 29].

Consequently, Locke's principle, 'All our knowledge comes from the senses', contradicts the fact, '*A priori* knowledge exists'. Anyone, therefore, who accepts Locke's principle and wishes to be consistent, must deny human beings the knowledge of any universal, necessary proposition.

317. But to grasp the implications of denying any kind of universal, necessary proposition, we should note that, if *universal, necessary* propositions are eliminated, the possibility of any certainty is eliminated and complete scepticism reigns.

First, we have no experience of anything which does not fall under the senses.

If we eliminate universal, necessary propositions, it is obvious that we no longer have any principle from which to deduce non-sensible truths.

Anything not falling under our senses cannot be deduced, by means of a *principle*, from what falls under our senses. For example, I deduce from geometrical shapes drawn upon a beach that some unseen human being has been there. To do this I rely on the principle: 'No effect occurs without a sufficient cause.' If I eliminate this principle, I am no longer able to deduce from the geometrical shapes the existence of a human being who has drawn them on the sand. All principles are necessary and universal of their nature, otherwise they would not produce necessity in any consequence.

I deduce the existence of other people's souls and the existence of God from their effects by the principle of causality.

Once *a priori* knowledge is eliminated, together with certainty about everything which does not fall under my senses and the possibility of knowing what does not fall under my senses, only the outward appearances pertaining to the senses remain. The whole world shrinks to a heap of appearances; to myself, I am merely an appearance. The consequence of this reasoning is universal, boundless, sceptical idealism. Such is the inevitable outcome of Locke's principle: 'All our knowledge is derived from the senses.'

Furthermore, even sensible appearances will not endure. I am not even certain of these.

To be certain of anything, I always need a necessary principle; certainty is simply an inevitable necessity to which my intellect yields assent. I cannot possess certainty about simple, sensible phenomena, unless there is a prior, necessary principle in my mind whose authority assures me of their existence.

If I were to say to myself: 'I am certain that I am being modified, that I perceive sensations in my senses,' my reason, reflecting upon my presumption of certainty, would immediately ask: 'And why are you certain that you perceive something?' If I were to reply: 'Because it is impossible not to feel what I am feeling,' my reason would retort: 'This is a universal principle, an *a priori* principle; it is the principle of contradiction. But who assures you of it? It does not come to you from the senses because the senses do not provide you with anything which contains *necessity* — as this principle does — or *universality* with which the principle you have employed is endowed. To trust the senses unfailingly, you must resort to a necessary, universal principle, to an *a priori* principle, to the principle of contradiction, in short, to reason, to me. The senses need to have their authority guaranteed by reason.'

318. Reason, therefore, does not have its origin in the senses. It needs to be necessary and universal; the senses are particular and contingent. No certainty is forthcoming except by means of

a necessary principle not derived from the senses, that is, a principle which cannot be otherwise and is, therefore, universal. Certainty which did not occasion necessity would be very curious. 'I am certain that this is how things are, but they could also be different!' Isn't this a contradiction? Consequently, if we believe rationally in the senses, we must have a *reason* for believing in them. This reason cannot originate in the senses; if it did, we would lose our way by resorting to reasons *ad infinitum*.

The destruction of *a priori* knowledge, therefore, brings with it the destruction of *a posteriori* knowledge which only exists through the agency of a necessary, universal reason, not originating from the senses. So the principle, 'All human knowledge comes only through the senses', finishes in absolute, universal doubt. But even this is nonsense. There cannot even be doubt without a rational principle, independent of the senses, which constrained us to doubt.[239] The real conclusion is complete and total destruction of everything we know. Not only is it impossible for human beings to be certain; it is impossible for them even to doubt. Reason is an impossibility, and the principle deprives mankind of intelligence, its special prerogative. Either we must deny a fact as luminous as 'Man is a rational ens', or we must abandon the ruinous principle, 'All human knowledge comes from the senses.'[240]

[239] Doubt always implies some certainty because it is a negation of certainty. Doubt and certainty are relative ideas: the former cannot be conceived without the latter. To say, 'I doubt', is to affirm something. In order to rule out certainty and affirmation completely, we should need to cease thinking. The very act of negation would contain an affirmation, because the act with which we deny cannot be included in the total denial.

[240] Descartes, therefore, is incorrect when he says: 'The senses are simply sources of error.' He ought to have said: 'The senses are sources neither of error, nor of truth, nor of doubt.' On their own, the senses are incapable of producing thought, which is always exhibited under one of these three modes: truth, falsity or doubt. These are modes of thought and not sensations. To say that the senses mislead us is to attribute to them one of the modes of thought. But if the senses were capable of possessing one of the forms of thought, they could also possess all the others. It would be absurd to say that the faculty enabling us to *affirm* error was different from that enabling us to affirm truth. The senses are not sources of error, as Descartes maintains, nor are they sources of knowledge, as Locke maintains. They produce no knowledge

319. These final consequences, which are not drawn even by Hume, are none the less necessary. Once the principle is accepted, we cannot call a halt; all consequences must inexorably follow their course. Its fecundity must be totally exhausted; if it is an erroneous principle, this fecundity finally brings about the destruction of all that is true, of everything that is. Amidst such destruction, the very principle is engulfed and along with it those who proclaim it.

Article 7

Attempts to refute Hume's scepticism

320. Hume denied a fact which Locke accepted: 'There is *a priori* knowledge', that is, necessary, universal knowledge, because he found that it clashed with Locke's theory, summed up in the following proposition: 'All our cognitions draw their origin from the senses and from reflection upon the operations of the spirit.'

Hume could have been refuted by proving, as all facts are proved, that *a priori* knowledge exists. Reid and Kant chose to follow this path.

It would, however, have been difficult to persuade a sceptic like Hume, who was deeply prejudiced in favour of his own ideas, that universal and necessary propositions do exist and are not, in fact, figments or suppositions of our imagination.

No matter how often you insist with such a philosopher that these propositions are accepted as absolutely necessary and universal by all mankind, he will probably reply: 'I do not deny that fact which, indeed, I am trying to explain. Rather, I maintain that this fact comes about as the result of a mistake which everyone commits inadvertently, due to the extreme affinity and proximity between ideas of *conjunction* in time and ideas of *connection* between cause and effect. Because of their proximity, great care must be exercised in distinguishing them from

whatsoever, no idea, no truth; they merely furnish our mind with the *matter* of knowledge with which our mind forms a judgment. To do so, it must inevitably possess some universal idea.

[319–320]

one another and, up to now, society has been unable to do so. Ordinary people especially, who represent the great majority of mankind, cannot sustain the first idea without slipping into the second. It is extremely difficult for them not to switch from the sensation created by the sun in the different points in the heaven to the belief that the sun moves, although the sensation of motion is different from real motion and is merely apparent. Mankind, therefore, easily confuses appearance and reality, and falls into erroneous judgments. This is what happens in the case of the principle of causality. People take it as necessary and universal, but it is so only in appearance.'

One might have replied that raw experience is totally different from necessity; even when I see the sun rise every day of my life, I do not conceive the contrary as impossible, as I do with the proposition: 'There is no effect without a cause.' Even if the experience were repeated indefinitely, even if I were convinced that it would continue for ever in the same way, I could never be persuaded that the opposite was impossible, unthinkable, an inherent contradiction. Consequently, analysis of contingent propositions obtained from a long, sustained experience and analysis of necessary propositions such as 'There is no effect without a cause' is perfectly adequate to enable us to distinguish between these two series of propositions and avoid any confusion between them. We do not exchange the supposed universality and necessity of the former for the intrinsic universality and necessity with which the latter are clearly endowed.

Article 8

How Hume's scepticism could have been refuted more effectively

321. However, a shorter, more convincing approach when refuting philosophers of this kind would be to follow their line of argument and start from what they themselves admit and recognise as undeniable.

The fact which they acknowledge is that all accept the proposition, 'There is no effect without a cause', recognising and using it as necessary and universal. But while admitting this, they deny that the proposition is necessary and universal; they say that it is only apparently so.

If we start from the fact which they admit as true, we could put the following argument to them:

You admit that the proposition, 'Every effect must have a cause', is necessary and universal only in appearance. But I shall prove to you that this could not even *appear* to be true to human beings unless they had *a priori* knowledge which is not sense-based, that is, truly necessary, universal knowledge.

Let us assume that the proposition, 'Every effect must have its cause', is merely the limited result of experience and, when strictly formulated, is expressed as follows: 'Certain occurrences repeatedly precede certain others.' My question now is: for human imagination to have been able to transform this empirical proposition into the rational proposition, 'Every effect must have its cause', what concepts do we need? Obviously we could not have been guilty of such a confusion unless we had 1. the idea of *possibility*; 2. the idea of *cause*; 3. the idea of *necessity*; 4. the idea of *universality*. None of these ideas, however, can be derived from the senses, as even our opponents concede. In other words, it is impossible to have 1. the idea of *possibility*, because the possibility of a thing does not fall under the senses; 2. the idea of *cause*, because only effects fall under the senses; 3. the idea of *necessity*, because the senses show what is, not what must be; 4. the idea of *universality*, because sense experience is limited to a given number of things and repeated only a given number of times. It follows that the problem we face in accepting the principle of causality as *true* is also to be faced in accepting it as *apparent*. If human beings had only sense experience, we could not have formed, or even assumed and imagined, such a principle.

What escaped Hume in this argument is the realisation that we must go beyond the senses, not only to imagine as *necessary* the axiom, 'Every effect must have its cause', but even simply to imagine it as *possible*, simply to conceive it. Because Hume did not see this, he grants that mankind only imagines it to be true. But this admission is sufficient to ruin his entire theory. In order to have the idea of something, it is not necessary that it should really subsist. All that is needed is that I should think it.

Mankind thinks *necessity* and *universality*. Therefore, these ideas are within us whether they are applicable to external things or not. Their origin needs an explanation; the senses do not provide it; consequently, we either deny the principle, 'All ideas come from the senses' or deny not only that the principle of causality is true, but that it is considered as true by anyone. We have to say that it has never been thought by the human mind, never imagined and never spoken of. But how would you rule out a principle without thinking it, without naming it? The sceptical argument based upon the famous axiom, 'All our knowledge comes from the senses', is essentially self-contradictory.

Article 9

Reid rejects Locke's principle and acknowledges the existence of *a priori* cognitions

322. The two propositions accepted by Locke, 'All human knowledge comes from the senses and from reflection devoid of ideas' and '*A priori* knowledge, that is, necessary, universal knowledge exists', were incompatible, as we saw, and the former destroyed the latter.

The first proposition was a philosopher's *theory*; the second was a *fact* of nature.

This destruction is proof that Locke's theory had run its bitter course. The philosophers who found it at this stage were in a position to assess it. One of these, the Scot, Reid, was in no doubt — as we have already seen (cf. 99, 116) — that the wrong path had been chosen, and that people were being led to absolute nihilism. This is essentially repugnant to human nature and mankind had no option but to retrace its steps.

Reid, unlike Hume, focused on the second proposition and maintained with all the greatest philosophers down the ages that '*a priori* knowledge, that is, necessary, universal knowledge, is an undeniable fact; Locke's theory is false because it cannot be reconciled in any way with this luminous fact.'

Having rejected Locke's principle, Reid had to replace it with something that showed how *a priori* knowledge was possible.

[322]

Reid did not concern himself unduly with showing the possibility of *a priori* knowledge in general. He went no further than explaining how we acquire knowledge of the existence of bodies, which is based upon some elements of *a priori* knowledge, and which Berkeley and Hume had denied [*App.*, no. 30].

With this in mind, he set about analysing the way in which we form the idea of bodies, and thought he had to distinguish three successive stages in the acquisition of this knowledge: 1. the *impression* made upon our sense organs by real exterior entities; 2. the *sensation* which immediately arises in our soul, granted this automatic impression; finally, 3. the *perception* of the existence and sensible qualities of bodies which occurs in our spirit simultaneously with sensation.

Sensation has no feature making it similar to the outward *impression*, just as the *perception* of the existence of bodies has no similarity to sensation. These three things occur in succession; this is the essential fact. One cannot be called the cause of another because all three are entirely different. The reason why these three things occur in succession is beyond our grasp; it is a mystery.

What we can say is that, as *sensation* cannot be the cause of the *perception* of the existence of bodies, we must admit in the spirit itself some innate activity or instinct which leads the spirit, immediately after sensation, to judge of the existence of bodies. This instinctive judgment, which is not the effect of sensations (which are simply associated with the judgment chronologically), is responsible for the immediate knowledge or thought in our spirit that bodies are something and exist furnished with certain qualities.

Article 10

Reid's theory does not avoid scepticism

323. Reid considered that his theory had put paid to *idealism* and *scepticism*. In fact, he evaded neither, as I shall show.

Idealists and sceptics start from the principle: 'We cannot know anything beyond sensation.' The idealists conclude from this: 'To say, therefore, that bodies exist is a gratuitous affirmation; all that we know to exist are sensations; there cannot be anything other than sensations.' The sceptics, who are more logical, go further and conclude: 'As a result, we have no principle of reasoning which warrants our moving from sensation to the knowledge of anything else, bodily or spiritual.'

Reid mainly had the idealists in his sights. He felt that the destruction of idealism would lead to the collapse of scepticism, and argued as follows: 'It is an undeniable fact that everyone has knowledge of bodies. Such knowledge, which cannot come to us from sensations, must therefore follow from an inner faculty of the spirit, from an *instinct* which, as soon as sensations arise, ensures that the spirit has an inner perception of bodies.'

However, as soon as he accepts — and, in fact, takes as the basis of his system — that *sensation* has no connection with the *perception of the existence of bodies* and that these two things, *sensation* and *perception*, are so distinct that they have not the slightest similarity to each other, how can he be sure that the immediate *perception* of bodies is not a delusion? What assurance is there that the perception of bodily entities corresponds to the entia themselves? This would seem an unjustified assertion, and the arguments about *sensations* would seem to have the same force when transferred to its *perception*.

The reason why idealists and sceptics conclude that we cannot be sure of the existence of bodies was this: 'Sensation, which is purely subjective, has no connection with the real existence of bodies. The common view that supposes the existence of bodily substances external to us with their own objective existence, independent of our modifications, is worthless.'

Reid replies: '*Bodies* are not perceived through *sensations*, but through a *perception* which occurs instantaneously in the spirit when sensations are experienced. Sensations then are quite unlike perception.'

But, granted this, it remains to be proved that this immediate *perception* of bodies is true. Instead, Reid has sought a better explanation of how the common error originates. According to him, people are driven to perceive bodies through a blind instinct, through a law of their nature. There is no reason pointing them in that direction other than mere, inevitable necessity. Yes, we may reply, it is perfectly obvious that everyone accepts the existence of bodies. By your admission, they cannot do otherwise. *Nature*, not *reason*, impels them to do so. Common sense is nothing but blind faith, a universal illusion which mankind passively accepts without knowing what kind of authority presents and imposes it upon us. Reid's system, therefore, does not solve the problem of idealism and scepticism. All that has been done is to set it back one stage. The problem which arose over *sensation* is transferred to immediate *perception*. Common sense remains involved in doubt and without authority [*App.*, no. 31].

Reid wished to apply his views on the immediate perception of bodies to principles of reason such as causality. According to him, we perceive them immediately by an inexplicable insight, by a natural instinct which sets them before us and arbitrarily forces us to give them our assent. He succeeded in explaining their origin, but did not succeed in endowing them with any rational authority to which, as human beings, we must bend our free assent.

Article 11

Kant derives his scepticism from Reid's principle as Hume had derived his from Locke's

324. Locke had unwittingly introduced the principle of scepticism into his teaching; it was to burgeon under Hume.

Reid, in his desire to refute Hume's scepticism, which was rooted in Locke's principle, denied the principle but replaced it by another which contained the seed of the disease itself. He planted it deeper, all unknowingly. It was destined to grow, and did in fact grow under Kant's direction.

The fact, '*A priori* knowledge exists', which was denied by Hume and vindicated by Reid, was accepted by Kant.

This fact is attested by all mankind. However, common sense, which has the authority to establish such a fact, cannot offer any explanation for it. All say, 'We know necessary, universal propositions', but do not say how they know them, nor explain why they are impelled to give them their assent.

Reid had said: 'This assent, by which all assert necessary, universal propositions is a natural, instinctive judgment which cannot be explained. We must simply affirm it as a mysterious fact.'

As we saw, this meant admitting the existence of *a priori* knowledge in us, but simultaneously denying its authority and veracity. This was the path Kant chose to follow.

Article 12
Kant's teaching: distinction between the form and matter of our cognitions

325. Kant's teaching can be summarised as follows.

We have no knowledge prior to *experience*, but Locke was wrong in asserting that all our knowledge comes from the senses.

Our knowledge is: 1. partly *a priori*, that is, necessary and universal; 2. partly *a posteriori*, that is, contingent and particular. We have to explain how experience, which furnishes us with both these cognitions, is possible.

A priori knowledge, that is, necessary, universal knowledge, has no connection with sensations. It arises, therefore, from within us, as Reid says, and develops from the very depth of our spirit on the occasion of sensations.

Nevertheless, we still have to investigate how this last fact, that is, the arousal of *a priori* knowledge in our spirit on the occasion of sensations, is possible. Reid was content to note the fact, but it must also be analysed. In addition, we have to discover the *conditions* by which it is determined. This is the point at which Kant's particular contribution begins. He analyses *perception* in so far as it contains *a priori* knowledge which Reid had previously accepted but not described in detail nor differentiated according to all its species.

326. Kant set about showing that when sensations occur, the human spirit *does* actually perceive external entia which, however, are not simply presented to it by sensations. External entia are not, as sensists claim, a cluster of sensations; they are entia, and are made up of two distinct elements, that is, 1. sensations, and 2. qualities posited by the spirit itself. Kant calls these qualities *forms*, as he had called sensations *matter*.

It follows that entia of the sensible world, in so far as we perceive them, are made up of *matter* and *form*. Matter is provided to us by sense, and consists of everything contingent and particular in these entia; form is provided by the understanding and consists of everything necessary and universal in them. In a word, *form* posits the *a priori* element of cognitions, *matter* posits the *a posteriori* element.

I perceive a tree and, in doing so, experience not only the sensible modifications of my bodily organs which, as subjective modifications or sensations, posit nothing outside myself, but also admit, with the activity in my understanding, something external to me. This has its own independent existence, independent of me and any modifications in me. According to Kant, in order to be able to accept this tree as external to me, to represent it to myself, and in a word to form it for myself, I must — with the activity of my spirit — add necessary, universal notions to sensation. No solid objection to this proposition can, in fact, be raised because (ignoring the forms of sensitivity, that is, *space* and *time*), I have to add at least the universal notion of *existence* or that of *possibility*. I have not perceived a tree with my understanding until I have judged that it *exists* or *can exist*.

327. Kant set himself to discover and describe with philosophical thoroughness all the universal notions which contribute to the formation of a corporeal ens as conceived. He reduced them to fourteen, two of which he named forms of the external and internal sense. These were *space* and *time*. The other twelve he called forms of the intellect or categories, that is, twelve universal ideas into which it is always necessary to locate, as in classes, real, perceived entities. In fact, our understanding, in perceiving what is real, merely places them in one or other of these classes: to perceive something real with our understanding is to classify and judge it.

The four general classes, each of which he sub-divides further into three minor subdivisions, are *quantity*, *quality*, *relationship* and *modality*.

According to Kant, it is impossible to perceive anything without perceiving it as furnished with a certain *quantity* and a certain *quality*, without perceiving some *relationship* such as substance or accident, and some *mode* of existence such as contingency or necessity.

[327]

Placing something real in these four classes is a necessary *condition* without which intellectual perception is impossible. This is a *condition of experience*, the experience through which we acquire our cognitions. Experience is impossible and thinking is impossible, unless we assume that the understanding, in perceiving what is real, carries out such a classification.

But carrying out such classification is the same as judging real things under this fourfold division; judging them is the same as furnishing them with the four predicates of *quantity*, *quality*, *relationship* and *modality* which, as universals, cannot originate in the senses, but are generated by the understanding in the act of perception. By means of these predicates, real entities acquire their being as objects. These predicates can, therefore, be called the *form*, and sensation the *matter* from which results the intellective *object*.[241]

Article 13

How Kant tries to avoid the accusation of idealism

328. Kant claims to have avoided idealism and scepticism in this way, but he refuted it in one sense only: by stating that Berkeley's idealism and Hume's scepticism were too narrow.

He transferred the idealism of Berkeley from the senses to the understanding itself.

Berkeley had said: 'Bodies have no real existence outside us; they are nothing but our sensations.' This was a consequence of

[241] It should not be thought that the distinction between the *matter* and the *form* of our cognitions is a discovery of Kant; it is ancient, and well known in Italy. Genovesi taught it in his letter to Antonio Conti in which, after examining whether *ideas* are the same as *perceptions*, he concludes: 'These reasons show clearly that ideas are the *forms of our perceptions*, the majority of which, that is, the first and simple forms, the basic elements of its knowledge, are received, not created by the mind. So let us go along with this view, which appears the most likely.' *Ideas* united to *sensations* by means of a *judgment* lead to the perception of bodies. These perceptions are composed of three elements: 1. pure ideas, simple apprehension of a thing (*form*), and 2. sensations (*matter*); 3. a judgment of the actual existence (*bond between form and matter*) which unites in a single object *what is felt* and the *idea*. However, all this will be discussed later.

Locke's theory: 'As we possess only sensations, we can only define the idea of bodies, which we have, as a cluster of sensations.'

Kant defines bodies as: 'A union (a synthesis) of intellectual forms and of sensations.'

Both come from us: intellectual forms from the activity of our understanding; sensations from the receptivity of our sense. We know nothing real; we do not even know whether anything real in itself and external to us is possible.

· This consequence comes straight from Reid's theory. He had said: 'The bodies which we perceive are not our sensations alone; an instinct of our understanding induces us to add an object to them.' The admission that we perceive this object by a blind operation in our spirit enabled Kant to conclude: 'It is therefore simply a product of our spirit.'

Kant states: 'I am not an idealist, because I do not accept that bodies are mere sensations as Berkeley does.' He accepts the title in a loftier sense, that is, he aims to be a transcendental idealist: this is the same as saying: 'I am not an idealist at Berkeley's level.'[242]

Article 14
Kant tries to avoid the accusation of scepticism

329. Kant also says that he is not a sceptic. According to him, scepticism consists in the rejection of the correspondence between our ideas and *entia* external to us. He does not reject such a correspondence. He analyses the objects thought by us and finds that they result from two elements, an empirical element (sensations), and a rational element (intellectual concepts). If these two elements do not unite, there is no thought object. But we can speak about thought objects. There are not two things, therefore, the thought object and the concept of the object, about which we may debate whether any correspondence exists. There is only one thing, of which my concept is one part, my sensation the other. Reid said: 'There are only

---

[242] *Critique of Pure Reason, Elementary Critique*, Part 1 and Part 2, division 1, bk. 2, c. 2, section 3.

external objects, not *ideas* of those objects.' If he had been faithful to his principles, he would have said: 'There are no objects which are not ideas.'

To perceive something, says Kant, is the same as saying that my understanding sees it as endowed with a certain quantity, quality, relationship and modality. I could not see it unless I placed it, with a judgment, into these four classes, that is, by assigning to it a quantity, a quality, some relationship at least with itself, and a mode of being.

Now, our understanding could not assign such universal notions without having them within itself. They do not come from the senses. It follows that our understanding of itself partially creates its object. In other words, it gives the object its *form*; the *matter* is provided by the senses.

This is really what Kant means when he says:

> The categories constitute concepts, dictate *a priori* laws to phenomena, and with phenomena impose laws upon nature, as the union of all phenomena, if nature is considered from a material point of view, *natura materialiter spectata*.

Elsewhere, he writes:

> Synthesis, generally speaking, is, as we shall afterwards see, the mere operation of the imagination — a BLIND but indispensable function of the soul, without which we should have no knowledge whatever, but of the working of which we are seldom even conscious. But to reduce this synthesis to conceptions is a function of the understanding, by means of which we attain to knowledge, in the proper meaning of the term.[243]

Consequently, the issue of scepticism is completely banished from critical philosophy because the sceptic asks: 'How can we be sure that entia correspond to the concepts we form of them?' Critical philosophy states: 'Concepts are not actually a representation of entia but part of them, that is, their formal part.'

330. It appears, however, that Kant by offering this justification takes undue advantage of his readers. His apparently serious explanation is his usual way of pulling the wool over peoples' eyes.

---

[243] Transcendental Logic, *Analytic*, bk.1, c. 1, section 3.

Everyone knows, of course, that scepticism consists in denying the certainty of things in themselves, independently of any modifications in our spirit. To reduce scepticism to the question: 'Do perceived *entia* correspond to our concepts?' is to alter the question.

Kant tells us that we are sure of *phenomena* only, that the objects of our thought are derived, relative to form, from our limited spirit, that we do not even have the idea of things which exist in themselves and not in us (that is, the ideas of *noumena*), that we do not know whether things in themselves are possible. In doing so, he involves us in such universal idealism, in such deep, subjective illusion that we are enclosed in a circle of inescapable illusions without hope of attaining reality. Truly, this does not make us unsure of what we know, and cannot therefore be called *scepticism*, but it does proclaim that we are incapable of any knowledge. Kant, by rendering all true knowledge of real things impossible and absurd, produces a much sadder scepticism than usual. This is perfected scepticism, consummated under the new title, *critical philosophy*. In this way, mankind itself (which exists purely to know) is eliminated and the work of modern philosophy is fulfilled.

Kant himself admits that criticism is an essentially negative teaching, but compares philosophy before his time to the rash, impossible venture of the Tower of Babel. The human spirit lies humiliated in the dust. This is the final outcome of its wisdom. After centuries of meditation, of delusion and self-congratulation as it proceeded arrogantly to conquer truth, it comes to the end of its journey, when it hoped to gather in the abundant harvest of its labours, and concludes by admitting its own impotence and nothingness. And it prides itself upon this as its greatest and ultimate discovery!

Article 15

The basic error in critical philosophy

331. The basic error in critical philosophy lies in its having made the objects of thought subjective.

These objects are the result of sensations (matter) and of

[331]

intellective forms. Sensations are modifications of our feeling and, according to Kant, are insufficient to constitute an argument for believing in the existence of an external cause that may have produced them. To be able to draw such a conclusion, one would have to accept the efficacy of the principle of *causae*.

However, the principle of cause and all the other forms, which do not originate in sensations, emanate from our spirit. They do so, Kant says, precisely because they do not come from sensations. Kant finds nothing midway between the origination of knowledge or some of its elements from sensations, and origination from our spirit. However, such an argument by exclusion is patently arbitrary and false because of the imperfect enumeration of possible cases. Such is the fundamental error of this school and the original sin of all the German philosophies which appeared after Kant's and took their direction from him.

The assumption — upon which Kant builds his system and for which he offers not the slightest evidence — that anything within our understanding which is alien to sensations must necessarily originate from the thinking subject, was due to his failure to notice that being has two modes (one *subjective*, the other *objective*) and that in both, being is identical.

Being in the objective mode is being which makes itself known, and makes itself known as it is, even when it is subjective. But because being is identical, knowledge is efficacious and true.

External things have subjective existence (to which extra-subjective existence is reduced). If we wish to know them, we must add to them objective existence which is their intelligibility. This objective existence is the part that does not come from sense; the subjective part comes from sense but is not known without objective existence because nothing can be known if it has no intelligibility. However, this does not change things because being is identical in the two modes; it is simply illuminated, it is known.

332. The fact is that we perceive external things, as it were by means of an instrument suitable for the purpose, by the idea of existence. When we form the judgment: 'Such and such a real entity exists', we apply the universal predicate of *existence* to the particular subject, that is, to the sensible action we experience. However, it does not follow from this that with our

activity we introduce *universal existence* into the thing perceived. We merely find in it its own *particular existence* and introduce this particular existence, which we have not created but
recognised, into universal existence. In other words, we place
the thing in the universal class of existing entia; we know them.

If the existence which we perceive in affirming a given real
thing were exactly the same as that which we have in our intellect when we perceive a real entity, we would have to introduce
into the perceived real thing a universal existence because existence is universal in our intellect. However, this is not the case.
We do not introduce a particular existence into a real thing
determined to the thing alone. We already see it there because
we know its own subjective existence by means of its objective
existence.

Kant's failure to distinguish between the prior concept of the
mind, which is always universal, and the thing, always particular, conceived by means of this concept, led the author of critical philosophy into another error. He considered that the
intellectual concept and the thing corresponding to it were one
and the same. For him, the whole universe was a product of
human understanding and human sensitivity. The understanding posited the *form*, and sensitivity the *matter* as two ingredients required to constitute all the entia of the world. He should
have realised that the part contributed by the intellect in
knowledge is confined to *making known* what the thing contains without contributing anything to it. He would have done
this if he had considered how the objective form, which is in
the mind, restricts itself to the measure of sensible, subjective
real things.

333. This observation on the idea of existence must also be
made on any other idea and especially on the twelve Kantian
categories to which, in Kant's view, all universals are reduced.

To show more clearly the truth of our observation, I shall
apply the argument I have expounded to *quantity*, one of the
four main ideas or categories.

The idea of quantity which I have in my mind is not, in fact, a
quantity of the same type as that which I perceive with the help
of my senses in a material ens, for example, in a house. These are
two entirely distinct modes of quantity.

This distinction is obvious. Although the two modes of

quantity, that which I have in my mind and that which I perceive in the house, are both designated by a single term, they nevertheless are different in character. The quantity which I have in my mind is characterised by a universality void of any measurement; in the case of the house, I do not, in fact, perceive universal quantity, or possible quantity applicable to other entia, but a determined, proper and individual quantity of the house itself, indissociable from the house. This quantity is therefore contrary to the idea, as the particular is contrary to the universal, and the ideal to the real. One excludes the other. The quantity which my mind conceives is not exactly that which I perceive by sense in the house, although I know the latter by means of the former. Critical philosophy errs, therefore, when it assumes that in perceiving external entia, we introduce into them the idea of quantity in our mind. The argument used is similar to that of Condillac when he points out that we refer and attribute to bodies the sensation of colour which exists only in ourselves. But regardless of Condillac's argument, that of Kant, which is similar to Condillac's, — although applied to ideas instead of sensations — is seen to be false as soon as the distinction between *universal concept* and *particular attribute* is grasped, that is, rendered particular by the sensible determinations proper to the perceived ens.

The same argument must be applied to the idea of *quality* and that of *relationship* (I shall deal with modality later on), and to their subordinate ideas, as well as to any idea we may wish to use to judge some real thing by attributing to it the quality expressed by the idea. It will always be necessary to distinguish, between the *idea* and the real, *particular quality* in the thing we recognise. The idea is the rule according to which we form our judgment; the *particular quality* in the external thing which we recognise is the result of our judgment; it is that which we have come to know by means of that judgment. It is not true, therefore, that our intellect inserts its idea as such into the thing, although it uses its idea to *know* what is in the felt thing when it is understood. It places what is felt into its idea and thus makes the external, real thing a true, complete *object* of cognition.[244]

---

[244] Our communication with external reality is through *sensation*; Kant seems to have ignored this. Consequently, he was unable to reconcile the

334. The truth of this distinction appears even more clearly when we consider what we do in pronouncing a judgment upon things, when we say, for example, 'This house is large.'

Let us analyse the statement. It contains nothing indicating that we have built the house, it says nothing about any size we have given the house. The meaning of the words presents simply an operation of our spirit with which it recognises the size of the house.

If we look more closely at this operation, we see that it assumes the *idea* of size which we use to recognise the *real size* of the house. The idea of size, therefore, is not the size of the house, because one is ideal and the other real. The ideal size is an instrument, as it were, by which we know the real size. Particular, real sizes are infinite; ideal, universal size is one and immutable.

Common sense bears witness to this. The whole of mankind, all the schools, ordinary folk everywhere have distinguished between the *idea* of a quality and the *quality subsisting* in a thing. They acknowledged that the idea can be present in our mind even when the subsistent quality does not exist. Kant, when accepting *a priori* knowledge, that is, necessary, universal knowledge, started from common sense and said to Locke: 'The existence of such knowledge is undeniable because people everywhere accept it'. Can he not admit now that the distinction of which I am speaking — between the idea of a quality and the particular quality shared by things — is also affirmed by common sense.[245] Kant, who devised a theory to explain a fact posited by common sense, also has to make room in the theory for other facts which relate to the same issue and are equally attested to and posited by human common sense.

Finally, if there were no true difference between my idea and the corresponding part of the house, I would be unable to tell one from another. In this case, why has everyone made the

following two truths: 1. that we know what is real through *concepts*; 2. that sensible real things are different from our knowledge of them. Unable to reconcile them, he sacrificed the latter to the former.

[245] Reid is inclined to deny my view that this is posited by common sense; the impartial reader will judge. The difference of opinion, however, about the witness of common sense shows that its authority is not always sufficiently self-evident to convince all individuals, as some claim.

distinction? What is the basis of such a distinction? This is the ideological question.

Article 16

Another error of the school of critical philosophy

335. Another error of the school of critical philosophy is this: Kant gratuitously assumes that each time we perceive something external with our understanding, we are also obliged to perceive *intellectually* its *quantity*, its *quality* and its *relationship*. This shows that he had not inquired deeply enough into the nature of the intellectual act with which we perceive things.

In fact, to perceive some reality with my understanding, I have to judge that it exists. But I do not need to judge about anything else; I do not need to assign specifically to the reality any quantity, quality and relationship. I can suspend judgment on all these matters and still perceive the thing intellectually, provided I say to myself, 'It exists.'

The judgment which I make in the first act of intellectual perception could be expressed as follows: 'Something exists which modifies my senses'. Here I implicitly assume that the thing must certainly be endowed with all the conditions of existence.

I do not need, however, to decide to conceive intellectually these *conditions* in the thing. The complex of sensations provides my spirit with the means to determine its object adequately enough to enable me to form the judgment, 'It exists'. I do not have to search with my understanding for the mode or particular determinations of this existence. Indeed, I can prescind from particular sensations, or sensations of any sort. I do this when, for example, I am thinking of a sensible object in general, or of an ens and nothing more.

Kant's error here consists in assuming that the four categories, quantity, quality, relationship and modality, are conditions of intellectual *perception* or, as he says, of experience. In fact, they are merely conditions of the *existence* of external things.

Certainly, no bodily thing can exist without quantity, quality and relationships but all these things, which are in it or belong to it, do not have to be intellectually perceived by me together with it for me to be able to say that I have perceived or conceived it. In fact, there are always many properties concealed in things which only time and study reveal. Nevertheless, the thing could have been perfectly well perceived without any thought of these properties or qualities.

To sum up: examining what is required by the act of our understanding when it perceives some bodily thing, we see: 1. that an agent has had an impact on our senses; 2. that our understanding pronounces judgment upon its existence.

The judgment, pronounced by the understanding on the existence of the agent as the producer of the sensations is the act of intellective perception.

However, the mind does not need to pronounce similar judgments on the quantity, quality and relations of a thing in order to perceive it, still less to conceive it. The understanding can conceive and perceive things without having to conceive and perceive their *quantity*, *quality* and *relationships*. These are conditions for the existence of things outside the mind in their real, particular existence. They are not, as Kant claims, conditions of intellectual perception. The understanding, even without the use of the ideas of quantity, quality, relationships, can perceive things. But it cannot perceive them without the use of the idea of existence.

When the understanding has perceived something proffered by the senses, it can also examine it and gradually discover its quantity, its qualities and its relationships. This is how we perfect our knowledge. Knowledge exists by means of a judgment upon subsistence; it is perfected by means of more particular judgments made about what has already become the object of our spirit.

336. It was inevitable that Kant should fall into the error to which I am referring; it is a consequence of the fundamental error outlined in the previous article.

He did not observe that there exists in the real thing some real, particular qualities corresponding to the four ideas of quantity, quality, relationship and modality. He imagined them as emerging from the mind to form part of the *thing* (which he no longer distinguished from the *object* of the mind) through an illusion on our part, by which we attribute to the thing what actually belongs to us.

Once this distinction was removed, he was unable to

[336]

distinguish the *conditions of the existence of external things* from the *conditions of the perception* and *of the ideas of those things*.

In Kant's view, things are for the most part not only known, but created. It follows that the conditions for things to exist and to be perceived must be the same. But the truth is that we do not posit anything of our own *in things*; we add to them with our act of perception what is needed to render them *objects* of our mind. The thing as it is in itself is one thing; the thing becoming the *object* of our mind is another.

Once the verbal ambiguity is dispelled, we see that there is some quantity and particular qualities in things, and some *quantity* and universal *qualities* in the mind. The former are something *real*, and must be present in things which otherwise could not exist; they are conditions of their existence. The latter are something *ideal*; they are in the mind and are the knowability of real qualities, the rules by which we judge things after perceiving them but not conditions necessary for perceiving them. Both, however, are identical relative to *being*, different relative to the *mode of being*.

Article 17

Objection answered

337. What I have said about the way intellectual perception takes place may cause the reader some doubt, which I must now dispel. This will help me clarify the nature of intellectual perception on the clear knowledge of which the whole question of the origin of ideas ultimately depends.

The doubt I refer to is not wholly new. I have mentioned it when expounding Aristotle's views on the question in hand.

I stated that the intellectual perception of external, material things consists in a judgment through which our spirit says to itself: 'An ens exists corresponding to my sensations.' Now someone may reply: 'The judgment is either pronounced by the understanding or not.' If not, the understanding does not perceive anything because intellectual perception is simply this judgment. If it *is* pronounced, the understanding necessarily perceives sensations upon which, or at least on the occasion of which, it pronounces its inner judgment of the existence of something corresponding to them. But if the understanding perceives sensations, judgment is not needed for intellectual perception because the mind first perceives sensations and then judges them.

338. This objection is due solely to a confusion of ideas about the faculties of the spirit and to a failure to distinguish the names which philosophers normally apply to them. It is met by a clear description of intellectual perception, which I am about to give, and a listing of the faculties in us which combine to produce it.

Let us recall the definition of the intellectual perception of corporeal things: 'It is a judgment through which the spirit affirms as subsistent something perceived by the senses.'

Analysing this act of the spirit, we find that it cannot take place without the following:

1. The body to be perceived acts upon our senses and occasions sensations in us. This sensible body is what has to be judged as existent.

2. To judge it as existent, we must have the idea of *existence* which is the universal applied to the same body when we say: 'It exists' — this universal does not come from the senses.

3. Finally, an act is needed in which we consider the effect of bodies upon us from the part of the operating principle. We consider this principle as existing *in se*, distinct from us. This amounts to classifying it in the class of existent things and formulating the judgment: 'What affects my senses, exists.'

It is clear from this analysis that perception involves the concurrence and co-operation of three different faculties:

1. The faculty of feeling what is sensible.

2. The faculty which possesses the idea of *existence*, that is, intuits being, which produces the predicate of the judgment.

3. Finally, the faculty which unites *predicate* to *subject*, and thus introduces the *copula* into the judgment, that is, forms the judgment itself.

Whatever these faculties are named, the distinction between them should always be maintained. They should never be confused.

If we call the first *bodily sensitivity*, the second *intellect* and the third *reason* or *faculty of judgment* and keep rigidly to these names, the following observations will, I feel, constitute a valid, complete solution to the proposed objection.

[338]

Sensitivity perceives the action of the body sensibly and passively (sensations); the *intellect* possesses within it the *idea of existence* (wherever it gets this idea, it has to possess it, as we saw, before the judgment of which we are speaking can take place). There is no doubt that as long as one *potency* possesses separately the complex of sensations (or whatever it has undergone), and the other power has only the idea of *existence*, no judgment is forthcoming. We do have, of course, the two elements making up a judgment, that is, subject and predicate, but the judgment is not formed as long as one is separated from the other. It is their synthesis or union which constitutes judgment, and it happens like this.

Sensitivity and *intellect* are two faculties of one and the same perfectly simple subject (the rational soul). This subject unites, in the simplicity of its intimate feeling, the two distinct elements bestowed upon it by its two distinct faculties. In other words, *myself*, who is on the one hand modified by *sensitivity* through which I feel the sensible agent acting upon me, am the same subject who, on the other hand, possesses the *idea of existence* in my intellect. This would not be sufficient, however, because the external agent and the idea of existence could both exist in a simple subject beside each other without uniting, without their revealing their connection to the soul. It is also necessary for this simple subject, which possesses these elements of judgment — the sensible element (matter) and the idea of existence (form of the judgment) — to possess a power or efficacy enabling it to focus its attention on what it experiences and what it has in itself. This subject therefore 1. is aware of having simultaneously what it experiences in its sensitivity and what shines in its intellect, that is, the idea of existence; 2. compares the sensible entity with existence; 3. perceives in the sensible element an existence which is merely a particular *realisation* of that ideal existence which it first conceived only as possible. These three operations, which we distinguish for greater clarity but which occur swiftly and even instantaneously in the depth of the intimate feeling of a sentient and intelligent ens, constitute the third of the faculties already mentioned, that is, the faculty of judgment, which is a function of *reason*.

In answering the proposed objection, therefore, I maintain that, in accordance with the names given to the three faculties, it is not the *intellect* which judges. Consequently the intellect is not the faculty which perceives, but that which provides *reason* with the means to perceive, that is, the rule by which to judge. This means and rule consists in the idea which serves as predicate in the formation of a judgment. What we are describing is termed *intellectual perception* because the intellect, although it does not specifically perceive, provides intellectual perception with its main, formal part.

339. It is not difficult now to offer a more explicit definition of *intellectual perception*: '*Intellectual perception* is what our spirit makes of something felt when it sees[246] this contained in the universal notion of existence.'

Article 18

Kant's philosophical achievement: he saw that thinking was simply judging

340. Kant's main achievement, I feel, was in seeing more keenly than any other modern philosopher, the essential difference between the two operations of our spirit, *feeling* and *understanding*.[247]

The distinction he made between these two operations enabled him to analyse the second, that is, *understanding*. It could not have been subjected to accurate analysis unless it were

---

[246] Terms derived from the sense of sight and applied metaphorically to indicate the operations of the other senses are the source of endless ambiguities and errors, as we shall repeatedly have the opportunity to observe. Nevertheless, I do not think that the same can be said of the verb *to see*, applied to the mind. Moreover, it can be said that this is now its proper sense. Common usage has changed its original, metaphorical meaning.

[247] He was aware that *understanding* was essentially different from *feeling* but he never really grasped the true nature of intellectual operation. What he grasped was that *understanding* was something active, *feeling* something passive. 'All *intuitions*, as sensuous,' he says, 'depend on affections; *concepts*, therefore, upon functions' (*Transcendental Logic, Analytic*, vol. 1, chap. 1, section 1). He called anything produced by the senses 'intuitions', somewhat inaccurately. This general habit of philosophers of speaking about other senses in *metaphorical* language taken from the particular sense of sight was the cause of frequent errors.

first isolated or separated from all other related or associated operations.

Accurate analysis of *understanding* enabled Kant to discover a most important truth. All the operations of our mind are ultimately reduced to judgments: 'We can reduce all acts of the understanding,' he writes, 'to judgments, so that understanding may be represented in general as the faculty of judging.'[248] This is true, however, only of the fleeting operations which the mind performs after it is first constituted; it does not hold good for the primal intuition.

Article 19

Kant clearly recognised the problem of assigning the origin of human cognitions

341. Kant had grasped that every function of our understanding came down, in the end, to a *judgment*. He was able to see, in a more general and more pr ofound way than all other modern philosophers before him, the precise difficulty in explaining the origin of human knowledge.

He recognised straightaway that our understanding could not *judge* unless it possessed notions, or concepts as he calls them, because judgment means submitting the particular to a universal concept. He said to himself: 'I can see very well how we can have the representation[249] of something particular through the senses, but I do not see at all how we can have *concepts*, that is, universal notions which have to serve us as attribute and predicate for the ens represented to us. The problem, therefore, can only consist in explaining these *anticipated concepts*, that is, those necessarily presupposed to sensations.'

He concluded that his first task was to analyse the *function of judgment* and indicate all the concepts it required. This he proposed to do in the part entitled: *Transcendental Analytic*:

> Thought is certainly cognition by means of *concepts*,
> but concepts, as predicates of possible judgments, relate to

[248] *Critique of Pure Reason, Transcendental Logic*, div. 1, bk. 1, section 1.

[249] The senses actually represent nothing. They merely give something felt to the spirit.

some representation of a yet undetermined object. Thus the *concept* of body indicates something — for example, metal — which can be known by means of that *concept*. It is therefore a *concept*, for the reason alone that other representations are contained under it, by means of which it can relate to objects. It is therefore the predicate to a possible judgment; for example the concept *body* is the attribute in this judgment: 'Every metal is a body.' All the functions of the understanding therefore can be discovered, when we can simply indicate the functions of unity in judgments.[250]

Article 20
The distinction between analytical and synthetical judgments

342. Kant, had realised, more clearly than any other modern philosopher, that the general mode of all intellective operations and, therefore, of intellectual perception, is judgment.

This shining truth could have led him straight to a full knowledge of intellective perception if he had carefully focused on it without too much care for regularity and system. Let us see instead where his thoughts led him.

Having fastened on to the principle: 'Thinking is judging', he set out on his philosophical itinerary from this sure point, and began to investigate the nature of judgment.

This inquiry convinced him that there are two possible species of judgment. Our mind operates in two different ways: either it divides an idea into a number of parts (*analysis*) or it combines a number of parts into one concept (*synthesis*).[251] Thus, some judgments are analytical, others synthetical.

[250] *Critique of Pure Reason, Logic*, div. 1, bk. 1, section 1.

[251] Kant maintains that no philosopher before him had thought of this division into *synthetical* and *analytical* judgments (*Critique of Pure Reason*, Introduction 6). This, it seems to me, is a customary boast of philosophers: they all claim to have been the first to see the most important truths. But the two operations of our intelligence, that of combining and of dividing (synthesis and analysis) were admirably described by Aristotle and were, after his time, more or less familiar to all philosophers. These two ways of operating cover, in fact, Kant's two species of judgments. In the *Phaedo*, Plato clearly describes *synthetical a priori* judgments (p. 13, 14), although he does not call them that.

Analytical judgments are those by means of which we assign to a subject a predicate which is essentially inherent to it, and merges into something identical to it. For example: 'A triangle is a three-sided figure.' This judgment merely explains the word *triangle*, asserting what it is, neither more nor less, that is, a figure with three sides.

Synthetical judgments are those in which the predicate is not contained in the concept of the subject but is something more than that expressed in this concept. For example, when I say: 'This man is white', I add the predicate *white* to the subject *man*, which does not contain it because there are also black men and men of other colours.

Kant noted the different propriety and task of these two species of judgment formed by the human mind when he wrote:

> The former (analytical) may be called *explicative*, the latter (synthetical) *augmentative* judgments because the former add in the predicate nothing to the idea of subject, but only analyse it into its partial ideas, which were thought already in the subject, although in a confused manner. The latter add to the idea of subject an attribute which was not imagined in it, and which no analysis could ever have brought out or discovered.

Article 21

How Kant posed the general problem of philosophy

343. Having established the difference between *analytical* and *synthetical judgments*, the two types of operation of our intellect, it was necessary to explain how such judgments could be formed in our mind. Clarifying the generation of these judgments would explain the acquisition of ideas and every other function of the mind.

Kant began therefore by noting that every *analytical judgment* implied a prior *synthetical* judgment. I can only break down what I have already built up. When I make the *analytical judgment* 'A triangle is a three-sided figure' I have to know beforehand the worth of the word *triangle*. Otherwise I could not define it as I do with this judgment. But to know the worth of the word *triangle*, I must 1. have in my mind the *concept* of triangle; 2. know that this name was given to this *concept*.

But how can I have the *concept* of a triangle[252] if I have not united in my mind the idea of a figure with the idea of three sides, that is, unless I have first said to myself: 'Is a figure with three sides possible?' But saying: 'A figure with three sides is possible', is simply to utter a synthetical judgment because the determination, or predicate, *three-sided*, does not form part of the *concept* of figure. In fact, there are figures with a various number of sides. We cannot, therefore, form an *analytical judgment* without presupposing the formation of a *synthetical* judgment. We cannot divide a concept without presupposing that we have intuited it united with all its parts. In other words, we have formed a synthetical judgment.

On the other hand, assuming that I already possess *concepts* as a result of these *synthetical* judgments, there is no difficulty in understanding how the *concepts* can be broken down into their elementary parts to generate *analytical judgments*. To do so, all I need to do is focus exclusively on some element of them, from which the concept is derived, and transfer my attention in turn from one element to another.[253]

Any difficulty, therefore, in explaining the operations of the human mind can lie only in attributing a sufficient cause to synthetical judgments.

344. Kant now focuses all his inquiry upon synthetical judgments, and first sets out to determine which they are.

He claims to have found two kinds: those relating to experience and those made *a priori*.

Empirical judgments, those derived from the experience of the senses, are all synthetical.[254]

---

[252] The concept of triangle in general, referred to here, is not to be confused with the mere sensation of a physically existing, particular triangle.

[253] This is the extent to which reflection can reach. For the rest, when I conceive separately the single elements of a concept which I am analysing, I must also be able to conceive these elements with the existence and union they have *in se*. To do this, I need to carry out a synthesis. Analysis, therefore, always presupposes synthesis.

[254] *Critique of Pure Reason*, Introduction 4. Kant calls these judgments synthetical because in them predicates are furnished by experience (we are speaking of empirical judgments) and are not contained in the concept of the

In fact, sensible experience provides the accidents which are not necessarily contained in our primal concepts. For example, I know from experience that certain men are white. I had not included the predicate *white* in my concept of *man*, but added it from outside. I use it therefore to form a *synthetical* judgment.

Kant sees no difficulty in the formation of such synthetical judgments because, he says, they are buttressed by experience 'which is itself a synthesis[255] of intuitions.'

> But to synthetical judgments *a priori*, such aid (of experience) is entirely wanting. If I go out of and beyond the conception of the subject A, in order to recognise another predicate B which is not contained in it but nevertheless united with it, what foundation have I to rest on to render the synthesis possible if I have here no longer the advantage of looking in the field of experience for such a predicate?[256]

Here Kant located the core of the difficulty with which we are dealing:

345. To enable the reader to understand the argument more clearly, I now summarise my findings to show how Kant endeavours to state his case.

thing. For example, when I see a white horse, I attribute to that horse whiteness not contained in the concept of *horse*, but given by sight sensation. But if the predicate is given me by experience, where do I get the subject to which to attribute it? The subject *horse* is an abstract which I would never have unless I had seen horses. But because the concept is abstract, it cannot be given by the senses. This is where the real difficulty lies; it does not consist in explaining where we find the *predicates of subjects already conceived* with our intellect but in explaining how we *conceive subjects*, or rather how we form concepts of them.

[255] Ignoring the inappropriateness of the word *intuition* used to signify everything real furnished by the five senses, I would merely point out that this proposition would merit extensive proof from Kant. Nevertheless, it can have a true meaning as long as this synthesis of intuitions does not go so far as producing the idea of existence. However, if we discard this idea, we cannot have any *synthetical judgment* suitable for analysis; in fact, a judgment of any kind is impossible. Kant therefore concedes to sensitivity more than a careful examination warrants. This shows the weak side of his philosophy and its *sensist* origin.

[256] *Critique of Pure Reason*, Introduction 4.

1. *Synthetical* judgments, it is claimed, are those in which we attribute to a subject a predicate not contained in the concept of the subject itself.

2. Assuming that we already have within us the concept of subject, we cannot derive from it the predicate we wish to add to it, because it is not contained in the concept. It follows that this predicate must come from another source.

3. This source can be sensible experience. When the predicate is such that it can be given to us from sensible experience, the possibility of our synthetical judgments is obvious. These are *empirical synthetical judgments*.

4. However, there are certain *predicates* in this species of judgments which cannot be given by the senses.

5. The difficulty consists, therefore, in showing the source of such *predicates* when, on the one hand, they are not given by experience, and on the other, are not contained in the *concept* which we have of the subject to which we attribute those predicates. Without these predicates, we cannot form *a priori synthetical judgments*. The universal problem in philosophy, according to Kant, must be stated as follows: 'How can synthetical judgments be presumed or preconceived?' or 'How can synthetical *a priori* judgments be formed?'

Anyone can see that in this series of five statements there is one which merits careful verification and solid justification. The fourth, the existence of *a priori* predicates not contained in the concept of the subject or — and this is the same — the existence of *a priori* synthetical judgments.

Do we really form *a priori* synthetical judgments? If we do, are they the judgments indicated by Kant? This is one of the foundation questions in Kant's whole edifice. It is a fact which must be proved. Its importance is such that we should dwell upon it for a while. It is, so to speak, the invisible leverage point which CRITICISM requires to raise the universe.

Article 22

Is it true that we make *a priori* synthetical judgments?

346. Kant claims that we make certain *a priori synthetical*

judgments, and puts forward examples by way of proof; there was no other way in which to prove such a statement of fact.

I shall, therefore, examine all the examples of *a priori* synthetical judgments produced by Kant. If I succeed in showing that they are not genuine, it follows that *a priori* synthetical judgments do not exist, or that Kant has wrongly included them in his list and misunderstood them. In this case, he built his system on a false basis.

To understand what I am going to say, note carefully which *a priori synthetical judgments* I deny. They are judgments in which an attempt is made to add to a presupposed subject a predicate which is neither contained in the concept already formed in the mind nor furnished by sense experience.

1. In Kant's view, the judgments of pure mathematics are all *a priori* synthetical. He first cites as an example the proposition $7 + 5 = 12$ which he claims is such a judgment.

The only reason he gives is this: the concept 12 cannot be derived from the sum of the two numbers 7 and 5, except by means of some external sign such as the fingers. The need for such external signs in addition is seen much more clearly (he adds) if we choose larger totals.

But this reason is useless for his purposes. Our need for some external sign to derive the number 12 from $7 + 5$ does not prove that the concept 12 is not comprised in the concept of the sum of the two numbers. On the contrary, it proves that it certainly is comprised in it. If it were not, we would be unable to deduce it even with the help of signs which add nothing to the concept but simply help us to recognise the same thing under two different *forms* or expressions. Note carefully that the *form* of a concept is one thing, and the *concept* itself another. In short, either we need the senses to conceive separately the number 7 and the number 5, or there is no *absolute* necessity for them in order to add the numbers together and obtain 12. The concept of 12 units, therefore, and that of seven plus five units is merely the same thing conceived by different acts of the mind. This gives the concept different *cogitative forms* in which the thing itself exists in equal measure.[257]

---

[257] The truth is rather that in nature there are no *collections*, but only separate individuals. Any numerical concept, therefore, implies something

347. 2. Pure geometry, says Kant, is full of *a priori* synthetical judgments. His example is the proposition: 'A straight line is the shortest distance between two given points.'

He claims that the concept of a straight line does not include the quality of being the shortest, and that sight alone cannot furnish such a proposition.

It is impossible to agree with this. Whether or not sight is necessary for us to deduce the shortness of a straight line, it seems obvious that this quality is of necessity included in the notion of being straight. All that is required is the pure concept of straightness and curvature to find, after analysis, that the concept of straightness contains the quality of the greatest possible shortness in relation to all the curves that terminate in the same points.[258]

348. 3. Kant claims that there are *a priori* synthetical judgments even in the physical sphere. He gives the following proposition as an example: 'In all changes that occur in the corporeal world the quantity of matter always remains the same.'

However, this proposition is necessary only on the assumption that by 'changes that occur in the corporeal world', we understand changes in forms and constituents, as happens in actual life. But if we add such a concept to the expression 'changes that occur in the corporeal world', it is obvious that the judgment is analytical. The immutability of the quantity of matter is a concept contained in the idea of the kind of changes mentioned in the proposition.

349. 4. Finally, Kant claims that even metaphysics (if, in

over and above what is in nature, or in sensation, precisely because it is the concept of a *collection*. This shows that in every concept of any number at all, the mind truly contributes *unity* by means of which it unites separate individuals and turns them into a collection. It can therefore be fairly said that in the concept of *number* there is always a corresponding *a priori synthetical judgment*. Kant's mistake, however, lies in looking for the synthetical judgment in the summation of 5 and 7 instead of looking for and finding it in the concept of 5, of 7, of 12 and of any other number, as I said.

[258] On the other hand, in the concept of every *line*, we can find a truly *a priori synthetical judgment*. Having the concept of a line is to think a possible line. But *possibility* does not lie in the physical line; it is a predicate furnished by the mind.

fact, it exists) cannot but consist of *a priori* synthetical judgments. His example is the famous proposition: 'Everything that happens must have a cause'. This, he claims, is one of his *a priori* synthetical judgments. I do not agree but, because the proposition deserves the most careful attention, I shall apply myself to examining it in detail in the following Article.

Article 23

Is the proposition, 'That which happens must have its cause', an *a priori* synthetical judgment in Kant's sense?

350. Kant claims that 'the idea of a cause lies totally outside the concept of event, and indicates something entirely different from it. Consequently this idea is not contained in the concept of what happens.'[259] According to Kant, in such a judgment a predicate (having a cause) is added to a subject (what happens). The predicate cannot be given by experience because experience does not indicate *causes* but only successive *facts*; nor is it contained in the concept of subject. As a result, he concludes, we have here an *a priori* synthetical judgment.

In my opinion, Kant needs to carry out a more painstaking analysis of the judgment, 'What happens must have its cause.'

I maintain that the concept 'what happens' contains the concept of *cause*. As far as I can see, the concept of *effect* and that of *cause* seem to me to be related in such a way that one is necessarily included in the other, that one cannot be had without implicit possession of the other.

Indeed, *effect* means 'what is produced by a *cause*'; *cause* means 'what produces an effect'. The definition of each of these two concepts, therefore, necessarily involves the other. One cannot be defined without understanding the other.

Kant, on his part, assumes that I already have the concept of subject, that is, of *effect* but, in making this assumption, he must also assume that I have implicitly the concept of *predicate*. If one is to exist, the other is absolutely necessary.

[259] *Critique of Pure Reason*, Introduction 4.

The judgment of the common sense of humanity, 'Every effect must have its cause' is not synthetical, therefore, because it is a judgment which has the predicate (cause) already contained in the subject (effect).

I am well aware of the objection that will be raised. It will be said that this judgment is made by mankind independently of the idea of *effect*, but solely with the idea of *what happens*. The judgment put forward as *a priori* synthetical was not: 'Every effect must have its cause' but: 'Everything that happens must have its cause.'

I feel the force of the objection. However, when we perceive something which occurs again, when, for example we see a tree in autumn bending under the weight of fruit which had not been seen the previous winter, we either see the new crop in its essence, and nothing more, or we consider its *beginning* to exist. In the first case (in the simple idea of the existing thing thought without its exterior relationships), there is no idea of effect or cause. In the second case, we come to consider it as an effect of some cause (however we arrive at this). Only at this second stage do we say: 'That fruit must have a cause', but we say this precisely because we have conceived it as an effect. In the second case, we have applied the general principle: 'Every effect must have its cause.' This principle, therefore, cannot be applied before the new crop is conceived as an effect, that is, until we have thought it with a concept so made that it contains the concept of cause. The concept of *effect* (subject), therefore, does not precede the concept of *cause* (predicate), nor is it ever independent of it. Rather, as soon as we conceive effect, we conceive cause implicit in it.

The difficulty cannot lie, as Kant maintains, in explaining how we pass to the idea of the predicate (which, he says, is not contained in the subject), but consists in our forming the idea of the subject itself (effect) which contains the concept of predicate.[260]

In other words, the universal proposition is necessary, and the *a priori* judgment can only be: 'Every effect must have its cause.'

---

[260] Kant could not have found an *a priori synthetical judgment* in the proposition, 'What happens must have a cause', but he could have found such a judgment in the intellective conception of 'Whatever happens'.

This is not an *a priori synthetical judgment* in Kant's sense, because the concept of predicate (cause) is contained in the concept of subject (effect).

351. Let us now apply this *a priori* proposition: 'Every effect must have its cause.'

How is this done? As follows: 1. we perceive an event; 2. we recognise it as an *effect*; 3. we conclude that it must have a *cause* because this concept is called for and required by that of *effect*.

The difficulty to be explained in these stages is not found at the first stage because we perceive a sensible event with the help of the senses. Nor at the third, that is, in finding the *predicate* of our judgment, as Kant claims, because, having conceived the event as an *effect*, we have implicitly posited a *cause*. The entire problem consists in explaining how we can take the second step and think of an event under the concept, *effect*. In other words, how we find the *subject* of the judgment, 'Every effect must have its cause', applied to a particular event.

Regardless of its explanation, however, we can take as fact the following proposition: 'We conceive any event whatsoever as an effect.' For the moment, I am not looking for an explanation; but the fact is undoubted.

This fact allows us to see the place occupied by Kant's proposition, 'Everything that happens must have its cause', amongst philosophical propositions.

Expressed in this way, the proposition does not express an *a priori judgment* but the *application* of an *a priori* judgmenet. The *application* generally made of an *a priori* judgment is only a fact. It is not a principle.

This is the order of these different propositions in their relationship to causality:

A priori principle: every effect must have its cause.

General fact: every event is considered by us as an effect.

General application of the a priori principle: everything which happens must have its cause.

Let me repeat. We need to explain the general fact: 'How does it happen that we conceive every new event, not only in itself, but also in its concept of effect?' If we succeed in explaining how we consider everything new that happens from this viewpoint, we also offer an adequate explanation of why we attribute a cause to this event.

352. Let us briefly analyse the universal judgment: 'Every event is an effect.'

Whenever a new event occurs, something begins to be which previously was not. I conceive two successive moments: in the first, the thing was not, in the second, it is.[261]

Starting from this observation, I argue as follows:

We cannot conceive the operation unless we first conceive *existence* (the existing operant).

Existence itself is an *operation* (an act). When the *existence* of a thing begins, therefore, and I consider this *existence* as an *operation,* I necessarily affirm some *existence* prior to the thing. This existence is precisely what we call *cause.*

It follows that an event is conceived as an *effect* when it is considered as *beginning to exist,* that is, when its *new existence* is thought as a *change* or, again, as *an operation.* This operation cannot be thought on its own but, to be thought, must be seen as preceded by another *existence* because the concept of operant being is included in the concept of operation.

The following, therefore, is the sequence of our conceptions:

1. We conceive *coming into existence,* a concept which includes that of *change.*

2. The concept of change contains that of *new operation.*

3. The concept of *new operation* contains that of *prior existence.*

4. The concept of *prior existence* contains that of *cause.*

Consequently:

1. The concept of *cause* is included in that of an *existence* prior to the *operation.*

2. The concept of *operation* is included in that of *change.*

3. The concept of *change* is included in that of *coming into existence.*

The entire difficulty, therefore, consists ultimately in explaining how we form the concept of *coming into existence,* that is, the passage from non-existence to existence. If we have the concept of this passage, we have the concept of change included in it; in the concept of change, that of operation; in the concept of operation, that of an existence prior to it; and, in the concept of

[261] The fact that I am aware at one and the same time of these two stages and compare them is due to the unity of my intimate sense.

an existence which necessarily precedes the first operation of a subject (which is precisely what exists), the concept of *cause*.

How, then, can we conceive the passage of a thing from non-existence to existence?

If we suppose that we can conceive the *existence* of real entities which fall under our senses, the passage of a thing from non-existence to existence presents no difficulty. It is administered to us from the senses with an act of judgment. We see, we touch, we feel what, in a word, we previously did not see, touch, feel, and could not sense.

The comparison we make of these two moments constitutes, in fact, the concept of the passage of one ens or of one entity from non-existence to existence. However, this implies, as I said, that we possess the faculty of conceiving the *existence* of that entity (that is, of that event). If we had only sensations, without the power to conceive something existent outside, that is, distinct from ourselves, we could never conceive the passage intellectually.

This analysis leads to the conclusion that the sole remaining difficulty in explaining the idea of *cause*, lies in the question: 'How do we perceive entia in so far as they are furnished with existence? How do we conceive existence? What is the source of the idea of being?' This is the problem of ideology.

Article 24

Shortcomings in Kant's way of stating the ideological problem

353. Kant stated the problem of ideology as follows: 'How are *synthetical a priori* propositions possible', that is, those judgments in which the predicate is not contained in the concept of the subject nor furnished by experience? The problem could also be expressed in this way: 'How is it possible for us to occasionally attribute to a given subject a predicate which does not come from experience, and which is not contained in its concept?' In formulating the problem in this way, it would seem that if we could find the *predicate* either in the *concept of the subject* or in *experience*, the difficulty would be solved.

[353]

First, if we could find the *predicate* in the *concept of the subject*, we would by implication already possess the *concept*.

The pity is that the problem lies precisely in our forming the *concept of subject*, in thinking things *as existing*, in transforming them into *objects* of the mind and therefore *subjects* of our judgments.

If we assume that we have formed the concepts of things, there is no difficulty in analysing and connecting them in any way whatsoever. The nub of the issue, then, consists in explaining how we form the *concepts of things*. Certainly we cannot form such concepts unless we think *existence* in these things. This implies that we have the *idea* of existence which cannot however come to us from mere sensations because sensations are particulars, nor from the concepts of things before we have formed them.

354. Second, Kant's way of presenting the ideological problem implies that there is no problem if we can find the predicate through sense experience.

It is certainly true that sense experience can, in a certain way, provide us with a predicate. Thus, when I judge a wall to be white, I am prompted by sense experience to apply the predicate *white* to it. Nevertheless, I must first have the concept of this particular subject to which I attribute whiteness, that is, I must have thought it as something existent. The difficulty, therefore, reappears: 'How can I think an ens, that is, conceive something real as existing?' I cannot derive the idea of existence (which I always need to enable me to form the *concept* of anything) by abstraction from the concept itself because I cannot abstract anything from a concept which I have not yet formed.

To summarise: even if I could find a predicate by resorting to sense experience or in the concept of subject, the difficulty of explaining the acts of our understanding would remain if it is necessary for me to have formed already a concept of the subject to which I then add the predicate. I would still need to ask how I had put together and formed this concept. The problem cannot consist in discovering the origin of a predicate to be attributed to a subject of which the concept is already formed, but in discovering the origin of the concept of the subject.

[354]

Article 25
Further clarification of the ideological problems

355. The problem: 'How is the object of thought formed?' where the object is subsequently to be the subject of judgments or, in a nutshell, 'How are concepts formed?', sums up the entire issue under discussion. I shall now proceed to analyse it as thus formulated, just as I have done up to now when it was formulated in different terms.

The formation of the concept of a thing involves an intrinsic judgment through which we consider this thing objectively, that is, in itself, not as some modification of ourselves. In short, we consider it in its possible existence.

As there has to be a predicate and a subject in every formed judgment, we first have to discover in our intrinsic judgment which is the *predicate* and which the *subject*. The next problem is the source of the *subject* and the *predicate*.

In our case, the *predicate* is simply *existence*. Perceiving a thing objectively is merely to perceive it in itself, that is, in the existence it can have. The subject is the thing which has fallen under our senses, that which has acted upon them.

Granted this, it is clear that the *subject*, prior to this judgment, is not something which has already been perceived by us intellectually. Indeed, the judgment itself is the act of intellectual perception. The *subject*, therefore — if we wish to call it that prior to the act of judgment — is merely the real entity perceived by the senses. It is, therefore, something of which we have no *concept* but only *sensation*. It is the felt element.

The greatest attention needs to be paid to this factual distinction, that is, first there are subjects in our judgments of which we have no *concept* prior to the judgments themselves, but only *sensation*. This simple observation is the golden key to the whole philosophy of the human spirit.

In fact, if we wish to express such judgments, which are the first made by our understanding, we say: 'What I feel exists.' I perceive intellectually by adding the predicate of existence to what I feel. I therefore take as *subject* of this judgment what is left when the predicate has been removed. But what remains when the word *exists* is removed? Only 'what I feel'. In other words, what I feel and do not, as yet, perceive as having an existence *in se*, that is, as something which does not yet exist for me in the immense throng of existent things.

It is this analysis of the primal judgment of our understanding in the formation of concepts, this purely mental division of the predicate 'existence' from the subject 'what I feel', which reveals the secret of the operation of our intelligent spirit.

The analysis of this primal judgment which enables us to form *concepts* of things, that is, ideas, reveals a *subject* — if it can be called this when isolated in this way — which is furnished by the senses alone and of which we do not, as yet, have any intellectual concept, and a *predicate* (the idea of existence) which cannot be furnished in any way by the senses and cannot, therefore, be explained by any thinkers who endeavour to derive all human knowledge from the senses alone.

The ideological problem consists therefore in discovering 'How the primal judgment with which we perceive intellectually what we feel, and hence form concepts of it, is possible.'

Article 26

Are primal judgments, through which concepts are formed, synthetical in Kant's sense?

356. The primal judgment, by means of which we perceive things and then form concepts from them, is achieved through a *synthesis* between the predicate, which is not provided by the senses (existence) and the subject furnished by the senses (complex of sensations).

In one respect, therefore, this primal judgment is *synthetical* and, as such, makes the formation of *analytical judgments* possible. Their function is merely to analyse the concepts of things which we have formed by means of the synthesis.

However, Kant does not use the word *synthetical* in this valid sense. Before I proceed any further, therefore, I feel I should point out the germ of the error, which lies in the ambiguous nature of this word.

The word *synthesis* means *union*. The expression 'synthetical judgment' means, therefore, 'a judgment which unites something to a subject without finding it in the subject itself.'[262]

However, the words *union, to unite* are metaphorical or at least conjure up the image of *physical unions*. We need to explain, therefore, right at the start, in what sense these unions can express how sensations and ideas are joined in purely immaterial operations.

When I say: '*I unite* a predicate with a subject', I may understand that I insert this predicate in the subject as I put a precious stone in a ring, or as I fit a wooden beam into the house which I am building. The stone and the beam are only in the ring or the house because I put them there. This is the sense in which Kant understands it.

Kant also assumes, as we saw, that in certain judgments the predicate, which I introduce and consider as an integral part of the subject itself, does not emanate from the *concept of the subject* and is not given me by experience.

He therefore concluded: 'It is I myself, it is my mind which places in the subject something which is not in the subject *per se*. My spirit, as though sending it out from itself, partly creates this subject for itself. That is, it creates the predicate in the subject. At times, I consider this predicate as a necessary part of the subject. I myself, through the activity of my spirit form or construct for myself the subject of which I am thinking even when something appears necessary and essential to the subject as the result of an illusion and deception on the part of my nature.'[263]

The entire argument is, in fact, coherent but it is unfortunately based on two gratuitous, false suppositions:

First false supposition: the attribute which we give to a subject is not found either in experience or in the *concept* of the subject

---

[262] I do not say in the *concept of the subject* but in the *subject itself*. I want to avoid giving the impression that we can think it possible to form the concept of the subject before forming the judgments whereby we perceive things, and hence forming concepts of them for ourselves.

[263] It really is humiliating for us to be presented with a philosophy which would always have us believe that we are inevitably and essentially deceived not by our fellows but by our own nature and by the author of our nature, if indeed the Creator survives in such a system! Can there be any greater humility in philosophy! It not only humbles mankind, but nature itself and God.

itself. On the contrary, when we assign an attribute to a subject, this attribute, if not given us by experience or by reasoning based upon experience, is always found in the *concept* of the subject itself.

Second false supposition: when we form a synthetical judgment, we unite the predicate with the subject in such a way that the predicate itself becomes an integral part of the *subject* although it forms an integral part only of the *concept of the subject*.

357. If we cannot take the word *synthesis* in the material sense attributed to it by Kant when we form a judgment, let us see what meaning the word has when it is applied to the operations of our spirit. This will serve to throw greater light upon the way in which intellectual perception occurs in us. An exact description and analysis of this perception is the key to the success of these investigations.

When we perceive a body intellectually, we attribute existence to it or, to put it more accurately, we conceive it in itself, in the existence it has, and not in its relationship to us.

There are three elements to this perception:

First element: everything pertaining to the body which comes to us through the senses (what is felt);

Second element: existence in all its universality, which is the idea;

Third element: the particular, real existence which we perceive in the body, and which we *attribute* to it by means of a judgment.

Existence in all its universality (at which stage it is still *ideal*) can be called *predicable*; the *particular, real existence* can be called *attribute*.

Kant, as I have already mentioned (cf. 322–323) confused the *predicable* with the *attribute* already predicated and affirmed. He confused the idea, which we predicate of a number of things (for example, the *idea of existence in all its universality*), with the particular, real *quality* which we attribute to the sensible body (for example, the particular, real existence) with which the bodily entity is endowed. He made these two things one. That is, he supposed that *idea-existence* and *thing-existence* were the same mode, although we call the second *subsistence* to distinguish it from the first. He failed to realise that the *existence* of an ens is particular to itself and not in any way applicable to other entia. *Idea-existence*, however, which is still not applied, is universal and applicable to infinite entia, to all those of which we can think. Particular existence is multiple, that is, there are as many different existences as there are existent things, and cannot strictly be called *existence* because it is inseparable from the existent thing. If we are to be precise, only the word *ens* can be used to express it. On the other hand, existence in all its universality, as it is present to our intellect, is one and unchangeable, and to it alone the word *existence* properly refers.

358. It may be objected that the existence which is in the perceived ens is itself either perceived or not perceived by our intellect. If it is not perceived, nothing can be said about it; if it is perceived, we have two ideas, one of existence in all its universality (predicable) and the other of particular existence (attribute).

I rebutted this objection earlier (cf. 324–326). However, it is so important to grasp the answer that I consider the solution worth restating in different words. I hope this will help the reader understand more deeply the intimate nature of the act carried out by our spirit when it perceives intellectually.

First, we must be careful to speak with propriety. The difficulty will then soon disappear.

The word *existence*, taken on its own, refers only to an idea. No *ens* whatsoever is said to have existence until we have conceived it. Before we conceive a material ens, therefore, this ens exists although we do not know it. Relative to us, it remains totally unexpressed.

If this material ens impinges on our senses — assuming that our intelligent spirit is inactive and that only sensations subsist within us — it would begin to have some relationship with us. The effect of this upon us would produce some sound which, however, would never be a *word* expressing what we had undergone and the cause which produced it. The sound would not be a sign of a judgment; it would not express an ens as it is in itself. It would be the involuntary *effect* of what we had undergone, of the feeling produced in us by that agent. It would not yet be perception of an ens. Inarticulate animal sounds are examples of what I mean, or exclamations of pleasure and pain which, although conveying no message in words, are instinctive effects of our animal experiences. All the articulated words which can be cited, for example, *ens, body, mind* etc., express already formed intellectual concepts. At this stage, therefore, I would not have perceived the *existence* of the ens, but only experienced the passion produced in me by its action.

But in activating my faculty of knowledge (reason), I assume that this agent, passively perceived by my senses, comes to be known in itself, that is, intellectually. What happens in the intellective act of my spirit?

I simply make an interior comparison between the experience undergone by my senses in particular (or, more exactly, the term of this experience) that is, the *felt element* and the idea of *existence*. I find a relationship between what is felt and the *existence* of an agent different from myself. I say to myself: 'What I feel is an agent which has existence (in a certain degree and mode determined by the senses).' In this way I form a judgment which constitutes my intellectual perception of the corporeal ens. Through this judgment, I consider this ens as posited in the immense host of entia, if I may speak in such a way. And I contemplate it from a universal point of view; I contemplate it as having an *existence in se*, independent of me, of my experience and of any other ens.

From this analysis of intellectual perception I conclude that 'intellectual perception is merely the vision of the relationship between that which is felt (the term of the experience) and the idea of existence'.

I can now resolve the objection set before me.

The *intellect*, if defined as the faculty of universal existence, merely intuits universal existence. It has no other ideas than this.

Reason, if defined as the faculty which applies the universal idea to external sensible things, is the faculty, possessed by our spirit, of seeing the relationship between what the senses provide and the idea of existence present to the intellect.

It follows that no corporeal ens can be intellectually perceived unless the following three factors are verified:

1. A universal idea (existence) in the *intellect*.
2. The effect of a particular entity acting on *sense*.
3. A vision of the relationship between the agent perceived by sense and the universal idea — an act of *reason*, a perception.

If any one of these three elements is missing, perception cannot exist in us, nor therefore the concept of a corporeal ens.[264] If we now assume that we have perceived through our sense the action of a particular corporeal agent and, to use an inexact expression, 'the particular existence of that ens', we would still not possess the concept or the idea of this ens. We would only have the sensation, the action. The particular ens, therefore, or (inaccurately) the particular existence is not *per se* knowable, it is not a concept. It is merely a sensible element from which the concrete idea or perception arises. This concrete idea or perception is 'the vision of the relationship between this particular agent in sense or (inaccurately) its particular existence, and the universal idea of existence'.

I conclude therefore: there are not two ideas of existence, one particular and the other universal. Only the following ideas exist:

1. A single idea of *existence*, which is universal existence.

2. Many perceptions and concepts of *existing entia* which consist, as I said, 'in the vision which our spirit has of the relationship between what is perceived in particular by sense and the idea of existence'.

359. Having resolved the problem put to me in this way and analysed more thoroughly the act of our understanding, it will now be clear how I can apply the word *synthesis*, or union, to a spiritual act.

The act of understanding or intellectually conceiving a corporeal ens consists in 'seeing the relationship between the particular agent as it is perceived by the senses and the universal idea of existence'.

It does not consist in our positing and uniting our idea (in our case, existence) in an ens, but in simply conceiving the relationship between it and our concept of existence by means of the unity of our intimate feeling. Perceiving a relationship does not mean confusing or mingling the two terms of the

---

[264] Eliminating the *idea*, and leaving only the real, as Reid did, comes down to the same thing. Reid removed the idea, Kant removed the real and left the idea. Both agree that entia are immediately perceived by our spirit. Reid says that the immediate objects of our spirit are *real objects*; Kant says that they are, in part, *concepts*.

relationship in a single thing. This would be a material species of union; it would be like that in which two liquids are poured into a vessel, or two ingredients mixed in food. On the contrary, when we conceive a relationship, the two terms are kept separate and are united only by an act of the spirit which considers one relative to the other and consequently finds a relationship between them. This relationship is a mental entity which in no way disrupts or alters them, but simply acts as a light to the spirit itself, forming what we call perception, knowledge and concept.

Accordingly, I call the primal judgment of our spirit, which gives rise to intellectual perception, *synthetical* and *a priori* because a spiritual union is formed between one thing given by the senses, which becomes subject, and another which does not enter the subject in so far as the subject is furnished by the senses. It is found only in the intellect, and is the predicate.

360. Note that while I say that this predicate does not exist in the subject furnished by the senses (that which is felt) I do not say, as Kant does, that it does not exist in the *concept* of the subject.

In fact, the predicate certainly does exist in the *concept* of the subject. The formed *concept* of the subject is simply the *sensible* subject to which the intelligible predicate has already been applied.

To say: 'The predicate does not exist in the concept of the subject' is entirely different from saying: 'The predicate does not exist in the subject.' The former is Kant's phrase, which contains the ambiguity and the error; the latter is the only one I accept and recognise as exact.

In a word: the subjects of our judgments are either furnished by our senses alone or already conceived by our intellect. In the second case, we have the *concept* of the *subject* of our judgment; in the first case, we have somehow the subject of the judgment, the subject in potency, which will become subject when the judgment has been made, but we do not possess its *concept*. Only when we add the predicate to the subject and form the judgment do we finally acquire, through this very judgment, *concept* of the subject.

These are *primal judgments* which constitute our perceptions of real entia from which we have concepts or *determined ideas*.

If, for example, we say: 'This man is wise' we make a judgment in which we already have the concept of the subject (this man). It is not, therefore, a primal judgment. But if we say 'What we are feeling at this moment with our senses exists', then 'What we are feeling at this moment with our senses' is indeed a subject of an already formed judgment but not of a judgment formed by the senses alone. Consequently, we do not have the *concept* until we have completed the judgment and said to ourselves: 'It exists'. Only then have we begun to perceive it intellectually.

The judgments, therefore, which enable us to form *concepts* or the ideas of things are *primal*, that is, the first we form of those things. They are *synthetical* because we add to the subject something which is not in it or, more precisely, we consider the subject in relationship to something external to it, that is, an idea in our intellect. Such judgments can still be rightly called *a priori* in that, although we need the *matter* of such judgments to be furnished by the senses, we find the *form* of the judgments in our intellect alone. In these synthetical *a priori* judgments lies the ideological problem, the first problem in philosophy.

Article 27

How Kant solved the epistemological problem

361. Every error in philosophy is due perhaps to the poor way in which the problem is stated. I think it is much easier to solve a problem than to state it correctly. In fact, it cannot be correctly stated unless one knows it through and through. And this is impossible unless it has been worked out in one's own mind.

We have seen that Kant stated the problem of ideology in the following way: 'How are synthetical *a priori* judgments possible?' By synthetical *a priori* judgments he understood those in which we ourselves introduce the predicate into the subject without its being included in the *concept* of the subject and without its being derived from experience.

[361]

Kant started from a false assumption. He began from the existence of such judgments. Having mistaken the first step, he had no choice but to construct the system of critical philosophy using an argument which can be summed up as follows:

'If there are *synthetical a priori* judgments, that is, judgments in which the predicate is not derived from experience nor found in the concept of the subject, we must derive it from within ourselves.

'Consequently, there exists deep in our spirits an awesome energy from which emanate the predicates of the species of things whenever we experience sensations.

'The nature of these predicates, which are not given to us by experience and are *a priori*, is inevitably endowed with two features peculiar to *a priori* knowledge, that is, *necessity* and *universality*.

'These predicates must be endowed with *necessity* because they are essential to our perception of entia, and they must possess *universality* because all perceived entia must be seen by us furnished with these predicates.

'If real entia can be perceived by us only when furnished with predicates, the predicates must appear to us as integral, essential parts of the entia we have perceived. It is the energy of our spirit which, from deep within, supplies these predicates in entia, and so to a certain degree constructs and forms for us perceived entia. In other words, it transfers from itself into them what they need for subsistence. It does not see in them that which is present of its nature, but that which has been placed there drawn from itself. And it sees itself in them.

'Granted these principles, ideology has to deal with two principal points:

1. It has to search for these predicates, that is, it has to seek and enumerate all the *necessary*, *universal* predicates without which the entia perceived by us would not exist. These predicates, because they possess the characteristics of necessity and universality, cannot have been given to us by experience.[265] They are, therefore, *a priori*. Nor are they to be found in the

---

[265] Kant's reasoning here is incorrect. It is not, in fact, the case that all *necessary*, *universal* cognitions are *a priori*. Only the *necessity* and the *universality* of these cognitions is *a priori*.

concept of subject.[266] Thus they pertain to synthetical judgments.

2. It has to describe the way our mind applies and transfers these predicates to entia, and constructs for itself the objects of its cognitions.'

The first of these two inquiries is called by Kant: *Analytic of conceptions*; the second: *Analytic of judgments*. Together they constitute the analytical section of *Transcendental Logic*.

362. First, in his attempt to discover and gradually elicit all the *concepts* (or predicates) which are used to form the *synthetical a priori* judgments previously mentioned, Kant thinks he can demonstrate that there are twelve of them, for which he preserves the Aristotelian term: categories. As sensations occur, our intelligence extrudes from within itself these twelve predicates or categories, as constituents in objects themselves. The objects result, therefore, from two elements: 1. from these *pure concepts*; 2. from *intuitions* of sensibility as he calls them, that is, sensations clothed in the forms of space and time.

The second task was to discover how this composition of pure concepts (categories) and intuitions of sensibility (sensations) comes about, so that they are like two elements making up the object itself.

In this inquiry, Kant thought he had established the need for a mediator between the (completely pure) categories and the (completely empirical) sensations in such a way that the latter could be seen in the former. He found the mediator to be *time* which unites with the pure concepts of the intellect (categories) and with sensations.

---

[266] The following contradiction in Kant's thought should be noted. He maintains that these predicates come to form part of the ens we perceive. But he describes ens, as perceived by us, as originating from two elements: 1. from intellectual concepts; 2. from empirical intuition: 'This extension of concepts beyond the range of our intuition is of no advantage; for they are then mere empty concepts of objects' (*Transcendental Logic*, Introduction 4). But those intellectual concepts are pure. They are the *predicates* of synthetical judgments. However, if pure concepts are the predicates of *synthetical a priori* judgments, how can he assert that the predicates of *synthetical a priori* judgments are not to be found in the concept of the perceived object? This concept is impossible unless it contains the pure concepts which are the conditions of our experience and of all our conceptions.

He assumed that time, in uniting with the categories or predicates, produces certain notions which are closer to sensible things (although still pure). He called them *schemata*, which are mid-way between completely pure, universal predicates and fully constructed objects.

He distinguished, therefore, the following different steps which our pure intellect takes in engaging with sensibility.

1. The intellect contains *categories* or fully universal predicates.

2. When these *categories* are considered united to *time* (which is the form of our inner sense, or the condition according to which we feel internally), the union gives rise in our minds to *schemata* which are in substance less universal predicates of categories.

3. If we unite these *schemata* to sensations, the subsequent union of these *schemata* with sensations (which Kant calls *empirical intuitions*) produces the real entities — or external world — which we think.

Thus, Kant solved the problem of ideology and philosophy coherently with the way in which he had formulated it. He had answered the question he posed: 'How are *synthetical a priori* judgments possible', that is, how do we form for ourselves the objects of our thought?

Article 28

Kant did not understand the nature of intellectual perception

363. It would appear, from what I have said about the way in which Kant formulated the problem and therefore about the way to solve it, that he formed an inaccurate, material concept of intellective perception.

In fact, intellective perception, as I have analysed it, is simply 'the vision of the relationship between an idea (existence) and that which we perceive with the senses'.

In this operation, the idea (existence) does not mingle with what we perceive with the senses, nor does it merge with it, but remains completely distinct. But it does apprehend the *relationship* between what is felt and this idea, a relationship which, as we shall see more clearly later on, enables us to know sensible entia.

On the other hand, Kant assumed that the universal idea (the categories) was so closely merged with what we perceive with the senses that together they formed the external object of our thought. He committed this error through his failure to distinguish the *predicate* from the *attribute* (cf. 330–332), that is, the particular element which really is in the known ens[267] from the universal element which is the type of which the particular is the realisation. For example, quantity in general, as a type, is certainly not the same as the quantity present in the real ens, although the second quantity has a singular *relationship of identity* with the first. This relationship makes the second quantity knowable, and constitutes it as known. 'The possibility of such a relationship of identity between the particular thing in the known ens and the universal thing in the mind' is the real issue which Kant should have formulated, but did not succeed in grasping.

Article 29

Kant admits too little and too much that is innate in the human mind

364. Kant's thought is merely a development of Reid's theory.[268] In Kant's view, our spirit has nothing innate prior to sense

---

[267] The particular element in an ens is only intelligible by means of the universal element in our mind; the former is not in itself an *idea* but the term of a *judgment* which unites it to the universal idea.

[268] Reid's thought that our spirits do not contain any *ideas* but only *perceptions of entia*, so that our spirit immediately perceives the entia themselves, was already present in the work of Arnauld: *Traité des vraies et fausses idées* (On True and False Ideas). However, in the work of this adversary of Malebranche, one sees, perhaps, even more clearly the link between his system, which has no room for ideas, and Kant's thought. Arnauld, in stating that there are no *ideas* between entia and ourselves, but that we immediately perceive entia themselves, said that our *perceptions* are of their nature representative and modalities of the soul. It is the soul, therefore, which has the *modes* (forms) of all entia. Anyone can see how close this is to the system of transcendental philosophy.

experience. When the spirit is provided with the *matter* of its cognitions by the senses, it is obliged to accept it in accordance with certain laws, to endow it with *certain forms*. Together, the *matter* of the senses and the *forms* which the spirit adds to them form external objects.

These *forms*, in relation to the intellect, are the *twelve categories* or pure concepts already noted, that is, predicates which our spirit adds necessarily and universally to the data of experience.

The best image of the human spirit in action, Kant says, is that of a prism which breaks up the light, as I mentioned earlier (cf. 256–257). The white is broken down by the form of the prism which splits it up into seven colours. In the same way, the sensations in our spirit take on all the forms of our spirit itself and are transformed into external entia which then seem to be things distinct from us and totally independent.

From one point of view, this way of considering the human spirit results in too little that is innate, as we have seen when discussing Reid; from the other, it endows the spirit with an energy which creates the external world, but is nevertheless subject to inexorable laws. Thanks to these laws, it simultaneously and continuously emanates from itself and involves itself in a profound, inextricable, necessary illusion, and in a fearful inevitability from which it can only escape by means of practical philosophy, another necessary, fatal illusion [*App.*, no. 32].

Article 30

Conclusion

365. I placed Reid in the ranks of philosophers who admitted too little that was innate in the human spirit, and Kant in the school of those who admitted too much, although Kant's system is a development of Reid's.

Effectively Reid did not foresee Kant's consequences, and considered as innate only an instinct for judging the existence of bodies. He did not realise that, once this was conceded, it was impossible to call a halt. Kant's was the only possible conclusion, and he had the courage to reach it. It takes courage for a man to condemn as deceitful the very nature of things.

CHAPTER 4

The steps taken by philosophy through Plato, Leibniz and Kant, and the work still to be done

Article 1

Epilogue to the three systems

366. Plato, more clearly than any other philosopher, and after him Leibniz and Kant, experienced to some extent the difficulty present in explaining the great fact of ideas.

The minor philosophers who overlooked this difficulty and whom I mentioned in the preceding Section — however meritorious their contribution to other branches of philosophy — cannot aspire to a place with those who attempted to discover and produced a solution to this particular problem. Our three philosophers, however, who concentrated their finest intellectual efforts on pursuing the discovery of such a noble truth, played an outstanding part in the history of the solution of such an important and capital problem.

It is also true that the question, passing from one of these philosophers to the next, made progress in the following way.

We saw that in attempting to assign a cause for facts given by experience, we must not put forward a cause greater than the effect. In this case, something in the cause would be superfluous. We have also seen that where a number of causes are put before the mind as equally capable of explaining the effect in question, the least or most simple cause offering an explanation is to be considered the most likely (cf. 26–28).

All three philosophers posited something innate in their explanation of the fact of the origin of ideas. This was sufficient for the explanation they intended to offer. At the same time, however, they posited an excessive, somewhat arbitrary degree of innateness.

Later contributors benefited from their predecessors in that each one whittled down to some extent the superfluity of his predecessor. Progress was gradually made, and the correct boundaries of the problem were set little by little. All the signs were that, in their hands, philosophy had chosen a path leading to perfection and truth which it would finally have reached if, before reaching its goal, it had not been overtaken by extraneous, fatal misfortunes and had not dealt itself a mortal blow.

Leibniz posited less that was innate than Plato who posited innate but forgotten ideas. Leibniz wanted only tiny vestiges of ideas which, in accordance with some kind of harmony, would have the power to relieve and reinforce one another (cf. 293–294).

I have already pointed out that these vestiges of ideas make no clear sense. All that can be admitted about the different ways in which ideas are present within us is applicable only to the state of *non-reflective* and *reflective* ideas (cf. 288–292). The question about the degrees of intuitive force can be set aside because it refers to the subject rather than the object.

But Leibniz's thought, which envisages tiny, insensible perceptions, shows very clearly the need he felt to remove the excessive feature of Plato's theory by accepting less of what was innate than Plato and Descartes acknowledged. But he could think of no other way of analysing ideas and isolating what was innate in them than by imagining them as devoid of light and feeling in the depth of our soul.

Kant came on the scene soon afterwards and had more success. He took advantage of a distinction which, although very ancient, was ignored by modern thinkers: the division of ideas into their *formal* and their *material* parts.

Conscious of the importance of this distinction, Kant regarded as innate (cf. 324–326) only the *forms* of cognitions, and left sense experience to provide their *matter*. This was an excellent thought and when viewed in relation to the spirit of Plato's philosophy seems to be the key with which to penetrate Plato's own intention. Plato himself perhaps was unclear about his aim and unable to communicate it exactly and coherently.[269]

---

[269] In a few passages, Kant adopts the mantle of Plato's interpreter. For instance, in dealing with his *three* ideas or concepts of reason, and relative to the understanding of Plato's philosophy, he makes the following observations:

'Let me say that it is nothing unusual, in conversation and in writing, to understand an author better than he understands himself by comparing the

Kant, by restricting what is innate in us to the pure *forms* of cognitions, introduced into the human spirit less of what was innate than all his predecessors. Nevertheless, he realised the necessity of admitting just enough for a full explanation of the fact of ideas and human cognitions [*App.*, no. 33].

367. Kant introduced seventeen *forms* into the human mind to explain the fact of cognitions: two for sense (internal and external) twelve for the intellect (*pure* concepts or categories), and three for reason (*ideas*).

This entire list of forms was excessive; the formal element of reason is much simpler. He did not succeed in expressing sufficiently well the subtle division between the *matter* and the *form* of knowledge, and extracting the purely formal element devoid of anything material.

This species of metaphysical chemistry which I have attempted convinces me that these Kantian forms are no more the *formal elements* of human knowledge than the four elements of *Empedocles* are the simple substances from which various bodies are derived. But just as progress in chemistry broke down the ancient elements of water, earth, fire and air into a greater number of principles, so metaphysics, in happier but opposite sense, offers as the final result of its analysis a much smaller number of formal elements of human knowledge. Finally, it reduces to the greatest simplicity — to one alone, the form both of *reason* and of *knowledge*.[270]

various things he has to say on a given subject. He may not have sufficiently determined his concept, and thus have reasoned, or even thought, in a way opposed to what he intended' (*Critique of Pure Reason, Logic, Transcendental Dialectic*, bk. 1, section 1, in Cav. Mantovani's translation into the vernacular).

[270] There is something inherently absurd and contradictory in the multiplicity of the *forms* of understanding and knowledge. If, in fact, I use the word *understanding* to refer to something determined, and the word is not a vague term with no specific meaning, and I use the word *knowledge* to express something which has a single essence enabling it to be distinguished from any other, it is inevitable that understanding and knowledge have only one single *form* which determines these things to be what they are. The *form* of a thing is what constitutes the *essence*, that which makes it what it is. But a thing cannot have a number of essences or a number of forms. This would be as much a contradiction as saying that a thing can be many things, that a thing can be what it is not. What Kant calls a *form*, therefore, has to be something subordinate to the first and true form of *understanding* and *knowledge*. They

Kant, therefore, admitted too much that was innate. Let us look more closely at how this came about and prepare ourselves for the path we shall have to follow in the next Section when, putting aside examination of others' conclusions, I shall set about fulfilling my other obligation to the reader: that of presenting the *theory of the origin of ideas* which, in my view, conforms to the truth.

Article 2

The superfluity of Kant's forms and how they are all reduced to a single form

368. Kant sets forth and describes his forms in the most systematic way: one form for the external sense, one for the internal sense; the intellect has precisely four, but each is sub-divided into three: finally, reason has precisely three, neither more nor less.

The orderliness which Kant's philosophy everywhere exhibits — it seems to have been devised using a set-square and guidelines — is calculated to alert the scholar to examine with greater care whether such a symmetrical and restricted arrangement is natural. In its other works, nature is usually simple, and fruitful in a more abundant and majestic manner than is the case with impoverished, presumptuous human imagination.

369. At this point, I make no claim to undertake a detailed inquiry into the Kantian forms. Although he said that he would deduce the categories strictly from the forms of judgments — always an extremely happy idea — he did not keep his promise. He presents us with a ready-made table of categories, claiming on his own authority it was perfect. Nowhere, that I can recall, does he attempt to demonstrate that the number of such categories resulting from the forms of judgment is precisely twelve, and assigned three by three with perfect distributive justice to each

may be what Kant calls partial and derivative forms, but they are not what we are seeking, the form which constitutes the nature of the understanding. As pure form, it is not multiplied except by union with something external and real.

[368–369]

of the four fundamental forms. But Kant, by not justifying the symmetrical inference of the categories, left us in doubt, as Aristotle (whom he criticises[271]) also did, whether they are correctly deduced and enumerated, that is, whether they are the only twelve classes into which all human knowledge should inevitably be placed and divided. It would, therefore, be out of place to undertake a detailed critique of this division (which is just as arbitrary as the ancient division) of the most universal ideas of the human understanding.

370. It is immediately evident that, at times, he confuses the outward form which our ideas are given by different views of mind and language with the ideas themselves. He groups and classifies the same concept differently because its outward form is different. This facilitates the symmetrical arrangement of the division. For example, in the form of *quality* he discovered the sub-division of *infinite judgments*, which are, in fact, no different from *affirmative* or *negative* judgments except in the outward *form* of speech.[272]

---

[271] In *Transcendental Analytic*, bk. 1, c. 1, he refers to 'the guiding thread for the discovery of all pure concepts of the intellect' and attributes it to the nature of judgment. Later, however, he does not deduce the forms from judgments but merely sets them out in a table. He does not bother to show the *necessity* for twelve, or that they cannot be more or less, or different, or in any different order from that in which he presents them.

[272] Kant puts forward the following example of infinite judgments, 'The soul is not mortal'; he claims that this judgment differs in *form* from: 'The soul is immortal'. Now if 'by form', we mean the outward trapping of words, I agree with him, although in itself the word *immortal* is perfectly synonymous with *not mortal* and therefore does not differ in the inner, conceptive *form* of which I am speaking. The forms which arise from speech are too numerous and merely apparent. One form of the mind is displayed and clad in a number of external ways. Let us take as an example a negative attribute which does not have only one opposite (as, for example, 'mortal' which has only the one opposite 'immortal') but a number of opposites, such as colours (affirming, for example that a body is not *green* does not, in fact, affirm that it is red). Such a case is complex, and comprises two pairs of judgments. The first pair, 'It is not green' and its opposite 'It is green', and the second pair, 'It is red' and its contrary 'It is not red'. When complex judgments are reduced to simple ones, only *affirmative* or *negative* judgments can be made (whether one affirms or denies with probability or certainty). The class of *infinite judgments* is merely a mixture of the two forms of judgment and does not produce any new, original form.

371. In the same way, Kant seems to omit ideas which determine the classes of human knowledge and could have been placed in the categories solely because he feared that they might exceed the established number and ruin the desired, regular arrangement. Thus, *continuous* and *intensive quantity* ought to be put into the category of *quantity*, where he puts only discrete quantity because it furnishes him with the three sterling classes of *unity*, *plurality* and *totality*.

372. At times, he endeavours to preserve the regular symmetry by doing violence to certain ideas. He tries to reduce these ideas to those which have had the good fortune to be honoured as *categories*. For instance, he wants to reduce *truth* to *plurality*, and *goodness* to *totality* as though the abstract idea of plurality could contain the notion of *what is true* and the abstract idea of *all* could contain the notion of the *what is good* [*App.*, no. 34].

373. In the ideas which he calls *ideas* of reason, which are forms of the absolute, he confuses what is truly *absolute*, as God is, with what is relatively absolute, such as the *human* soul and the *universe*. In the end, all ideas of the absolute must, according to Kant, finally be reduced to one, indivisible idea, that is, to the *ens of ens*, to God.

Thus Kant's three *ideas*, or *forms* of reason, are reduced to one.

374. However, the very idea of God, considered as *form* of reason, as Kant presents it to us, is ambiguous.

God is to be taken either as a subsistent being or merely as a pure idea of our mind. For the sake of its own satisfaction, our mind thinks as possible and necessary a species of hypothesis about the final cause.

This final cause, seen as a pure, undetermined, abstract hypothesis, which the mind needs for its own satisfaction, is not what we call God. Kant, therefore, when referring to God in the *Critique of Pure Reason*, does a kind of sleight of hand, using in a different way from normal a term considered venerable by mankind in order to deceive his readers and ward off the ignominious title of atheist.[273]

---

[273] In Kant's *Pure Reason*, God is viewed merely as a type in our mind of a most perfect being, an ideal, an exemplar. This does not permit us to come to any conclusion about his real existence.

In truth, God, if considered as real Being, could not be a natural form of our reason, in this life here below, without being at the same time the matter of our thought because we can conceive God only according to likenesses based upon the finite beings which we experience. The form of our reason here below is *ideal being*, a rule through which, when forming judgments, we come to know real entia. The *form* of our knowledge must therefore accommodate itself to all objects of knowledge, and cannot be one of them.

Granted this, let us see what universal, formal elements there are in the idea of a first cause, which is the Kantian idea of God.

Analysing the idea of a first cause, we find within it two other more elementary ideas which go to form it: 1. the idea of cause in general; 2. the idea of the cause of all causes or of all that is (finite).

The cause of all that is, is found only through the application of the idea of *cause* in general to all that is.

The idea of cause contains the principle: 'Every event must have its cause.'

The application of this principle to the complex of all events (to the universe) produces the proposition: 'The complex of everything finite (the universe) must have its cause'.

This proposition is merely a consequence of the principle; it is contained in the principle as though in a seed. It does not, therefore, offer any new *notion* which informs our mind, different from the notion of cause in general. Hence the idea of a first cause cannot be an *originating form* of the human mind, different from the notion of cause in general.

However, the idea of *cause* in general is already included by Kant in the twelve categories.

None of Kant's three ideas of reason, therefore, can truly be called the form of our intellect. Kant confused in these ideas the *matter* of thought with what pertains to the *form*.

375. Let us now examine the twelve categories which Kant calls the forms of the intellect, and the two forms of the internal and external sense. Let us see whether they are all truly *originating* and primal *forms* of our mind, as Kant claims.

I note first that Kant's twelve categories cannot all aspire to the same status in such a way that each may be independent of the others and thus *sui generis*; they cannot be reduced and aligned under each other as minor classes under major ones.

[375]

Take the *form* of *modality*. It has under it the three categories of *possibility*, *existence* and *necessity*.

Now compare this form with the other three, that is, the forms of *quantity*, *quality* and *relationship*.

I am perfectly able to conceive a *possible* or *existent* ens without having to know its *quantity*, its *quality* and *relationships*.

In this case, my intellect is conditioned by the law of having to think such a being either as *possible* or as *existent* or as *necessary*;[274] but my intellect is not in any way obliged to furnish this ens with the forms of *quantity*, *quality* and *relationship*.

If an act of the intellect can, therefore, be posited without need of the three forms of *quantity*, *quality* and *relationship*, these, by implication, are not *necessary* and *essential forms*. They do not inform and constitute in its proper nature the operation of the intellect. Consequently, these are not the forms which we are seeking. We are looking for those forms by which the intellect is intellect, and through which intellectual operation exists, that is, the forms which constitute the proximate, essential and necessary term of the intellectual act.

It follows that the form of modality is independent of the forms of *quantity*, *quality* and *relationship*. Hence the understanding, with the single *form* of modality, can carry out some of its acts without need of the other forms.

On the other hand, we cannot think of the *quantity*, *quality* and *relationships* of an ens unless we have previously thought it either as *possible* or *existent*.

All three forms of *quantity*, *quality* and *relationship* depend therefore on the form of *modality* which is greater than the other three. These can only occur in thought by means of, and subsequent to, modality.

We are justified, therefore, in concluding that Kant's first three forms, *quantity*, *quality* and *relationship* cannot be considered as original and *essential* forms of the understanding because its existence and operation can be conceived without any need of them.

---

[274] What is *possible* is always *necessary*. This threefold division is therefore defective. The exact division would be 1. possible; 2. existent, with subdivisions of a) contingent, b) necessary. But in this case the systematic threefold classification would be sacrificed.

376. The same is true for another reason. Is it necessary for every ens to have a determined *quantity* and *quality*?

To affirm this categorically, as Kant does, is to convict critical reason of extremely dogmatic self-assurance and rashness and endow it with the power to decide a question which cannot possibly be determined *a priori*.

Kant could have said: 'To maintain that every possible ens must be endowed with a fixed *quantity* and *quality* is a claim that goes beyond the forces of reason because, in order to make such a claim, we would need to examine all possible entia as well as examining the infinite Being, of which we have no positive and adequate notion.' In this case, he would have displayed a modicum of true or certainly apparent philosophical modesty. He would have shown some self-consistency. But he has none, although nothing pleases and gratifies him more than being able to criticise reason and rail against the philosophers he scornfully calls dogmatists, that is, against all those who openly profess something as certain. However, he had pronounced judgment on the issue and affirmed that *quantity* and *quality* were among the first-born forms of the human understanding, without which the understanding could not think of anything at all. This was blatant audacity, and revealed the barrenness of critical philosophy, shorn of the mask of philosophical humbug.

We must conclude, therefore, that *modality* alone is the only one of the Kantian forms which may be called an *original form* of the human understanding — a form which informs the intellect and the knowledge proceeding from the intellect. Let us see whether modality contains anything we are seeking.

377. I first note that when I think and judge that something *exists*, I do not necessarily perfect my *idea* of the existing thing.

Indeed I can have an *idea* as perfect and determined as required, even though the ens corresponding to it does not really *exist*.

Consequently, the judgment that the thing of which I have the idea really exists is an act intrinsically different from the one whereby my intellect possesses and contemplates the idea. The judgment adds nothing to my *idea*, no new notion informs my mind through the judgment.

Real and external *existence*, therefore, the term of my judgment, cannot be any *original form* of my understanding, which contains only the *idea* of the thing. The idea neither increases nor diminishes, nor undergoes any alteration from the subsistence or non-subsistence of the thing itself.

The *form* of the intellect, therefore, can only be an *idea*, not the *subsistence* of the thing. Hence, *existence*, one of the three categories, *possibility*, *existence*, and *necessity*, cannot in any way be an original, essential form of our understanding when considered separately from the other two.

378. Let us see if the other two, *possibility* and *necessity*, have the characteristics of originating, essential forms.

The idea of any thing whatsoever (in so far as it does not have any internal repugnance) is what is called the logical *possibility* of the thing.

Now, it is of course impossible to perform any act of understanding without the form of *possibility*.

However, when I think of the *possibility* of a thing, I am not required to think explicitly of its absolute *necessity* if this necessity refers to the thing thought and not to its possibility. If the necessity refers to the possibility, it is not distinguished from the possibility, of which it is an abstract quality.

Necessity cannot, therefore, be an original, primal *form* of my understanding because it is not the object and universal, immutable term of my understanding.

This leads us to conclude that, of all the twelve Kantian forms, the human intellect has only one, *possibility*. Let us see what it is.

379. I said that the *possibility* we are discussing is the *idea* of any thing whatsoever. In fact, possibility must always be thought of any thing, because the possibility of nothing cannot be thought.

Possibility, therefore, is indissociable from any thing whatsoever; on the other hand, it may be united to any thing whatsoever.

For us to be able to conceive possibility, therefore, it is not necessary for the thing we are thinking of to be determined to a genus, a species or an individual. It only needs to be something, an ens, even perfectly undetermined.

The *idea* (possibility) of the *undetermined ens* is the sole original, essential form of the human intellect.

380. Let us see now how all of Kant's nine first forms of the intellect are reduced to this alone, as to their formal principle,

and how the other two categories of *modality* (*existence* and *necessity*) either have nothing formal or are elements already contained in possibility. Let us begin with these.

If by existence we mean the idea of the existence of a thing *in all its universality*, this is comprised in the idea of *undetermined ens*.

If by existence we mean the actual subsistence of an ens, this is only the term of the *faculty of judgment* and does not add any form to the *intellect*.

The analysis of *possibility* enables us to discover *necessity*; what is possible is necessarily so. In this sense, necessity is comprised even in the *idea of ens in all its universality*.

However, if by *necessity* we mean a *real, necessary ens*, we have to say of this what was said universally speaking about the *actual existence* of entia.

381. With the three categories of *modality* reduced to the single form of the *idea* of *an ens in all its universality*, let us see how the three which come under the heading of *relationship*, that is *substance*, *cause* and *action*, are reduced to the same form.

I have already shown that the entire intellectual content in the ideas of *substance* and *cause* is nothing other than the idea of *existence* and of ens in all its universality (cf. 52–54, 347–348). Kant, therefore, in placing *substance* and *cause* in the categories, or original, essential forms of the human intellect, did so because he failed to analyse the categories sufficiently to discover what was pure form in them.

Note, relative to the idea of *action*, that both the understanding and the *senses* perceive *action*, although the latter do this by experiencing it in their own way.

Particular action, in so far as it is perceived by sense, cannot be placed in the categories. This is reserved solely for *action* conceived by the intellect or — which amounts to the same thing — the *concept of action*.

But how does it come about that the *particular action* perceived by sense becomes *universal* when it becomes the object of the intellect? This depends on the understanding's power to consider the particular action experienced by sense as *possible*, that is, repeatable an indefinite number of times. It is, therefore, the addition of *possibility* which transforms the action into a *universal concept*. The same holds good when I consider what constitutes the nature of action in general, and I abandon consideration of the particularities of the different species of action.

The concept of action, therefore, when subjected to analysis, is found not to be an entirely pure form of the intellect. Rather, it is made up of 1. a *material* element in so far as it refers to acts experienced by our sense; and 2. of a *formal* element in so far as our intellect adds the form of *possibility* and thus abstracts and universalises particular actions.

The only formal element, therefore, in the idea of *action* is possibility, that is, the idea of ens in all its universality.

382. Undertaking a similar analysis, we are able to reduce Kant's *quantity* and *quality* to the form of ens in all its universality by separating their *material* element from them, and retaining only their *formal* element. Such an analysis, however, leads us to the conclusion that these concepts contain no formal element apart from the idea of *possibility* or — which amounts to the same thing — of ens in all its universality.

Indeed, even the term of my sense has a certain *quantity* and a certain *quality*. But *quantity* and *quality* perceived by my sense are not in the least the form of my intellect. *Quantity*, therefore, and *quality* as concept and, according to Kant, as form of my intellect, are not particular quantity and quality, but quantity and quality considered in all its universality.

If we adopt the same approach to quantity and quality as we did to the concept of *action*, we can see how we arrive at *quantity* and *quality* in all their universality. When I perceive a particular quantity and then think it purely as *possible*, I have by this operation alone made it *universal*. If I remove from this idea, or possible quantity, the features which specify it, and thus generalise it, I have in it quantity in general.

Quantity or *quality*, therefore, are not naturally the object of my intellect as though they were an intrinsic form of the intellect. To become such an object, they need to be informed by another form. The form which my intellect adds is, in fact, that of *possibility*.

Quantity and *quality* are *per se matter*. My intellect, by informing them, makes them into one of its *concepts*.

This *concept* of quantity and quality, therefore, (when analysed) has nothing formal in it except the *idea of possibility* or *ens in all its universality*.

[382]

Thus, Kant's twelve forms are reduced to one single, pure and true form.

383. There is no need, at this point, to mention what Kant calls forms of the external and internal sense, that is, *space* and *time*. These do not pertain to the order of intellectual things. Such a question can only involve their concepts.

The formal element in such concepts, therefore, is *possibility* alone, or the idea of *undetermined ens*. What has been said proves this.

384. There is, however, another difference to note between the nature of Kant's multiple forms and the nature of the single form with which we are left after all the others have vanished. Kant's forms all come from deep within the subject and are therefore subjective. But the true form is essentially *object*. This difference in nature is of infinite importance, as we shall see; at this point I can only forewarn the reader of the diversity.

I conclude: the human mind has no innate *determined* form. Kant's seventeen forms have no true foundation, and are completely superfluous in the explanation of the origin of ideas.

On the contrary, the human mind has a single, *undetermined* form: the *idea of ens in all its universality*.

The idea of *ens in all its universality* is pure form, and has no material element associated with it; it is not subjective, but rather *per se objective*. It is so simple and so elementary that it cannot be simplified further, nor can anything more elementary be conceived which may be capable of informing our cognitions. At the same time, it is infinitely rich in promise.

Truly, it is impossible to imagine any act whatsoever of the mind which does not need this form, and is not natured and informed by it. If the *idea of being* is removed, human knowledge and the mind itself are rendered impossible.

Having reduced what is innate in the human mind to the *minimum* possible, I now have to show how this minimum is nevertheless sufficient to explain fully the origin of all our ideas. This will form the argument of the following Section.

Appendix

1. (Preface, 3)

[Value of ancient philosophy]

Note that in modern times philosophy has endeavoured to stage a revival. Human vanity and self-love grew so inordinately, especially in the second half of the last (18th) century, that the entire philosophical heritage was solemnly spurned and abandoned. The sophists who wrote before and during the French Revolution adopted a lofty, insolent tone which showed how they thought, and tried to persuade others to think, that all their predecessors were stupid victims of immeasurable prejudice and corruption. This explains the profound contempt they displayed for all ancient writers, especially those who expounded the traditional teachings of Christianity.

This contempt for ancient philosophy, and to a greater extent for the Fathers and other Christian writers, was communicated to the general public, and instilled a prejudice which can be dispelled only very slowly. It has still not entirely disappeared and operates to the detriment of true, sound teaching. For my part, however, I want to point out here, once and for all, that whenever I can, I quote authors who witness to the tradition of the truths expounded in the present work.

On the other hand, I do not intend to use authorities to settle questions. I would be quite happy if intelligent persons, who may be averse to such authorities, or have bowed to standard prejudice about them, or have little or no regard for them, were to concentrate solely on the arguments and judge tradition accordingly. In fact, there is no other way of laying aside false prejudices and the lack of esteem felt for these authors. Only personal experience of a philosopher's work and careful attention to his judicious reasoning together with true, profound arguments enable us to decide whether an author is serious and worthy of honour. This is the way in which to revise judgment on our predecessors. We do not abruptly rise against them, but show appreciation of their fine, subtle research, their noble judgments, their solid arguments. And we point out that apparently new questions and difficulties about human knowledge which seem exclusive to our age were not unknown to the ancients.

Our prejudices arise, of course, because so few of the ancients are known and studied; our unbridled passion for independence and for total control of our lives has broken the thread of tradition. But we have to believe that people born prior to the 18th century also had eyes and ears, tongues, feet, hands and heads, as we do. Thought is not in any way a modern discovery, nor has any machine been invented to make our thinking more effective, swifter and reliable, less subject to the delusions springing from human passions and the allure of human malice.

2. (107)

[Reid and ideas]

Dr. Reid would like to banish *ideas* from philosophy because he finds them somewhat awkward. To do so, one would have to discover how to eliminate the term *idea* from all vocabularies, remove it from all languages, forbid common sense from uttering or thinking it. But, it is in fact a term very frequently used, as much by ordinary people as philosophers, in both scientific and everyday speech.

What exactly is Dr. Reid proposing? The title of his work would have me believe that his sole aim is to defend the principles of common sense against philosophy which is bent on their destruction. Is he, perhaps, the kind of person who sets out to defend common sense but begins by opposing it?

Claiming that one's own philosophy adheres to common sense may be true if we wish merely to express what we intend, but it is at least presumptuous, if we mean that our own philosophy is actually in accordance with it. Whatever the philosopher claims, he remains nonetheless what he is, a poor fallible mortal, a mere individual. One will tell you in all earnestness: 'My philosophy is that of common sense.' That is certainly not the case: it is neither more nor less than your philosophy.

338 *A New Essay concerning the Origin of Ideas*

Another will boldly say: 'All the others are guided by their prejudices; one should follow reason alone, as I do.' These are rash and empty words; a person will at most follow what he considers reasonable, but he cannot act as reason itself, he is not the personification of reason. Even if the whole of mankind (setting aside revealed truth) were to tell you with one voice: 'This is truth', you would be entitled to reject such a bold statement and reply frankly: 'Mankind is corrupt. As soon as you speak you are lying! What arrogance leads you to claim that what you think is truth? Say: "This is my opinion"; do not say: "This is truth." Such an expression is for God alone'. However, a person, either on his own or in a group always tends to see himself as greater than he is. The cheating politician speaks on behalf of the nation; every newspaper always assures you that it speaks for public opinion; every demagogue declaims for the sake of the people and defends the people's rights against its inhuman oppressors.

I wanted to mention this when speaking about the philosophy of Dr. Reid because he is so modest and circumspect. My remark in such circumstances is all the more effective and shows how easy it is for a philosopher to promise more than he can achieve, and how common a defect it is among those who rely upon themselves for their arguments. The Fathers and so many writers of the Catholic Church, it must be said in all justice, are the only ones whose deep, genuine modesty is universal, sustained and sufficient to allow a person to attain truth.

Moreover, the problem of the existence of ideas which Dr. Reid raised is extremely important and extremely difficult, and for such a great man to have simply highlighted the problem is of incalculable value.

The scholastics, however, had already seen this. They realised that the object of our thought, when we are thinking about real things, could not be the idea but must be the real thing itself. As a result, they said: 'We think about something, but because it is external to us, we need, in order to think about it, an idea (or image) to make it present to our spirit.' I must admit that this explanation, taken in its most obvious sense, is unsatisfactory. It is always possible to reply that we think about something external to us by means of an idea. In this case the object of our thought is in the last analysis something not present to us. It is

[*app.* 2]

not absurd, therefore, that my understanding, as though going outside itself, should grasp an object remote from it. But if this is feasible and possible, what use is the idea? Is it necessary? The reason which persuaded me to accept the idea was merely the need to confine the spirit within itself, so to speak. Now, on the other hand, the idea is itself an instrument by which the understanding ventures forth to grasp the external object which is different and distant from itself. The question was not *how* our understanding could make the external thing its term and object, but whether it was possible for the external thing itself to be this term and object. If this does not involve contradiction, I have no need of the idea. All I need, when sensations occur, is to let my understanding range freely over them and grasp the external objects as they are, and thus perceive them. This is the objection we can raise about the solution proposed by the scholastics, when taken in its original sense. In my view, however, the schol astic or Aristotelian solution admits of an interpretation which makes it more plausible. I intend to present it elsewhere when I have dealt with other concepts essential to a clear understanding of it.

Later still, I shall give the solution which I think allows for Dr. Reid's problem over ideas. I shall show that such a difficulty arises partly from philosophers' lack of clarity in expression, and certainly from the erroneous understanding of certain philosophical expressions. For example, when I say that an idea expresses something as its image, portrait, type, sign or indication, I am using expressions which are to be interpreted with great caution. Otherwise they produce the most serious misunderstandings. Let us briefly see how this occurs.

Recall what was said earlier about the identity between representative and common idea, and you will understand what I mean in saying that an idea is something representative. Let us analyse this statement under both its aspects.

1. *Everything representative is common or universal.* In fact, whatever is representative of something is also representative of all similar things, since a number of things that are similar to a third are similar to each other. There can be only one exception to this: that is, when only one thing can be similar to what is representative.

2. *What is common or universal is representative.* On the

other hand, a thing is representative of another only in so far as it has some quality in common with it. Thus a portrait is representative of the persons who resemble it, not in so far as it is an individual picture. As individual, it is a strip of canvas, some priming, oil, and particular colours mixed and prepared in the oil. In all these things which constitute its own, individual, real existence, the portrait cannot be like any actual thing. When considered merely in its individuality, it exists only in itself, has no relationship (since it abstracts from such relationships) and consequently represents nothing. It is therefore intended to represent persons only by virtue of what it has in common with them, that is, in virtue of exerting on our spirit an impression similar to that offered by the faces of such persons. It is ourselves who find the likeness between the portrait and such persons because we compare the impressions made on us by the picture and the persons, and find them similar. Discovering the similarities in these impressions is exactly the same as ascertaining some common quality in them as, for example, the flesh pink of the colouring or the expression on the face or the curve on the lips, and so on. Now, *common quality* means, in fact, that what is in one subject is also in the other. This common quality is thus one single thing which *we* see in a number of subjects. But although it is a single thing in us, we assign it to two or more subjects determined and individuated by their own features and by their real existence. We do this by means of different intellectual acts of our spirit. This single thing is thus a *single species* in us, by which we see a number of things when they act individually upon our senses. This is how we recognise that such things resemble each other. Seeing two or more similar things means 1. seeing a number of things *by means of a single species* through which we are shown their similar elements and 2. receiving the particular, individual impressions which each of them produces in us and through which we see these things in so far as they exist individually in themselves without any relationship of similarity between them. Now, it is clear, merely by observing things in so far as they exist externally to us and in themselves, that they are not similar since none of them goes outside itself; each is absolutely confined to its own existence. If, therefore, we see similarities in them, if (which amounts to the same thing) we see their similar qualities through a single species, we have to admit that, in this respect, we do not see them as they are in themselves, in their proper, real existence. We see them by means of a *species* which is in us. We call this species *idea*, which is representative in the sense that it is a quality replicated in many subjects.

Here I cannot discuss further or clarify this issue which belongs to the treatise *on the nature* rather than the *origin of ideas*. However, I had to demonstrate the existence of ideas so fiercely assailed by the Scottish philosopher. To demonstrate the origin of ideas, we must be sure that they actually exist. Otherwise we are in danger of constructing a theory upon a non-existent 'fact'. This has frequently happened to poor sages here below.

3. (120)

[Degerando and Galluppi on judgment]

The efforts that people make when they are beset on all sides by a problem are worth consideration. They try every possible way out, overturn every obstacle to free themselves and escape from their predicament. They even go so far as to alter the notions of things; they deny the most commonly accepted definitions; they cast doubt on even the most obvious truths. They then become very watchful of others and will almost certainly find the slightest slip if this is in any way helpful to them. They adopt the same approach as they do when falsifying the meaning of so many other words and distorting so many ideas.

Among other efforts made by philosophers to evade the problem which I raise against Reid's theory is their attempt to deny the definition of judgment. Degerando tells us that judgment cannot be a comparison of ideas because, if it were, ideas would have to precede judgment; Reid's argument, on the contrary, shows that judgment necessarily precedes ideas.

Degerando's view does indeed point to an inaccuracy in the common definition although it provides no answer to the objection which I raise against Reid. I think this is the place to point out both the valuable aspect of Degerando's view and its defect.

[*app.* 3]

Degerando argues thus:

> When we affirm to ourselves the existence of an external
> object, we form a judgment. Now, this judgment on the
> existence of external objects cannot be produced by the
> comparison of two ideas. In this comparison I find rather
> the relationship existing between ideas, but do not thereby
> venture outside my spirit. I never succeed in judging, by
> the comparison, that something outside me actually exists.
> Consequently, the judgment by which I assert the reality
> of some external object cannot consist merely in a compar-
> ison of my ideas.

This argument (assuming that we are speaking of the reality of
bodily *entia*) brooks no reply. Up to this point, therefore,
Degerando's reflection is true and can be fittingly used in
argument.

However, the consequence from such a reflection is this: 'The
definition which sees a judgment as a mere comparison of ideas
is therefore inadequate.' That is all that can be inferred from the
argument, nothing else.

There still remains the other definition of judgment which I
usually adopt: 'Judgment is an operation of the spirit by which
we attribute a predicate to a subject.' This is a broader definition
than the former, 'Judgment is the comparison of ideas.' My definition says nothing about ideas nor does it stop at comparisons;
it speaks of *predicate* and *subject*. To reduce it to the definition
criticised by Degerando, we would need first to demonstrate
that *predicate* and *subject* were necessarily in every case two
ideas. Now this is precisely what I show not to be the case. I
maintain instead that only the *predicate* must in every case be an
idea, not the *subject* which may be a feeling, a complex of sensible qualities, a felt element. By means of this view I explain the
primal judgment to which we resort when judging the real
existence of things outside us. I show that this does not arise
from linking two ideas, but from linking the real, felt element
(in which form it is not yet an ens for us but a complex of sensations) and the idea of existence. It is the second linking
which enables us at one and the same time to judge the real
existence of external objects, and form some concept of them.

Degerando, however, did not see this intermediate link

between saying: 'Judgment consists in the comparison of two ideas' and saying: 'A judgment occurs without the need for ideas.' He did not see that there is another proposition between these two: 'A judgment is sometimes formed by linking an idea and a feeling.' So, having shown by means of a sound argument that defining judgment solely in terms of a comparison of ideas was inadequate, he felt justified in establishing that judgments are made even independently of ideas, that is, by a simple act without the need for two elements (predicate and subject), from the mingling of which the act results.

He endeavours to establish that 'there are elementary judgments which consist in the mere perception of objects' and that our knowledge arises from these.

> Our first act of cognition is both perception and judgment; perception because its object is seen; judgment because it is seen as real.
>
> (*Histoire comparée*, vol. 2, c. 10)

I shall use Baron Galluppi's own words to criticise this strange statement, that is, the words of one who is basically in agreement with the French philosopher.

> If simple perception of objects (as Galluppi says with his usual common sense) is merely perception, why give two names to a single operation of the spirit? This only gives rise to equivocation.
>
> Degerando says: 'Primal knowledge is a judgment because the object is seen as real.' The spirit, I repeat, associates the idea of reality or existence with the notion of object. It says to itself: the object which I see is real; but this operation presupposes the ideas of object and of reality or existence. Consequently, it is a secondary operation relative to perception or idea, which ruins Reid's theory. There is no intermediate view: either the mind focuses on the mere sight of an object and has a perception, or it focuses on the object's reality and immediately unites two ideas and forms a judgment. But the second operation occurs after perception and implies it.
>
> (*Philosophical Essay on the Critique of Knowledge* by Pasq. Galluppi, Naples, 1819, vol. 1, c. 1)

Galluppi then turns back to the view that simple perception is the initial operation of our spirit and that the *simple apprehension* (the idea) of objects is prior to a judgment about their real existence. However, this theory cannot be sustained after the comments Reid made upon it.

Having demonstrated that the initial operation of the spirit cannot be a simple intellectual perception (an idea) Reid concluded:

> Thus, the initial operation of the mind is a judgment. However, this conclusion was too hasty and could not be accepted; judgment without any prior idea was inconceivable.

Degerando, aware of this difficulty wrote:

> In that case, let us change the definition of judgment. Let us form one that suits us, that is, one which incorporates the two systems. Other thinkers insist that the initial operation of the spirit is a *judgment*, although this does not mean judgment without perceptions. Let us accept then that the spirit begins from a single operation which is both judgment and perception. Let us imagine a simple judgment, a judgment as simple as perception.

Galluppi came along subsequently and found Degerando's solution contradictory. In fact, simple perception can never be a judgment because, in simple perception, the two terms of a judgment cannot be discerned. Nor can a judgment ever be simple perception because in reducing the two terms to one, the judgment would be destroyed or even rendered it impossible. Degerando's intermediate solution is as self-contradictory as saying that two is one or one is two.

Escape from such an intricate maze is possible by asserting with me that: 1. the simple intuition of *being* is innate in human beings, and that consequently, 2. if we exclude the natural act which renders us intelligent, the first operation of our spirit is a judgment which unites sensations with the idea of being and thus forms the ideas of bodies.

According to this theory, a judgment is not the union of two ideas, but of a predicate and a subject — the subject is the felt reality. It is therefore a union of idea and felt element. Prior to such a judgment, we do not have the simple apprehension or *idea* of things but only the *sensation*. We form a judgment on their real existence, and from this judgment and subsequent persuasion of their real existence, we derive their *simple perception* by abstracting or excluding entirely from our persuasion of their existence.

We must therefore either admit that the problem of the origin of ideas is inexplicable or accept the proposition to which we seem so reluctant to subscribe: there is within us some primal, natural form of information. I trust that as this work develops, the truth will emerge in all its clarity.

4. (152)

[Applying names in ancient times]

The most ancient data we have referring to the imposition of names is the famous passage in *Genesis* (c. 2, 19) where we are told that Adam gave their names to all the animals God created. After this account, the sacred historian adds: *Whatever Adam called every living creature, that was its name.* In explaining this passage, Eusebius says that Moses wished to indicate how the names assigned to the animals expressed their nature: 'When he says, "That was its name", what else did he mean except that these were the names that nature recommended they be given?' (*Praep. Evan.* vol. 9, c. 6). Now the names given to the different animal species created by God to signify their nature, are in fact merely *common names*. Thus, the most ancient, authoritative document surviving on the early formation of language clearly demonstrates that the first names given to things were common, not proper names. Hebrew traditions and the opinions of the rabbis corroborate Eusebius's opinion. Anyone wishing to see this collective evidence, needs only to consult Giovanni Buxtorfio Junior (*Dissert. Philologico-theologicae* 1, §24) or Giulio Bartolucci (*Biblioth. Magna rabbin.*, vol. 1) or other writers.

Moreover, it is not only the ancient Hebrew texts which assure us that *common* nouns, which signified the *nature* or *quality* of things named and not their individuality were the first and most ancient. This is the view of all the ancient world and the fact presented by ancient languages. I do not have enough time now to offer the countless proofs which these languages offer. All I would say is that Plato's *Cratylus* is substantially given over to proving this very point, that is, that in very ancient times, names were given to things not arbitrarily but rationally. If we have to assign new names, we too must try, as the ancients did, to form and assign names which express the qualities and nature of the things to be named. Finally, in using names that have already been assigned, we should be careful to employ them with complete propriety so that they do, in fact, correspond to their meaning.

Because ancient names were common and referred to *common qualities, species, essences,* the ancients clung to the firm, universal opinion that the fullness of wisdom consisted in the study of names, which had to be jealously and immutably guarded. They were to be handed down to the children as they had been received, a precious and sacred heirloom which contained the deposit of religion and wisdom, and the key to human happiness.

Superstitions associated with the use of certain names came from the same source. The reverence which the old showed for these names, and the importance they gave to keeping them intact and handing them down to their descendants, was later transformed into blind, indiscriminate veneration. Such excess, to which every human passion is always inclined, allows the imagination to run riot and produce the most capricious effects.

5. (154)

[Common and proper names; abstraction]

A common noun, even before it becomes proper by convention, is occasionally used to refer to individuals. When this happens, the indetermination of the noun is usually corrected by external circumstances connected with the act to which it is referred. Meeting someone by himself on the road and wishing to talk to him, I shout across to him: 'Man, listen to me'! Upon hearing my voice, he stops and turns towards me, rightly applying to himself the common noun *man* because there is no-one else on the road. If there were, others perhaps would have turned towards me because the noun was common to them all. However, if this had happened, I would soon specify the man to whom I was speaking by waving my hand, or merely by the way I projected my voice, or by other signs suitable for restricting the common noun to one individual.

Now the first names given to things must, in fact, have been essentially *common*, though used and considered by those who uttered them as *proper*. In other words, nouns, although they indicated only a *common feature*, were always taken as united with individuals to which they were tacitly referred. Our spirit, in its primal state, is still not accustomed to dwell on abstractions and goes directly to the reality of objects.

The order of ideas pondered by the human mind is as follows: 1. The mind has the idea of being but neither reflects upon it nor gives it any thought until it has considered everything else. The series of ideas dependent on reflection does not start here. 2. Next the spirit acquires perceptions of individuals through the senses. These perceptions consist of a) common notions (ideas) and b) the proper, real, sensible element. Human attention dwells and focuses on this twofold term of perception. 3. *Abstraction*, whereby human attention focuses solely on more *common* notions, begins only later.

We name only the idea on which we reflect, not the idea to which we give no attention. Thus, our first named ideas are those applied to individuals. It was this, I think, which led to Smith's error. He inferred that our first words must have been proper nouns, which history and, therefore, reason shows not to be the case. He had not observed the nature of ideas applied to individuals and presumed that we think of individuality with the aid of simple ideas alone. Instead, the ideas by means of which we think of individuals are common notions linked to the proper, real element. I maintain that, although the first named ideas are not simple but applied to individuals (perceptions or memories of perceptions), this naming is referred to the common notions included in them. These are, therefore, common names which, as a result of their users' intention and external circumstances, are made suitable for naming individuals.

If the first named ideas are individuated, the second are abstractions, that is, ideas of common notions included in individuated ideas. The next operation of the human spirit is to separate these common notions, isolate them and finally give them a name.

As I said, individuated ideas are named after their common content, and as common refer to individuals solely because of what is implied by the spirit of their user who does not employ them without mentally referring them to individuals. This means seeing what is common in individuals. We now need to see what is common in isolation from individuals and name it in this state.

Two questions therefore: 'How can the spirit carry out our first abstractions?' and 'How can it name them?'

Obviously, if we assume the power of abstraction to be present in the spirit as it operates (in other words, if we assume that the first difficulty is solved) there is no longer any difficulty in understanding how the human spirit can name the abstractions it has conceived.

It can name them both by using common nouns such as *man, animal* etc. and by using nouns indicating abstractions such as *mankind, animality* etc.

Relative to common nouns, which it already possesses, the whole difficulty for the spirit consists in finding out how it begins to use them as merely common nouns, that is, without referring them to determined individuals. Knowing how the spirit can do this means knowing how it is roused to its first abstractions. It therefore depends entirely upon the first of our two questions.

Once we suppose that the spirit has managed to reflect upon the abstract qualities of things envisaged in isolation from their proper qualities, there is no difficulty in forming nouns referring to abstraction. In fact, a person can name any idea whatsoever provided he grasps it by concentrating his attention on it. Everything depends, then, on the first question: 'How is the human spirit moved to carry out its first abstractions?'

To do this, a person needs assistance from some *external sign* (language) which indicates the abstract thing separate from everything else. This sign must be suitable for focusing its attention and concentrating it purely on the abstract quality. It is thus impossible for an isolated person to invent a language to serve that purpose merely by thinking it out.

[*app.* 5]

6. (155)

[Applying names]

Captain Cook's observation, which Dugald Stewart puts forward in favour of Smith's view, serves — rather remarkably — to prove the opposite. While on the one hand it confirms the view I am putting forward, on the other, it offers an example of the vast difference there is between using facts and using them properly.

Smith and Stewart claim that the savage was the first to form *proper* nouns, which he then converted into common nouns by applying them to a number of similar things. These nouns, applied to many similar things, took the place of species and genus. This, according to Smith and Stewart, is the process by which human beings come to form genera and species.

Captain Cook thus described his landing on the small island of Wateeoo on his voyage from New Zealand to the Friendly Islands.

> The inhabitants were afraid to come near our cows and horses, nor did they form the least conception of their nature. But the sheep and goats did not surpass the limits of their ideas; for they gave us to understand that they knew them to be birds.

He adds:

> It will appear rather incredible, that human ignorance could ever make such a strange mistake, there being not the most distant similitude between a sheep or goat, and any winged animal. But these people seem to know nothing of the existence of any other land animals, besides hogs, dogs and birds. Our sheep and goats, they could see, were very different creatures from the first two, and therefore, they inferred that they must belong to the latter class, in which they knew that there is a considerable variety of species.

Personally, I think it more likely that Cook, who did not speak the language of the islanders well, misunderstood them. Indeed, I am convinced that the islanders, who were certainly endowed with their five senses, had in fact seen that the rams and goats looked more like pigs and dogs than birds.

[*app.* 6]

However, as Mr. Stewart has no difficulty believing this account, I merely observe that the story in no way proves the transition from proper to common nouns; rather, the story mentions only common nouns. The islanders possessed the names of the species but not the names of the individuals, and applied them to those individuals which were either comprised in the species signified by those names or could somehow be reduced to that species. Applying a common noun to a number of individuals does not extend its meaning. However, even if we were prepared to imagine that the islanders did extend the significance of the word *birds*, the extension would be from a less extended to a more extended species, and thus be from species to species, not from individual to species. This final transition is the real difficulty: it is not solved by Cook's account.

Moreover, when a word is accepted in common parlance as referring to a species of things, and the same term is then used to indicate an object not contained in that species, it is more correct to say that the person using the word is mistaken over its meaning or over the judgment he makes about the object to which he applies the word, than to say that the term has been given added meaning. If I see a camel and call it a horse, I have made a mistake about the species of animal or about the meaning of the word *horse*. The word has not and cannot be given greater meaning until it is received into common speech.

7. (177)

[Ideas and reality]

Following Reid's comments, Galluppi and Degerando tried to combat the way the ancients viewed ideas, that is, as *representations of objects*. They said that if this definition of ideas were accepted, there would be no means of knowing whether the representations were true. In other words, it would be impossible to tell whether the idea and the object represented conformed to one another. As a result, scepticism was inevitable. Galluppi writes:

[*app. 7*]

Ideas are true not because they are in conformity with objects but because they act immediately on objects and grasp them. Degerando says: In the case of primal truths, ideas invest and immediately grasp objects: I go along with his views.

(*Critica della Conoscenza*, vol. 1, pp. 38, 41)

The scholastics (I have already referred to this, 106) had seen the difficulty and said that the idea was not the *object* of our thought but merely the *means* whereby our spirit thought an object. This solution, however, when taken in its most obvious sense, shifted the difficulty a stage further back without solving it. The same may be said about the theory of Galluppi and of others I have mentioned.

The sentence: *Ideas grasp and invest external objects* is bizarre and poetic; it is unnecessary and moreover false and absurd.

Note simply that it is not enough to know whether ideas seize and grasp objects themselves, as our philosophers put it. We also need to know whether this is merely accidental in the case of some ideas, or whether it constitutes the very nature of ideas.

If investing and grasping really existing objects is essential to ideas, it ought to be true of all ideas. Granted something, what is essential to it can never be lacking because it is this which forms the thing.

If, then, investing and grasping really existing objects by the idea is merely accidental, the first difficulty reappears. It is still necessary to show 1. what an idea is; and 2. how it manages to grasp and envelop an existing object (upon which it is not dependent for its being because the object is accidental to it).

I maintain that ideas cannot all be such as to envelop and grasp the object, which exists for them, and that their association with the object is not essential to them.

To prove this, I use all the arguments which show the diversity and independence of our *idea* relative to the *actual thing*. For example, the white in my thoughts is different from and independent of the real white of a wall. This is true not only of the idea of whiteness in general, but also of the *idea* of whiteness as applied to an individual wall. The idea is different from the real, subsistent wall.

Saint Augustine establishes in similar vein the distinction between the idea and the real thing thought in my idea. He

[*app.* 7]

notes that if my idea invested and grasped the object, it would inevitably follow that the thing could not change unless the idea I have of it also changed. Thus, I love Paul because I think he is honest; he might change, unknown to me, and become dishonest while I go on loving him as before. I love Paul, therefore, as my spirit thinks him, and not *as he really exists*. In other words, I love Paul in the way that he is in my idea, not as he is in himself. It follows that I do not grasp and take him in himself. If he were always in my spirit as he is in himself, I would no longer love him for his uprightness after he had become evil. On the other hand, I may alter my view of someone without his having changed at all; I may wrongly think him wicked after considering him good. In this case, *in illo homine nihil mutatum est; — in mente autem mea mutata est utique ipsa existimatio, quae de illo aliter se habebat, et aliter habet* [nothing is changed in him — in my mind, however, my past and present opinions of him have changed] (*De Trinitate*, bk. 9, c. 6). In short, our ideas, if they invested and grasped fully the really existing object, would necessarily be in conformity with it: we would then be infallible. In avoiding the danger of *scepticism*, we would swing to the other extreme and bestow *infallibility* on the human spirit.

We cannot say, therefore, that our ideas, *per se*, invest fully and grasp the really existing object. But we believe that, by means of them, we invest the object and grasp it fully when we refer such ideas to really existing *entia* experienced by us. To be certain that we are not mistaken in such a belief, we now need some demonstration or argument which I shall endeavour to expound later.

For the present, I merely add another comment to throw light on the difficulty under discussion. I would ask: 'When we refer ideas to really existing things, or rather *believe* that our idea or, more accurately, our thought invests and grasps something that really exists, does this depend upon the idea? Is it an element which goes to form the idea itself?'

By no means: the *idea* is completely different from the *belief* in the existence of a real ens corresponding to the idea (cf. 60, 64, 90, 98). Our idea is perfect and entire even without this belief. Moreover, the belief adds nothing to the idea. It merely imparts to our spirit a belief which is not an idea. Our spirit then comes to know of the real existence of an object through an act entirely different from that by means of which it has the idea. In this way, the operations of the intelligent spirit are two essentially different acts: 1. that with which it has the idea of a thing; 2. that with which it believes that a real thing, existing *in se*, corresponds to the idea. This distinction of the two main operations of the intellect is of the highest importance.

8. (177)

[Nominalism]

What a sterile theory *nominalism* is for mankind! It maintains that all metaphysical and ethical sciences based upon universal principles are essentially vain. But what branch of knowledge does not require universal principles? Every form of knowledge is impossible in *nominalism*; every noble enterprise, every good in society is declared absurd and fanciful by this system. The consequences of certain doctrines are so far-reaching that, considered in themselves, they seem to be purely intellectual games reserved for a few speculative thinkers whose clever insights make them lose touch with the real world! But this is not the case. Nobody can lose touch with the real world as far as the effects of his thinking are concerned. The error inserted into a seemingly abstract and purely speculative theory, gradually penetrates practical issues, where it develops and produces its consequences. It becomes involved in the human affairs of human beings, in the structure of society. Greatly to our surprise, it corrupts human life, disrupts the order of society and spreads its harmful effects everywhere. It will spread from the ethereal spirit of the most rapt metaphysicians to the labours of peasants and the toil of artisans, leaving its traces, its damage and corruption everywhere.

Present-day *nominalism* is derived from *materialism*. Generally speaking, *nominalists* have always been *materialists*. Hobbes thrust nominalism forward vigorously. After Hobbes, those who denied the existence of abstract ideas most zealously were La Mettrie (*L'homme machine*), Helvetius (*L'Homme*, vol. 1, section 2, c. 5), the author of the *Sistema della natura*, (c. 10) and others of a similar tendency. Locke, on the other hand, located the difference between human beings and beasts in the human faculty of abstraction (bk. 2, c. 11, par. 10).

Locke accepted abstractions and universal ideas for the same reason that materialists denied them, that is, because they are the great divide separating animals from man. Materialists wished to remove this divide; Locke recognised it, and at least wanted to establish it on a sound footing.

If we are endowed solely with the power of perceiving sensible individuals, human beings are reduced to sense because sense presides over the perception of individuals. Consequently, reason is ruled out. Whatever the principle of bodily feeling, it is always such that its identity, at least, must cease with the dissolution of the material organ. This explains: '*The death of man and of beast is one*' (*Eccles* 3: 5). Stewart certainly did not see the close connection between *nominalism*, an abstract and theoretical system and *materialism*, a practical system. If he had, he would not have been a nominalist. This is what I like to think. It is a dubious compliment, but here I have to say that he has acted unthinkingly, like someone who has done little to work out the consequences of his principles. And it is a compliment I am paying him.

In general, I must say that there are certain philosophers nowadays in need of a friend to dissuade them from writing against scepticism — which is the final result of materialism itself — or who would, at least, insist that they write about it more competently. The best friend could be the respectful, careful study of the great masters whom the Church possesses in all these matters, her Fathers and Doctors.

9. (178)

[Stewart's opinion about Reid's concept of universal ideas]

When discussing Reid's opinion on universal ideas, Stewart comes to the following conclusion:

> The long experience I have had of the candor of this excellent author, encourages me to add, that in stating his opinion on the subject of universals, he has not expressed

himself in a manner so completely satisfactory to my mind
as on other occasions
(*Eléments de la Philosophie de l'esprit humain*,
chap. 4, section 3)

I would go further. I feel it is difficult to reconcile Dr. Reid
with himself at this point. Certainly Stewart, in attempting here
to speculate about this excellent thinker's opinion, has difficulty
in bringing it into line with his principles on ideas. This is what
Dr. Reid says about universal ideas:

> An universal is not the object of any external sense, and
> therefore cannot be imagined, but it may be distinctly con-
> ceived. When Mr. Pope says, 'The proper study of man-
> kind is man', I conceive his meaning distinctly, although I
> imagine neither a black nor a white man, neither a crooked
> nor a straight man. I can conceive a proposition or a de-
> monstration, but I cannot imagine either. I can conceive
> understanding and will, virtue and vice, and other attrib-
> utes of the mind; but I cannot imagine them. In like man-
> ner, I can distinctly conceive universals, but I cannot
> imagine them.

If we are to take this passage in its obvious, ordinary sense, it
would appear that Dr. Reid recognises that universal ideas are
objects of thought, not mere names. Yet this would contradict
his theory of ideas; he has denied that our thought has objects
distinct from itself and distinct from external things. Consequently, Stewart endeavours, with great subtlety it must be
admitted, to give Reid's passage a meaning reconciling it with
other passages by the same author. However, I feel that his
interpretation is very unsatisfactory. It states:

> It appears from this passage, that by *conceiving* universals,
> Dr Reid means nothing more than understanding the
> meaning of propositions involving them.

But to realise that this is not compatible with Reid's view, we
need only to indicate that, in the passage cited above, Reid distinguishes between conceiving a proposition and conceiving
universal ideas; he states that as we conceive propositions, so we
conceive universal ideas. What is more, I have already shown
that universal terms would be of no use to us unless we linked to

them truly universal ideas (cf. 162–167). Thus we either have to look for a better way of reconciling Dr. Reid's theory of universal ideas with his own theory of ideas or to accept that one of the two is false. On the other hand, it seems obvious to me that it is impossible to come up with a true theory of ideas before solving the question of universal ideas which so preoccupied all the ancient philosophers. This observation must at least cast grave doubts on Dr. Reid's theory.

10. (196)

[Conceptualists and universals]

The careful reader will readily notice that, although I consider *nominalism* a totally untrue system, I do not subscribe to *conceptualism*. Nor do I like to call myself a *realist* because this word, along with *nominalist* and *conceptualist*, does not express single, precise opinions, but rather a body of various opinions. In fact, according to John of Salisbury, realists were divided into six different categories, and conceptualists and nominalists also had their different factions. The acceptance, therefore, of such a vague title would either be useless, or involve supporting a faction and taking sides without clearly understanding why. As I have remarked elsewhere, the history of philosophy will never come to perfection until we begin to classify philosophical systems by providing an exact description of their views, not by labelling them with the names of their authors or factions. (*Part of a letter on the classification of philosophical systems* in *Introduction*, etc., 4, 1).

However, let me indicate briefly what I mean by saying that I do not subscribe to the conceptualists' position. It is clear that this name can be aptly used to designate those who define a universal as a mental concept in such a way that nothing the mind thinks with a universal exists outside the mind. This form of subjectivism is far removed from my view.

I take a universal idea and subject it to analysis. Such analysis furnishes me with two elements from which my idea is derived:

1. the quality thought of; 2. its universality, which St. Thomas also distinguishes and calls *intentio universalitatis*.

I maintain that there is, corresponding to the quality thought of, a reality in the individual thing; corresponding to the universality thought of, there is nothing real in the thing: this *universality* is solely in the mind.

Universality is not, properly speaking, the quality thought of, but a mode which it takes in the mind; it is necessary to make this distinction very clear.

How does the quality thought of become a *universal* within me? When my spirit has perceived any quality whatsoever, it has the power to replicate this quality in an indefinite number of individual entities by means of a corresponding number of acts of thought with which it thinks that quality successively or simultaneously in an indefinite number of individuals. This power derives from two principles; 1. from an intuition of *what is possible*, possessed by my spirit, and 2. from the iterative capacity of acts of the spirit.

The power of replicating acts of thought, and thus imagining the quality as indefinitely replicated, is a faculty unique to the spirit. It is the spirit, therefore, which, by means of its faculty, adds the character of *universality* to the quality which it thinks of. This universality signifies only the possibility which a quality has of being thought by us in an indefinite number of individuals.

I cannot resist adding that if Degerando had clearly seen the difference between maintaining that *universal ideas* are pure concepts and admitting that only the universality of ideas exists solely in the mind while the *ideas* themselves, relative to the qualities they express, have a real correspondence in things, he would not have said that St. Thomas was a *true conceptualist* (*Histoire comparée* etc. 2nd ed., vol. 4, p. 498), a title which he claims also applies to Ockham (*ibid.*, p. 582), who is very far from holding the philosophical ideas of St. Thomas.

11. (209)

[Stewart's understanding of *general ideas*]

Stewart seems also to have been led astray over the existence of universal ideas by his failure to notice that *relationships* between things are resolved into *general ideas*, and are the basis of *common* nouns. In fact, a common noun designates an ens by both a *common quality* and by a *relationship*. When I utter, for example, the common noun *man*, I indicate the individual in a *genus* formed by the common quality *humanity*. On the other hand, when I say *son*, I indicate the individual in the genus formed by the relationship of filiality, which also is common to a number of individuals.

To conceive a *relationship* is to have a *general idea*, one of those ideas which form genera and give rise to common nouns. If Stewart had noted this, he would not have thought that he had demonstrated the non-existence of *general ideas* by replacing them with the idea of relationship, nor that a reasoning is understood without any need for *universal ideas* but only by means of *ideas of relationship*. He says:

> From what has been said, it follows that the assent we give to the conclusion of a syllogism does not result from any examination of the notions expressed by the different propositions of which it is composed, but is an immediate consequence of the relations in which the words stand to one another.

The fact, accepted by both parties and proving the *necessity* of general ideas, is this:

> ...in every syllogism the inference is only a particular instance of the GENERAL AXIOM

(not mere signs, therefore)

> that whatever is true universally of any sign, must also be true of every individual which that sign can be employed to express.

In a syllogism, nothing is predicated of the sign, but always of the thing indicated

[*app.* 11]

Admitting, therefore, that every process of reasoning may be resolved into a series of syllogisms, it follows that this operation of the mind furnishes no proof of the existence of anything corresponding to general terms, distinct from the individuals to which these terms are applicable.

(Eléments de la Philosophie de l'esprit humain,
chap. 4, section 2)

12. (fn. 135)

[Bossuet and truth and falsity]

If in Bossuet's time some scholar had appeared who, instead of taking a different road from that into which philosophy had been directed by Descartes, had chosen solely to move it forward along the same route, to be magnanimous in welcoming and preserving truths which had already been explained, to verify them and add to them, he could have developed this opinion without departing greatly from what was then known. Merely by bringing together and clarifying such truths, he would have brought great benefit to philosophy. This development might have run as follows.

The intellect was defined as 'the faculty of knowing what is true and what is false.' It only remained, therefore, to discover what truth and error were. Clarifying this would have brought philosophy an endless benefit, and could have been done, as I said, without venturing too far from knowledge already possessed.

In fact, Bossuet defined what is true and what is false as follows: 'The truth is what is, error is what is not' (chap. 1: 16). According to Bossuet, therefore, truth is ens. The intellect is thus simply the faculty by which we perceive ens, as Bossuet himself says.

Along these lines, it was necessary to endeavour to demonstrate carefully that

1. Sense perception could in no way grasp ens (cf. 52–62) but only the things accidental to ens.

2. This *idea* must consequently have been planted within us by nature (cf. 51).

[*app.* 12]

3. Substances are perceived by the perception of ens itself.

4. Substances are therefore perceived by our intellect alone (cf. 48–50).

5. The idea of ens shorn of all the determining factors coming through the senses is the *most universal idea* of all.

6. All other ideas receive their character of universality from the idea of ens.

7. All ideas are furnished with this characteristic which constitutes the nature of ideas (cf. 90–98).

Finally, we would have learned and established that the intellect is not only 'the faculty of what is true and false' but that it alone is 'the faculty of ideas', which cannot pertain to the senses. In brief, all the truths which I have tried to expound in this work could have been elucidated step by step.

13. (227)

[Wolff and notions]

A symptom of error occasionally concealed in an accepted theory is uncertainty in expression and undue concern to justify it by the use of intellectual subtlety. This shows the authors' perplexity and how, deep in their conscience, they hear the murmuring of a voice alerting them to the hidden error which they would discover if they were brave enough to listen to this voice. There is perhaps no philosophical viewpoint more readily accepted than that which posits the operations of the human understanding in the following order: 1. idea; 2. judgment; 3. reasoning, and there is perhaps no other in which we find, when reading philosophers' explanations, such obvious manifestations of this symptom of hesitation.

I have already pointed out how, in the age of Bossuet, there were some who doubted the correctness of the order (cf. 219) and how Fortunato da Brescia (cf. 89), to evade the difficulty he felt, was cautious enough to add to the definition of the idea the express phrase: 'The idea, to be such, must not contain any judgment' — as if the idea could cease to contain what it actually contains because a philosopher ejects it from his definition. However, all these indications, which show how authors realise the mistakes they have made, are valuable. They make errant philosophers into witnesses to the truth and reveal the extent of its hold over human beings. It will be helpful, therefore, if I mention the efforts Wolff made to retain for *notions* the status usually assigned them by making them constitute the first operation of the human understanding.

Wolff did not grasp the force of Plato's statement: 'Thought is merely an internal conversation.'

He distinguished between the notion thought only by the intellect, which he called *cognitive intuition*, and the same notion expressed in words or signs, which he called *symbolic knowledge*. According to him: 'In *symbolic knowledge*, the first operation of the intellect (the notion along with pure perception) is merged with the second' (*Psychol. Ration.*, para. 398). This does not occur in purely *intuitive knowledge*. This distinction is simply flight from the difficulty. When I express a notion in words, why do I have to express it in the form of a judgment? Am I obliged to express in words more than is contained in ideas? In that case, if I express in words something not contained in ideas, I am using meaningless words which are unrelated to the mind. This would be a lapse into an absurd *nominalism*. For example, if I wish to express my notion of a triangle, I shall say: 'A triangle IS a three-sided figure.' Now the verb 'IS', which expresses the possible existence of the triangle, is not, in fact, a mere external word but corresponds to something in my mind, that is, the notion itself perceived as something distinct from me.

'But,' says Wolff, 'the word IS does not merely indicate that a triangle is seen as a subject but rather expresses the in-existence of three sides in this subject. But purely intuitive knowledge does not consider this connection. By this knowledge, qualities are represented in a thing as being different from each other and different from the thing in which they are found. (*Psychol. Emp.*, para. 331). On the other hand, in *symbolic knowledge*, they have to be expressed as linked and in-existing in the subject. Symbolic knowledge, therefore unlike intuitive, includes a judgment.'

I would like to make the following observations on Wolff's argument:

    1. I deny that the word 'IS', in the quoted proposition, has

the force which he attributes to it. The statement: 'A triangle is a three-sided figure', corresponds exactly to this other statement: 'What I conceive and call by the word *triangle* is a three-sided figure.' The word 'IS' thus expresses nothing more than the existence of the notion of a triangle in my mind, without involving the slightest alteration in that same notion expressed exactly as it exists in my mind with the words 'three-sided figure.' If, on the other hand, I were to say: 'This figure which I conceive HAS three sides,' the verb 'HAS' would in that case express the in-existence of the three sides in the imagined figure. However, the verb 'IS' does not refer in any way to such in-existence.

2. According to Wolff, in *intuitive knowledge* the qualities of a thing are perceived as separate from each other and as separate from the thing itself. Is this possible? Is this actually how our first knowledge of things occurs? The opposite seems to be the case; we first perceive the thing furnished with its qualities and then, by a process of abstraction, we separate out all these things and we consider them one by one. My experience would seem to bear out that our first knowledge of things comes about in this way. Furthermore, I have already shown (cf. 55–61) that the opposite is impossible. In our first perception, it is quite impossible that we intellectually perceive accidents apart from the subject in which they exist. It is different for the external sense which perceives only accidents, not their concepts. Wolff may have been led into error here by his failure to distinguish sufficiently the characteristics of *sensation* from the characteristics of the *idea*, although he establishes the *universality* of notions which, according to him, are the object of our intellectual first operation. From this universal characteristic, he would have found it easy to form a very accurate concept of intellective knowledge relative to which it is impossible for us first to conceive initially the accident in isolation from the subject and then unite it to that subject, as Wolff maintains. In fact, when we perceive the accident of a subject we either know from the very beginning that it is an accident (and in that case we conceive it in relation to its subject), or we do not know this (and in that case we form a subject from the accident itself, that is, we conceive it as something independent, possessing *being* and a *mode of being*). This amounts to conceiving a *subject* (ens) and a

predicate (a mode of that ens). Consequently, the basis of Wolff's theory is impossible.

This can also be proved from a study of Wolff's own writings. He defines the first operation of the intellect: *Prima intellectus operatio est plurium* IN RE UNA *singillatim facta repesentatio* [The first operation of the intellect is the representation of a number of things one by one in ONE SINGLE THING (*Psychol. Emp.*, 330). He inserts the word *singillatim* [one by one] to show us that we perceive piecemeal all the qualities of the thing of which we have an idea. Let us ignore the fact that this successive perception of several existent qualities in a thing cannot as a series of intellectual operations be the first operation of the mind. My question is: where do we perceive these various qualities? *In re una* [in one single thing], our philosopher replies; all of them in the thing of which we have the idea. But in that case we do not perceive them in themselves separate from the thing, but as qualities or parts pertaining to the thing; qualities and parts which exist in the thing, not apart from it. But this means attributing them all to the thing itself; it means *judging implicitly* that they belong to it. Perceiving those conditions, parts or qualities individually, as Wolff claims, would make what I am saying even more obvious. It would mean that for each of them we make a particular, internal judgment enabling us to assign them to the thing to which they belong.

However, I am not asking Wolff to go that far, and I willingly forego the assistance he so generously awards me in putting my case. I merely say that all the qualities, of whatever kind, whether they are perceived as either united or in isolation from one another, are perceived through the first operation of our intellect in a real, or imaginary, or merely possible subject. Thus, in our first intellective operation, we always perceive two things: 1. a being (subject); 2. a mode of being (predicate); and we perceive these two things together. Consequently, a judgment is included in this first operation.

For these reasons, Wolff's distinction between *intuitive knowledge* and *symbolic knowledge*, introduced to defend the received order of intellectual operations, is without foundation. It is one of those ingenious makeshifts which, by their vacuity, reveal the feebleness of the system which they are intended to bolster up.

[*app.* 13]

14. (230)

[Truth within us; Plato's observation]

When I set out to find the characteristics of electric or magnetic fluid, I am still ignorant of what they are. However, having discovered them and wanting to know if these are indeed what I am looking for, it is sufficient to know if they have the *true* characteristics of the current. As soon as I know they are true, I know that they are precisely what I am seeking, because I am seeking only truth, whatever it may be. I must therefore have within me the power to distinguish what is true from what is false. In other words, I must have foreknowledge of *truth* in order to recognise it in its particular acts, wherever I find it. To have *prior knowledge of truth* is the same as having its type within me. By means of this type, I am able in comparing different views to know which is in conformity with the type and therefore true, and which is out of harmony and consequently false. The fact is that unless I had within myself foreknowledge of the distinctive characteristics of truth, I could never recognise it as truth when I encountered it and would therefore lack the faculty to discern truth from falsehood. The possession in my mind of the distinctive characteristics of truth is identical with knowing it as it is. It means having before me the features, a certain type, an exemplar, a prior concept, a form of truth.

It is on these grounds alone that Plato's observation is conclusive in stating that we have to accept that the true *face of truth* is present in us. Otherwise we would not be able to form any judgment (and I shall show that this face or primal type is simply the innate concept of being, THE SOLE FORM OF REASON). However, it is not conclusive in stating that we have necessarily to accept in us as many types as there are judgments, or as the ideas acquired by such judgments. As I have said, as soon as we have within ourselves the *sign* enabling us to recognise truth and error, we are able to apply it to an infinite number of things, to anything we wish. From this point on, we have the faculty for judging, discerning and savouring the truth which everywhere presents the same appearance. In short, we have the power to judge things through our possession of a *rule*. One rule alone is adequate for all things because in all of them we are seeking *one thing alone*, what is true and what is false; in short, what IS.

If we wish to analyse Plato's statement in greater depth, we can undertake a threefold investigation: 1. sometimes we seek and learn truths, whatever they may be, by using our reason as occasion offers; 2. sometimes we seek new truths related to something already known under some other aspect; and lastly 3. sometimes we seek truths already included in certain ideas even though we have not reflected upon them or perceived them clearly and individually.

We carry out this third sort of investigation whenever we analyse some idea. In this case, we add nothing to our stock of knowledge (analytical judgments), but merely attempt to grasp in fragmented, divided form that which we already possess in combined, united form. We acquire or increase only our *reflective* knowledge; initially we possessed intuitive, *spontaneous* knowledge of it. In analyses of this kind, we investigate what we know in one mode in order to understand it in another. Knowing it in the second way, that is, knowing it in analytical and differentiated form, serves different purposes unavailable to synthetical, undifferentiated knowledge. The type of argument devised by Plato cannot apply to this sort of investigation which does not attempt to discover a completely new truth but to find the components, as it were, of something already known as a whole.

If we wish to consider the parts of this whole as new truths when known as parts, this third kind of investigation can then be reduced to and classified with the second kind.

The second species of investigation takes place when we are looking for something which in itself is totally unknown to us but which refers, nevertheless, to something which we do know. For example, if I wish to measure the specific gravity of various bodies, I set out to investigate something of which I am completely ignorant. However, I do know about the bodies to which gravity relates, and I am aware of the general notion of gravity. So when I discover, as a result of experiments, the unknown, specific gravity I am seeking, I can certainly know that it is the result I am seeking because I know the bodies to which this gravity must belong. The relationship between the gravity being sought and these bodies specifies what I am

[*app.* 14]

seeking and fixes it for me so firmly that, as soon as I come across it, I recognise it as what I am seeking although I did not know it previously. Certain external features mark off and indicate the thing so clearly that it cannot be mistaken for others when it is found, even though it was previously unknown. Let us imagine that someone says to me: 'The person I shall greet is the one you must seize.' I do not need to know the man by sight to be right; I only need to recognise him from the description I have been given which marks him off unerringly. In this kind of investigation, therefore, when I am seeking and discover some truth, I recognise it as what I have been searching for, not because I knew it previously, but because I knew beforehand its relationship with something I already knew. This relationship acts as a sign which, provided the relationship is quite determined, enables me to recognise what I am seeking. Thus, all so-called determined algebraic problems lead me to find a result completely new to me simply because I have been given the conditions serving to determine the result fully. Plato's argument, therefore, has no place in an investigation of this sort either, because I do not need any prior knowledge of this truth to recognise it when I find it. All I need to know is some relationship suitable for connecting it with something previously known.

But in the first of the three kinds of investigation which I outlined, we do not seek determined truths which we have set out to investigate, but merely seek, or rather discover, the truths which we encounter, as occasion presents while our intellective faculties develop. For example, as soon as we come into the world, we receive a large number of sensations from the realities surrounding us. Because we are open to such sensations and endowed with reason, we say something to ourselves whenever our sensories are stimulated. For example, we say to ourselves: 'There is something external to me' or rather, especially when we are particularly affected, we inevitably begin to think and say with each sensation: 'There is something here, something else there, and so on.' This internal message, not yet expressed in words, is an assent to what comes before our mind. We assent to the existence of external real things; this internal assent is a judgment enabling us to know of the existence of entities that are distinct from ourselves. In other words, we attribute

[*app.* 14]

existence to them just as we attribute existence to ourselves, and thus produce objects for ourselves (synthetical judgments). It is in these primal judgments, where we need to have some prior conception of existence, that we require some sign or indication enabling us to know that the existence of bodies is a truth. Here, Plato's argument is solid; in this third kind of investigation, or rather in these discoveries of truth, we need something innate within us to distinguish the truth intuitively, almost at sight. We do not know it through its relationships with other truths which, in our assumption, are still unacquired.

The fact is that all the problems we have been discussing disappear if we suppose that from the beginning we have impressed within us the distinctive, common *note* of truth (as we shall see, this note is the idea of existence). By this *note*, we apprehend the first truths which come to us, not because we are seeking precisely these truths, but because we are looking for all truths in general. Or rather, we are alert and watchful to receive them from any source whatever because reason desires nothing more keenly than these truths. We grasp them in a natural way, as things congenial to our mind. Grasping determined truths is, as I said, the same as judging that something is true. Perceiving bodies with our reason means judging that it is true that bodies exist or (which amounts to the same) assenting internally to their existence. When we have reached this stage and come to possess a number of truths, we can easily explain how the second type of investigation is possible. Known truths are related and enable us to determine other, still unknown truths which can thus become the particular object of our curiosity and our investigations. It is precisely at this point that *investigation* into truth begins; the first category of investigations is more accurately defined as perception or discovery. In the same way, in the third kind of investigations it is not difficult to explain how to obtain the ideas we analyse.

Plato, who did not differentiate between the three ways in which I carry out my investigations, or at least find the truth, extended the difficulty of which we are speaking to every investigation into truth, although it is present only in the first kind. This explains why his solution failed to be true and perfect.

[*app.* 14]

15. (230)

[Plato and innate knowledge]

One cannot expect someone like Plato, who was the first to explore the origin of ideas in such depth, to have honed the doctrines he discovered to the ultimate degree of linguistic precision. Original thinkers who first make a discovery are so content and exultant over their success, are so captivated by the new truths which fill their minds with such freshness, that they make no further effort to purge them of any error or inaccuracy they may and often do contain. Such thinkers have no doubts about their own discoveries and, entranced by their unexpected beauty, have no further vigour to work at them, or to entertain any doubts about their perfection. They accept their discoveries as they are and idolise them. Systems originate in this way and I think that something of this kind happened to Plato over the origin of ideas.

Nevertheless, reason in such men, working imperceptibly in their quiet moments, guides them unconsciously nearer the truth. In certain passages, Plato comes so very close to it that, if these were the only ones to survive, we would have no doubt that he had found it

In the *Theaetetus*, to explain how we bear our cognitions around with us, yet still have to investigate them, he says that they can be *possessed* without being *had*. We are, in this respect, like someone who keeps birds in an aviary without actually having them in his hands. Take the example he gives of someone who knows arithmetic or the art of calculation. This art comprises all our cognitions of numbers; it represents, so to speak, the aviary of such information. So the person who knows only the art of arithmetic possesses all the results that can be obtained from numbers but does not have them to hand. He possesses them as a person possesses the birds he feeds in an aviary. They flutter about freely and belong to him only in the sense that he is able to catch them when he wishes.

But let us listen to Plato himself:

Socrates: ...There is an art you call arithmetic.
Theaetetus: Yes.

[*app.* 15]

Socrates: Let us grant that this is a kind of hunt for cognitions about all numbers, odd or even.

Theaetetus: Very good.

Socrates: With this skill, the arithmetician has under his control all cognitions about numbers which he communiates to others.

Theaetetus: Yes.

Socrates: Passing them on, he is said to teach; receiving them, to learn; having them in his possession in that aviary of his, to know.

Theaetetus: Certainly.

Socrates: Now take note of what I am now going to say. The expert arithmetician knows all numbers, doesn't he? We cannot deny this if he has in his mind all knowledge of numbers.

Theaetetus: Naturally.

Socrates: And yet does not such a person sometimes count either the numbers themselves in his head or some external things that have a number.

Theaetetus: Of course.

Socrates: So counting, then, is merely trying to find out what some particular number amounts to?

Theaetetus: Yes.

Socrates: It would seem, then, that the man who, as we have already established, knows how to handle numbers, is trying to find out what he knows as if he had no knowledge of it. Do you see the contradiction involved?

By this system of his, Socrates explained this contradiction and showed it to be merely apparent. The arithmetician *knows* all the results of his art but only *in potency*. He does not know them *actually* and therefore, when he wants to know them, has to try to go looking for them, using all his skill. The ambiguity hinges entirely on the word *know*. Saying that the arithmetician *knows* all the results of his art is not an accurate expression, as Aristotle later stated. In strict accuracy, we can only say that he *can know* them. In other words, he has the means to get to know them, the art of discovering them. This linguistic inaccuracy led to Plato's system being discredited. His desire to assign to the word *know* the meaning *possess knowledge of*, that is, have full control of it, instead of assigning to it the meaning *have knowledge of*, that is, have it at its own, true level of meaning, led him to state that we *know* from birth, that is, we have *innate ideas.*

Leaving aside such an inaccuracy and the error into which it led Plato, and accepting only the spirit of the dialogue between Socrates and Theaetetus, we can see how close Plato came to the truth. In the dialogue, it is irrefutably demonstrated that there must be in man some innate *knowledge* which potentially comprises all other knowledge, just as arithmetic comprises the whole science of number. This knowledge contains, in a word, the *art* of distinguishing and recognising truth wherever we encounter truth, and consequently a full explanation of the cognitive faculty or reason, which is only the *art of discovering different cognitions.*

Having reached this stage, what else should Plato have done to bring the theory of the origin of ideas to perfection?

He needed only to discover the nature of this primal art or *originating knowledge* which virtually comprises all other cognitions, just as arithmetic comprises all the information about number. He had grasped perfectly well that, to discover some knowledge about arithmetic, to solve arithmetical problems, some art was needed. In other words, it is necessary to possess principles and know how to pass from such principles to the desired results. And what is true about arguments concerned with limited subject of numbers is true about arguments concerned with any other subject. Any use of reason is merely the exercise of an innate, *primal art* which cannot be learned; all other arts are learned by reasoning. Presupposing, therefore, complete ignorance of reasoning, it would be quite impossible to learn the art of reasoning. Plato had clearly realised that prior to any knowledge acquired through reasoning, there has to be some innate knowledge providing us with the *mode of reasoning.* The study of this primal knowledge was the path Plato still had to travel to arrive at the full discovery of truth.

16. (246)

[Aristotle and judgment]

I have already pointed out that Aristotle's mistake may have

[*app.* 16]

been occasioned by a solecism of the kind Plato was so addicted
to. He attributes, perhaps, to the word *judge* a wider meaning
than is appropriate, or uses it in two essentially distinct senses:
1. in the sense of producing in the animal an *instinct* to tend
towards certain things which as a result are designated as good
or else to shun others which are called *bad*. This creates a species of *de facto* discernment between relative *good* and *bad*
which can be mistaken for and confused with rational judgment; 2. in the sense of the association our intellect makes
between a *predicate* (positive or negative), that is, a universal,
with some individual or at least less general *subject* than this
predicate.

Only the second operation is truly intellectual; the first (inclination towards certain things or aversion from others) can be
unaccompanied by any act of knowledge, and is due to instinct
in animals and aroused by sense. Moreover, the things pursued
or shunned by *instinct* are not, in fact, good or bad in themselves
prior to, and independently of, instinct. They are called *good* or
bad to show that the instinct pursues or shuns them. Goodness
or badness in this case is relative to the desire of instinct.

This observation makes it easy for us to grasp the infinite
difference between *instinctive discernment* and *judgment*.
Instinctive discernment is the cause motivating us to say that
some things are good and others bad in such a way that goodness is the effect of this discernment. *Judgment*, on the other
hand, is not prior to the goodness of things but subsequent to
them; it is not the cause of the goodness of the things which it
judges. The goodness of things, on the other hand, is the cause
of the judgment which declares them good — *judgment* is an
effect. In short, judgment arises from reason; instinct operates
blindly and without reason. Judgment must conform to things
as they are, good or bad. Instinct does not conform to things,
but things to instinct, and this accidental suitability is what we
call their goodness. However, when we use the word *good*
about things pursued by instinct, we form a judgment by asso-
ciating a *rational judgment* with an *instinctive discernment*.

My conjecture regarding the misuse of the term *judge* by
Aristotle will be proved and demonstrated by a comparison
with other passages from his works. For example, he maintains
(in bk. 3 of *De Anima*, lect. 11, 12) that *affirmation* and *denial*

pertain solely to the mind. He says that sense, when apprehending what is sensible, *judges it in its own way*. When sense is attracted or repelled, it pursues or shuns what is sensible as though it *were affirming it* as good or bad. He does not say that it *affirms* what is sensible as such because this operation (as St. Thomas says in his comment) is proper to the intellect alone; rather, it carries out an operation which, relative to its effects as *pursuit* or *flight*, resembles an intellectual *affirmation*. *Facere affirmationem et negationem est proprium intellectus... sed sensus facit aliquid simile huic, quando apprehendit ut delectabile et triste* [Affirming and denying operations is proper to the intellect... but sense does something similar when it apprehends something as desirable or unattractive]. A little further on, Aristotle, although he had previously attributed judgment also to *phantasy* (*De Anima*, bk. 3, lect. 5, 6), nevertheless subsequently removes *affirmation* and *negation* from it and of course *knowledge of the truth*, which is proper to the intellect alone. *Nam cognoscere verum et falsum est solius intellectus* [knowing what is true and what is false pertains to the intellect alone], as the Angelic Doctor explains. We have to say, therefore, that Aristotle might have imagined a species of judgment that did not *affirm* or *deny*. This judgment would not involve giving or denying assent, but be formed without any opinion about what is *true* or what is *false*. In short, Aristotle retains the word *judgment* but then removes what is essential to the concept which the term expresses in ordinary language. I have to say that I do not think it acceptable to use the word *judgment* to refer to an operation in which no affirmation or negation is made and which does not have what is true or false as its object. I would call this operation, — as, I feel, the rest of mankind would — either mere *feeling*, or experiencing an *instinctive movement*, and nothing else. This feeling and this movement will certainly produce in the animal the same external actions or movements as rational judgment reproduces in us, although the seemingly identical nature of the effects is not on this occasion able to prove the identical nature of the proximate cause which produced them. I shall reserve the term *judgment* to refer to this cause in us in so far as we act rationally; the term *feeling* or *instinct* will refer to this cause in animals.

What more is there to say ? In other passages, where Aristotle reverts to the normal use of language, the philosopher takes judgment as equivalent to stating what is *true* or *false* (*De Anima*, bk. 3, lect. 5). This, it would seem, is the meaning he assigns to *judging* when he uses it in its correct sense and attributes it to the understanding. On the other hand, when he attributes it to feeling or phantasy, he intends it in a figurative or metaphorical sense.

This vagueness in his manner of speaking was one of the reasons preventing our philosopher from explaining the formation of ideas in a thorough, clear manner. By his misuse of the word *judging*, he deprived his followers and himself of the chance to face the difficulty inherent in the question. In fact, we are accustomed to give the word *judgment* the meaning of *affirmation* and *denial* of a predicate relative to a subject, and occasionally forget, when we attribute this word to sense, that we are not speaking of a similar operation. But once we conceive sense as a faculty of judgment, we have no difficulty in explaining the acts of our understanding. Our reasoning runs like this: the difficulty of which we are speaking lies entirely in the understanding; it does not lie in sense, and consequently not in judgment because sense judges. The difficulty has vanished. In fact, however, the difficulty is in the understanding because *judgment* resides in the understanding. Transferring judgment to sense would indeed remove the difficulty. The understanding will then judge without difficulty because it receives judgments already formed from sense, and has only to perfect them, give them a form, render them more explicit and obvious. In this way it will have its very own *affirmation* and *negation*. Knowledge of what is true and what is false will conventionally begin here. But this is to confuse and disguise the issue, not to solve it.

17. (247)

[Aristotle's *common sense*]

This was Aristotle's theory: in the human being, there is something called *common sense* which judges sensations. It alone can do this because it alone feels what all the other senses feel. But even a *particular sense* feels and judges in a more restricted field, that is, it judges the various sensible things which it can perceive. Hence, Aristotle's rather vague proposition: *Sensus proprius participat aliquid de virtute sensus communis* [the more particular sense shares to some extent in the power of common sense]. How this power-sharing could come about is a mystery.

It was equally difficult, in Aristotle's philosophy, to explain how *common sense*, which is single, could have a number of potencies and several essentially different operations. It required real ingenuity to explain this feature by sound, lucid arguments although it could easily be evaded by use of an example. Aristotle therefore opted for this second, much easier way. He found a suitable exemplar in the image of a centre and of radii which all meet at a centre. So common sense, which is essentially single, receives sensations from the different sense organs. In so far as it receives many modifications, it *feels*; in so far as it is one, it *judges* (*De Anima*, bk. 3, lect. 3, 4). It seems that for a long time philosophers were quite happy with this solution. Nevertheless, it would have been simple to note some important differences between the centre of a circle and common sense: the centre is inactive and, although the terminus of many radii, it does not judge them, it does not act upon them and it does not actually receive them in itself. Finally, it does not constitute a centre of itself, but only because our minds refer the radii to that point. *Per se*, it is only a point. All the linear connections it acquires are due to our thinking, not to something actually connected with it.

But even in the concept of circle, centre and radii, we still have to explain how thought is able to create a multitude of relationships in a single thing such as a circle. The very likeness of a centre taken to explain by *analogy* the thought of universals or of relationships between things is no clearer than thought itself, since it is merely a particular instance of thought. When we have explained how we perceive relationships and universals, we have explained how a point is for us a centre and terminus of a number of lines. But a centre is inexplicable unless the first explanation is presupposed. The example is therefore misleading, and only appears to clarify the problem. It provides no

[*app.* 17]

explanation of the way in which a single faculty can both feel the sensible things proper to various sense organs and judge them, that is, compare them to one another, note how they are alike and how they differ, and judge them as pleasing or displeasing. All these are real operations: they are not mere relationships which we link to common sense by means of our understanding, as in the case of a centre which we view as the terminus of a number of lines. Even if it were easy to understand how a single thing may have multiple relationships with other things, it is nonetheless difficult to grasp how a potency may have a number of terms and, while remaining a *single potency*, bring about numerous essentially distinct operations, if by potency we mean a particular force of the soul, a force specific and separated by the unity of its term or its specific operation. There is no doubt that *feeling* and *judging*, if two essentially distinct operations, as Aristotle in fact holds, require distinct faculties. The potency of feeling is named after the act of feeling just as the potency of judging is named after the act of judging. If feeling and judging are essentially the same thing, why attribute *judgment* to sense? This is non-sense, as the English would say. It means attributing to sense something which is not sense. In this case, the word *judgment* could be banished from human language and replaced by sense or sensation, without anyone noticing the difference, which is patently impossible.

What kind of argument persuaded Aristotle to endow the sense with the faculty for judgment?

> Not only do we feel but we also feel that we feel and, feeling we are feeling, we judge what we are feeling. Now, we feel that we feel either with the very sense whereby we feel or with another. If it is with another sense, I repeat the same question. How do we feel that we feel what we are feeling through this sense? Through a third sense, perhaps? If so, we would prolong this series of senses *ad infinitum*, because we would always have to repeat the same argument. We are therefore obliged to state that we feel that we feel with the same sense whereby we feel and, consequently, we use this same sense to judge.
>
> (*De Anima*, bk. 3, lect. 2)

This argument may seem ingenious. However, if we take just

one of its fallacies, we see that it is based upon a false assumption, that is, that in a sense, the feeling of the feeling is inevitably contained. What does the expression 'to feel we feel' mean? It can have no meaning unless it means a *reflection* by the soul on its own sensation. When the soul turns in upon itself to discover its own condition, and finds it is experiencing a feeling, we normally say that it feels it is feeling. But this reflection by the alert mind upon itself is, strictly speaking, thought. The soul, therefore, *thinks it feels*, it does not *feel it feels*. It thinks about its own *sensation*. In this case, *sensation* is the object of this thought. On the other hand, *thought* itself is the act.

We must not therefore confuse the object of the act with the act itself. *Sensation*, which is the object, is external and passive; thought, by which we reflect on this sensation, is internal, active and voluntary. Thus, when we say *we feel that we feel*, we are using the first *we feel* metaphorically in the place of *we think*, and the second *we feel* in its literal sense to express the actual sensation. Sense *qua* sense does not feel it feels, it *feels*, and nothing more. A sensation arises simultaneously with the modification occurring in a bodily organ and does not involve any reflection upon self. If a sensitive organ then receives the same or another stimulus, it is activated again, but nothing is produced similar to reflection. We have only a new impression and sensation which our mind finds similar to the first, but completely distinct in its essence from the first. However, because we are also endowed with the faculty of thought, it is often impossible not to think contemporaneously about it, not to notice it, not to register it. Whenever we notice sensations, we not only feel, but think we are feeling sensations; we never just experience a feeling and describe this metaphorically as 'feeling we feel.' It is very easy, therefore, for us to attribute what we experience within ourselves to entia endowed with feeling alone.

This I think is what happened in Aristotle's argument. Having noticed that every time we realise we are feeling, we are also thinking, that is, reflecting on our feeling, he assumed that reflecting upon self was the essential characteristic of sense. He was thus led to endow sense with a corresponding reflection inseparable from judgment because, when I reflect upon what I feel, I am merely making a judgment upon myself. I say to

[*app.* 17]

myself, 'I am experiencing a sensation.' This is to form a judgment, to think.

18. (250)
[Sensible perception and abstraction]

St. Thomas states the problem in all its force:

> A nature endowed with the intention of universality, let us say the nature of man, has a *twofold being*, that is, material being in so far as it is in natural matter, and immaterial being in so far as it is in the intellect. In so far as this nature has being in natural matter, it cannot be endowed with the intention of universality because it is individuated by matter. The intention of universality is present to it only in so far as it is abstracted from individual matter. But it cannot be really abstracted from individual material as the Platonists claim. There is no natural, or real, man unless he is flesh and blood. — It remains true, therefore, that human nature, outside the individuating principles, has no existence except in the mind.
>
> (*De Anima*, bk. 2, lect. 11)

This passage means: 'You maintain that the intellect, when it perceives a particular object, merely perceives exactly what the senses perceive, except that it divides in the particular what is common from what is individual. Then, setting aside what is individual by abstracting it, it perceives only what is common. This way of explaining how the *term* of sense becomes the *object* of the intellect would not meet with any objection if this division, which you assume the mind makes, were real. In other words, there would be no objection were we dealing with a real being where what is common and what is individual could be divided up as a cake or a pie is cut in two, with one half being cast on one side and the other being used for some purpose. It has to be said, however, that the division made by the understanding between *what is proper* and *what is common* is not a real division but a metaphorical division, so to speak. The understanding does not, in fact, extract what is individual from a real being, leaving behind only what is common in the way we extract lees from wine, leaving behind pure wine. We are not dealing with any real abstraction and division. When a particular ens is perceived by the understanding, it does not undergo any alteration.'

Anyone who thinks he has explained how our understanding perceives what sense puts before us by saying simply that the understanding *abstracts* the universal from the particulars may be quite happy to accept such an analogy or a likeness despite its unsuitableness. But he has not put forward any real explanation for perceptions and intellectual intuitions. The word *abstraction*, therefore, is a metaphor which may satisfy the shallow-minded but it does not contain any new light likely to clarify the workings of the understanding. But if we abandon this *analogy* of abstraction and division, which cannot properly be applied to any particular sensible thing, from which nothing can be abstracted, nothing divided, what remains to be said about the way in which the understanding perceives things?

The following points are certain:

1. No particular sensible entity undergoes any alteration or division of any kind when perceived by the understanding. Consequently, the word *abstraction* does not throw any new light on the explanation of intellectual acts when it is understood as an operation dividing what is common from what is proper, in any particular sensible thing.

2. An ens, in so far as it is in the understanding, has a *completely* (not partly) different existence from that which it has in real nature.

3. The existence which an ens has in the understanding is *universal* although in its own nature what is real is *particular*.

4. Consequently, any object, in so far as it is *universal*, exists solely in the understanding; this object of the understanding, this *universality*, is entirely different from and has no connection with the terms of sense, which are *particulars*. Stated in this way, the difficulty of explaining how the mind can receive its objects from sense, in the way Locke and Condillac understand this, receives its full force. St. Thomas saw the difference between the terms of sense and the objects of understanding so clearly that in refuting the error of those who accepted that the acting intellect was external to us and communicated with us by means of sensible phantasms, he was

able to show the impossibility of the error. The object of the intellect is in no way part of these phantasms, as the word *abstraction* might implicate. It is an object completely immune from phantasms and consequently completely different from them. There is, therefore, no true communication between the *idea* of this intellect and the *sensible phantasm*. This shows the shrewdness of the holy Doctor. He was not deceived, as the Arabs were, by the metaphorical connotations of the word *abstraction* (See comment of St. Thomas on the book *De Anima*, lect. 7, 10).

19. (251)

[Aristotle, St. Thomas Aquinas and universality]

Aristotle, explaining the *formation of the objects of the intellect*, refers in passing to a DORMANT UNIVERSAL IN THE SOUL. In his attempt to show how all our ideas are derived from the senses, he maintains that *memory* is produced by *sensations* which leave the imprint of their traces, and that when a number of memories are compared, *experience* gives rise to the deduction of principles or *ideas*. But, as though dissatisfied by the term *experience* which is confined to particulars, he adds, 'from experience and from every universal dormant in the mind' (*Poster.* 50, bk. 1, final chapter). At this point, our philosopher, contradicting his premises, needs to add to experience some other element in the soul. Despite the vagueness of Aristotle's views in this passage, St. Thomas's comment and explanation of the origin of ideas could not be more accurate and precise. Knowing how to describe the fact exactly, already means great progress on the way to explaining it. St. Thomas points out that *experience* can only be of particular things and that, consequently, one needs to proceed further and draw out principles from some universal: ULTERIUS EX UNIVERSALI QUIESCENTE IN ANIMA [further from the universal dormant in the soul]. He also points out that this universal is produced by an operation of the soul through which the soul receives something which is in reality particular, as though it were a universal: (*quod scilicet accipitur ac si in omnibus ita sit, sicut est experimentum in quibusdam).* Outside the soul, therefore, there is nothing universal; the soul adds *universality* and receives as *universal* what is *in se* particular. Moreover, this *universalised* object is described by Aristotle as UNUM PRAETER MULTA [one beyond the many]. According to St. Thomas, it is the intellect alone which adds this specific *unity* to *many individuals*. This unity has nothing to do with the many; it is outside them, PRAETER MULTA. This *universal* is therefore not part of those individuals, not something really extracted from them, but independent of them. In short, it is an *idea* completely different in nature from that of subsistent individuals, which are *particular substances*. It seems to me, therefore, that St. Thomas, in affirming that there is nothing in the intellect which did not previously come from sense, did not exclude from the intellect the *form of universality* which the intellect adds to things. It draws this form, which makes it the intellect it is, from within itself. Later, we shall see what this form is. This interpretation becomes certain, and even obvious, if we come to consider the *light* which St. Thomas grants to the intellect for its very existence, as we shall see.

20. (252)

[Intellect, soul and sense]

To overcome this difficulty, the scholastics resorted to saying that the mind perceives particulars *per quamdam reflexionem* [through a kind of reflection]. Anyone can see that although the pronoun, *quidam, quaedam, quoddam* is respectable enough, it is also often used as a plank for shipwrecked philosophers. It cannot always calm the human understanding in its desire to find sounder arguments. As I see it, the difficulty is the same as that noted relative to common sense. The solution is as follows: sense and intellect are potencies of a single subject. The same *myself*, modified by sensations, thinks about them. There is no need, therefore, to assume that the understanding, a particular potency, perceives sensations, as if sensations were perceived by two potencies. Consequently, there is no need to assume two species of phantasms, one like the other. This would mean multiplying entia unnecessarily, and lead to infinite progression. It is sufficient for us to concentrate upon the unity of MYSELF, a unity which contains sensations, ideas and thoughts. Aristotle assumed that sensation from an external organ was one thing, and that sensation conveyed to the common centre was another. Thus there were two potencies, *proper sense* and *common sense*. The fact is however that there is no sensation in the external organ separated from the soul; it is always the soul alone which feels. There is only one kind of sensation, and no bodily senses other than organic senses. However, because it is always the soul alone which feels, it follows that the soul simultaneously participates in several sensations (from this point of view, it could itself be called a *common sense*). The soul also reflects on these sensations, and thus thinks. The understanding is the faculty of thought; it does not perceive particular sensations; the soul, which is the seat of understanding, perceives them. It is not sensations, but the judgment which the soul makes on them which is called *intellectual perception*. The soul, which makes this judgment — and subsequent judgments — is to this extent considered as endowed with the potency of *reason*.

21. (271)

[Aristotle and innate universals]

The obstacle to discovering the truth of problems are the confused ideas sometimes jumbled up with them. In order to trace accurately the development of the errors made by an author, we need to know where the obscurity and confusion in his ideas are located. Thus on a number of occasions I have noted in Aristotle's arguments passages where he seems not to grasp very clearly and simply the thread of his argument. Let me give an example. The question of the origin of ideas consists entirely in explaining how we can have universal conceptions when all that the senses provide are sensations or particular perceptions. If we can discover how to conceive a single idea, a single universal, the question is resolved.

We need to know that we require a universal from the moment of the first judgment formed in our mind; no judgment can be formed without an idea. The nub of this issue, therefore, consists wholly in the first step our mind takes in its first and simplest judgment. But philosophers who have not realised properly that the problem lay wholly in explaining the first step taken by reason blithely skipped over the initial stages of reason, unaware that the core of the problem lay here, and reached the final stages and arguments when reason establishes scientific principles. They then undertook to explain the formation of these principles, and did so very well. But the only real problem was the first step in the argument which they supposed without any explanation. On occasions, Aristotle falls into this error. He comes up against the nub of the question, but in the wrong place — at the final stages rather than at the first stage.

The passage I quoted from Aristotle shows this clearly. In it, he endeavours to explain the origin of the *principles of the sciences and arts* as if the difficulty lay in their formation rather than in the formation of the first popular, common ideas from which reasoning moves. This is more obvious in Themistius' paraphrase of the passage from Aristotle. 'The universal,' he says, 'is the work of the mind and is formed by it.' But how is it formed? This is the problem at issue. He replies: 'By induction because it is characteristic of the mind to unite, to gather together and, as Plato says, to *put an end to undefined things.*' (In passing, let me say that in this passage Aristotle appears to agree with Plato in admitting that it is the proper role of the intellect to *determine* anything *undetermined* which pre-existed in the mind. This would confirm my conjectures on Aristotle's acting intellect).

Aristotle, according to Themistius' paraphrase, describes as follows the induction enabling the mind to collect and unite universals from particulars. Note the whole passage:

> This induction takes a long time. A great distance elapses between the perceptions received from the senses and their interconnection. The senses immediately begin to form phantasms but only when they are well versed in it does the force of the soul called intellect appear and reach its conclusion (the universal). A long period and a great deal of knowledge is required for this because whatever is diffuse and scattered can only be unified and reduced to one over an adequate length of time.
>
> (*Poster.*, bk. 2, c. 36)

[*app.* 21]

The whole difficulty of explaining how the mind forms universals is here considered by Aristotle as consisting in the formation of *scientific* principles which are certainly formed by means of repeated observations over a long period. For example, to establish the universal principle, 'Peruvian bark dispels fever,' it was required 1. that those who worked upon the discovery had already reached the age of reason; 2. that they repeated the experiments over and over again and from them arrived by induction at the general proposition, 'Peruvian bark dispels fever.' Aristotle illustrated his views with an example similar to this taken from medicine.

However, those who accept innate ideas have no quarrel with such an argument; in fact, the whole step taken by Aristotle is out of place. He attempts to explain the formation of scientific principles as though the difficulty lay here. But the real difficulty and whole question does not consist in explaining this kind of scientific universals. It is found in the explanation of the *universal* itself, even the most apparently ordinary and obvious one. In fact, before we can form the universal proposition, 'Peruvian bark dispels fever', we must already have a number of other universals formed in our mind. All the terms in this proposition without exception express universality. The words *Peruvian bark* do not, in fact, express any particular fragment of bark, but the *species* of bark. These words express all possible barks of this species. It is therefore an *idea*, a *universal concept* because it refers to a species, not to something subsistent. Similarly, the word *fever* does not refer to a fever picked up from Sempronius or Caius, but refers to any fever, to the species of illness called fever. At this point, we can see that the question: 'What connection is there between these two universal ideas, Peruvian bark and fever?' is entirely different from 'How can we possess universal ideas of Peruvian bark and fever?' The first is a *medical* question, which is answered after a great deal of experience and as a result of more or less lengthy induction which gives it some degree of reliability. The second question involves *ideas* and is intended to explain a non-scientific, but common fact: that of the existence in the human mind of the universal ideas, *Peruvian bark* and *fever*. These universal ideas are to be found in the human mind, not after a long period and as a result of long experience and extensive inferences, but as soon as we first begin to use our reason. The infant, as soon as it begins to talk, names *fever, bark* or in short, substantives which express species of things, not mere subsistences. What we wish to know is how this child moves so rapidly from particular, individual and subsistent things which he perceives by the senses to species, that is, to *ideas* without which speech is impossible. This is the issue. Aristotle (or Themistius) shuns this question, which aims at explaining the origin of the *first universals, and transfers it to the formation of scientific principles* which are the *final universals* and presuppose the formation of the first universals of which they are only a prolongation.

The explanation put forward to our question about the formation of universals is erroneous when it concludes: 'Thus, gradually and imperceptibly, this inference is formed' (from which scientific principles are drawn) 'and its very continuity conceals its beginning and end. As a result many people hold that man's nature possesses inborn information, independent of any study or intellect to produce it and stimulate it. This is untrue.' These words reveal the standard attitude of thinkers who wish to deduce everything from the senses. They resort to affirming that this operation, so slow and imperceptible, cannot be observed and that, consequently, some imagine that universals are innate in us. They try to establish their theory by disseminating obscurity. All ideas are imperceptibly derived from the senses by a process that evades one's gaze. I maintain, however, that this development must be infinite because development from the particular to the universal requires infinite progression — as such it has no bounds. Individuals, however multiplied, can never form or exhaust a *species* even if they progressed indefinitely.

To explain, therefore, how *ideas* are derived from *sensations*, it is necessary to suppose the possibility of actual infinite progression whose ultimate end would be *ideas*. This end, however, would never be attained; if it were, the progression would come to an end, which belies the assumption, and the ideas would not be produced. In short, between sensations and ideas there is not merely a difference in gradation but in essence; a gradual transition from one to the other is impossible. As I was saying, therefore, Aristotle's argument is unreasonable. He says: 'There are no innate ideas because scientific principles are derived from ideas inductively'. This is rather like saying 'Cut stone is not the work of nature because *we* build houses with it.'

22. (280)
[Leibniz confuses reality and possibility]

The high esteem in which I hold Leibniz is the reason I am so hard upon him. Every careless turn in his argument deserves to be pointed out so that we may see how the slightest inattention leads to error. And error, however slight and scarcely percept- ible it may be, always produces greater errors. This is especially the case with more logical and nimble minds.

Here, Leibniz, after stating that naked faculties are a mere abstraction, appeals to fact and claims that in the whole universe there is not a single dormant potency, that is, a potency which remains without an act, and in a state of naked, pure potency. This passage is wildly astray. He was speaking of the nature of potencies considered in themselves, and asserted that their nature was such that they were always associated with an act. In other words, he was speculating metaphysically whether a potency totally shorn of act was *possible*. We were in the realm of possibilities. Now, to prove it is impossible, he resorts to reality by asking: 'Where in the universe will we find a potency devoid of act?' But this means abandoning his first argument to relapse into the realm of reality; he appeals to experience to prove what is and is not possible. Experience, however, only witnesses to what is and what is not; it indicates facts alone. Consequently, it is useless in determining what is possible. Even if it could do this, it would be impossible to truly affirm or deny by means of observation the non-existence in the whole uni- verse of a pure potency which does not, for at least a single moment, abide in this state of pure potency — if such a thing is possible. It is impossible to investigate them all, or submit them all to observation at every moment of their existence. Observa- tions of this kind would enable us at most to induce a conjec- tural argument from analogy to prove a general, but still not absolutely necessary, fact. Leibniz frequently confuses the two worlds, the real and the possible.

Because such confusion has important consequences for this thinking, I hope I shall be forgiven if I mention another passage where the same association of *fact* and *possibility* can be noted, and where fact is called upon to prove possibility. In one passage he states:

> I maintain that naturally a substance could not exist without action.

Immediately after, he adds:

> and that there are no bodies without movement.
> (*Nouveaux Essais*, etc., Preface)

The first of these two propositions is abstract, but the second, dealing with bodies, becomes concrete and consequently not a *necessary* proposition like the first. If he had merely stated that bodies have to act because they are substances, and proved that they were substances and that every substance had to act, all would have been proved. But to say that all bodies move, and to add, 'Experience is on my side, and we only need to consult Boyle's famous book against absolute rest to be convinced' (*ibid.*), is to resort to what occurs in the real world in order to ascertain the stable, eternal relationships of the ideal world.

This becomes obvious on the occasions when Leibniz is guilty of arguing in a vicious circle. Thus, to prove that the understanding always thinks, he resorts to the need for each potency to have an act of its own — he resorts to fact. Experience does indeed show no examples in nature of potencies without action, but Leibniz' question, 'Does the intellect always think?' posited in this way is truly the question about the possibility of a potency totally shorn of its act.

Later, we shall see why Leibnz did not distinguish sufficiently between the *ideal* and the *real* world. We shall see that the very nature of his philosophy prevented his affirmation of such an important distinction.

[*app.* 22]

23. (290)

[Leibniz and sensation]

This argument of Leibniz seems wrong to me. It is not, in fact, absurd to suppose that our organs, in order to produce a sensation in us, must be touched with a certain degree of force. If this degree of force is absent, the sensation does not occur; it begins only when the external impression has reached the degree of force required to produce a sensation in the organ. The impact upon the bodily organ and the corresponding sensation or perception which occurs in the soul must not be confused. That any external force, however small, acting upon our bodily senses, should produce some physical impression on them seems patently obvious. The phrase, 'external force', refers to something which is acting, to a small or great extent (according to its strength or weakness). Consequently, when what acts is applied to that on which it is called to act, it will undoubtedly produce some effects.

But are we obliged to believe that there is always some sensation in the soul corresponding to this slight action exerted upon the external sense organs? I have no doubt that every wave moved by the sea, moves the air slightly and that the air moved by the wave has an impact upon my ears. I go further: I am willing to believe that not only each wave, but each drop making up the wave moves the air proportionately to its own movement, and that the tiny wave movement is transmitted throughout the whole body of the atmospheric air. It affects not only my ears but the ears of persons further afield, decreasing as it goes. But it does not follow from this that the impact on my ear will be sensible for me, nor a perception for my soul. Experience shows that the impression of external things on the sensible parts of our body in the extremities of the tiny nerve ends should come from outside. It is important that the tremor or impact, however slight, should be transmitted to the brain. Once the link between nerve and brain is severed, sensations do not occur. Nor will every tiny impulse affecting the external nerves be sufficient to produce the amount of movement needed over the whole length of the nerve to arouse a sensation. It could be, that the impression of the external sensories has to have a certain degree of force merely to enable it to be transmitted and directed to the brain.

However, ignoring this, how did Leibniz acquire this view of his which I have refuted? Its source is an application of the *law of continuity*, to which he resorted a great deal. It is not my intention, at this point, to investigate this law or to assign its limits. The following observation should suffice to show clearly the wrong use the great philosopher made of it. What connection is there, I wonder, between the *impression* produced in the bodily organs and the corresponding *perception* in the soul? According to Leibniz's theory, these things are, by nature, totally different; one cannot be the cause of the other. One is certainly subsequent to the other, but it is a question of coexistence, not of cause and effect. Why, then, should I have to *perceive* every slightest *impression* formed in my external organs? Not by the law of continuity, because there is no scale of degree between the *impression* and the *perception*. They are things which are, by nature, different, arising as they do from completely different sources. Even if the law of continuity were to apply in this instance, it would apply only relative to the series of *impressions* on the one hand, and to the series of *perceptions* on the other. In other words, the same law would have to establish that a strong impression is impossible except through a series of prior, weaker impressions. Similarly, a strong perception would be impossible unless it were preceded by all the minor degrees of the same perception leading up to the strong force perception.

The *law of continuity*, therefore, will at most be applied separately to the series of *impressions* made upon the bodily organs on the one hand, and on the other to the series of *perceptions* of the soul. It can never be applied to the transition from one of these two series to the other because they are completely different in nature. Consequently, it is not at all absurd to suppose that the series of *perceptions* begins when the series of the degrees of *impression* is already well under way. In other words, perception does not arise in our spirit until our organs are moved by a certain degree of force. This is a law of nature which cannot be conjectured or deduced *a priori* but discovered only through experience. And constant experience convinces me that for every tiny impact which external things produce upon my

[*app.* 23]

bodily organs, there is certainly no corresponding perception in my spirit: perception only occurs when the impulse has a certain power. It may be, of course, that the degree of force required is more or less dependent on the difference in sensitivity of the organs with which different persons are endowed. I am willing also to admit that perception may be present without our being aware of it. In fact, we are continually having perceptions of which we are unaware because our attention is focused on other things and distracted by them. Nevertheless, it is essential that I should be aware of them when I turn my attention to them. If not, I would have to say that they are not present within me. I could not even say that they existed. Thus, however much I intend to smell the perfume of a flower, if I do not smell it I can only say either that the flower has no perfume or, if it has, that I have a cold in the nose or cannot smell anything. In other words, although my organ is always able to receive an external impression, it is not always able to receive it in such a way that there is a corresponding perception of the scent in my spirit. This can be said with at least a high degree of probability because I could on occasion be unable to focus my attention upon the perception. Experience shows that I have to acquire the ability to focus my attention on observing something occurring within me.

But this ability to focus our attention upon ourselves and direct it where we wish varies a great deal from person to person. Not everyone knows how to observe human nature, and only a few are alert and ready enough to reflect upon everything which occurs fleetingly and occasionally within them. The majority cannot do so. This explains the difference between philosophers and the masses, and between different philosophers. Again, one of the truly important circumstances which make it difficult for ordinary persons to focus their willed attention upon what happens to them individually is the minuteness and tenuous nature of the sensation. Highly vivid sensations draw our attention to themselves — violently, one might say — and tear it away from less vivid and strong sensations. On the other hand, if we wish to focus specifically upon them, we have to employ increased, inner, spontaneous vigour to counteract their own lack of power to stimulate and attract us. Because of this, it is indeed difficult to observe the minutest sensations within us. When we do observe them, we do so more easily if we dissociate ourselves from all other powerful impressions and we withdraw to somewhere dark and quiet where we can concentrate on ourselves. It is impossible, therefore, to assert categorically at this very moment that we do not have, for example, slight sensations of the very distant sounds of which neither we nor those around us can be aware however much we apply ourselves to listening for them. I conclude: the whole purpose of this long note is to bring out the difference between 1. *unreflected* sensations and 2. *minute* sensations. Leibniz confuses them, speaking now of one and now of the other as though they were the same thing. They, must however, be distinguished very carefully. From this distinction flow important consequences in the history of the human spirit. But I cannot deal with them here without straying too far from my original intent.

The reason we are not aware of our sensations, whether great or small, is that we do not *reflect* upon them, we do not focus our attention upon them, we do not think about them. *Unreflected perceptions*, therefore, are all those of which we are not *aware*. We do not know that we are having them. If asked whether we are having them, we are inclined to say no. Nevertheless we do have them.

The *smallness* of sensations is simply one of the many circumstances which very often deter us from reflecting upon them. We can indeed be aware of small sensations although this occurs in different persons according to their ability to reflect upon themselves and observe what is going on within them. *Small* sensations are not always or necessarily *unreflected*, that is, sensations of which we are unaware and cannot speak. Nevertheless, very frequently, they lie within us unobserved, *unreflected*. For this reason small sensations may be confused, as the great Leibniz confused them, with *unreflected* sensations. Again, we sometimes find highly vivid, powerful sensations which remain unreflected while all our attention is focused on a more interesting and powerful object. This explains why Archimedes, absorbed in solving a scientific problem dear to his heart, was unaware of the din created by the Roman army when it entered Syracuse.

[*app.* 23]

24. (295)

[Leibniz and *virtual knowledge*]

Leibniz, to express what he considers innate, sometimes uses the expression *virtual knowledge*. This would seem to imply that he admitted only knowledge contained in some principle. Consequences are said to be contained *virtually* in principles because they can be deduced from them. However, a number of passages by our philosopher demonstrate that he accepted all innate cognitions as existing *per se*, not *virtually*, in the sense that they were contained in other cognitions. He says, for example:

> Actual knowledge (of the most difficult sciences) is not innate, but is what we may call virtual knowledge. It is like the figure traced by the veins in marble before it is revealed by the sculptor's hand.
>
> (*N. Essais, etc.*, bk. 1, c. 1)

This shows the difference between Leibniz's *virtual* knowledge and what this word *virtual* may seem to mean at first sight. If the sculptor, instead of outlining the statue by using the veins in the marble itself, had only a mechanical *rule* expressed, say, by some mathematical formula, he would have carved a statue without knowing what the eventual outcome would be. In such a case, he would have *virtual knowledge* of the statue because the statue is *virtually* comprised in the rule. In other words, the rule used by the artist has the power to lead him infallibly to the creation of the desired statue, although the statue does not exist in the rule and does not make itself known. The rule and the statue are entirely different things. But this is not how Leibniz understands *virtual* knowledge which he uses to signify *outline* knowledge, that is, like the statue designed from the veins in the marble. This is a highly inappropriate *analogy* which led the great man astray.

25. (298)

[Internal judgment and external object]

Leibniz himself says: 'Sensation occurs when we apperceive an external object.' Remember, however, what I have already noted. If we *are aware* of perceiving an external object, we are forming an internal *judgment*. We judge that there exists, external to us, an object distinct from us. We utter an *interior word* as, for example, 'It is this thing'. Forming an internal judgment that an object is external to us exists is the same as placing that perceived object in the class of entia and attributing to it *existence*. But in attributing *existence* to something perceived by the senses, we merely compare the sensible term with a universal because existence is an idea, the most universal of all ideas. Until I judge that the perceived term exists externally to me; until I know that anything particular perceived with the senses belongs to the universal class of beings; until, in short, I consider myself and the said term as two distinct entia or things, but as sharing existence, I cannot be aware that I perceive an external object. Being aware of perceiving it presupposes my knowledge that it is something, and knowing that it is something is the same as considering it as one amongst possible entia (of a given nature). Without this, I would have only *sensible perception* without being *aware* of having it. I would not know what I am, what perception is, what its term is. It is certainly difficult to imagine a state of spirit with only *sensible perception* and nothing more, without any thought to make us aware of the perception, or to make us know it. As human beings endowed with reason, we frequently carry out a cognitive act upon our sensations and their term simultaneously. Separating the two is the narrow pass to be traversed by anyone aspiring to make some progress in this philosophy of the human spirit.

26. (299)
[Leibniz and presentiment]

On this subject [of presentiment], Leibniz points out 1. that animals are easily caught because they do not have the ability to draw universal and necessary consequences from things; 2. that empiricists are subject to numerous errors because they rely upon experience alone. Statesmen and leaders, over-reliant on experience, are subject to similar mistakes. Wiser people, besides using experience, attempt to get down to the reason for things in order to judge when it is opportune to make exceptions. Leibniz adds:

> Reason alone is able to lay down sure rules, and provide the missing element for uncertain rules by finding exceptions to them, and finally find certain connections in the power springing from necessary connections. This often provides a means of foreseeing an event without any need to experience the sensible link between images to which beasts are reduced. Indeed that which justifies the internal principles of necessary truths also distinguishes mankind from animals
>
> (*N. Essais*, etc., Preface)

A comment on this whole argument of Leibniz.

First, the principles of prudence governing a wise person's activity are based upon prevision of certain events, but not upon an absolute prevision or, as the philosophers say, apodictically necessary prevision. In this case, prevision is only relatively or hypothetically necessary. For example, knowing that the nature of the sun is to shine, I foresee that it will shine tomorrow. However, this prevision, although founded upon knowledge of the sun's nature, has no inner necessity. It is true only on the hypothesis that the sun continues in its orbit without undergoing any changes. This could also happen, because it does not involve any contradiction. Leibniz, therefore, confuses *apodictic* with *hypothetical* necessity. Only apodictic necessity exhibits the full power of reason because reason owes nothing to the senses for its firm, absolute necessity but owes it all — let it be said in passing — to the infinite force of an unlimited, supra-sensible truth. Pascal fell into an error somewhat similar to that of Leibniz when, as I have already remarked (*Opusc., Fil,* 5: 1, p. 93), he included among the first principles of reason, *space, time, movement* and *matter,* and affirmed in refuting the Pyrrhonists that knowledge of these things is as solid as any knowledge obtained by rational argument. *Space, time,* etc., are not *principles* of reason; they are merely positive *data* of experience. The *principles* of reason have an inner necessity; data have an *arbitrary* character because they are chiefly dependent upon the will of the creator, either to be in one form rather than another, or certainly to be or not to be, and to be the subject of our experiences in some way. In a word, the principles of reason are apodictically necessary; the primary data of experience are hypothetically necessary, that is, constituents of arguments which we make about a certain genus of things because they are given to us as such, not *per se.* A comparison between Pascal's error and Leibniz's, can be made as follows:

I. First, the following must be established:

1. There are absolute principles of reason, such as the principle of contradiction, which are apodictically certain.

2. These principles, when applied to some genera of contingent things produce other principles of hypothetical necessity which should be called *primary data.* These can be nominated as *space, time, motion,* and so on.

3. Using the principles and primary data, other consequences of a double hypothetical necessity are deduced which require two hypotheses, that is, 1st. data of *space, time,* etc.; 2nd. data from *bodies,* etc.

Pascal confuses the apodictic necessity of *principles* of reason with the *hypothetical necessity of primary data.* Leibniz went a step further, and confused the *apodictic* necessity of principles with the *doubly hypothetical* necessity.

II. Moreover, Leibniz's argument is directed at proving that we cannot derive all our cognitions from the senses because they never give us necessary, universal cognitions which we must extract from deep within our reason. This may be proved not only by necessity mingled with our reasoning, that is, by merely apodictic necessity, but also by any degree of hypothetical necessity, because the senses can never provide necessity of any kind. Leibniz's argument as a whole, therefore, is on the right lines, but the following partial mistake may be noted. He equated animal with empirical behaviour. This, I maintain, is wrong. Even the behaviour of empirical people is based upon a reason, a principle, which has its own universality and necessity, and to this extent cannot be deduced from the senses. In fact, empirical people are guided in their activity by similar cases; they begin, therefore, from the universal principle of *analogy*. This principle, although the cause of frequent error, is nevertheless universal or is, at least, taken as such. Empirical people also err by placing too much reliance on experience and unduly widening the scope of its applications: 'This is how it has been, so this is how it is going to be.' But they could not succeed in unduly extending the scope of the results of experience, that is, the universalisation of similar instances, if they relied solely on the senses. They use their reason and add *universality* and *necessity*, derived from themselves, to facts. They may indeed err in this, but they do so by transcending the senses and show that they themselves possess a conception of *universality* and *necessity*. Beasts do not behave in this way. Without rules, they follow their instinct or habit from which they acquire a tendency and an inclination to repeat certain actions, to prefer some and shun others. The behaviour of even a pragmatist cannot be confused with that of an animal lacking reason.

27. (302)

[Kant and the foundation of all knowledge]

It really is odd to see how Kant gratuitously accepts this principle and believes that it requires no proof whatsoever. He sets about constructing his philosophy upon this initial foundation: 'There can be no doubt that all our knowledge begins with experience.' These are the opening words of the *Critique of Pure Reason* in Mantovani's Italian translation. No reason is given anywhere in Kant's work for this non-*critical* and highly dogmatic basic principle except the following question which comes immediately after:

For how is it possible that the faculty of knowledge should

be awakened into activity except by means of objects which affect our senses, and partly of themselves produce representations, partly rouse our powers of understanding into activity, to compare, to connect, or to separate these, and so to convert the raw material of our sensuous impressions into a knowledge of objects, which is called experience?

He then confidently concludes:

In respect of time, therefore, no knowledge of ours is antecedent to experience, but begins with it.

It is clear, therefore, that the entire principle of critical philosophy was received by its author as a truth generally accepted in his age, that is, as a definitive judgment which consequently needs no further proof. In other words, *critical* philosophy is based entirely on a principle not subjected to *any critique whatsoever* and accepted as a mere *prejudice*! If this first proposition were to be investigated and found unreliable, it would bring about the downfall of Kant's whole vast enterprise. What can be stated for the moment, however, is that the reason given by Kant to verify such a principle is inadequate. He asks: 'Is it possible for our faculty of knowledge to be awakened into exercise by anything other than external objects?' The question shows that he assumes as already proven 1. that there are external *objects* independently of our faculty of knowledge; 2. all our cognitions are formed by the exercise of our faculty of knowledge. If there were any innate knowledge, the cognitive faculty would not need to be stimulated to form them; he supposes, therefore, as true what he intends to prove.

Moreover, a similar supposition is immediately denied him by a number of thinkers from Descartes onwards. Descartes holds that understanding lies in essential activity, in continual thought. He denies that he needs to be stimulated by external things in order to think. Leibniz also was to reject it most vehemently. According to him, sensible entia cannot stimulate the mind to think, because they cannot have any real communication with it. Every action of the spirit proceeds from an inner activity, from instincts which are intrinsically subject to some determined development. Again Malebranche, with all those thinkers who deduce the spirit's ideas from direct action

[*app.* 27]

upon it by God, would deny Kant his principle. To claim that all such opponents should be ignored is going too far. Nor is it in keeping with Kant's usual method of stooping to confute the views of philosophers much less important than those of whom we are speaking. On the other hand, if the first proposition needs no proof, it must be said that critical philosophy as a whole needs none because the whole kernel of critical philosophy is contained in that proposition. In fact, it amounts to saying: 'It is certain that Descartes, Leibniz, Malebranche, etc., and all those who accept the existence of innate notions, or notions derived from some being other than bodies, are wrong.' If we accept such a proposition as true, we need to resort to Kant's system to explain how we acquire cognitions. Kant therefore begins by positing as certain a principle which renders his system necessary. This means accepting that the system is true from the outset prior to any proof. Such an error is common amongst philosophers. They begin by establishing a proposition which seems obvious and implicitly contains their theory, yet dispense themselves from proving it. Next, they deduce their theory from the proposition. The theory is now declared proven, although it has been deduced from an assumed principle passed off as accepted.

28. (309)

[Locke and abstraction]

As I have already observed, Locke's inexact description of *abstraction* was the source of his inaccuracy. Let us suppose, he says, that I see a pear tree in my garden. Comparing it with the other trees in the same garden: 1. I note something which it has in *common* with all the other trees to which I compare it; this common element furnishes me with the idea of the *genus* which is expressed, if I so wish, by the word *tree*; 2. I note that the tree which I observe has something in common with certain determined trees. From this common element, which is common to one class of trees, but not to all trees, I form the idea of the species to which I give the name: 'pear tree'; 3. finally, I note that, in addition to the features common to all trees and to the features common to all pear trees, my tree has something of its own, not common with other trees. From this, I have the *individual idea* of that tree, which I do not name because I do not need to name it individually. Now, if we ignore the inaccuracies in this derivation of an individual idea, I maintain that, if I were to form the idea of the genus of trees by selecting the features common only to all the trees submitted to my experience (and in the case before us, to all the trees planted in my garden), this generic idea would contain nothing over and above the element common to the trees which I have examined. I could therefore apply the name *tree* only to that determined number and to the actual trees I have seen. This idea would be of no use to me in designating a possible tree, or an existing tree that I had not seen, but only heard about. This, however, runs counter to the use of the word, which expresses genus. It is easy to see that, in using the word *tree*, I am indicating something common not to ten or twelve individual trees, nor to all existing trees, but to all the trees imaginable and, therefore, of all possible trees. It follows that in the idea of *genus* expressed as a common noun, there is always included the idea of a *notion* applicable to an infinite number of beings, that is, the idea of their possibility which transcends all the limits of experience.

Furthermore, the idea of *genus* does not have extension based on the number of individuals subjected to my sense experience. A person who had examined all the trees in the world, one after the other, would perhaps have an idea of the *genus* of trees that was more precise but certainly no more extensive than that of someone who had never set foot out of his house or left the tiny confines of his garden. Both persons would refer to the *tree* as a genus, assigning to the word a notion as extensive as the notion of possibility, which has no limits of any kind; both would apply this word *tree* to all those trees which God might create, as well as to those he has already created. The same remark may be applied to the idea of *species*. From this, it is clear that these ideas contain an infinitely greater extension than that which all sense experience could provide. Consequently, we have to resort to another source adequate to explain the notion of *possibility*, which forms part of every common idea, constitutes the

[*app.* 28]

common idea's great extension and does not in the least have its source in the senses.

29. (316)

[Hume and *a priori* knowledge]

Hume divided human cognitions into two classes: 1. those which consist in simple relationships of ideas, such as all reasoning in pure mathematics, and 2. those which deal with facts, such as the proposition: 'There is no effect without a cause.' He was concerned to eliminate this second type of *a priori* cognitions whilst leaving the former intact. However, even assuming such a distinction, one of these aspects of *a priori* knowledge could not subsist without the other. Hume's dialectic, based upon Locke's principle, is a kind of corrosive acid capable of dissolving everything; *a priori* knowledge vanishes completely and all *a posteriori* knowledge connected with it. My argument is, I think, utterly clear, and unanswerable. Hume's distinction between *a priori* knowledge which consists in simple relationships between ideas and *a priori* knowledge which deals with facts, would not affect the argument in any way even if it were sound; both would be equally doomed to destruction. What is more, the proposition, 'There is no effect without a cause', considered in all its universality, is a simple relationship between ideas like any proposition in pure mathematics, as, for example, 'Two things which are equal to a third are equal to one another.' That proposition, if applied to some particular effect or cause, involves the practical realm, just as the propositions of pure mathematics do when they are applied to bodies and thus become the source of applied mathematics. The proposition which is true in theory is also true in practice, provided care is taken to calculate all the practical elements in order to modify the result of the purely theoretical proposition. If I wish to calculate the thrust of a vault which I intend to build in order to discover the thickness of the supports which I have to provide, I start from theoretical propositions, from simple relationships regarding the nature of arches, gravity, movement, *etc.*; and even prior to this I begin from simple numerical calculations, in short, from the propositions of pure algebra and geometry. The certainty, therefore, of those universal, necessary propositions which are *simple relationships of ideas* and of those which *refer to facts* is intimately connected. If the first certainty exists, so does the second; they constitute a single certainty. Propositions which involve facts are merely applications of theoretical propositions which express a simple relationship of ideas. The theoretical propositions communicate their power to the factual propositions whose certainty cannot be shaken unless the certainty of theoretical propositions, communicated to the factual propositions, is shaken.

Assuming, therefore, that our *a priori* knowledge is divided into propositions which are only simple relationships of ideas and propositions which refer to facts, it is obvious that Hume cannot have examined closely enough the link between these two series of propositions. He assumes their mutual independence, although the second group are only derivations from the first; he assumes the presence of *a priori* propositions referring to facts without their being applications of antecedent propositions, that is, of meaningful, simple relationships of ideas, which is false. He was led astray by the outward form of the proposition 'There is no effect without a cause', which in referring to effects seems to refer to facts. But a careful examination shows that it refers to *effects* in general, to effects which are mere ideas. It does not refer to this or that real effect, in which case alone it would refer to facts. In short, it merely expresses a relationship between two ideas, that is, between the idea of *cause* and the idea of *effect* in exactly the same way as a similar relationship is expressed by this example: 'The number two is less than the number ten' or 'The angles of a triangle are equal to two right angles.' When these mathematical propositions are applied to a number of real things — for example, to a number of persons and to a particular triangle — they refer to reality in exactly the same way as the proposition, 'Every effect must have its cause', refers to facts when applied to a particular, actual effect.

Finally, Hume's distinction is false.

The universal principle from which these concrete propositions (that is, propositions dealing with facts) is derived, is mixed with the concrete propositions themselves. Consequently, the concrete propositions, too, have a certain *a priori* element. Nevertheless, *a priori* knowledge always lies in the principle itself. In other words, it lies in propositions which, although applicable to facts, express a simple relationship of ideas and as such are necessary and universal. Human cognitions, therefore, are certainly divided into *a priori* and *a posteriori* cognitions, although *a priori* cognitions cannot be divided, as Hume attempts to divide them, into 1. propositions which express a simple relationship of ideas and 2. propositions which deal with facts. The second kind of propositions are *a posteriori*, although they need the others if they are to be deduced on the occasion of external experience. Such experience provides particular facts to which general propositions can be applied and used to form a judgment about facts.

Finally experience, corresponding to the calculations of applied mathematics, bears witness to the truth and efficacy of the ideal propositions which surveyors use to rule nature and ensure its obedience.

30. (322)

[Reid on principles and ideas]

We have already seen that Hume's classification of universal truths also led to the elimination of *a posteriori* knowledge (cf. 315).

Reid was particularly concerned to demonstrate those principles which assure us of the reality of external bodies. Rather than principles, they should be called *applications of principles* to the real existence of things. These applications have the form of multiple judgments.

Moreover, such judgments were considered by Reid as *necessary, blind* instincts of nature.

Consequently, his teaching did not succeed in actually defending the *principles of reason* and their unshaken authority. On the contrary, he inevitably fell victim to a number of contradictions, as follows.

First contradiction. — *Universal principles* depend upon

our idea of the *essences* of things (cf. 307). If we denied any knowledge of their essences, principles too are ruled out. Unaware of this, Reid agreed with Locke on this point and maintained that we have no idea of the *essences* of things (*Essays on the Powers of the Human Mind*, Essay 1, c. 1). However, when he later discussed how we perceive the existence of bodies, he said that, thanks to a law of our nature laid down by God, we are led to add a *subject* (substance) to attributes, and then admitted that we possessed a *vague notion* of the nature of things or of their *essences* (*ibid.*, Essay 5, c. 2). This is an example of the same inconsistency noted in Locke.

Second contradiction. — Reid eliminated ideas. He accepted the operations of the spirit which, in his view, immediately conceives *real objects*. This implied the destruction not only of universal ideas but also of universal conceptions; it meant reducing intellectual knowledge to pure subsistent individuals. Reid states specifically in some passages that mere *possibility* is *nothing* because, he maintains, that which is merely possible does not exist, and that which does not exist is nothing. This argument was inevitable from the moment he ruled out *ideas* and left in place only what is real. *Possibilities* were eliminated because they are only ideas. But it was impossible to be consistent when saddled with such a system. This would have been beyond the power of human beings who need to think the *possible* in all their conceptions; no intellective act is feasible without the idea of the possible. The following passage from the Scottish philosopher clearly shows him in open contradiction with all that he taught elsewhere on the subject of essences, on the possible and on objects of the mind. He says openly:

> We know the ESSENCE of a triangle and from that essence can deduce its properties. It is an UNIVERSAL and might have been conceived by the human mind though no individual triangle had ever existed (*we are in the realm of the possible*). It has only what Mr. Locke calls a *nominal essence*, which is expressed in its definition. But everything that exists has a *real essence* which is above our comprehension; and, therefore, we cannot deduce its properties or attributes from its nature, as we do in the triangle.
>
> (*Essays on the Powers of the Human Mind*,
> Essay 5, c. 2)

[*app.* 30]

I should point out also that Reid certainly does not take Locke's *nominal essence* as a mere *word*. He states explicitly that words, if they do not express thoughts, are mere sounds and useless (*ibid.*, Essay 5, c. 1). He also says that there are *general concepts*, and that this *generality* is not found in the conception itself, that is, in the act of the mind, but in its *object* (*ibid.*, Essay 5, c. 2).

In Reid's view, therefore, there are *universal objects* which are not ideas or mere possibilities. They are not existent things, and yet not nothing. What can they be?

31. (323)

[Reid criticised in Germany and Italy]

My criticism of Reid is generally accepted as solidly based. My observations had their counterpart in Germany. Buhle writes:

> The main drawback of Reid's philosophy is the vague, undetermined concept of *fundamental truth*. As Reid sees it, a fundamental truth is one enabling a person to reason and act prior to any observations from which to deduce this truth through abstraction. Accordingly, without being fully aware of it, we act most of the time almost by instinct in accordance with that truth. The rigorous idea or the only certain idea, as Feder has stated in his excellent critique of Reid's philosophical theory, is that it is a JUDG-MENT which necessarily arises from the simple ideas of subject and attribute.

Feder's observation is the very one which I have repeatedly put forward (cf.119). There were quite a number of German thinkers who realised that Reid 'made no contribution to the advancement of the cause of philosophical dogmatism, and in particular to that of empirical realism' (Buhle, *Histoire de la philosophie moderne*, vol. 5, c. 12).

In Italy, Galluppi, an outstanding thinker, showed clearly that Reid's system offered no protection against scepticism, but rather opened the way to it. The reason was Reid's having distinguished between *sensation* and the *perception of bodies* while denying that there was any likeness whatsoever between them. The two facts would have arisen in us contemporaneously without any reason. To remedy this defect, Galluppi eliminated the distinction and carried over to *sensation* everything that Reid had said about *perception*. Reid had assumed that *perception* enabled us immediately to perceive bodies as existing beings. Galluppi said that this immediate communication of our spirit with exterior things is achieved purely by *sensation* alone. Sensation, far from being merely *subjective*, as Reid had considered it, was essentially *objective*, something that Reid had said about perception. Galluppi endowed the senses with an aptitude for perceiving the existence of bodies, an obvious example of sensism.

However, it is impossible to attribute the perception of the existence of bodies to the senses alone. Note that it is impossible to say that we have perceived bodies as existing until we have said to ourselves: 'These particular beings exist.' To say this, it is absolutely essential that we have the prior *universal idea of existence* which, according to Galluppi, comes about after perception of bodies by an operation of our mind on these perceptions. But these perceptions of existent beings assume this idea which, as universal, can never be derived from particulars. I willingly grant to Galluppi the immediate communication of our spirit with the body, that is, our body; I grant that through our acquired sensations we experience within us some *action* of the external bodies but not that these are sufficient to enable us to perceive beings existing in themselves; the *sensations* of bodies must not be confused with *judgment*. We perceive bodies by means of an operation of the understanding which adds *existence* to the action of bodies upon us through sensations, and considers bodies as entia which act upon us in a manner determined by the sensations themselves.

32. (364)

[Lessons from the history of human wisdom]

If we combine this final result of Kantian philosophy with

the systems dealt with in the *Saggio sulla speranza* (*Opusc. Filosof.*, vol. 2) and in the *Breve esposizione della filosofia di M. Gioia (ibid.)*, which posited the basis of human happiness in a continuous illusion, we see what lessons can be learned from the history of human wisdom. Full of confidence, man sets off, promising himself that he will discover truth; no truth, however recondite, will evade his inquiries. Meanwhile, his passions raise a murmur of protest, fearing to be denied the heady sweetness of the senses. Man reassures them and promises them that the truth still to be discovered will confirm all sensible pleasures. By this promise, he relies upon an unknown result which he keeps in view as that which must constantly govern all his inquiries. However, truth does not bow to the self-seeking intentions of such a philosophy which, in turn, disdains such behaviour from truth. Then, when every effort has been made to persuade truth to serve its ends, when it has been subjected to all manner of flattery and blandishments, when it has been threatened with being called inhuman, barbaric and cruel if it does not resign itself to the violent instincts of degenerate nature (which does not recognise its own baseness), what does philosophy do in the last resort? It focuses earnestly upon itself and ponders its vicissitudes, then, dejected at its inability to get the better of truth, to corrupt it, or to find a true system which rules out order in enjoyment and replaces justice with sensual pleasure, finally pulls itself together.

At this point, it no longer boasts, as it did at first, that it is setting out on the assured conquest of truth. The discovery of truth was no longer to be its aim; it had gone astray in choosing it. Twisting and turning along a different road, it takes pleasure in becoming shrewder and more cautious, and admits that initially in its naïveté it had sinned by rashness. Modest as it now is, its only aim is to teach people to doubt. Philosophy is perfectly convinced that replacing truth by doubt in this way will calm the passions aroused against its undertaking. Its journey along the new road of doubt is actually an easier one. Instead of spending its time in building, its aim is to destroy anything that would disturb the desires of the human heart, ever insatiable for the sensual pleasures of life. The development of doubt goes hand in hand with the development of unrestrained freedom and the never-ending growth of human concupiscence. The philosophy of doubt, essentially hesitant and restless — like concupiscence — has no aim beyond its own complete fulfilment. This consists in moving from *doubt* to *illusion*. Illusion is devoid of any uncertainty, which is always to be found alongside doubt. It is not *truth*, nor *doubt* either, but *illusion* which makes man blissful in possessing his heart's desires. Such must be the true aim of agreeable, humane philosophy. This is real progress! However, illusion does not yet completely satisfy us: from deep within there arises a reproach against anyone who tries to fool himself that he has not been created for truth. Philosophy wishes to go even further and actually devotes itself to dispelling this vexation. Illusion, it says, is not produced by human will. There is no need for self-reproach. On the contrary, it is a noble, happy effect inevitable in human nature. It is not man, but the nature of the heart which inevitably and foresightedly seeks to deceive itself because it wishes in this way to be perfectly happy; the nature of the human mind is so constituted that it is the wellspring of a universal, irreparable deception. Truth, which no longer exists for the mind, must not hold it back. Illusion alone, whether true or false, is the exalted object of intelligence itself. Yes, that is what happens. Philosophy cannot solve the great problem which it keeps proposing : 'How can man find happiness for himself on this earth?' without ending dismally, absurdly and madly by condemning as mendacious his own nature, the nature of all things, everything that exists but which, as mendacious, cannot exist. Mankind has to reach perfect *nothingness* before it succeeds in its rashness in satisfying its essential needs without God. Then, finally, whether it wants to or not, mankind will have to turn back.

33. (366)

[Kant's system of innate forms]

Let us set aside any historical investigation about the way in which Kant conceived the innate forms. I have already expressed my opinion about this in the chapter where I examine his writings. The system of innate forms may however be conceived in two ways: 1. the spirit possesses the *forms* innately (as though they are *universal and abstract ideas* called forms because of the way they are used in understanding real entia) — this is how Descartes or Plato introduced innate ideas; 2. the mind possesses a radical power so determined that, when it conceives the entia given by sense experience, it extrudes from itself and gives existence to forms which did not previously exist by uniting them with the matter furnished by sensible experience. This power generates of itself, without any seed one might say, or rather creates its own intellectual knowledge and along with it the world itself. I would merely point out at this juncture that if *forms* were understood in this second way, much more would be introduced into our spirits than in the first way. In this second way, the system of forms would err more on the side of excess than it would in the first.

Here, I cannot refrain from quoting some reflections of Antonio Genovesi in one of his letters to Conti where he deals with the system of forms interpreted in the second way. We see that Kant's system was substantially conceived and refuted in Italy even before it was brought over the Alps. Genovesi says:

> I am perfectly willing to admit that this production of forms of merely possible things may be due solely to the nature of the spirit. Nevertheless, no one will ever hold the view that a mind which knows absolutely nothing of existing things, of which it can find no trace within itself, of which it does not receive any vestige from external causes, can produce images or forms corresponding to these things. Here, I am at sea. This power is even greater than the creative force; after all, the creative force only produces what it understands. This power produces forms which it does not understand; nor does it produce things as possible, but as existing. This seems odd to me. It is as though a painter claims to have made pictures of things of which he had no idea. In addition, this means turning to the darkest, imaginable scepticism about the existence of bodily things. It is a denial of all the evidence of the senses; it is a betrayal of the clear feeling of consciousness.

34. (372)

[Kant's categories and his concept of truth]

In *Transcendental Analytic*, bk. 1, c. 1, section 3, Kant claims that the scholastic maxim: *quodlibet ens est unum, verum et bonum* [every ens is one, true and good] is already comprised in his categories of *unity*, *plurality* and *totality*:

> These claimed transcendental predicates are, in fact, nothing but logical requisites and criteria of all cognition of objects, and they employ, as the basis for this cognition, the categories of *quantity*, namely, *unity*, *plurality*, and *totality*. But these must be taken as *material conditions*, that is, as belonging to the possibility of things themselves. They [the scholastics] employed them merely in a *formal* signification, as belonging to the logical requisites of all cognition, and yet most unguardedly changed these criteria of thought into properties of objects, as things in themselves.

In this passage, one can see, as Kant admits, that his categories are not pure *forms* but have matter associated with them.

He was prevented from making a correct division between the *form* and the *matter* of thought by his having taken the objects of thought (in general) as purely *subjective* things, and thus confused them with the *modes* of the thinking ens. Having accepted the objects of thought as emanations of thought itself and nothing more, he confused what pertained to the *modes* of thought with *forms* of thought. Leibniz was led astray in the same way when, having drawn from the depth of the spirit both knowledge of universals and that of real entities, he mingled and confused the realm of abstractions with that of reality (cf. 296–299). But Kant went further and made one thing of the objects of thought and the forms of thought. He not only wanted every item of knowledge to issue from our spirit, as Leibniz did, but also the world, at least to a great extent.

Moreover, he miserably claims that the concept of *truth* consists in *plurality*. This is so, he says, because 'the *more* true deductions we have from a given concept, the more criteria we have of its objective reality' (*Transcendental Analytic*, bk. 1, c. 1, section 3), as though the *criteria* of truth were the same as *truth*, or *plurality* could not also be found among false consequences. *Plurality* is a kind of cupboard without contents, whereas *truth* determines and fixes a quality of the contents. For example, in the midst of *a number* of false judgments, truth determines the *one* which is true. Similarly, the attempt to reduce *what is good* to *totality* is pathetic quibbling, as though the idea of a *whole* offered also the idea of the goodness of this *whole*. Even if this were the case, the two ideas of *all* and *good* would still be as distinct as two entia of reason. It would not be right to confuse them and make them one.

35.

Preamble to the Ideological Works
[5th Edition, Turin, 1851–1853]

(1). Previous editions of my ideological works contained no general preface. Twenty-two years ago, when I published *A New Essay*, I did not foresee the works that would ensue nor did I think it useful to outline for my readers the method I intended to follow in presenting my teachings. This method, which was the only important thing I needed to mention, would be discussed in the works themselves. Moreover, method in my opinion is a corollary of knowledge and as such cannot be understood before knowledge

Many judgments have been passed, however, on my works, and I now think it necessary to write a few introductory words to this new edition for the sake of those who have either read and judged my works, or heard about them from others whose opinions they have accepted. A large number of those who have taken the trouble to examine my works have acknowledged in their own writings that I have succeeded, despite the difficulties of the subject, in making myself understood clearly enough. Others have interpreted the works so differently and in such contradictory ways that I have been called every kind of philosopher: sensist, idealist, rationalist, pantheist, dogmatist, sceptic. Finally, I was numbered amongst the critical school.

This last classification — the others are too far-fetched altogether — was made in a recent work by a distinguished professor of the University of Turin.[1] It has stimulated me to clarify the aim of my philosophical teaching in this preamble, where I shall explain the limits within which I can accept the classification and the sense in which I must protest against it. In fact, classifications of this kind, used in good faith by people who have certainly read my works, are often employed by others who have not. This could easily result in damage to the truth before public opinion.

(2). Emmanuel Kant was the first to make *critical philosophy* famous in modern times. For him, it meant a system halfway between *dogmatism* and *scepticism* — as if there could be a middle way between having and not having certain knowledge of truth. The concept is absurd, but the great sophist used his outstanding intelligence to create the appearance of having found this *via media*. According to him, the dogmatists were right because all human beings must assent to the first truths; the sceptics were right because nothing could be proved to exist in itself. Truth therefore was now relative to human beings, and as such ceased to be truth — what is not true *absolutely* is not true. Kant had given scepticism a new guise, in fact a disguise, called *critical philosophy* which, however, I unmasked in *A New Essay concerning the Origin of Ideas*, where Kant's scepticism is exposed for what it is.[2] I also showed that the consequences of every subjectivist system are inevitably subject to scepticism, even when those who profess the system are unaware of this. The philosophy of Galluppi, with whom I am ranked by Bertini, is of this kind. In this sense therefore I cannot be classed among *critical philosophers*. In fact, it was I who refuted the sophistry of their system, almost unknown at the time in Italy, in my *New Essay*

(3). Kant called his philosophy *critical* for another reason. Sitting as judge, and citing human reason to appear before him, he passed sentence on its worth and results. I have often observed that this judgment contains an intrinsic contradiction: while intelligence or human reason considered as a whole can

[1] *Idea di una filosofia della vita*, etc., G. M. Bertini, Etc., Turin, 1850, vol. 1, pp. 9 ss.

[2] Cf. 99–133; *Rinnovamento*, bk. 3, cc. 13, 30, 47; *Theodicy*, 140 ss., and many other places.

[*app.* 35, (2)–(3)]

certainly assert itself, it cannot criticise or condemn itself totally. Nevertheless I accept 'critique' in the sense that there are opinions, propositions, forms of speech and concepts which can and must be subjected to critique; intelligence as a whole judges a part of itself, that is, judges a particular faculty and the results of this faculty. I have defined my own understanding of 'critique' as 'an examination of different human cognitions carried out by means of the highest, most evident principle of reason in which we have first convinced ourselves that there is no possibility of error at all'. I wrote: 'To carry out a critique of reason at the same time as a critique of human cognitions would be absurd... This is precisely Kant's error. Reason can criticise particular human cognitions, but not itself, because it can never oppose itself.'[3] In *A New Essay* I said: 'The phrase "critical philosophy" contains something presumptuous and absurd because it implies that we can judge everyone else's reason, as if we were not human beings ourselves.'[4] The philosophy I propose therefore is certainly not 'critical' in either of the two meanings which Kant gives to the word.

(4). My philosophy is even less 'critical' if the word is understood as I use it in the work from which I have quoted: 'Critical philosophy believes that the truthfulness of human intelligence is not a final corollary, but a first theorem to be *proved* before anything else and defended against the scepticism that denies the theorem.'[5] Bertini, who attributes this philosophy to me, tries to demonstrate its uselessness by employing the very same reason I myself used to refute it. He says: 'The faculty we have to use for the demonstration is our own intelligence. But if this itself is suspected of error, how can we use it?'[6] Here Bertini and I agree.

(5). We also agree in our denial that philosophy can begin from a *demonstration* of the truthfulness of human intelligence and from a defence of this truthfulness against any scepticism which denies it But I go further: I maintain that philosophy cannot begin from *any demonstration*. In *A New Essay* I explained

(3) *Essence of Right (ER), Philosophy of Right,* vol. 1, p. 176, Durham, 1999.
(4) Cf. vol. 3, fn. 6.
(5) *Idea di una filosofia della vita,* etc., vol. 1, p. 9.
(6) *Ibid.*

this with greater clarity by asking and answering four interrelated questions: 1. What is the starting point in human development? Reply: *external sensation.* 2. What is the starting point for the human spirit? Reply: *information about being.* 3. What is the starting point of those who begin to philosophise? Reply: the point reached by their mind as they undertake this kind of reflection. 4. What is the starting point of philosophy as a branch of knowledge? Reply: the luminous point from which emanates the clear light of certainty and of truth for all other cognitions, that is, the *idea* of being.[7]

The first two questions do not concern us here. The third indicates the starting point of the philosophy which Friedrich Wilhelm Schelling called 'regressive', that is, all the work done by the human mind as it makes its way back, as it were, to arrive at the clear point where the intellective light, which explains all things, first sets out. The fourth question indicates the starting point of the philosophy which Schelling calls 'progressive'. Moving from the evidence provided by the discovery of this starting point, it progresses to all other human cognitions, which are justified and demonstrated by means of the power of that first truth. Finally, progressive philosophy explains in some way the enigma of the world.

In my opinion, therefore, there is no question of beginning philosophy with any demonstration whatsoever. A demonstration needs *principles*, and if we had to demonstrate principles, the process would be infinite. As I have so often said, we would never, in this case, attain any kind of knowledge.[8]

(6). For the same reason, I did not begin to philosophise by opposing scepticism, as Bertini supposes and I have said on many occasions. For example, in the third volume of *A New Essay* we read: 'I still do not intend to prove to the sceptics that a valid principle of certainty exists for human beings.'[9] We must first find a *self-evident light* and then use it to refute the sceptics. The refutation is a corollary, as it were. This is the method I have followed.

Consequently, while I cannot accept the *critical philosophy*

[7] Cf. vol. 3, 1469–1472.

[8] Cf. among other places, vol. 3, 1466–1467.

[9] Cf. vol. 3, 1061.

which Bertini imposes on me, I am happy to agree with him that it must be excluded.

(7). I wish I could agree also with the rest of his argument, but I do not think he has kept his promise. Although he accurately indicates the defect of *critical philosophy*, he seems to me to have fallen into the very same error. In his Preface, he presents his method and clearly explains that he has written the book as a direct refutation of the sceptics:

> This is what I have done with the sceptics. I followed them in their doubts to a point which they had to acknowledge as indubitable, if they were not to annihilate themselves as thinking beings. Basing myself on this unshakeable point and making use of appearances which they could not deny, I constructed a system of positive philosophy. A corollary of this is precisely the veracity of human intelligence which the sceptics attack.[10]

We see that Bertini begins by accepting the sceptics' *critique* of human reason in order to refute them with another critique whose results are more comforting. He thus justifies and rehabilitates reason. This kind of philosophising is *critical* throughout, in the true sense of the word.

(8). But I do not think he argues logically. He claims that the veracity of human intelligence is simply a corollary of the previous system of philosophy. But is a *system* possible before we know the veracity of human intelligence? Is there such a system of cognitions, which self-confessedly lacks certainty? As long as doubt persists, we cannot say that we know anything at all, still less possess a system of philosophy. Doubt is certainly not knowledge. Bertini's system of philosophy therefore, which claims to demonstrate the veracity of human intelligence as a corollary, does not merit the title 'system', much less 'system of positive philosophy'. We must first have deduced from the system the corollary which demonstrates that human intelligence, which has produced the system, is itself incapable of deception. Prior to this corollary, the system cannot claim any certainty; it is a hypothesis or postulate, nothing more. But in this case the system will begin with its corollary! The problem which Bertini

[10] *Idea di una filosofia della vita*, etc., vol. 1, p. 9.

wishes to solve last takes first place once more thanks to the inflexibility of logic.

(9). But there is a greater problem. The mind spontaneously asks how a *certain corollary* can be deduced from a *system of positive philosophy* which because of its own uncertainty is neither a system nor positive. Corollaries have always been considered certain if the principles from which they are drawn are certain; the certainty of the principles gives certainty to the consequences, but not vice versa. Nevertheless we have here a *system of positive philosophy* which cannot be harmonised with this logic. We are told that a corollary is required to demonstrate the truth and certainty of the system. But the corollary is deduced from a system which is itself uncertain. This corollary is nothing less than the veracity of human intelligence without which nothing, not even the least information, or even appearances, is certain. The veracity of human intelligence is deduced therefore from a system of *positive philosophy* devised by an intelligence which does not know whether it is itself true, still doubts its own honesty and grants its sceptical opponents the same doubt.

(10). However, I do not wish to comment on this obviously vicious circle in which Bertini has inadvertently entangled himself. I wish simply to observe that as long as this philosophy has not spoken its last word, that is, the veracity of human intelligence, it cannot claim to be philosophy, and still less positive philosophy. As Bertini says, the truth of the previous system must, by right of postliminy as it were, be derived from this final word, that is, from the veracity of human intelligence. In this way, the whole system is reduced to a critique of intelligence and therefore to the *critical philosophy* whose weakness Bertini himself has indicated.

(11). I could also add that my philosophy follows a path far removed in yet another way from that taken by Professor Bertini's critical philosophy. His starting point is doubt; he says that he began 'by following the sceptics in their doubt' which, strictly speaking, is the principle proper to *critical philosophy*. If, however, we begin by doubting intelligence, the only way left to arrive at a positive philosophy is to examine intelligence to see whether it provides just grounds for suspicion (however it may do this) or whether the suspicion is baseless. As I have said, whoever doubts is ignorant and cannot therefore have a positive philosophy. I myself did not begin from *doubt* but from *methodical ignorance*, as I showed in my first work on ideology, from which I quote:

> Descartes founded the philosophical edifice on the basis of the state of doubt. We must note two things here. First, at the beginning of philosophy, the supposed state of the human being is one of *methodical ignorance* rather than *methodical doubt*. If philosophy begins by indicating the origin of human cognitions, and develops by gradually deducing them from their first source, the nature of a philosophical treatise presupposes that prior to their origin these cognitions were not. But the absence of cognitions in human beings is called 'ignorance', and in this respect there is a clear difference between the character of Descartes' philosophy and ours: his philosophy has a *demonstrative* nature, and intends from the start to search for *certainty*; our philosophy goes a step further back, and begins not from *demonstration*, but from *observation* of the first facts which are the basis of demonstration itself and constitute its possibility. The first aim of philosophy therefore is *cognitions* themselves, not their *certainty*. We enquire about the existence and origin of cognitions and, as a corollary to this, about the principle of certainty.[11]

The true, natural beginning of philosophical thought cannot be doubt, which arises only when philosophical reflection sees that human beings are mistaken about many things, and asks itself whether it could be mistaken about everything. Those who accepted this possibility invented *scepsis* to make people doubt everything and affirm nothing. Consequently, when philosophical thought opposes this negative doctrine, it is not taking its first step. It has already made much progress.

(12). In distancing myself from Professor Bertini, I am not accusing him of having substituted another *critical philosophy* for Kant's. As we have seen, the word 'critical' can be understood correctly; a complete, positive philosophy (a philosophy that affirms as well as denies) clearly cannot be conceived until the sceptics' doubts have been examined and the veracity of

[11] Cf. vol. 3, 1477–1478.

human intelligence defended against them. Nevertheless, it does not seem reasonable to claim that a philosophy can be called *critical* simply because it leaves the sceptics' doubts to the end and solves them, or hopes to solve them, with its final word, or rather with a simple corollary of a preceding system.

(13). But I have still not dealt with the greatest difference between my system and the system under discussion. This difference is connected with the *luminous point* in which, to use a metaphor of my opponent, truth reigns.[12] According to Bertini, this point is the direct presence to our mind of the *absolute Ens*,[13] that is, God. In my opinion, however, it is the direct presence of *undetermined being*. This being lacks the determinations essential to God without which the concept of God does not exist. Bertini, therefore, maintains that all certain knowledge, every truth, is deduced from God himself present to the human spirit. I maintain that human beings have cognitions, truths and some certainty logically prior to the knowledge of God. For me, the knowledge of God is not naturally intuited but deduced by reasoning from being which is always present to the mind and, as fully undetermined, lacks the characteristics of divinity; it is equally susceptible of both infinite and finite determinations so that in adding the former, we acquire the idea of God, and in adding the latter, we form concepts of finite entia.

(14). What I have taught has also been understood, in varying degree, by all philosophers of any standing. My only merit here consists perhaps in greater coherence in its application and development.

Among these philosophers, I am pleased to name the great Charles Sacretan, who recognises that the only starting point for the human spirit is the one I have indicated.[14] According to him, even the most famous German philosophers had to begin from the same point, although they came to grief later.

[12] *Idea di una filosofia della vita*, etc., vol. 1, c. 12.

[13] *Ibid.*

[14] *Tel est le point de départ de la spéculation, c'est l'ÊTRE INDÉTERMINÉ, l'être qui peut tout devenir et qui n'est rien encore, l'être qui n'est que puissance d'être* [The starting point of speculation is UNDETERMINED BEING, that is, being which, although it can become everything, is as yet nothing; it is simply potency of being] (*La philosophie de la Liberté*, vol. 1, less. 11).

[*app*. 35, (13)–(14)]

(15). The starting point must be the *idea*, not *some real thing* understood differently from the idea.[(15)] Those who have begun from another light, and particularly those who have claimed to begin from God himself as directly and really present to the spirit, were forced into the most manifest contradictions. They had to turn surreptitiously to that very point of undetermined or ideal being which they had tried to avoid, and which is for human beings the pure, clear light from which all reasoning and certainty proceed. Bertini himself was forced to do this, as we can see: 'Philosophy begins from the *pure concept* of what is real, and consists solely in meditation on this concept.'[(16)] He then calls this concept, which he has to grant as the starting point of philosophy, the 'concept of what is real but most undetermined'.[(17)] But if we are to avoid equivocation, it is clear that the *concept of what is real* is not the real thing itself. When we take the *concept* of what is real as the starting point, we are not starting from what is real as such. Moreover, Bertini's 'what is real but most undetermined' can only be a *concept*, not what is real itself, because what is real is always determined. It is true

---

[(15)] To say that the idea is itself real, is to play with words. If real means 'something', the idea is certainly something — it is being and not nothing. But because being is both *ideal* and *real* (which are its two primal modes), we must ask: 'Is first evidence and logical necessity intuited by the human mind in ideal or in real being?' For example, it would be absurd to say, 'Undetermined being is real being', because real being, being existing in itself, is always determined. On the other hand undetermined being thought by the mind is certainly not nothing. Signor Bertini, therefore, is guilty of equivocation when he claims to have found something real in the concept itself (c. 4). He is taking 'something' and 'real' as synonyms. — For the same reason he equivocates when he says, 'The infinite is its own idea' (c. 6), meaning by 'infinite', God. If we are speaking about an idea which God has of himself, we are speaking about a non-existent thing. In God there is only his essence, knowable through itself, which is not an idea. If however we are speaking only about our idea of God, it cannot be claimed that these many, more or less perfect ideas are God himself. This would mean the existence of many Gods, a kind of Platonic polytheism. Finally, God is not known by us through a simple *idea* but by the addition of an *affirmation* asserting his *subsistence*. The *intuition* of the idea and its *affirmation* can certainly be united in a single act of the spirit, that is, in *perception*, but 1. Signor Bertini does not demonstrate that we have the *perception* of God, and 2. our perception itself would never be God.

[(16)] *Idea di una filosofia della vita*, etc., c. 3.

[(17)] *Ibid.*, c. 4.

that the *concept of what is real* is also *something*, but only in the same way as the *concept of what is ideal* is something; both are something but the concept of one is not the concept of the other; moreover, what is real is always something different from what is ideal. There are two kinds of something: that which is ideal, and that which is real. These two somethings cannot be made into one. Furthermore, although the concept of what is real but most undetermined is certainly something, it is not THE something (and much less THE real something); on the contrary, it is some particular, determined thing. It is not, therefore, that most undetermined something of which it is the concept.[18] On the other hand it is very true, as I have repeatedly said, that we can *argue* from the existence of the simple *concept* (of anything whatsoever) to the necessary existence of *something real* (for example, an intelligent being). This, however, does not in any way mean that the real thing to which we have argued is the *concept* from which we began our argument. Sophisms abound, as we can see, in the philosophical process under discussion.

(16). Signor Bertini affirms that philosophy begins from and is fully contained in reflection on 'the pure concept of that which is real but most undetermined'. Nevertheless, this concept is neither God himself directly present to the human spirit (on whom, he says, depend the veracity of human intelligence and all its other human concepts), nor is it the *idea* of God. On the contrary, it is the light by which, when determinations are added, both God and finite entia are known; in other words, it is that being which the scholastics call *most common*. It would be a serious error to confuse this being with God because God is certainly not the being common to all finite things — except for pantheists.

That which is directly and naturally present to the human

---

[18] Signor Bertini defines what he calls 'real concept' as 'a concept which clearly implies the existence of its own object' (p. 25). His example is 'the concept of what is real and most undetermined' which, according to him, implies something. But it is an error to say that the concept of what is real but most undetermined implies the existence of its object. The concept, although A something, is determined, while its object is THE something and totally undetermined. Signor Bertini does not see the great difference between a determined and an undetermined object. This accounts for the error in his argument.

spirit therefore is definitely not God but being at its most undetermined, from which Signor Bertini himself begins, whether he wishes to or not.

(17). Another proof that being at its most undetermined is the object of direct intuition by the human spirit is the following. Internal observation alone is sufficient to acknowledge what we directly intuit. We have therefore begun philosophy from *observation*.[19] This internal observation, which is simultaneously a reflection, makes us aware that the undeniable, luminous and very simple point where all our thoughts begin, and whence light and certainty come, is the information we receive from totally undetermined, modeless being. This, too, proves that the *observation* itself which we have used, taking it on faith as it were, cannot deceive us because it shows itself as that which cannot not be. In Signor Bertini's system, however, mere *observation* is totally insufficient to attain the principle of certainty (which for Bertini is not undetermined being, but God, absolute being); we also need *argument* and *demonstration*. But anything attained by argument and demonstration is *indirectly* present to our spirit, not, as Signor Bertini holds, *directly* present. The Hegelians, who like Bertini posited certain truth in absolute being, saw and admitted this. Thus, consistent with themselves in this, they said that truth is found solely in *what is indirect*, and waged a merciless and even ridiculous war on what they called *direct*.[20]

(18). Bertini was quite open about having attained God. He was

> aware of the principle that what is undetermined and real cannot objectively exist, and relied on the principle of contradiction and on all other principles presupposed in every reasoning.[21]

He himself puts the objection: 'What is the value of a result obtained by reasoning if the *principles* and intellectual faculties used are suspect?'[22] and replies:

[19] Cf. paragraph (11) above.

[20] Cf. *Introduction to Philosophy*, Discourse on the studies of the Author, 84, 63 [in course of preparation].

[21] p. 230.

[22] p. 234.

When philosophical reason, following its law, leads me from doubt to God, its only value and function is that of a *material condition*, not of a *logical principle*. The true logical principle is God.[23]

I must comment on this reply.

First, God is certainly not a logical principle; we use logical principles to reach him, and apply them to him when we wish to draw other truths from our knowledge of him. 'Logical principles' is the phrase used by the whole world for first judgments or *universal* propositions, that is, *ideal* propositions. From these we draw consequences whenever we apply them directly or indirectly to *realities*. We cannot change God into a logical principle; as absolute being, he is real and individual. Changing him in this way would lead to rationalism and atheism, errors which Signor Bertini opposes with all his might and often with great skill and success.

(19). Furthermore, Bertini's reply confuses the *material conditions* of a demonstration with its *formal conditions*. It is clear that the truth of a demonstration does not depend on its material conditions; and the existence of a philosopher who reasons, and his subjective faculty of reasoning are clearly material conditions. I agree with this.[24] But 'the principle that what is undetermined and real cannot objectively exist,[25] the principle of contradiction, and all the principles presupposed in all reasoning' are continually used by Bertini to support a demonstration of God's existence, although they are not purely *material conditions* in the sense that even if false, God's existence could nevertheless be a true conclusion. They are *formal conditions* and must therefore be true if the conclusion is to be true. Their truth and certainty precede in the human mind the truth of the conclusion deduced from them and seen by means of them as necessary. Consequently, the existence of God is not the first

[23] p. 237.

[24] Signor Bertini describes these conditions very well on p. 50 of his book, but does not include amongst them the principle of contradiction and the other logical principles which he uses to arrive at the existence of God.

[25] I would say '*real existence*' or existence of being in itself, because even undetermined being is itself *object* of the mind. It has therefore an *objective existence* different from that of the mind, although in the mind.

certain truth guaranteeing all other truths. The only truth here (which perhaps Signor Bertini had in mind) is that the existence of absolute being, when known, provides the philosopher with the possibility of answering the metaphysical objections which can be brought against truth and thus gives rest to the human spirit. But these objections cannot in any way weaken the certainty of the first logical principles against which they are made. Whenever a truth is *per se* evident and necessary, no objection can shake it or render it uncertain. I grant therefore that if we exclude knowledge of God, of absolute being, apparent contradictions may arise in our spirit which can however be fully solved by what is taught about that being. But antecedent to and independently of their solution, the first truths shine in our mind endowed with unmovable certainty. No objection has any force against what we know directly to be true and unable to be other than true, even if we cannot solve the objection specifically and directly.

(20). Bertini himself, perhaps unconsciously, was obliged to grant the presence in the human spirit of truths which are both certain and logically precede knowledge of the divine existence. He reasons as follows:

> That which is thought exists. — The existence of the object of ontology is therefore a point *unassailable* even by the most negative philosophers, such as nihilists, idealists and sceptics. Consequently, our doubter should start his meditation from this *evident* and *unshakeable* point.[26]

This point or, as Bertini later calls it, 'first truth', is certainly not a material condition or a postulate of human knowledge. If he admits that the starting point is this *first truth*, which can then lead the doubter *to the existence of God*, there is in the human spirit a truth which is certain and, in the logical order, precedes the truth of the divine existence. Throughout his demonstration of this existence, Signor Bertini speaks about *true* cognitions and *certainty*,[27] and goes on in this vein until he has

---

[26] *Idea di una Filosofia della vita*, p. 25.

[27] For example, on p. 26 he says that if we have the concept of happiness, we can answer the question whether 'Croesus, granted he exists, is happy or not'. According to Bertini, a doubter *certainly* has the concept of *non-being*, because without it he could not have doubted. In this way he convinces the

reached his conclusion about the existence of the absolute being. Clearly, the certainty of this conclusion depends on the certain truths which he has cleverly used as the basis of the conclusion and which precede the conclusion itself.

(21). Moreover: 1. anything deduced by argument is not *direct*; 2. his conclusion that we are 'endowed with an immanent, *direct intuition* of the absolute life of God'[28] invalidates the conclusion itself by making it greater than his premises. The direct intuition does not and cannot result from any of his arguments.

If we truly had direct intuition of God's absolute reality and life, the fact would be verified solely by internal *observation*; *reasoning* would not be necessary because we ourselves would be witnesses to the fact. Bertini's long, exhausting and often wise reasoning is clear proof that in this life, we do not directly see God himself, and that human common sense is not wrong in believing that we do not see him. The only legitimate consequence to be drawn from these laborious reasonings is that the existence of God is certain and necessary and is finally reduced to the *a priori* demonstration which I gave in *A New Essay*, and Professor Bertini has further enhanced.[29]

(22). We can easily be mistaken if we lose sight of the difference between intuitive or visual *direct knowledge* on the one hand and reasoned *indirect knowledge* on the other.

In fact, Bertini extends the meaning of 'intuit' too far when he says that 'knowing is seeing or intuiting the being of things'.[30] Not all *cognition* are *intuitions*. Even if we wanted to use the word in this way, we would need to explain it; for example, to avoid error, we would need to distinguish between intuition and different kinds of intuition. Equivocation is even more evident in Bertini's reasoning when he constantly says that

sceptic by making him *contradict* himself. He continually discusses *possibility* and *impossibility*. He supposes that *true* and *certain* results are obtained from the comparison and analysis of concepts, that appearances cannot be denied, that the infinite must exist if the finite exists, and that if the temporary exists, the eternal must exist (p. 32), and so on.

[28] p. 230.

[29] Cf. vol. 3, 1456–1460.

[30] p. 38.

'knowledge is a *direct vision*'.[31] He attributes *what is directly intuited* to all knowledge, and consequently argues that 'if knowledge is a direct vision, it follows that thought and knowledge of the *infinite* can only be the *direct vision* of the infinite'.[32] The equivocation is obvious.

(23). Certainly, *everything known* is in a sense directly intuited, otherwise it would not be known. But the expression, 'everything known', has a double meaning: it refers either to the thing *as it is in itself* apart from knowledge, or is *as it is known*. Sometimes the thing as known is not what it is in itself prescinding from our knowledge; it can in fact be something entirely different. This is the case with *undetermined being* known by the human mind; it is not entirely the same as *being in itself*, because nothing undetermined can exist in itself. In fact, undetermined being present only to the mind differs from being in itself (pure being), not only qualitatively, but totally; the difference is precisely in being, not in quality. The determinations lacking to undetermined being pertain to the *very essence of being in itself* (as Bertini grants). But an object from which something essential has been removed is no longer itself. Consequently, undetermined being, which we certainly know and think, is not God, who is complete, absolute being in itself; the identity is lost when our mind passes from one being to the other. But this will be discussed at greater length in ontology.

It may be objected: 'You determine undetermined being with your argument by beginning from its concept, and thus arrive at knowledge. In this way you directly intuit the absolute being which you already implicitly intuited in undetermined being.'

The objection disappears if we carefully distinguish the different modes of human knowledge. It is a common prejudice to believe that everything we know is always known in the same way. But first, a *determined object* can be known in two ways: 1. the

[31] *Ibid.* — There is also ambiguity in the word 'infinite' because it can mean a *determined* and an *undetermined infinite*, both of which are thought by the human mind. Thus, when Signor Bertini writes that 'the infinite is not only thinkable in itself but is the only thinkable thing' (p. 48), he enunciates a truth if he means the undetermined infinite. This is not the case with the determined infinite, which we think explicitly only as a result of reasoning, but do not need in order to think other things.

[32] *Idea di una Filosofia della vita*, p. 38.

object presents itself together with its determinations, or 2. we ourselves determine an undetermined object presented to our spirit by adding purely *logical determinations*. The difference between these two ways of knowing is immense. In the first, we know the determined object by a single act of intuition or *perception*. We do not yet think of the determinations separate from the object but of them all together indistinctly in the object with which they form a perfect unity. Later, by means of analysis, we can separate the determinations. In the first instance however all that is before our spirit is the *single* object fully determined in a perfect synthesis without any analysis. In this case, we do not have recourse to any *reasoning* in order to know the object. This way of knowing is aptly called either *intuition*, if the determined object is ideal, or *perception*, if it is also real.

If however the object present to our mind is undetermined, our spirit proceeds in a contrary direction and must itself add determinations to the object to complete it. Our spirit, which is now constrained to begin not from analysis but from dispersed elements and from ourselves, forms a synthesis of the elements by various operations of the mind. We think with separate acts the undetermined object and the determinations which we add to it. The determinations are taken not from the object present to us (it is undetermined), but from elsewhere. Substantially Bertini grants this, or certainly should grant it, because he himself begins from the undetermined concept of *something* and then determines it not with what he finds in it but with other mental and abstract concepts.[33]

Because we do not find the determinations we are seeking in the undetermined object that we want to complete by many operations of our thought, we have to extract them, as I said, from other objects. For this reason they cannot be determinations *proper* to the object which is determined in this way, but

[33] Anyone in possession of a real concept knows the objective existence of a thing by means of the concept. He can compare successively many mental concepts with this real concept and thus determine the first concept' (pp. 25, 26). This method allows him to form an idea of God from undetermined 'something': he 'uses the concepts of limit, life, perfection, entity, intelligence, activity, love, freedom, etc.' (p. 230), which are all abstract concepts, and different from the concept of something.

purely *analogical* determinations, that is, they are attributed to it by analogy. For example, Bertini himself attributes *life* to the undetermined object, *being*, but draws this concept of life from elsewhere, from among the living beings which fall under human experience.[34] Moreover, the life of living beings perceived by us on earth is certainly not the life of God. If we saw the life of God, we could compare it with the life of animals and human beings and note the difference. But because even Bertini finds this direct comparison impossible, he is forced to take the *abstract* concept of life (abstracted of course from the living beings of which alone he has *direct* knowledge) and determine it by other concepts which themselves are abstract. He then says: God must have life to the *highest degree*.[35] Very true, but the phrase, 'to the highest degree', indicates nothing determined; it is still a formal, logical concept. Aware of this and unable to turn to any other *direct knowledge* of other lives, Bertini tries to determine this *highest degree* of life by comparing the different grades of life of finite beings. The comparison results in his discovery that the greatest life consists in the *perception of oneself*.[36] But we are now at the start once more: the perception of oneself is still an abstract. He therefore makes an effort to determine this next *concept* (it is still a question of *concepts* and not of *reality* itself) and states that the highest degree of perception consists in intelligence,[37] which itself is an abstract concept. He must therefore find another concept to determine this concept; he must investigate the nature of the highest degree of intelligence. He says

> The highest degree of intelligence is proper to the person who understands all that is intelligible in the most perfect way, that is, understands the infinite. Moreover, there is no highest degree of intelligence unless that which is infinite and understood is that which understands.[38]

[34] He begins his analysis with the question, 'To which beings do we normally attribute life?' (p. 54).

[35] p. 53 ss.

[36] pp. 54–55.

[37] *Idea di una Filosofia della vita*, p. 55, 59.

[38] p. 59.

This is very true, but all these new concepts ('intelligible', 'infinite', 'identity') are abstract and consequently far removed from presenting the *reality* of the thing. At this point, Bertini stops. Unable to proceed further along this path, but wishing to complete the concept of divine life, he performs the same laborious task of mixing abstract concepts for the purpose of determining the concept of the highest love, a concept which is itself abstract and has to be forced into the concept of divine life.[39] But is it really true that if we had the *direct vision of the life of God*, we would need to stitch together these abstractions in order to think and know such a vision? Would we not see it perhaps as an extremely simple thing, just as simply and directly as we see a colour, or sense some smell or sound? Can empty abstractions, no matter how many we ingeniously combine, ever give us the *reality* itself of a thing? We have seen that Bertini, despite his great effort to determine one concept by another, has never been able to break away from the order of abstract concepts which need further determinations. Has he in fact given us the reality of divine life or shown us what it is in itself? Has he really persuaded us that we see it? I leave the reader to judge. The only thing I see is a large quantity of concepts, and I know for certain that the *reality* of the divine life will *never* be a complex even of innumerable concepts. Moreover, who can tell me how all these concepts become one in God, or can conscientiously say they have seen such a fact? Where is the *unity*, the living unity, of these concepts? Multiple concepts certainly cannot be necessary for this unity which is not in fact a concept but something very real, extremely simple and undivided. Give me this reality instead of concepts and I will grant that I see and directly intuit the infinite life of God.

(24). I do not deny that we can acquire *some* knowledge of the divine life by unifying many concepts, but such knowledge is not direct. The one, extremely simple divine life, so different from all other lives known directly by us, is given in this multiplicity of the concept as a kind of beautiful and useful logical formula, as a symbol or sign. But the nature of the formula is such that we cannot derive any clear result from it.

[39] p. 59 ss.

[*app.* 35, (24)]

Consequently the result, which is the divine life in itself, remains unknown. The sign or symbol (or symbols,) are sufficient 1. to make us understand that the divine life is *not* the life of any finite ens; 2. to instruct us not to confuse the lives of the finite entia we experience with God's life which we do not naturally experience, and 3. to demonstrate that the analogy between these two kinds of life allows us to apply the same word and a *common abstract concept* to them both. We can use the word 'life' for both of them, provided we acknowledge that the word contains an equivocation due to the analogy on which rests the common abstract concept expressed by the word.

This logical, thought-out manner of knowing the divine life cannot in any way be called a direct intuition or perception. The only thing we know directly are the signs, symbols and formula of this life, that is, the mixed concepts. But the *positive* meaning and the real result are known only in so far as we understand that the intellective signs have a meaning, that the formula has a result. But neither meaning nor result can be confused with anything else. This is enough for us to admit our ignorance and, while adoring, confess that one day, but not now, we will see what lies behind that mysterious veil.[40]

(25). Other observations could be made about Signor Bertini's theory, but perhaps even the few I have made may seem superfluous. There is much I could recommend about his writings, but I had no intention of passing complete judgment on them. I wished solely to defend what I teach in my ideological works, which are being reprinted, by clearing up some of the

---

[40] Sometimes Bertini seems content with an *implicit* intuition of God. But *implicit knowledge* is purely a *potency for knowledge*, not actual, direct knowledge. I certainly do not deny this potency. Indeed I maintain that we can argue inductively from the idea of being to the concept of God and prove his existence. But even if we grant a concept such as that of undetermined being which itself implies or virtually contains the concept of God, we still have to decide how and to what extent human intelligence can make explicit what is contained implicitly in this concept. The answer, I think, is this: human intelligence can make explicit the concept of God contained virtually in the concept of undetermined being in the way that Bertini posits, that is, by means of *simple*, *logical determinations*, which however do not allow us to see or communicate with the *reality* of the divine being.

ambiguities which seem to have been the cause of the main objections.

(26). Similarly, I must point out how far from the truth are those who have said, 'The starting point of his philosophy is psychological, not ontological.' I think I have stated frequently enough that the starting point of philosophy as the science of the human being is being, but *being* as *undetermined*.[41] The reason is clear and undeniable: *undetermined being*, which logically precedes all human cognitions, is their form; it is the springboard of human reasoning which can always be reduced to 'the faculty of determining being'. Hence, those who claim that fully *determined ens*, that is, ens with its characteristics of divinity, is always present naturally to the human spirit, are mistaken. Among other things, they do away with human reasoning by rendering it superfluous and inexplicable. Moreover, if determined being is God and, according to them, continually present and manifest to the human spirit, they must attribute divine being to all finite entia which are known only by means of being, that is, in so far as they are entia. But the only being which the human spirit can attribute to them, and thus know them, is the being which it intuits, God himself. This is pantheism.

(27). Those adversaries who believe that undetermined being is purely a production of the human mind are also greatly mistaken. They infer from this erroneous principle that starting from undetermined being is the same as beginning from a primal *psychological element*. Undetermined being however, although *absolutely being*, is not *absolute being*. The objectors therefore reveal their total ignorance of the *ideal mode* of being. Being, which is present to intelligences in this mode, is not confused with intelligences nor produced by them. No ens, and hence no human spirit, can produce another ens which possesses, if only in some respect, a nature contrary and infinitely superior to its own. *Being in itself* must certainly have its own determinations, but it also possesses another mode and power by means of which it presents itself to intelligences as something totally distinct from and against them. Consequently, nothing prevents being, in this mode, from showing itself as

[41] Cf. vol. 3, 1468–1472.

undetermined and without its term; this explains why it is called ideal. If, on the other hand, the human spirit had of itself enough power to *produce* being, although without its determinations, indeterminate being could be considered to have a psychological origin. But if this were the case, we would have no reason to deny that the human spirit had the power to produce being with its determinations; this second act is less than the first. This is what the German philosophers, from Fichte to Hegel, ingenuously admitted they wanted, although later Schelling drew back somewhat from this abyss, as can be seen in his new philosophy.

(28). The accusation against me therefore could reasonably be turned against my adversaries by demonstrating that, whatever they may say, it is their own error which errs through *psychologism*. Psychologism's great sin is to grant to the soul deformed in this way the power of making totally undetermined being present to the spirit.

(29). Consequently I reject the accusation that the first element in the order of knowledge is psychological; it is in fact totally ontological. But there can be two primal ontological elements: absolute, *determined being*, and ideal, *undetermined being*. According to me, absolute, determined being is the primal element for the divine mind; ideal, undetermined being, for the human mind. God's way of knowing is certainly different from ours, and we must be content with our knowledge without insanely attempting to usurp God's. If we are not content, we will renew our stupid, vain attempt to deify ourselves. As mortals, we must remember that we are not at the centre of the great ocean of being but in a little corner from which alone we direct our gaze on things.

(30). Being, although undetermined, is the *object* of human intelligence; the soul is the *subject*. I have always tried to distinguish these two things, which cannot be confused by anyone who has seen their absolute opposition demonstrated in *A New Essay* and elsewhere. I have posited all knowledge, every truth and certainty in the *object*, never in the *subject* soul. The existence of the intelligent soul and of the faculty of understanding and reasoning with which the soul is endowed are, as Professor Bertini has so rightly said, purely *material conditions* totally independent of the truth and of the force of every intuition and

[*app.* 35, (28)–(30)]

proof. This is the teaching in my ideological works, and it is certainly not psychologism. If our possession of truth is to be certain, then material conditions are indeed necessary but do not in any way constitute truth itself or the motives for certainty. Truth is totally independent of the human soul, although the soul is dependent on truth and cannot possess it without existing.

(31). As we have seen, the primal philosophical element of philosophy is the second of the two primal ontological elements mentioned above, that is, the *ideological* element. Because philosophy is certainly knowledge, it must begin from ideas; we are deluded if we think it can begin from any other point. But I entirely reject the other accusation that my philosophy is purely ideological. This comes about because my opponents pay such intense attention to my starting point that they no longer consider the whole corpus of my teaching. It will not be a waste of time therefore if I offer a brief comment on my teaching, sufficient to rectify the inaccurate judgment passed on it. A compendium of my work has been given elsewhere.[42]

As I have said, Schelling distinguished between *progressive* and *regressive* philosophy. 'Regressive' philosophy (or rather philosophising) begins from the accidental point at which the mind happens to find itself, and turns back to trace all the steps of its development. Guided by the law of the logical priority and posteriority of ideas, we attempt to reach that luminous point beyond which we cannot go and which is necessarily and clearly true. Having turned our reflection to this point and grasped it, we move in the reverse direction. This is *progressive philosophy* which, when completed, is not only philosophising but philosophy, that is, knowledge.[43]

For me, regressive philosophy is *ideology*, and the secure starting point of knowledge, because it searches for the first, evident truth, which cannot not be what it reveals itself to be. This is the secure starting point of human knowledge.

Reflection, equipped with this first, evident truth, progresses from this truth to all others.

[42] Cf. *Introduction to Philosophy.*

[43] I have distinguished these two parts in vol. 3, 1471–1472.

(32). But it is the intellective soul, that is, the intelligent human subject, which now progresses by acts of reasoning. Many of these acts, however, are subject to the influence of human free will and are erroneous. If *progressive philosophy* is to begin its journey with the certainty of not erring, it must first use the principle of truth and certainty it has discovered in order to indicate the *formal* and *material conditions* of intellectual progress. The formal conditions are the object of *logic*; the material conditions are the object of *psychology* because, as I said, the existence and nature of the soul, of human beings and of their faculties are material conditions of knowledge.

Both these sciences, which deal with the material and formal conditions of what is humanly knowable, lie between *regressive* philosophy and systematically *progressive* philosophy. I say 'systematically progressive' because both are certainly formed by progressive reasoning which begins and progresses from the discovered, immovable point. This point is pure light intuited naturally by human beings who have then exercised their reflection on it through ideological activity. The movement however remains partial and does not extend to all that is. Hence it cannot be called a system of philosophy.

(33). Systematic, progressive speculation can, with reasonable courage and cautious judgment, be undertaken by a thinker who fully knows and possesses the formal and material conditions of intellectual progress.

This kind of speculation will lead the thinker to *theosophy*, to the *theory of ens*. This theory includes 1. ontology, that is, the general doctrine about Ens; 2. theology, which is the doctrine about Ens with its own terms, which make it *absolute*, and 3. cosmology, that is, the doctrine about Ens with terms which are not its own and make it *finite* and *relative*. These three parts of theosophy are therefore doctrine about 1. Ens in all its universality, 2. infinite Ens and 3. finite Ens; in other words, theosophy is always doctrine about ens, which alone deserves to be called 'theory'.

(34). I fully agree that even in progressive philosophy there is a part which could in a relative sense be called regressive because it leads us from *undetermined being* (the luminous point) to *absolute being*. But this regression is simultaneously progression: progression because we begin from a definite, luminous point; regression because we arrive at another luminous point, a second stopping place as it were, which is the concept of absolute being, that is, of God. From here, for the reasons I gave above, we set out again on a journey of more precious discoveries: by meditating on this concept of absolute being we disperse all the antinomies which our human spirit encounters in its speculation. With this increase of light we not only possess truth and certainty, but do so without objections which may perhaps trouble our spirit but cannot extinguish the unassailable light of truth, whose direct necessity is seen by the mind. When our spirit has attained the concept of absolute being and has sufficient energy to speculate, it cannot only be certain of the truth but reconcile it with itself and possess it as it were in a kingdom of peace. *Theosophy*, which accomplishes all this, will also make all I am saying understood.

In conclusion, we can y that properly speaking *theosophy* is progressive philosophy, speculation *par excellence*, system.

(35). Such then is the outline of philosophy which I decided to flesh out. So far, only certain parts of it have been published. I believe I have a right, therefore, to ask people to abstain from naming it in prejudicial ways. As good custom dictates, let it be named after its birth.

Index of Biblical References

Index of Persons

*Numbers in roman indicate paragraphs or, where stated, an appendix (app.);
numbers in italic indicate footnotes. Bracketed numbers refer to the paragraphs
(roman) and footnotes (italic) of no. 35 of the Appendix*

General Index

Numbers in roman indicate paragraphs or, where stated, an appendix (app.); numbers in italic indicate footnotes. Bracketed numbers refer to the paragraphs (roman) and footnotes (italic) of no. 35 of the Appendix